PRESIDENTIAL ADVISORY COMMISSIONS

PRESIDENTIAL
ADVISORY
COMMISSIONS

TRUMAN TO NIXON

Thomas R. Wolanin

The University of Wisconsin Press

PUBLISHED 1975
THE UNIVERSITY OF WISCONSIN PRESS
BOX 1379, MADISON, WISCONSIN 53701

THE UNIVERSITY OF WISCONSIN PRESS, LTD.
70 GREAT RUSSELL ST., LONDON

FIRST PRINTING

PRINTED IN THE UNITED STATES OF AMERICA
FOR LC CIP INFORMATION SEE THE COLOPHON

ISBN 0-299-06860-9

Publication of this book was made possible
in part by a grant from the Andrew W. Mellon Foundation

To the memories of
Ewart K. Lewis and Robert G. McCloskey
Models of humanity and scholarship

CONTENTS

TABLES

PREFACE

MY INTELLECTUAL and personal debts to those who helped to make this study possible and to improve its quality are large, longstanding, and numerous.

Professor John D. Lewis of Oberlin College as a teacher, a colleague, and a friend has given to me most generously of his knowledge and his wise counsel. He has set standards of scholarly excellence and intellectual rigor that I hope I have approached.

Professor James Q. Wilson of Harvard University steered me away from several dead ends and gave me the benefit of his experience with interviewing techniques. He gave his time freely and was a challenging and constructive critic. At various stages, the manuscript was also read in whole or in part by Don K. Price, Michael Lipsky, Frank Popper, and David Fellman. I have benefited from the valuable comments that they all offered. In particular my colleague David Fellman has been a greatly appreciated source of assistance and encouragement.

The Brookings Institution generously made available to me a Washington, D.C., base of operations and the use of their facilities. Congressmen Lucien Nedzi of Michigan and Frank Thompson, Jr., of New Jersey gave me a unique education in American politics through service on their staffs.

Those who were interviewed for this study, who must remain nameless by the terms of our interviewing arrangement, gave their time magnanimously and were very candid and helpful in our conversations. Without their cooperation, the study could not have been realized.

My colleagues and friends Paul Dawson, Isebill Gruhn, Doris Kearns, Scott Van Doren, Charles Smith, Bill and Johanna Kramer, Mike and Jan Faden, Craig Liske, Bob and Andy Adler, and Steve and Monica Sinding helped in innumerable large and small ways with the substance and the mechanics of my work. They often provided a patient ear to listen to long discourses on commissions and were willing partners for much-needed hearts games. The expert editorial criticism and assistance of Mary Maraniss have contributed significantly to improving the quality of this work.

Without the support and encouragement of my parents, I never could have reached the point of even beginning this study. Finally, my wife, Barbara, has been the ultimate friend and patient helper throughout.

To all of these, I offer my deep gratitude. My name is visible on the title page of this work because I stand on their shoulders. The responsibility for all errors of fact and judgment is, of course, mine alone.

Thomas Wolanin

Madison, Wisconsin
September, 1974

PRESIDENTIAL ADVISORY COMMISSIONS

CHAPTER ONE

OBJECTIVES AND DEFINITIONS

PRESIDENTIAL ADVISORY COMMISSIONS generally have a bad public image. According to many commentators, commissions are created by Presidents primarily to avoid taking effective action; are packed and manipulated by the White House; have members who are inactive, uninterested, and ineffective in the work of the commissions; and have their reports buried or ignored by the White House. They are a sham and a waste of money.[1] The following is an example of this type of criticism:

> If you're pestered by critics and hounded by faction
> To take some precipitate, positive action,
> The proper procedure, to take my advice, is
> Appoint a commission to stave off the crisis.[2]

Another example is the following:

> The White House has responded to our spreading social chaos by appointing Presidential commissions to study the problems, then ignoring the recommendations. This has become the new political technique for sweeping problems under the rug while pretending to do something about them. . . . It takes most Presidential commissions at least a year to gear up. Their studies cost the taxpayers millions. Yet they keep coming up essentially with the same solutions, followed by the same inaction.[3]

One President admitted using commissions in the manner described by the critics, providing some justification for the widespread skepticism about commissions. Herbert Hoover wrote:

> There is no more dangerous citizen than the person with a gift of gab, a crusading complex and a determination to "pass a law" as the antidote for all human ills. The most effective diversion of such an individual to constructive action and the greatest silencer on earth for foolishness is to associate him on a research committee with a few persons who have a passion for truth—especially if they pay their own expenses. I can

3

now disclose the secret that I created a dozen committees for that precise purpose.[4]

The objective of this work is to provide a systematic study of presidential advisory commissions as political institutions, with a focus on the relationship between Presidents and commissions and on the widely voiced criticisms of commissions. Studying commissions as political institutions involves looking at their institutional characteristics and capabilities, their internal dynamics and decision making, and their role in national politics and policy formulation. This study will not attempt to assess the substantive merits of the findings and recommendations of the various commissions.

A definition of a presidential advisory commission is offered below, along with a list of the bodies that fit that definition. To that extent, this is a systematic study. It is not systematic, however, in the sense of having all of its generalizations based on data for each of the ninety-nine commissions. While some information was found on each commission, the discussion of any particular topic is usually based on data for about half of the commissions. Which half may be involved in the discussions of a given topic varies from topic to topic, depending on the availability of data. However, for each topic, a range of commissions representing the different commission sizes and subjects and the different administrations is drawn on.

Commissions are only one among many advisory techniques available to the President.[5] In addition, presidential techniques for "gathering, processing, evaluating, and interpreting facts and information for the decision making process"[6] are themselves only one among the several constellations of presidential techniques used to perform the whole range of presidential functions. Thus, commissions are a relatively small thicket in the presidential forest. Examining the thicket as a whole rather than one tree in it seemed to be the most worthwhile expenditure of resources. A case study of an individual commission seemed less warranted, for example, than the committee studies that have provided a foundation for the efforts of scholars examining the Congress. This study, then, attempts to learn what is typical about commissions rather than what is unique to a single commission; it is an aerial photograph rather than a ground survey of this largely unmapped terrain.

As an option completely under the control of the Presidents (with the exception of the few commissions created by statute), commissions are a presidential institution. The purposes for which commissions are created, the process by which the decisions to create commissions are made, the formulation of commission mandates, the choosing of commission members, the financial arrangements for commissions, the liaison maintained with commissions, and the responses to commission reports are the links between the White House and commissions which are major themes of this study.

Despite their common occurrence and the great public interest shown in many of their reports, there is only a very scanty popular and social science literature discussing presidential advisory commissions as political institutions.[7] The entire literature consists of two books devoted to commissions, a few essays by scholars and journalists discussing their strengths and weaknesses, and a few case studies of selected aspects of individual commissions.[8] There are no detailed case studies of all aspects of even one commission. Many of the existing works on commissions are long out of date. The existing studies are also deficient because none attempts to formulate a systematic definition of a presidential advisory commission, and they usually generalize about them on the basis of only a small collection of examples. Thus a need for a study of presidential advisory commissions clearly exists and has frequently been expressed.[9]

It is often claimed that commissions were first used by President Washington and have been one of the techniques available to chief executives ever since.[10] This view is in error. Washington's commission was a small group of men sent in 1794 to try to persuade the rebellious farmers of Pennsylvania to yield to the federal government during the Whiskey Rebellion. They were unsuccessful, and the militia were ultimately sent to end the rebellion.[11] This commission was a group of conciliators and negotiators who, upon failing in their task, advised the President that sterner measures were needed. They were an operational group dealing directly with a crisis, and therefore more analogous to Clark Clifford's mission to Detroit during the urban riot of 1965 at the behest of President Johnson than to presidential advisory commissions as they have operated in the twentieth century. President Tyler in 1842 sent a three-man commission to investigate a scandal in the New York customhouse.[12] This group also bears only a slight resemblance to presidential advisory commissions appointed to analyze broad questions of public policy.

While there are some eighteenth- and nineteenth-century American antecedents for presidential advisory commissions, as well as longstanding foreign models, particularly the British Royal Commissions, presidential advisory commissions are basically a product of the dramatic enlargement of the federal government in the twentieth century and the correspondingly larger role routinely played by Presidents, even in the absence of crises.[13] Theodore Roosevelt probably most deserves the title of "Father of the Presidential Advisory Commission." In implementing his stewardship theory of the presidency, he was the first to employ groups of nongovernment experts to examine problems of public policy.[14] He created the Commission on Public Lands (1903–4), the Commission on Inland Waterways (1908–9), the Commission on Country Life (1908–9), and the Commission on National Conservation (1908–9). Among the more prominent commissions created by his successors before President Truman were the Commission on Economy and Efficiency (1910–13), the Commission on Industrial Relations (1912), the Research Committee on Social Trends (1929–33), the National Commission on Law Observance and Enforcement (Wickersham Commission, 1929–31), the Committee on Economic Security (1934–35), the Special Committee on Farm Tenancy (1936–37), the President's Committee on Administrative Management (Brownlow Committee, 1936–37), and the Commission to Investigate the Disaster at Pearl Harbor (Roberts Commission, 1941–42).

This book will discuss the commissions created from the beginning of the Truman Administration (April 12, 1945) to the end of the first term of the Nixon Administration (January 20, 1973), a period that for brevity's sake is designated 1945–72 throughout. The period was chosen because, first, it seemed short enough to be manageable and long enough to provide some perspective on the development and behavior of the presidential commission, and second, one could not hope to find interview subjects for any period beginning much earlier, and the presidential documents for this period, while far from perfect, are much more accessible and well organized than those for an earlier period, and are adequate for the study.[15]

In addition, the earliest general work on presidential advisory commissions "as a governmental device" was Carl Marcy's *Presidential Commissions* (1945), which focuses on the years between 1900 and 1940.[16] The period that this work would cover was thus selected in part to pick up where Marcy left off. The other general work, Frank Popper's *The President's Commissions* (1970), shares with this study the perspective of describing and evaluating presidential advisory commissions "as an institution of the American political system."[17] However, Popper's brief work focuses almost exclusively on the 1960s, and is unsystematic in its approach.

Finally, this period was chosen because it is a recognizable era in American politics, marked by the general acceptance of the New Deal and welfare liberalism as the baseline of domestic politics and by the active undertaking of broad and continuing international responsibilities by the United States, including the maintenance of a high level of military preparedness and vigilance. The Full Employment Act of 1946 and the National Security Act of 1947 are notable landmarks indicating the beginning of this period which continued through the Nixon Administration.

Previous students of presidential advisory bodies have noted the lack of any systematic definitions or enumerations.[18] Arthur Macmahon expresses doubt that a definition is even possible. In his words, "Precision in terminology is alien to a development so fluid in essence as the institution of the advisory board."[19] Nevertheless, a definition is offered here, and a chronological list of all of the bodies which satisfy that definition appears as appendix 2.

The definition and list of commissions are not conclusive, because of the imaginativeness of Presidents and their staffs in continually devising new variants in advisory bodies, the plurality of titles used to refer to commissions, and the fragmentary and unorganized nature of the documents relating to the presidency.[20] It can only be said that the definition and list here are much more systematic and complete than any that have yet been offered.[21]

A presidential advisory commission is defined as: (1) a corporate group created by a public act, (2) which is advisory to the President, (3) all members of which are appointed directly by the President, (4) which is *ad hoc,* (5) at least one member of which is public, and (6) whose report is public.

In practice, "group" has meant no fewer than three commission members and frequently twenty or more. A "corporate group" is a body having an identity and an existence of its own. The separateness and identity of a corporate group is achieved by its being created by a public act.

"Creation by public act" means either that the commission was created by an official public act such as a statute, executive order, proclamation, reorganization plan, or directive or memorandum appearing in the Federal Register (in fact statutes and executive orders were the only official public acts used to create commissions), or that the commission was announced or recognized publicly by the President in a speech, press conference, letter, directive, memorandum, or White House press release at its inception.

An advisory body is "not legally capable of authoritative action."[22] A body is considered to be advisory if its public mandate gives its task as "advising," "studying," "recommending," "investigating," "gathering information," or something similar. It is of course apparent, as numerous studies have indicated, that the distinctions between "advising" and "deciding" or "choosing" are far from clear in practice.[23]

Being "advisory to the President" means that a commission reports to the President. It may also report to others. For example, the advisory commissions created by statute are required to report to both the President and the Congress, or to the President, who then transmits the report to Congress. A body does not qualify as advisory to the President if it reports only to one of the President's legal subordinates.

For the requirement that all members be "appointed by the President" to be satisfied, none of the members may be designated by position (for instance, "the Secretary of State") by statute, even if the occupant of that position is a presidential appointee. None of the members may be appointed by a subordinate of the President, even though the President may have appointed that subordinate or "approves" the subordinate's appointments. Appointment by the President which requires the "advice and consent" of the Senate, as in the case of the National Commission on Materials Policy (1970–73), does not disqualify a body.

When the President "appoints" the members of a commission, he usually neither has personal knowledge of most of the appointees nor is deeply involved in the screening process at any but its last stage.[24] Thus presidential "appointment" may in some cases be only marginally different from formal presidential "approval" of the appointees of a Cabinet member or someone else (which removes a body from the category of presidential advisory commission). However, *de jure* presidential appointment is felt here to signify a generally higher degree of involvement by the President with an advisory commission and to justify its use as a criterion of inclusion and exclusion to sharpen the focus on commissions and the presidency.

To be *"ad hoc,"* an advisory body either must have a termination date included in its mandate or must be instructed to undertake an advisory task of clearly limited duration. A termination and reporting date not more than three years later than the date of creation of a body is required for it to be considered *ad hoc.* Thus, the Atlantic-Pacific Interoceanic Canal Study Commission created by PL 88-609 (September 22, 1964) was excluded because its final report was not due until 1970. Bodies which had no termination date in their mandate but which were terminated by a separate public act of the Congress or the President within three years after their creation were not thereby considered to be *ad hoc.* All *ad hoc* bodies have had, as members, a single group of individuals who served for the duration of the commission, rather than sets of members with staggered fixed terms, as many permanent presidential advisory bodies have had. Individual members of presidential advisory commissions have, of course, left them for a variety of reasons and been replaced by new appointees for the duration of the commission, or their positions have been left vacant at the discretion of the President.

The requirement that at least one member of a commission be "public" means that he not be an employee of the executive branch of the federal government. The public member may be from the Congress, the federal judiciary, state or local government, or be a private citizen.[25] The converse, that an advisory commission have at least one member from the Executive Branch, is not required, and a presidential advisory commission may be composed entirely of public members.

For a commission's report to be "public," its findings and recommendations must be published and available to the public. The public report can vary in formality and elaborateness from a multivolume report published by the Government Printing Office to a letter to the President from the chairman of a commission that is made public and that sets forth the results of the commission's work in a few pages. Bodies which were consulted by the President without producing a document embodying their conclusions are excluded. Bodies whose reports were never released or which are secret are also excluded.

Thus presidential advisory commissions are public in three senses: they are created by a public act and therefore have a public mandate, they have at least one public member, and they make a public report.

Presidential advisory commissions as enumerated in appendix 2 are those which were *created* in the period April 12, 1945–January 20, 1973, thereby excluding any commissions created earlier but which reported after April 12, 1945, and including commissions created before January 20, 1973, but reporting afterward. Presidential advisory commissions must also have been created while the President was in office. Thus some of the advisory bodies created by John F. Kennedy and Richard Nixon while they were Presidents-elect but which did not issue their reports until after inauguration are also excluded.

The definition excludes from the enumeration of presidential advisory commissions the following members of the "presidential advisory system":[26]

1. the White House staff;

2. the President's permanent advisory institutions (e.g., the Council of Economic Advisers);

3. all interagency advisory bodies or advisory cabinet committees;

4. government agencies or private institutions which undertake an *ad hoc* advisory task for the President (for example, the report, *20th Century Minutemen,* produced for the President and sent to him in January, 1954, by the National Security Training Commission, which was an ongoing administrative body; or research contracts to RAND or the Brookings Institution); the definition requires that both the body carrying out the task and the task itself be *ad hoc* and coterminate;

5. advisory groups without formal mandates or reports, although they may work on some *ad hoc* tasks (for example, "kitchen cabinets");

6. advisory groups whose mandate, membership, report, and existence are secret; and

7. single agents or representatives of the President or consultants to the President who carry out fact-finding missions or perform in other advisory capacities, even though their missions and report may be public.

Other bodies not clearly excluded by the definition of presidential advisory commissions have also been excluded here to attain a more unified focus. They are:

1. *ad hoc* fact-finding or recommending bodies created in response to labor-management disputes under the discretionary authority granted to the President under Section 10 of the Railway Labor Act (45 U.S.C. 160) or Section 206 of the Taft-Hartley Act (29 U.S.C. 176) or by an independent exercise of the President's authority; for example, the Railroad Marine Workers Commission created by President Kennedy in February, 1962. There were more than two hundred of these bodies in the period under consideration;

2. White House conferences which are large groups of people (often several hundred) who meet for a few days to discuss some topic and to make recommendations to the President; for example, the President's Conference on Industrial Safety, June 2–4, 1952, or the White House Conference on Equal Employment Opportunities, August 20, 1965. The conference is usually preceded by the work of a small committee, which prepares an agenda and materials for the conference. The conference itself usually meets in a series of panels or committees, which make recommendations to the conference as a whole, sitting as a legislative assembly. The conference is often followed by another committee that writes a report based on the discussions of the conference and the proposals it adopted. The organization and dynamics of these bodies seem sufficiently unique to justify excluding them from the list of presidential advisory commissions and from detailed consideration in this study, although they do merit and have not received extensive analysis;

3. what might be called "citizen mobilizations," which are White House sponsored citizen groups with committees throughout the country whose purposes are to educate the public on some topic, mobilize public support for a government program, and carry out through private efforts some program which the President wishes to encourage; for example, the National Alliance of Businessmen (announced January 23, 1968), or the Citizen Food Committee (1947).

Various other government bodies which are called commissions are not included under the definition of presidential advisory commissions. In particular, all of the various international commissions in which the United States participates by statute, treaty, or executive agreement and which have a variety of fact-finding, administrative, coordinating, and conciliating functions are not included; for example, the Inter-American Tropical Tuna Commission (1949, 1 U.S.T. 23). Also, of course, the well-known regulatory commissions such as the Federal Communications Commission of the Interstate Commerce Commission are excluded.

Although the definition of presidential advisory commissions set forth here may appear somewhat artificial, it effectively distinguishes a set of bodies almost all of which fit the general mental image of a presidential advisory commission, and excludes very few bodies that fit the commonsense view.[27]

CHAPTER TWO

WHAT ARE THE GOALS OF PRESIDENTS IN CREATING COMMISSIONS?

THE COMMON VIEW of journalistic and academic commentators on presidential advisory commissions is that the primary purpose of the President in creating them is to evade issues and avoid taking action.[1] Representative of this view is the Art Buchwald column in which the following exchange with a White House aide, Harvey Troglodyte, takes place:

> "The purpose of a presidential commission has been misunderstood by a vast number of Americans."
> "What is its main function?" I asked.
> "When the President announces he is appointing a presidential commission to study something, he is saying to the American people he is very concerned, and he is asking for answers to questions that all Americans are entitled to know."
> "That's well put," I said, "What else?"
> "That's it," Troglodyte said. "By the time the commission has come up with the answers, the President is counting on the problem to have gone away."[2]

The evidence indicates, quite to the contrary, that commissions are created to be instruments of action, reform, and change, not of obfuscation and standpatism. The primary presidential purpose for the largest number of commissions is to formulate innovative domestic policies and to facilitate their adoption.

This chapter attempts to substantiate the central point made above as well as to explore the variety of purposes that have motivated Presidents to create advisory commissions since 1945. Any attempt to divine the motives or intentions of Presidents is a risky enterprise, and this is no exception. There is, however, no reason to begin with a presumption that in the case of commissions Presidents are motivated by a desire to evade their responsibilities and to frustrate the aspirations and hopes of the public that are focused on them. Presidents, like other people, are likely to have mixed motives or to perhaps not even be conscious of their motives. Unfortunately none of the Presidents whose administrations are covered by this study was available to be interviewed.[3]

However, since presidential purposes are less the reflection of the will of one man than quasi-collegial outcomes from the modern institutionalized presidency, the testimony of White House staff is quite valuable.[4] Their purposes are also in a sense "presidential" purposes. Interviews with them have been heavily relied on in what follows. Furthermore, presidential goals must be communicated to be acted upon. They are communicated (or sensed) not only within the White House but also in many cases by the commission members and commission staff. For this reason also, interviews with White House staff as well as with commission members and staff have been valuable.

Previous studies that have dealt with the goals of Presidents in creating commissions have been deficient in several respects. First, some of them have treated presidential purposes in a speculative or in a prescriptive manner. They discuss the goals that the President could possibly have had or should have had, rather than those he did in fact have. They tend to deduce possible or desirable presidential goals from the variety of problems faced by the President and from the purposes for which commissions seem to be appropriate. They deal with potential or logically possible motivations.[5]

Second, some of them deal with actual presidential purposes, but generalize from only a small number of commissions, usually those that have received the most recent public attention.[6]

Third, most of their authors confuse purpose and outcome. In general, they assume that if a commission serves a particular function or has some impact at its conclusion that this is a reflection of the purpose of the President who created the commission. It is a curious assumption of presidential omnipotence.[7]

Finally, none of these authors attempts to assess which expectations predominated in the creation of commissions. They provide us with a catalogue of purposes without a discussion of which of them seems to be decisive in the largest number of cases and which appear in only a small number of cases. Each purpose that is presented by them appears to have the same weight and to occur with the same frequency as every other.

The discussion which follows focuses on the purposes Presidents have had, so far as they can be learned, in forming the commissions studied here. The congruence between presidential purposes and the impact that commissions have had is treated separately in chapter 7, thus leaving open the question of the relation between purpose and outcome. Finally, a ranking of presidential purposes, in terms of how often one purpose rather than another seems to be dominant in the creation of commissions, is developed.

The judgments expressed on types of purposes for which commissions are created and on the predominance of some purposes over others are based on data, beyond the formal commission mandates, gathered for approximately one-half of the ninety-nine commissions. This data was drawn primarily from the interviews described in appendix 1. The interviews were extensively supplemented by information from public records and secondary sources as well as by inferences drawn from the political situations at the time the commissions were set up. The analysis which follows cites only a few commissions as typical examples and illustrations of each of the purposes, rather than offering lists of all of the commissions which are known or suspected to have had a particular purpose.

POLICY ANALYSIS

The stated goal for every presidential commission is to be a policy analyst.[8] They are instructed to make a study assessing a specific problem, to evaluate current efforts to solve it, and to recommend whatever actions they deem appropriate to more successfully solve the problem. The mandate of the National Advisory Commission on Health Manpower (1966–67) is a typical expression of this revealed purpose:

> . . . the Commission shall:
> (1) Make a comprehensive study and appraisal of the current situation and trends in the provisions of health care for the civilian population and the armed forces and their implications with respect to the current and prospective adequacy and utilization of manpower;
> (2) Appraise the current policies, programs, and practices of public agencies and private institutions and organizations and other factors which have a bearing on the requirements for, and the availability of, health manpower and the effective allocation and utilization of such manpower; and
> (3) Develop appropriate recommendations for action by Government or by private institutions, organizations, or individuals for improving the availability and utilization of health manpower.[9]

Perhaps surprisingly to many people, the stated goal of policy analysis is in fact the actual goal for the largest number of commissions. Based on the available evidence, well over half of the commissions were judged to have this goal as their primary purpose, and almost all of the rest had it as at least an important secondary purpose.

White House aides identify one of the important purposes of commissions as "to really find something out," "to take a fresh look at a problem," or to satisfy "a need for ideas."[10] An aide from the Eisenhower and Nixon administrations remarked, "The President doesn't have time to look into everything. He wants fresh ideas." Commenting on the President's Committee on Urban Housing (Kaiser Committee, 1967–68), a Johnson White House staff member said, "The Kaiser Commission was to deal with a specific problem—how fast could we build enough housing units to close the housing gap."

Commissions created primarily for policy analysis have been called upon to deal with a wide variety of questions, among them What federal policies should be pursued to maintain the nation's shipbuilding capacity? Where should the World's Fair be held? and Why is voting participation low in the United States and how can it be increased?[11] And among the prominent policy analysis commissions have been the President's Water Resources Policy Commission (1950), the President's Materials Policy Commission (1951–52), the President's Committee on Education Beyond High School (1956–57), the President's Advisory Commission on Narcotic and Drug Abuse (1963–64), the President's Commission on Law Enforcement and Administration of Justice (1965–67), the President's Commission on Postal Organization (1967–68), the President's Advisory Council on Executive Organization (1969–71), and the President's Commission on School Finance (1970–72).

The President's policy analysis goal in creating these commissions carries with it a number of expectations about what the commissions will actually do. The stated purpose for every commission and the actual purpose for this largest subset of commissions is formulated in terms of problems. The basic expectation is that every commission will recommend a solution for the problem it is dealing with. It is expected that no commission will write a report saying that the problem with which it was presented is insoluble or that the state of affairs it has been asked to remedy must simply be tolerated. It is assumed that for every problem there are solutions and that the commission will discover and recommend one of them.

Commissions are expected to evaluate the alternative solutions that they discover, or that are presented to them, in terms of some criteria of public interest, benefit, or welfare. It is important that they recommend one package from among the many that are available. The President needs, welcomes, and expects a choice reducing the many to one. This service is valuable to him, whether or not the recommended package is in fact substantively "better" than those which are rejected. A commission is also expected to present a rationale for its choice, however.

There are also expectations concerning the nature of the solution that is recommended. First, commissions are not expected to find "new" solutions in the sense of wholly original and never-before-considered or unheard-of ideas. A commission is not precluded from inventing unique and original solutions or from dusting off a hoary prescription, elevating a heretofore obscure proposal, or juggling several proposals into a new combination. In general, however, it is expected to pick one solution from the already established array of options.

Second, commissions are not expected to find that the problems they are dealing with are insignificant, or that no federal action is necessary to solve them, or that federal action cannot contribute significantly to their solution. The decision to have a commission implies a judgment that a problem is important, that some action is necessary, and that action by the federal government will probably be appropriate and effective. A President and his staff do not look for or invent problems and then ask commissions to tell them whether or not they should ignore them. If a problem is not yet considered important enough to require a response from the federal government, it is not ignored by conscious choice, it is simply nonexistent in the White House.

Third, it goes almost without saying that commissions are not expected to engage in fundamental critiques of or to recommend radical changes in the political, economic, or social order. They are expected to suggest proposals for ameliorating and reforming the status quo.

The commissions formed with the presidential purpose of policy analysis usually come somewhere in the middle of the process that begins with the initial recognition of a problem and ends with the promulgation of some government response to deal with it (or the final realization that the government cannot or will not take action). They follow some perception of the problem held by relatively narrow segments of the public and some specialized sections of the government. Creation of the commission indicates a relatively firm but still tentative decision to "do something," and the commission is expected to decide what to do within the broad boundaries of nonradical federal action.

WINDOW DRESSING

The second most prevalent purpose of presidential commissions is to be "window dressing," to help sell or market a proposal to which the President is already committed. Commissions created with this in mind are expected to facilitate the acceptance of a presidential initiative by the other political actors, usually Congress and the federal bureaucracy, whose consent is required for authoritative action. The President has already decided what to do in these cases, and the commission is meant to help him do it and, to a certain extent, to tell him how to do it. This purpose is almost always unrevealed at the time the commission is appointed, as are all of the purposes other than policy analysis. Window dressing was the primary purpose for about twenty of the commissions studied (a fifth of the total), and an important secondary purpose for almost all of the commissions. A key Truman aide remarked in an interview that some commissions were used "to build a case for something they were already convinced on." His view is echoed by a member of the Nixon White House who said, "Sometimes you appoint commissions to reach a foreordained conclusion and they have some political value."

What is the political value that these commissions are expected to have? "The process of having a commission enables a President to say that this eminent group of people or this cross section of the country approve of what he is proposing," observed an aide in the Johnson Administration. It is "a way to get the establishment to bless something," to "minimize the accusation that the decks are stacked," and to "dignify and give persuasive expression to the advocacy of ideas or to possible changes."[12] The President's purpose is to recruit a representative elite and to use it to support his program initiatives. In addition, the President wants to provide a forum and a context in which an elite consensus for his proposals can be generated. For a large number of the President's proposals, representatives of the nation's political and economic power centers or representatives of the constellation of interests involved in the policy area concerned lack the opportunity to form a consensus. Or if a consensus does exist, it is not articulated in a single document, by the most prestigious constituency representatives, from a highly visible platform, and with the accompaniment of an elaborate rationale. A member of the staff of the National Commission on Technology, Automation, and Economic Progress (1964–66) observed, "The role of the commission is to show a consensus where one was not apparent before."

Or the purpose may be to gain greater acceptance for a proposal that would be ignored, easily dismissed, or grossly discounted if it emanated from the White House. An Eisenhower aide remarked:

> To achieve credibility for some policy you might want a third party to work on it which is impartial. . . . It's too bad that the established institutions of government lack public confidence and you have to resort to these advisory commissions.

Endorsement by a commission is expected to increase the credibility and weight of a presidential initiative. Harnessing such a credible elite consensus to a presidential proposal provides a President with a powerful educational and persuasive tool. The President expects that these commissions in reaching a consensus which endorses his proposal will enable him to persuade and educate the Congress and the public.

In a system of "separated institutions sharing powers," persuading the Congress is usually the primary objective, because congressional consent is essential for most major presidential initiatives and is often not easily forthcoming.[13] Public education is generally seen as an indirect way to persuade the Congress. Truman's President's Advisory Commission on Universal Training (1946–47) is a good example of a commission created with the purpose of persuading Congress and the public. President Truman had first proposed a universal military training program in 1945.[14] He was personally interested in the idea, and the War Department and Secretary Marshall were very much in favor of it. It was rejected by the Congress. The President then created the commission in November, 1946, and noted that its "recommendations would go a long way toward dispelling the confusion existing in the public mind on this subject."[15] In his *Memoirs,* President Truman explained his purpose and the results:

> The plan submitted by the Commission in its report was a thoroughly studied elaboration of the views I had expressed to my Cabinet almost two years before. I had hoped that the publication of this report by a group of distinguished and representative Americans would move Congress to action, but again I was to be disappointed.[16]

Another commission created for primarily the same purpose was the President's Advisory Panel on Federal Salary Systems (1961–63), appointed by President Kennedy. A member of the panel explained his perception of the President's purpose:

> There are situations where the President can't count on his own political influence with Congress. He wants to mobilize political support. He wants to convince those in Congress who do not usually support him. It was probably thought that this eminent group, including a businessman like Clarence Randall, would be able to help the President convince some of the Republicans. Someone on the White House staff probably thought that such a group would look good and have legislative weight.

The objectives of window dressing and persuading Congress also show through in the letter inviting one of the members to serve on the panel: "The President intends to submit a proposal on Federal pay to the Congress in January. He feels the need, however, for your advice and the advice of others on the panel before firming up his proposal."[17] The President thus already had a proposal which only needed "firming up." The panel also did not have its own staff and was limited for the most part to reviewing the proposals presented to it by the Bureau of the Budget, the Civil Service Commission, and the Department of Defense.

An important aspect of persuading Congress and the public through a commission is the allaying or neutralizing of the fears or doubts that they may have about a proposal. White House counterarguments to the fears and objections voiced in Congress are naturally suspected of being less than candid. It is hoped that a commission saying much the same thing as the White House will solve this credibility problem.

The President's Committee on Foreign Aid (1947) provides a good example of this purpose. The editor of *The Private Papers of Senator Vandenberg* eloquently describes the situation that President Truman intended the committee to deal with:

> The Marshall idea fell upon a Republican Congress dedicated to reducing taxes and cutting government spending. There was deep concern, not only in Congress but throughout the country, that scarce American goods would be drained off the domestic market for foreign consumption. There was similar concern lest the United States strain its financial and material resources only to "pour its money down a rat hole," and it was asked whether success of the program would serve only to increase competition for American business.[18]

The bipartisan group composed of "representatives of the economic power groups" was intended to help the President meet the doubts in Congress about "this relatively novel and tough idea."[19] Or as a staff member of another commission put it, "This commission provided a useful service in dealing with some of the nitty gritty questions and problems that could become objections to the idea."

To carry out his policies, the President often needs to persuade not only the Congress and the public but also the federal bureaucracy he nominally heads. The theme of bureaucratic resistance to presidential initiatives is well established in political science.[20] Creating a commission can be intended as a way for a President to get "leverage on his government." This purpose is illustrated by the Committee on Population and Family Planning (1968), about which a Johnson aide said, "This commission was to take a problem that the administration had already recognized and assert a new priority for it in the government. It was a way to try to make the bureaucracy realize that you really mean business on this."

An important variant of the window-dressing purpose is that of persuading and educating the Congress so that it will not do something that the President is opposed to. This "holding-the-line" purpose is particularly evident for the periodic commissions dealing with foreign aid.[21] The President's objective is to prevent curtailment of a program which lacks a permanent domestic constituency receiving its benefits.[22] A staff member of the President's Citizen Advisers on the Mutual Security Program (1956–57) explained:

> There was a problem they had in selling the program on the Hill. There was always a substantial number of Congressmen who were against the program. The President may have felt that it was not understood properly. Getting a commission of this stature would help not only with the Congress but with business and other elements of the nation. "If Fairless from U.S. Steel says it's O.K., then it must be."[23]

Another example is the President's Commission on Veterans' Pensions (1955–56), which was created while Mrs. Edith Nourse Rogers (R-Mass.) was chairman of the House Veterans' Affairs Committee. She had the reputation of being openhanded on veterans' benefits, and the World War I veterans, "Oneies," were aggressively demanding what amounted to an old age pension. "The Oneies were knocking at the door," said one of the commission's staff members. "They were at the age and it was their turn." The commission was part of an effort to "beat off this raid on the Treasury," he concluded.[24]

The window-dressing commissions usually occur relatively late in the process of presidential policy initiation. The President's Advisory Commission on Universal Training (1946–47), in fact, came after the President's proposal had been completely developed and rejected by the Congress. The report of the President's Committee on Foreign Aid (1947) was rushed to the printer before all of the members had read the final draft, so that it could be available to backstop the Marshall Plan legislation then going before the Congress. These commissions also tend to have very limited staffs of their own, in contrast to the large staffs, sometimes numbering more than a hundred, characteristic of the policy analysis commissions.

It would be wrong to view these window-dressing commissions as simply rubber stamps. They are as independent as any other commission, as they must be if they are to serve the President's purposes.[25] There always exists the possibility that they will not endorse the proposal whose course the President is trying to grease with the commission's support. Or they may recommend substantial modifications in the President's proposal. This was the case, for example, with the President's Commission on the Health Needs of the Nation (1951–52). President Truman indicates what his purpose and the commission's recommendations were in his *Memoirs:*

> In a move to offset the propaganda of the opposition an Executive Order was issued on December 29, 1951, creating the President's Commission on the Health Needs of the Nation. . . . What the Commission was recommending basically represented a compromise between the compulsory national health insurance program requested in 1945 and throughout my administration, and the current system. . . . While the insurance program was not the same as the one I had proposed earlier, I felt that the Commission on the Health Needs of the Nation had accomplished a monumental task and that a workable outline for raising our national health standards was now available.[26]

The policy analysis commissions are also in a sense window dressing. First, as was discussed above, a general commitment to federal action ususally already exists when these commissions are created. They therefore are intended to smooth the path for the acceptance of some action. Second, while their primary purpose is to decide what the federal action should be and to defend their choice, they are also expected to assist in persuading and educating the Congress, the public, and the federal bureaucracy to accept the solution that they have formulated. This common combination of purposes for a policy analysis commission is illustrated by Eric Goldman's explanation of the purposes he envisioned for the National Advisory Commission on Selective Service (1966–67) when he recommended that it be created. "[W]hat I had in mind was that . . . an able and reasonably dispassionate Presidential commission might help pinpoint for the public both the deficiencies and the way they could be lessened if not corrected. This would help build a public opinion which favored, or at least was ready for, healthy change in the system."[27]

LONG-RANGE EDUCATION

About a half dozen commissions have been created when there was no short- or intermediate-range prospect of executive or legislative action to deal with the problem at hand. The President's primary purpose in creating such a commission is either to begin a long range support-building effort for solving a problem that is well recognized but on which there is little prospect of immediate action, or to elevate a problem to a prominent position on the national agenda. The commission is created to call attention to a problem and to establish a frame of reference in terms of which the problem should be debated and ultimately solved. It is intended to have an educational impact that will be manifest only in the distant future as measured by presidential time, that is, beyond the end of his current term.

The President's Commission on Immigration and Naturalization (1952) is an example of such a commission. It was created by President Truman shortly after the McCarran-Walter Act had been passed over his veto and while he was a lame-duck President, Adlai Stevenson having already been nominated as the Democratic Party's standard bearer for 1952. One of the commission's staff explained, "I looked at it as a ten-year proposition. . . . There was no reasonable likelihood that the Congress would take up a lameduck President's proposals. It was a long range educational effort directed at the people and at the Congress in particular."[28]

A good example of a commission designed to place a heretofore unrecognized problem on the national agenda is the National Commission on Higher Education (1946–47). In 1946, higher education was not widely perceived as an area in which the federal government did, could, or should have a major responsibility. The intention of the White House was explained by a Truman aide: "The Higher Education Commission was strictly a study commission to set goals and priorities in a noncontroversial field where you couldn't see the future clearly." A staff member of the commission noted, along the same line, "This guy was really looking down the road. . . . Truman was trying to lay down several large lines of movement for the years ahead and he chose education as one. . . . I heard him say privately that returning veterans were only a temporary problem and that he was more concerned with the long-term development of education."

Similarly, President Kennedy's Panel on Mental Retardation (1961–62) spotlighted and made legitimate this formerly taboo problem. This legitimization and symbolic elevation of a problem to the status of a "national goal," "national crisis," or "pressing issue" by presidential designation of a commission to study it is a minimal purpose for almost every commission. Creating a commission is a tangible expression of the President's concern for a problem and an indication that he believes that the Congress, the bureaucracy, the parties, and the public should also be concerned.

It is also expected that every commission will set out the terms in which the problem should be conceptualized and debated. While this purpose of legitimating and conceptualizing issues to begin a long-term process of public education is the primary purpose of only a few commissions, it is expected that almost every commission will at least serve it in addition to its major purpose.

CRISIS RESPONSE

Commissions are also created to meet crises, as a way for the President to satisfy a public expectation of action by him. Fewer than ten commissions were created with crisis response as their primary purpose, but several others had this as an important secondary purpose.

One of the major political dangers faced by every President is that he will be "caught out" on some issue, that he will be judged to have failed in his responsibility to act. Commissions dealing with various substantive problems are intended to safeguard the President from this danger. However, the expectation of a presidential response and the concomitant dangers of being caught out are most intense in crisis situations. Since the President is the national symbol of stability, predictability, and unity, there is a very strong expectation that he will act when events create widespread and intense anxiety because of their often violent and unforeseen nature.[29] Therefore crisis commissions have as their primary purpose to reassure the public that the President and the government are concerned and are acting. They are generally expected by the President to be more useful for their immediate symbolic value than for their ultimate findings and recommendations. A Johnson White House aide said, for example, of the National Advisory Commission on Civil Disorders (Kerner Commission, 1967–68), "The Kerner Commission was created in the wake of the riots. You can be damn sure that the President was not going to let the people think that he was not doing anything about the riots."

The National Advisory Commission on Civil Disorders (Kerner Commission,

1967–68), the President's Commission on the Assassination of President Kennedy (Warren Commission, 1963–64), the National Commission on the Causes and Prevention of Violence (1968–69), and the President's Commission on Campus Unrest (1970) are obvious examples of crisis commissions. A less well known but equally graphic example is the President's Airport Commission (1952) created by President Truman. One of its staff members explained the commission's purpose:

> This [commission] came up . . . because in January, 1952 there were three serious accidents of planes crashing around the Newark airport. There was an uproar in the press. This was a kind of emergency thing—don't just stand there, do something. . . . This commission had a hell of a lot of political inputs behind it. It was a public relations deal—o.k. chums we're doing something about it. It received a lot of publicity. Pictures were taken of the town fathers and the commission at the airport and were printed in the local press. The idea got about that the Great White Father was interested and doing something.[30]

These commissions are created *faute de mieux*. They represent the response of a President caught between the perception that he can and will act in a crisis and the constraints of his office and the limits of his power. They are palliatives. But they arise not so much from a desire on the part of the President to evade taking effective action in areas where there are remedies at his command as from the elevated and unrealistic, but pervasive, image of the President's powers and responsibilities.[31] As Howard Shuman, executive director of the National Commission on Urban Problems (1967–68) observed, "They [commissions] are sometimes established as acts of desperation. When all else fails, appoint a commission."[32]

ISSUE MANAGEMENT AND ISSUE AVOIDANCE

Another of the purposes for which Presidents create commissions is expressed well by Howard Shuman. "Commissions are generally established to buy time on an immediate and politically tender issue—or, as someone else has said, to treat the politics of a situation rather than the situation itself."[33] White House aides from each administration, commission members, and commission staff also describe one of the reasons for creating a commission as "to duck a problem," "to farm problems out for awhile to see what will happen," "to cool things down," or "to get off the hook on a problem." A commission, in this view, "takes the heat off" or is "a way of sweeping dirty problems under the rug."[34] It is difficult to assess the number of commissions for which this purpose was an important consideration in their creation. It seems to have been of some importance in the establishment of many commissions, particularly those in the policy analysis category.

The common theme of these various descriptions is that commissions are often set up to defer or avoid acting or deciding. There are, however, important differences between the two variants of this theme, deferring action and avoiding action.

Deferring action on a problem through the appointment of a commission can be a responsible and useful presidential technique. The politically most viable and substantively best decisions are not necessarily those that are made most quickly. Appointing a commission brings under presidential control the time at which and the form in which the President will have to commit himself more deeply and more finally on an issue. Creating a commission allows a President to choose a deadline, impose some preliminary structure on the issue, and to make tentative commitments. The commission is a means by which a President can feel his way into a controlversial, complex, or new area. Action is contemplated, and it will in the President's view be more effective because of the policy analysis, window dressing, and crisis management services provided by a commission.

Avoiding action can also be important to a President. As an Eisenhower White House aide, for example, said, "They [commissions] could be used . . . to put a problem on a shelf. White House aides were happy to be rid of some problem because there were always more of them coming down the hall. If you were rid of something for a year or two it might go away or administrations might change and it would be somebody else's problem." While seeking to avoid action could theoretically be legitimate in cases where there is no appropriate or effective presidential response to be made to a problem, it is difficult to imagine an example of this sort, given the public expectations focused on the President, the expansive conception of the office held by most modern Presidents, and the wide range of statutory and customary powers that have devolved on Presidents in the twentieth century.

Determining which of these two purposes, issue management or issue avoidance, is predominant in the creation of commissions to postpone action is next to impossible. It is most likely that the two are intertwined rather than discrete and separate. Presidents probably desire to have more information, a sense of the political realities, and more control over the form and timing of an issue, and at the same time hope to have the issue die down or be resolved without presidential action before the commission issues its report.

It is at least logical to assume that avoiding issues is not the predominant purpose. Most problems do not go away. A Johnson aide remarked, "At its cynical best, a commission can only temporarily stave off a problem." While appointing a commission may postpone a problem in the short run, it also makes it inevitable that the problem will return in a more salient form, embodied in a presidential commission report. There is also a not inconsequential possibility that the commission will make recommendations that the

President does not like but will find it difficult to directly disown or evade. The best way to ignore a problem is just to ignore it and not call more attention to it by appointing a commission. Appointing a commission in general implies a commitment to presidential action.[35]

OTHER PURPOSES

The major purposes, outlined above, for which commissions are created do not exhaust the presidential goals in appointing commissions. There are a number of other purposes which are important in particular cases although less common.

Commissions are appointed to restore congressional and public confidence in an institution or process of the federal government that is under a shadow of doubt or being attacked. For example, the President's Committee to Appraise Employment and Unemployment Statistics (1961–62) was created in response to doubts expressed about "the scientific objectivity of the agencies responsible for collecting, processing, and publishing these data."[36] In appointing the commission, President Kennedy stated that it was his "objective to maintain and enhance the quality of our statistics . . . so that the public may have the highest degree of confidence in them."[37]

A commission can be intended to serve the President as an independent check on the staff work being done within the executive branch. "It provides an outside check to make sure that the insiders are not overlooking something," explained one commission member.

It is not considered proper for some recommendations, particularly those dealing with the internal policies of the other branches of the federal government, to originate from the President. A commission can provide a more acceptable source for these recommendations. One of the studies done by the President's Advisory Panel on Federal Salary Systems (1961–63) made recommendations concerning legislative, executive, and judicial salaries. One of the commission's members remarked, "Legislative and judicial salaries were not the President's business. Congress could be expected to react violently and antagonistically if they perceived presidential interference. It was probably thought that they would not resent proposals coming from that panel as much."

Some commissions have been created from a desire to maintain the White House as a primary source of policy initiatives. The threat of a congressional study preempting the initiative was an important prod moving the White House to their formation. In other cases, direct suggestions from congressmen were important.[38] The President's Committee on Foreign Aid (1947), the Air Policy Commission (1947–48), the Missouri Basin Survey Commission (1952–53), and the National Advisory Commission on Civil Disorders (1967–68) are among the commissions set up either to head off congressional studies or at the urging of congressmen. At least two of the nine commissions created by statute were forced upon a reluctant President (Commission on Marine Science, Engineering, and Resources, 1968–69, and Commission on Obscenity and Pornography, 1967–70).[39]

The role of the Congress in prodding the President to form some commissions suggests two general observations about congressional-executive relations. First, in general, the Executive Branch is the primary source of policy initiative in American national politics, because of its institutional capabilities and its capacity to formulate integrated and coordinated national programs. The areas in which initiative is taken is a function of the institutional perspectives within the Executive Branch, for example a general bias in favor of federal governmental programs, and of the ideological goals and partisan calculations of the President and his policy-making appointees. However, prods from outside the Executive Branch are also an important stimulus for initiatives, and the threat of erosion of Executive Branch power through the preemption of dormant policy areas by the Congress is one significant prod.

Second, the role of the Congress in policy initiation is perhaps more extensive than is commonly believed. Critics of the Congress point to its increasing inability to deal with broad problems through the formulation and enactment of comprehensive policies and programs.[40] The role of Congress in the creation of presidential commissions suggests that the impact of Congress should also be assessed in terms of the degree to which it activates the executive, rather than solely in terms of how many comprehensive pieces of legislation it generates internally.[41] In these terms the Congress is perhaps a much more active and significant participant in policy initiation than is usually thought.

Another reason why Presidents create commissions is in order to satisfy or to not disappoint the persons who suggest them. The suggestion that the President set up a commission does not reach the White House as a disembodied message. It comes instead embodied in and articulated by persons often holding important positions within the administration or in public life and having personal or political ties to the White House and the President. Commissions were suggested, for example, by President Kennedy's sister, Eunice Shriver, in one case (Panel on Mental Retardation, 1961–62), and by John D. Rockefeller, III, and Secretary of the Treasury Fowler in other cases (Committee on Population and Family Planning, 1968–69, and Industry-Government Special Task Force on Travel, 1967–68). This fact not only assured the ideas a hearing within the White House but also increased the likelihood that they would be agreed to. Thus agreement by the President to create a commission may in part be a means to purchase quiescence from important individuals. As one White House aide put it, some commissions are created "because somebody gets to the President."

Commissions are also created at least in part simply because a problem exists and the option of a commission is available. "Sometimes these things [commissions] are just created by chance," observed a Johnson aide. The suggestion to have a commission is almost routinely raised when a problem confronts the White House, particularly a problem to which there is no obvious response in terms of already existing programs. Suggestions for commissions are continually in the air. Presidential commissions on inflation and Watergate have recently been suggested, for example.[42] "Creating a commission was almost always suggested as a solution to every problem in the White House. A very small number of those that are suggested see the light of day," remarked an aide who served under both Presidents Kennedy and Johnson. During the Johnson Administration, for example, commissions on Vietnam policy, creative federalism, and the Executive Office of the President reached varying stages of planning and commitment within the White House, but were all eventually rejected.[43] Given that the suggestion to have a commission is more often than not rejected, the great majority of commissions are probably created because they are seen to have special capabilities or advantages for accomplishing the President's purposes. However, since commissions are also a routinely available option, perhaps more routinely available as they have become more numerous and familiar and have demonstrated their utility, some of them are created for no good reason related to their special capabilities. A commission may simply be the last option remaining after all others have been rejected, or it may be seen to have the fewest liabilities compared to other courses of action being considered. An Eisenhower aide remarked, "My impression is that they [commissions] just sort of happen. Some problem is being pounded around among the staff members or Cabinet members, and someone says, 'Why don't we create a blue-ribbon commission on this?' "

The preceding discussion of presidential purposes has isolated the purposes in separate categories and expressed judgments about the relative numbers of commissions that fall primarily into one or another of these categories. This is, of course, a distortion of reality. For each commission there are in fact multiple and interrelated purposes that are rarely articulated fully and that are almost never ranked in an order of priority. As noted above, the expectation of policy analysis by a commission is usually accompanied by the hope that the commission will also persuade other political actors to accept its recommendations. Failing this, it is at least expected that a commission will conceptualize and focus attention on the problem and lay the foundation for solving it in the future. Thus the first three purposes discussed above, policy analysis, window dressing, and long-range education, are frequently goals for the same commission. Without detailed case studies of each commission, it is impossible to say in each case with any certainty which of the three is dominant, if in fact there is a dominant purpose. Almost every commission is also created to manage and structure issues, and there is also at least the faint hope in many cases that the issue will have died before the commission reports. Perhaps the best generalization is that commissions are expected to "do something" about a problem, but exactly what that "something" is is not necessarily clear to the President. Rather than having a single specific purpose, most commissions are probably considered to be potentially useful in several ways. In which of these ways the commission ultimately has an impact depends in large measure on the commission itself, on whether or not it develops what seems to be a workable solution, supports it with a persuasive argument, and is unified in its position. It also, of course, depends on the political context at the time the commission reports.

A good example of the multiple and interrelated purposes for which a commission is created and the lack of clarity of presidential purpose is the President's Committee on Civil Rights (1946–47). Following the end of World War II, there were a number of especially frightful racial lynchings in the United States. Pressure for federal action was focused on President Truman and on the Civil Rights Section of the Department of Justice by the then-existing civil rights organizations. President Truman also feared a post-war reaction comparable to the one that had followed World War I. However, the President and the Civil Rights Section lacked the authority to deal effectively with this crisis. So, in part, the committee was created as a symbolic response to this crisis, since no other response was available. Creating the committee was also perhaps, in part, a symbolic gesture to the liberals in the Democratic Party, who were not yet convinced that Truman was worthy of Roosevelt's mantle. The racial lynchings were also the subject of critical propaganda abroad, particularly from the communist countries, and appointing the committee was a way to respond to that criticism.

In addition, the committee's mandate and Truman's *Memoirs* make clear that the President was committed to seeking an expanded Federal role in protecting the civil rights of individuals and planned to seek legislation for this purpose. Another purpose of the committee was therefore to build support for this legislative initiative, a window-dressing purpose.

However, the President lacked a clear idea of the scope and nature of the civil rights problem and of the kind of legislation that was most needed and that would be most effective. The committee therefore also had a straightforward fact-finding and policy analysis purpose.

Finally, one of the White House aides closely involved in the creation of the committee expressed the view that it was also part of a general strategy of public education "to turn the tide of public opinion" and "to put segregation on the defensive." These various purposes were neither distinguished clearly from each other nor explicitly ranked in importance.[44]

Commissions have multiple purposes. These purposes are often interrelated.

The dominance of one purpose or several results less from a hard, clear choice by the President when the commission is created than from the evolution of presidential needs and problems and the way in which the commission perceives and does its job. When it is created, a commission is a bag of possibilities. Some of the possibilities are more salient than others, but all of the possibilities may not be clearly perceived and their relative importance may change over time.

In sum, commissions are intended to formulate solutions for problems; to build interest group, congressional, bureaucratic, and general public support; to legitimate and conceptualize new problems and to arouse public concern for them; to prevent action that the President views as undesirable; to serve as a symbolic response to a crisis; to manage issues; to evade issues; and for a number of other less-frequent purposes. In only a small minority of cases does the dominant purpose of a commission seem to be to evade having to act. In the cases where a commission is a symbolic crisis response, it is argued that this is more the result of the lack of other options in the face of public expectations than of presidential unwillingness to act effectively.

Three themes characterize the basic purpose for the overwhelming majority of commissions. First, they are intended to analyze problems. This generally means that they are expected to propose changes in the current state of affairs and action by the President and the federal government. They are a manifestation of the "future-oriented" character of modern government, intended to help it choose from among "alternative futures."[45]

Second, they are intended to be a forum in which a consensus will be reached among the constituency representatives who are commission members. This consensus will then be a means to persuade and educate various publics, most often the Congress, to the wisdom of the commission's or the President's proposed initiatives.

Third, they are expected to manage issues by placing a presidential structure and deadline on them. In short, commissions are usually intended to be a technique of innovative presidential leadership. They are conceived of as a way for Presidents to do things, not to avoid doing things.

CHAPTER THREE

WHY A COMMISSION?

ALL OF THE PURPOSES for which Presidents create commissions could be served by a variety of other presidential actions: creating a task force or interagency committee, sponsoring a White House conference, giving a speech, delivering a message, issuing a proclamation, embarking on a presidential trip, inviting congressional and public figures to the White House for briefings and discussions, persuading a friendly congressional committee chairman to hold hearings, or encouraging a foundation or university to undertake a study. All of these options are often chosen to deal with the same problems and to accomplish the same purposes for which commissions are created. Indeed, one or more of these other alternatives is often being used simultaneously with the operation of a commission.[1] The questions, then, that are the focus of this chapter are What are the unique and defining characteristics of commissions from the point of view of the White House? What special capabilities do commissions possess? and In what circumstances and for what kinds of issues are commissions particularly suitable and useful?

The underlying assumption of the chapter is that the President's choice of a commission rather than some other tactic to accomplish his purposes is rational and is based on a judgment that commissions have unique characteristics and capabilities.

THE UNIQUE CHARACTERISTICS OF COMMISSIONS

In their public statements announcing the creation of commissions or responding to their reports, Presidents ascribe to commissions a number of characteristics. These characteristics are asserted to set commissions apart from other governmental techniques and to make them unique. Similarly, White House staff, commission staff, and commission members attribute unique characteristics to commissions.[2]

First, commissions have members and staff who are said to be *competent* and *qualified* to examine the problem with which the commission is concerned. They are competent for one of three reasons or for a combination of them. They may be "technical experts" whose professional careers have been largely devoted to the study of the commission's problem—for example, Richard Scammon, the chairman of the President's Commission on Registration and Voting Participation (1963), or Stephen Spurr, a member of the President's Advisory Panel on Timber and the Environment (1971–73).[3] They may be billed as men of wisdom who, while not experts in the field, will bring their competence as generalists to the problem. They are "the best minds." Kingman Brewster, President of Yale University, in his service on the President's Commission on Law Enforcement and Administration of Justice (1965–67) might be an example of this type. Or they may have been practitioners in some aspect of the commission's concern, or have dealt with or been affected by the problem under consideration; the competence of the commission members and staff may be said to derive from their work experience. Thomas Cahill, Chief of Police from San Francisco, who also served on the President's Commission on Law Enforcement and Administration of Justice, is an example of this type.[4]

Second, commissions are *representative.* They are described as being a demographic cross section of America (men, women, blacks, whites, business, labor, academia, etc.) and representative of the major interests or areas of knowledge involved in the issue under consideration.[5] Implicit in this characteristic is the belief that a commission will take into account more points of view than would normally be available in the process of policy formulation in the Executive Branch. Thus the commission is said to be more "democratic" because broad membership gives it better channels to the public and a better sense of public needs and attitudes than Executive Branch policy makers.

Third, commissions are *prestigious.* One of the most common adjectives used by Presidents to describe commissions is "distinguished."[6] Commission members are said to be the most "eminent" and "high-status" experts and representatives. They are in effect the public symbols of their field of knowledge or their constituency. The most striking example of this is George Meany, President of the AFL-CIO (since 1955), who served on eight commissions, including at least one created by each of the four Presidents preceding Nixon.[7] During most of that period, a public opinion poll question asking for the identification of "Mister Labor" in the United States would have produced at least a large percentage, if perhaps not a majority at all times, for the name of George Meany. Similarly, the other commission members are generally the "Misters" of their respective fields. Thus presidential advisory commissions are often referred to as "blue ribbon commissions."

Fourth, presidential advisory commissions are highly *visible.* Creating a commission represents a White House decision to treat a problem in a public way. "If you want public discussion . . . public participation, and public exposure, then you have a public commission," said a Kennedy White House aide. Commissions have high visibility primarily for two reasons: the eminence and prestige of their members, and the fact that they represent an extraordinary action by the President giving them a presidential mandate. Although there has been a trend toward establishing an increasing number of commissions per year since 1945, their creation is still a significant event, at least to the specialized public most concerned with the problem at hand. Actually, between 1945 and 1968 only about three commissions a year, on the average, were appointed. Despite the outpouring of twenty commissions in the first year of the Nixon administration, a new commission is hardly an everyday occurrence.[8] Even if it were, the daily actions of a President are still front page news.[9]

Fifth, commission members are generally drawn from outside the Executive Branch of the federal government. They are *"private citizens"* who will bring "outside judgment" and "outside thinking" to bear on the problem.[10]

Sixth, commissions are *ad hoc.* In contrast to almost all other government organizations, they are defined by their impermanence.

Finally, when taken together, all of these six characteristics of commissions—their competence, representativeness, prestige, visibility, non-executive-branch membership, and limited tenure—define the most important special attributes of commissions, their *independence* and *objectivity.* The commission is alleged to have no vested interest in the programs and policies of the Executive Branch because it is temporary and because most of its members are not employed in the Executive Branch. They are a group of temporary "outsiders." The reputed integrity and prestige of the commission members is to guarantee that their actions will not be guided by a hope of future preferment from the President. The representativeness and high visibility of commissions is also felt to assure that they will not be dominated by Executive Branch or single clientele points of view. Presidents disavow any intent to influence them. "I should like to emphasize," said President Eisenhower concerning the Commission on National Goals (1960), "my desire that the inquiry be conducted free of any direct connection with me or other portions of the federal government."[11] The commission is also unbiased and unprejudiced because its members are "neutral experts" and "nonpartisan," or because it is balanced and bipartisan, composed of representatives of all points of view. This balance will result in an objective report, since the commission reproduces in microcosm America's pluralism or the marketplace of ideas through which self-interest and antagonistic views are metamorphosed into the truth and the public interest. So with regard to the federal executive, commissions are said to be an objective and neutral third party.[12]

THE SPECIAL ADVANTAGES OF COMMISSIONS

Presidential advisory commissions have three kinds of general advantages or capabilities because of their special characteristics. They have a unique ability to engage in policy analysis and to formulate innovative recommendations.

They have an unusual capacity to persuade other political actors to adopt their recommendations and agree with their findings. And they are effective as a forum in which their members can be educated and thereby form a consensus or be brought into closer agreement with the policies of the President.

Commissions are innovative analysts because of a number of factors that are inherent in "temporary systems."[13] All commissions are temporary. Their termination is either linked to the passage of a period of time specified in their mandate or to a future event, the completion of their report. Most often these two conditions for the termination of commissions are combined. They are expected to disband after a specific period, provided that their report is completed. If it is not completed, their life is extended briefly.[14] Although the time limit is not rigidly enforced, it does represent White House expectation and is a strongly felt constraint on commission members and staff.[15]

Temporariness, for the commission, means that it is a new institution whose members are brought together specifically to serve in it and will disband after a limited and specified time. Institutions of this kind are free of the "historical baggage" that encumbers most permanent institutions.[16] They are unencumbered also by routine action and goal accomplishment responsibilities (other than producing their reports). They need not be preoccupied with institutional maintenance. The original definition of the commission's goals in the mandate from the President and in the President's personal charge to the commission is usually relatively clear and sharp. Some ambiguities, of course, exist, and further goal specification and operationalization is usually necessary in the course of the commission's work.[17] But compared to the perception of goals in most permanent organizations, commission members and staff have a good idea of what they are supposed to do.[18] All of these factors are likely to produce a sense of beginning with a clean slate, of optimism, and of a high probability that their efforts will be crowned with success.[19]

The boundaries of the commission are clear. Commissions operate apart from the permanent institutions of the federal government. They are usually somewhat isolated physically and socially because of their newness and temporariness. This also tends to increase their consensus on commission goals.[20] Also, the relatively small size of commissions heightens their ability to focus on and accomplish their task.[21] Thus commissions are well-defined institutions, set apart from the daily concerns and problems of the government, with clearly defined tasks, manageable numbers of people to perform them, and deadlines.

These conditions are likely to foster more intensive and concentrated work on the part of the participants.[22] In this environment, members of the temporary system are more easily socialized to be concerned with the group's goals. A sense of group identity and *esprit* often emerges, providing further incentive for concentrated work toward the commission's objectives. Commission participants will often communicate with each other more freely because a feeling of equalitarianism and openness is likely to prevail. The commission members and staff tend to use and draw on each other's capacities more fully.[23] Therefore, in the commission context, innovative ideas are more likely to be entertained and adopted, because of the new environment that is intensive but nonthreatening and cooperative, because of the detachment from the permanent institutions of government, and because members are uprooted from their normal routines.[24] A staff member of the President's Commission on Law Enforcement and Administration of Justice (1965–67) recalled that the "commission provided a great opportunity to brainstorm on an intensive basis for a long period."

Thus commissions are likely to promote harder, more focused effort, more interchange and feedback among the group members, and more free-wheeling and original ideas. Every commission does not, of course, live up to this potential. But the institutional format of *ad hoc* commissions does make it more likely that they will be successful policy analysts.[25]

Presidential advisory commissions are more capable policy analysts also because they can attract highly qualified membership and staff. There are very few cases of refusals to invitations tendered to prospective commission members by the White House. They invite the best, and they get them.[26] The staff of the commission is also generally of very high quality.[27] Those who were interviewed for this study seemed very knowledgeable and articulate about the substance of their commission's work and had ample qualifying education and experience. The comments of commission staff members about the performance of their staff colleagues were also generally very favorable and laudatory. A staff member of the President's Commission on Law Enforcement and Administration of Justice (1965–67), for example, commented, "This Commission had a spectacular staff."[28]

The prestige and visibility of this presidential-level forum, as well as the compelling nature, for commission members, of an invitation from the White House, make the commission a superior mechanism for recruiting the best available talent to focus on a problem. A staff member of the President's Commission on Heart Disease, Cancer, and Stroke (1964), in the course of describing his interest in and commitment to the substantive thrust of the commission's mandate, also said, as an aside, "I would have taken the detail of a White House commission on anything, for the sheer prestige, even on garbage collection." Not only does the commission promote more intensive, focused, and innovative work, but it also attracts better people to do it.

A commission also, in general, has better access to governmental and private sources of data and expertise. The appendices to commission reports listing the witnesses, advisers, and consultants they have called upon are usually an impressive "Who's Who" of the commission's field of concern.[29] The presidential status of commissions also provides them with the leverage to pry information from the agencies of the Executive Branch that otherwise might be jealously and judiciously kept under wraps. "We had White House authority and could get anything we wanted" is a typical statement from a commission staff man. The commission can also get agencies to undertake studies that they would otherwise not do.

For example, at the request of the National Advisory Commission on Selective Service (1966–67), a questionnaire was sent to each local draft board member soliciting background information, and the Census Bureau conducted a study of the records of a sample of two hundred local boards to examine the uniformity of their draft classification decisions. Both of these studies, as well as others that were done with the reluctant cooperation of the Selective Service System, yielded information that led to criticism of the operation of the system. This information would not have been forthcoming had the inquiring group not had White House sponsorship and status. In the words of a staff member,

> We couldn't have got near some of the information unless we had been a presidential commission and they knew we would go to the White House if they didn't give it to us. This is especially true of the Census Bureau study of Selective Service records.

Not only do commissions have superior people working under conditions likely to promote effective problem analysis, but they also have better data to work with.

Finally, commissions are particularly capable as policy analysts because they are an integrative forum, a framework within which a wide variety of intellectual and constituency interests can be focused. The commission is a mechanism that permits an interdisciplinary and multi-interest effort to be directed at a problem. Satisfactory solutions for some problems are not available, because a context in which all of the relevant sources of expertise and all of the affected interests could meet has been lacking. There rarely exists a forum that brings together the most prestigious experts and constituency representatives in a format likely to promote sustained, focused, and creative effort aided by a highly capable staff and the best available information. Attorney General Katzenbach, chairman of the President's Commission on Law Enforcement and Administration of Justice (1965–67), somewhat rhapsodically observed that commissions "can be essential links in the chain of public and professional understanding, in weaving a unified fabric of knowledge, in giving sinews to strong but fragmented impulses to public action."[30]

The second major capability that commissions have is the ability to persuade and educate the public. As Felix Frankfurter observed, ". . . commissions are admirable means for taking the nation to school."[31] This ability is the product of the publicity they can generate for a problem and for their proposals to solve it, the increased impact that their findings and recommendations have because of the prestige of the commission, and the higher legitimacy attached to proposals from a commission because of the belief that the methods employed by commissions are superior to those normally used within the Executive Branch.

One of the first steps leading to the adoption of an idea as authoritative policy by the government is its circulation within the relevant policy community and the creation of a broad appreciation for the existence of the problem. A familiarity with a problem and with the proposals for solving it is a necessary prerequisite to agreement to adopt the proposal. This is all the more true if the problem is new or the proposal represents a substantial departure from the status quo. In politics, one of the most deadly responses in a discussion of a problem or proposal is, "I never heard of it." It seems that problems and proposals, particularly those that are departures in public policy, have to be lived with for a while before they are adopted. The rhythm of American politics does not appear to be congenial to a sudden broad enthusiasm for a proposal which will lead to its quick adoption. Problems and proposals for solving them have to be lived with for a time before action is taken. For example, the idea of a guaranteed income, negative income tax, or income maintenance first surfaced in the mid-sixties as a major issue of public policy. It was advocated in various forms by, among others, the National Commission on Technology, Automation and Economic Progress (1964–66), the National Advisory Commission on Rural Poverty (1966–67), the National Advisory Commission on Civil Disorders (1967–68), and the President's Commission on Income Maintenance Programs (1968–69). In the form of the Nixon Administration's Family Assistance Plan it came close to being adopted, and now has a prominent place in the debate over how to remedy the "welfare mess."

Commissions have the ability to focus attention on a problem, to broach a proposal in a policy community, and to see that thinking about it permeates that community more rapidly. In most cases commissions are capable of capturing the attention of at least the policy community in question, and they are often capable of reaching a much more extensive public as well.

The prestige and visibility of commissions give them this capability. Since at the presidential level they are an extraordinary occurrence and deal with important problems of public policy, and since they are composed of the best known and most highly respected experts and constituency representatives, their interest for and access to the media are enhanced. They also package their proposals in an attractive format. Special care is taken to assure that a report is persuasively written and well illustrated. Professional writers and art consultants are frequently engaged. Extensive, often free, distribution of the report is arranged, usually with the cooperation of the White House. For example, a staff member of the President's Commission on Heart Disease, Cancer and Stroke (1964) reported, "A copy of the report was sent to every doctor in the country. A copy was sent to every hospital in the hospital association and to members of the American Association for the Advancement of Science." Unfortunately, comparative public opinion data that would permit more concrete illustrations of the ability of commissions to increase effectively the public perception of a problem and to propagate a proposal for its solution is lacking. The available evidence from the interviews and comment in the press that have followed commission reports indicates that commissions appear capable of making others aware of a problem and of expanding the numbers of people who have heard of the solution advocated by the commission.[32]

Commissions are particularly useful as persuaders not only because they are a mechanism for expanding public awareness of an issue and their solution for it. They are also more likely, as a source of communication, to engender a positive response from those they are attempting to persuade. For example, speaking to General Bradley, chairman of the President's Commission on Veterans' Pensions, in hearings on the commission report, Congressman Edmondson (D-Okla.) said, ". . . seeing your name on this report adds a great deal of weight to it and to its conclusions. . . ."[33] Others have spoken of the ability of commissions "to bless," to give "validation," and "to legitimize" the ideas contained in their reports.

It has been amply demonstrated that the "worth" or "weight" of a statement is not independent of an evaluation of the source of the statement by the audience. According to Lane and Sears,

> For any given message, the better the reputation of the source the more likely people are to agree with the message. A substantial amount of evidence shows that a message attributed to a credible (positive) source is more likely to be believed than the identical message attributed to a less credible (negative) source.[34]

In the selection of their members, commissions are weighted with those who are prestigious and respected in the constituency that is most likely to be opposed to the commission's or the President's proposals, or that occupies a strategic position in the policy process. Thus, for example, the membership of President Truman's Committee on Foreign Aid (1947) was composed largely of men with high standing in the constituencies of the Republican Party. A majority of the members were men with high positions and strong reputations in the business and financial community. Republicans, largely for fiscal reasons, were skeptical of the Marshall Plan proposal that was under scrutiny by the committee.[35] The Republicans had a majority in both houses of the Congress, and their consent was also required for adoption of the program.

If the opinions that a commission tries to change are too intensely held or if the change they try to obtain is too great, the audience is likely to disparage the commission members or to distort the commission's position to more closely conform to their own.[36] The prestige and reputation of commission members therefore do not guarantee that they can sell anything to the skeptical or to those in strategic positions. But having a commission with credible "name" members, sanctioned by the President, does make it more likely that the commission's message will be favorably received by the target audience.

States, governments, and laws are perceived as authoritative either because they are perceived to be effective, to be doing what we want done, or because they are legitimate, a source that we respect sanctions their actions and impact. The general study of the sources and limits of political authority is one of the grand traditions in political science. However, the study of why the analyses and preferences of some persons rather than others on questions of public policy are accepted as authoritative is not nearly as well developed. We seem to lack an important baseline for the understanding of public policy formation. The problem is not particularly troublesome when a policy that is advocated is in agreement with the preexisting policy preferences of the audience. It is not hard to understand, for example, why 75 per cent of the American public supported (in 1967) federal funding for job training for the poor.[37]

The difficulty appears when one asks why one interpretation of and prescription for dealing with a novel, complex, and uncertain policy problem is accepted rather than another. The relative communications advantage possessed by some advocates is part of the explanation. The communications advantages of commissions were discussed above. The recognition and trust of the source of a point of view (which was also discussed above in relation to commissions) is another part. How easily a new policy problem can be analogized to old and familiar problems is also a relevant consideration. Is a student sit-in at a public university, for example, more like trespassing or more like constitutionally protected speech? But in this case one can ask why one analogy is chosen rather than another. It seems that these factors do not singly or in sum explain why in general some people's opinions are accepted as authoritative.

Another set of considerations also seems to be very important. Some policy analyses are accepted over others because they were arrived at in the way that policy analyses should be arrived at. That is, there is a public ideal of the process against which the actions of government decision makers is measured. Thus if the findings and recommendations of a commission are reached in this legitimate way, they are more likely to be accepted as authoritative. Or perhaps more accurately, reaching findings and recommendations in this way, or at least giving the appearance of doing so, is a minimal condition for their acceptance.

This public ideal seems to contain two elements, to both of which commissions, because of their unique characteristics, conform. The first element is suggested by David Truman in his discussion of the "rules of the game."[38] There is a public expectation that decisions will be reached in a "democratic" and "fair" way.[39] This implies that all of those who are affected by the decisions should have an opportunity to participate in making the decisions either by actually making them, by having their representatives make them, or by presenting their views to the decision makers. The representative and public nature of a commission's membership seeks to satisfy this norm. Representing the views of a cross section of the nation and of those with a knowledge or interest in the area, a commission's decisions can be perceived as democratic and fair. In addition, commissions, in general, aggressively solicit the written or personal testimony of all those who have an interest in the commission's area of concern.[40] Truman observes:

> Basically the creation of advisory committees marks a recognition of those "rules of the game" in the United States that prescribe that individuals and groups likely to be affected should be consulted before governmental action is taken. Such consultation is in most cases prerequisite to the action's being accepted as "fair."[41]

The first element of the public ideal for the process of policy analysis, being suggested here, is procedural, in the sense of specifying who shall be heard and who shall participate in deciding.

The second element of this ideal is epistemological, and it defines the public expectations concerning the intellectual process by which findings and recommendations will be arrived at. Charles Lindblom argues that theorists "preach" a model of administrative decision making that is both impossible to attain and probably undesirable in its consequences if it were attainable. This is the "rational-comprehensive" method which is characterized by a full clarification of all the relevant values and their priority, and a comprehensive analysis relating all possible alternatives to the desired objectives, with a heavy reliance on theory.[42]

It is suggested here that not only do theorists in public administration measure administrative decision making against this normative model, but that also, the politically attentive public similarly evaluates the search and decision-making processes of commissions, as well as other agencies of government, according to a watered-down version of this standard. The public's image of an objective and expert decision maker seems to be of one who considers all of the available evidence and policy options. Since commissions, for the reasons described above, are reputed to be expert and objective, and since they make extensive and frequently well-publicized efforts to gather information, they also fulfill the conditions of this aspect of the public's ideal of how decisions should be made.

Because they conform to the normative ideal, to the public's expectations, the decisions of commissions are probably generally perceived as legitimate, properly made. Therefore they are more likely to be acceptable as authoritative statements. Presidents and their staffs are also probably not immune from the belief that the best decisions are likely to be produced by a body acting according to the normative ideal. Therefore the choice of a commission to undertake policy analysis possibly also reflects the President's desire to have a model decision-making mechanism, not only because the public is more likely to be persuaded by it but also because he believes it will produce the best decisions.

Making decisions in a manner that conforms to the expectations embodied in this normative ideal does not, of course, guarantee that a commission's definition of a problem and its proposals for solving it will be accepted. It only increases the likelihood of acceptance. It prevents an easy discounting or discrediting of a commission's work. But the commission must still compete with other interpreters of public problems who advocate different solutions and who often also possess a similar legitimacy and their own communication and prestige advantages.

While positive proof of the existence of the normative ideal described above cannot be offered, the nature of attacks on commissions provides some indirect confirmation. If commissions are persuasive in part because their decision-making processes are perceived to conform to a public standard, then an effective way to discredit a commission would be to demonstrate or intimate that its processes did not in fact conform to that ideal. If commissions are questioned in terms of the ideal, it is evidence for the existence of such an ideal and for its importance as a source of the persuasive power of commissions. Indeed, questions about the processes of commissions, in contrast to straightforward disagreements with the substance of their recommendations, have often been framed in terms of the elements of the normative ideal. President Truman's Civil Rights Committee (1946–47) was attacked as unrepresentative and therefore in violation of the "rules of the game" component of the normative ideal:

The pretty-sounding theory behind the selection was the choosing of members representing all groups in American life, yet we find to our immediate dismay that not one fair-minded, representative Southerner was appointed to the committee! The South, in other words, was permitted no word in its own defense as the committee worked out a plan to wreck Southern society.[43]

President Truman was compelled to defend the impartiality and objectivity and by implication the "rational-comprehensiveness" of his Commission on the Health Needs of the Nation (1951–52).[44] In hearings before a special subcommittee of the Senate Interior and Insular Affairs Committee in 1954, the President's Materials Policy Commission (1951–52) was challenged on the grounds that its members and staff were not fully qualified to examine the problem because of their lack of training.[45] President Eisenhower's Commission on Veterans' Pensions (1955–56) was questioned in hearings before the House Veterans' Affairs Committee on the background and qualifications of its membership and staff, the representativeness of its membership, its diligence in soliciting the opinions of those interested, and the independence and objectivity of its staff and members.[46] It was also intimated that the report was the product of staff work rather than of the commission members and that therefore the report should not be evaluated in terms of the prestige, expertise, and representativeness of the commission members.[47] The legitimacy of the Commission on Heart Disease, Cancer, and Stroke (1964) was challenged on similar grounds.[48] These examples, which could easily be multiplied, indicate that the normative ideal of government decision making seems to exist and that commissions can gain in their persuasive power if they conform to it.

Commissions are capable of being effective persuaders because, also, their work uniquely reaps the combined benefits that accrue to governmental and nongovernmental reports. Commissions are at once intra- and extragovernmental. The aura of officiality and authoritativeness that radiates from the federal government increases the impact of their work. A statement prefaced by "A government report says . . ." has a special ring of truth and objectivity. This is perhaps a product of the sovereignty of the federal government or of the great power attributed to it.[49] In addition, commissions have at least the image of being disinterested, independent, and objective. In terms of the aphorism that "Where a man sits determines where he stands," commissions are perceived to "sit" outside of or apart from the normal operation of government and therefore to "stand" for detached and unbiased analysis and judgments. They are thus less tainted by "politics" and not likely to engage in "whitewashing" the government. Commissions enjoy the happy circumstance of being persuasive because they are hybrids (some would say bastards) that simultaneously are and are not part of the government establishment.

In sum, commissions are uniquely capable of analyzing problems because they are temporary systems; they can recruit well-qualified members and staff; they have unusually good access to expertise and data; and they serve as an integrative framework for an interdisciplinary and multi-interest consideration of problems. Commissions are also particularly capable of persuading others to accept as authoritative their findings and recommendations because they can command a wide audience for their reports; they can call upon the prestige of their members and of the presidency to increase the likelihood of a favorable hearing; they have a decision-making process that conforms to the public's ideal of how decisions should be made; and they enjoy the benefits of being both inside and outside the government.

The two most important capabilities of commissions are to engage in policy analysis and to persuade others to accept their findings and recommendations. In chapter 2 it was argued that the two most frequent purposes of Presidents in creating commissions are to investigate and propose solutions for problems and to persuade and educate various publics to the wisdom of the commission's or the President's proposed initiatives. Thus commissions are most capable of doing that which Presidents most often intend them to do. If we assume that Presidents in general have the wisdom to choose the best tool for a job, this congruence between commission capabilities and presidential purposes is not coincidental, but rather argues for the view that the dominant purposes of Presidents in creating commissions are to analyze and to sell policies. If a President wants to do something else, then he, in most cases, will not set up a commission. Since commissions are most suited to be means to certain ends, it is reasonable to expect that those ends are the ones for which commissions are most often created.

What time of year a commission report will be issued is largely under the control of the White House. Thirty-four of the ninety-nine commissions reported in the months of December and January, and only seven reported during July and August. This probably indicates a desire to use commission reports in conjunction with the President's legislative program being introduced to a new session of Congress, and to avoid having commissions report during a time when Congress is usually in recess and public attention is not focused on government. This again supports the view that commissions are primarily intended and capable of serving as policy analysts and salesmen.

In addition, it is fairly obvious that the special characteristics of commissions enable them to perform effectively some of the other purposes of Presidents in creating them. The prestige and visibility of a commission makes it particularly useful as a symbolic crisis response when other courses of action are not available. The *ad hoc,* "temporary system" characteristic enables a commission to be an effective mechanism of elite education, discussed in chapter 2 as one element of the window-dressing purpose.[50]

Finally, the commission does not seem to be particularly capable of serving as a mechanism for avoiding action on a problem. All of the factors that increase the analytic capacity and persuasiveness of commissions assure that they will return problems to the President in a salient, public, and prestigious package with all of the trappings of good staff work. If the problem is an albatross around the neck of a President and he foists it onto a commission, they will return it to him as a millstone.

THE CIRCUMSTANCES IN WHICH COMMISSIONS
ARE PARTICULARLY USEFUL OR SUITABLE

The capabilities of commissions as policy analysts and persuaders seem most appropriate for problems that involve an intellectual redefinition of a situation, an inability of the federal executive branch in general or the White House in particular to deal with a problem, or an undertaking of a major new responsibility by the federal government. Commissions are also particularly appropriate in the arena of domestic problems rather than national security policy and foreign affairs, except in those areas where the Congress feels itself competent and asserts a major policy-making role.

When the problem is one of reformulating a federal program or commitment or of conceiving a new approach to a problem, the analytic and persuasive abilities of commissions are particularly useful. Roughly a third of the commissions dealt with in this book were created in a context calling for a basic rethinking of federal policy in some area.[51] Five examples to illustrate the role of policy innovation follow, one from each administration.

The federal government has been involved with the problem of the supply of critical resources for national defense needs since the Revolutionary War, when the supply of tall oaks for ship masts was a matter of concern. The nature of this problem was radically altered after World War II. One of the most important changes was the Cold War division of the world into two camps. The strategic resource position of the United States was modified by its leadership of and its ties to the "Free World," and the President's Materials Policy Commission (1951–52) was instructed to give consideration to this new dimension of the problem.[52] In addition, in a war like World War II, the entire economy and all resources were part of the nation's warmaking potential. A "comprehensive policy" or intellectual framework with which planning on this massive scale could be undertaken was also needed, and the commission was also expected to develop such an approach.[53]

Materials policy had to be rethought once again in the Nixon Administration. Preserving and enhancing the environment replaced maintaining the warmaking capacity of the "Free World' as a central policy concern. The National Commission on Materials Policy (1970–73) was established primarily to recommend federal policies that would "strike a balance between the 'need to produce goods' and the 'need to protect the environment.' . . ."[54]

Under the Eisenhower Administration, the President's Commission on Veterans' Pensions (1955–56) was called upon to deal with the problem of veterans' programs operating in a fundamentally altered context. The requirement of a large standing army had become the norm in the cold war, and military service was required of a large proportion of the male population. Conditions of service in the armed forces had greatly improved in the previous decades. A variety of programs to protect the economic security of all citizens had been instituted. Under these new circumstances, what were the obligations of the federal government to veterans? In what circumstances should military service be the basis for special privileges and benefits, and what benefits? This was another problem of intellectual reformulation and reorientation.[55]

President Kennedy created a President's Advisory Panel on Federal Salary Systems (1961–63) to help formulate and sell "comparability," the basically simple idea that the salaries of public employees ought to be on a par with those of employees in the private sector doing similar work. This was a radical departure from the traditional concepts that had guided federal pay practices. The government's ability to pay and notions of an adequate living wage had guided it, without any systematic or explicit relation to wages in private life.[56]

Finally, President Johnson's Commission on Income Maintenance Programs was confronted with the problem of formulating a national incomes policy. Of particular importance was the commission's task of examining the existing federal programs for providing economic security. These programs represented a variety of intellectual and practical approaches to the problem of poverty: human resources development (e.g., job training), social insurance (e.g., social security), cash income transfers (e.g., public assistance), and income-in-kind (e.g., food stamps).[57] The commission's problem was how to supplement, modify, or replace these approaches with an intellectual and practical approach that, if implemented, would assure every citizen of receiving a minimum adequate income.[58]

New approaches need the staff capabilities that commissions have. A framework that is conducive to innovative thinking and that provides a forum for an interdisciplinary and multi-interest approach is desirable for rethinking policy. New policies also need the exposure, prestige, and legitimacy that an effective commission can confer on them.

The new policies that commissions formulate and are called on to advocate are often "new" only in that they represent a departure from the established way of doing things in the federal government. In the world of ideas they are often more like dowdy spinsters, old but unused. For example, the President's Commission on Immigration and Naturalization (1952) concluded that the national origins quota system "applies discriminations against human beings on account of national origin, race, creed, and color," and it recommended that this system be abolished and replaced by a "unified quota system" which would place a general limit on immigration, without regard to national origin, race, creed, or color.[59] This was by no means a new idea. It was alive in the early twentieth century when the great debate on limiting immigration was taking place.[60] It had, however, never been adopted as national policy, and it represented a fundamental departure from the established policy. Commissions established with a view toward policy innovation are not expected to blaze new trails on the frontiers of knowledge. They are expected to change the orthodoxy of the federal government or to suggest one where none exists.

Commissions are also particularly used and useful for problems and in circumstances marked by federal Executive Branch incapacity. When the federal bureaucracy cannot do a job, the stage is set for calling upon a commission. In specific, the bureaucracy is often unable to be innovative or self-critical, to engage in basic reformulation or reevaluation of its goals, or to reorganize itself, and it often lacks credibility or clout as an advocate. Approximately a third of the commissions studied were created in circumstances characterized by this kind of bureaucratic incapacity, and a good number of them were also expected to perform the function of policy innovation discussed above.

The basic incapacity of bureaucracy is its inhospitability to innovation and change.[61] "If he [the President] asks the bureaucracy for suggestions," said a White House aide, "they will recommend more of their ongoing program."

The bureaucracy is the problem here in two ways. First, it is incapable of engaging in the uninhibited policy analysis which the President on occasion wants. Second, the misdirection or ineffectiveness of bureaucratic performance are often the reasons why re-analysis of a problem is needed. If bureaucracies are incapable of creative thinking in general, they are particularly incapable of thinking about themselves in the self-critical way which could lead to a basic reorientation of their policies or goals and to reorganization of their structure. These two strands are obviously intertwined, since it is that federal agency whose performance is inadequate which is often also the primary source of governmental expertise on the substantive problem, and therefore the logical source from which to solicit proposals for change.

Attempts to remedy this inability of bureaucracies to engage in creative self-evaluation and self-criticism through an institutionalized planning capacity in the operating agencies have generally proved unsuccessful. These planning units are usually either dumping grounds for misfits who cannot do the agency's work and who spin their wheels formulating idle plans, or, if they have a good staff, their time and energies are siphoned off to meet crises and to help with day-to-day operations.

This general incapacity to plan reorienting change is manifested in and reinforced by a number of specific maladies for which commissions can be and have been the remedy. A strong and pervasive agency point of view ingrained over a long period of time and supported by a forceful leadership in the agency leads to rigidified thinking and an inability to reconceptualize agency programs and goals. The abilities of a commission as an innovative policy analyst are particularly called for in this situation. For example, there is the case of the Selective Service System and the National Advisory Commission on Selective Service (1966–67). Bradley Patterson, the executive director of the Commission, explained:

> President Johnson set up this Commission by Executive Order in July of 1966, just a week after the following exchange has taken place before the House Armed Services Committee:
> "The CHAIRMAN. Now, General Hershey, my last question: If you were a member of this committee or a Member of Congress, what changes would you recommend today in the Selective Service law?
> "General HERSHEY. I would recommend no change." Now, if President Johnson had any private convictions that perhaps some changes were needed, he could not very well turn to his own executive branch staff to find out what they were; this is the kind of situation that is tailor-made for the convening of a Presidential public advisory commission. With no disrespect for the honorable and distinguished service General Hershey had rendered this Nation, I believe the President wanted to find a way to throw up for public discussion, and his own consideration, some alternatives to the existing way of doing things.[62]

Rigid agency thinking and a diminution of the capacity to innovate can also result from the domination of an agency by strong clientele groups.[63] A member of the President's Materials Policy Commission (1951–52) noted, "It would have been impossible to get objective recommendations on materials from the Interior Department because it is so influenced by mining and other interests." A commission is shielded by its own prestige and by the protection of the White House from domination by interest groups. Commissions are new, and interest groups lack established access to them. Commissions have good information-gathering and analyzing capability in most cases, and do not need to rely heavily on interest groups for this kind of service. Commissions are also *ad hoc,* and therefore lack the institutional maintenance problems that give clientele groups leverage over established agencies.

Federal agencies are also often incapable of marshalling the kind of staff expertise that is available to a commission, and they are therefore less capable of innovative planning. For example, in response to a question about what the President's Commission on the Status of Women (1961–62) could do that could not be done in the Women's Bureau of the Department of Labor, a member of the staff of the commission who also had long service in the Women's Bureau said, "The Women's Bureau couldn't have done the report. At that time, the Women's Bureau had become a traditional government agency. Their staff could not have tapped the expertise brought together on this commission."

Agencies also often overlook or lack access to sources of opinion and information in the public that commissions can draw on. A staff member of the President's Advisory Commission on Universal Training (1946–47), for example, said:

> They [the commission members] added a great deal to the technical judgments of the War Department and the Executive Office. It was very important in this case to have a commission. There was no chance for this proposal to succeed unless it reflected the views of the society in which it was to operate. The commissioners had channels to the private community and could bring to bear a sense of the popular reaction—the kind of things that the military don't immediately take into account.

Because commissions are often better able to recruit a more expert and diverse staff than is available to an agency and because they can develop superior access to the public, the depth and breadth of the inquiry and analysis is likely to be greater.

The bureaucratic incapacity may be that an agency is not satisfactorily performing its statutory functions. It is simply ineffective. For example, the Department of Housing and Urban Development during the Johnson Administration seemed to be incapable of reaching the goals for new housing construction, particularly of urban low-income housing.[64] A Johnson aide said, "We had asked HUD this question [how to close the housing gap] , and they had given us a half-assed answer."[65] The ineffectiveness of HUD was an important factor leading to the creation of the President's Committee on Urban Housing (1967–68). Ineffective agencies rarely have a passion for trenchant self-criticism, and a commission can evaluate agency programs and suggest reforms.

Bureaucracies are often ineffective because of a fragmentation of federal efforts dealing with the problem that needs attention. This situation often calls for an intellectual definition or redefinition of the problem to prepare the way for a concerted effort directed at it, as in the case of income maintenance programs. This, it was argued above, is one of the circumstances in which commissions are particularly appropriate and in which they have frequently been used.

In addition, the usual response to fragmentation of federal efforts in a certain area is an attempt at reorganization. Reorganization is, of course, also a technique for attempting to increase executive control, to improve performance, or to redefine the goals of a single agency.[66] Restructuring federal programs is the logical follow-up to rethinking a problem. It is hoped that the new structure will reflect the new conception of the problem and deal with it effectively. In general, competing agencies, or competing bureaus or divisions in a single agency, are also incapable of agreeing on how they should reorganize themselves. Deciding how to redefine the boundaries of the "policy space" of bureaus is not something that those involved can accomplish dispassionately, quickly, or effectively.[67] Reorganization and its planning are more effectively done in a context that is out from under the weight of bureaucratic inertia and that dilutes the bureaucratic instinct for self-preservation and aggrandizement. A presidential commission allows the interested agencies to be heard, opens a "legitimate channel" for discussion of changes, and provides a forum in which presidential and public values can have a greater impact on the recommendations for reorganization.[68] *Ad hoc* bodies are generally useful in initiating reorganization and organizational innovation.[69] A variety of task forces and interagency committees are used for this purpose. Commissions frequently make suggestions for reorganization with their recommendations for new policy directions or their reconceptualization of a policy problem. The reorganization proposals from commissions are usually on the order of "shake-ups" to reorient an agency toward the new goals defined by the commission, rather than major reshufflings of peak agencies. The most important exception was the President's Advisory Council on Executive Organization (1969–71), which proposed sweeping changes in the organization of the Cabinet departments and the independent regulatory agencies.

In addition to their limitations on policy analysts and innovators, executive agencies are also hampered, in some cases, by an inability to be effective policy salesmen. Proposals emanating from the Executive Branch, quite satisfactory to the President, may lack credibility in the Congress or some sectors of the public. These proposals are therefore more easily dismissed or ignored. In some circles and for some issues federal agencies are widely suspected of being narrowly self-seeking and overoptimistic or even conspiratorial and lying.[70] The attitudes of many college students toward the Defense Department in the later years of the Johnson Administration is an example of this situation. The Administration was interested in draft reform. But, "Where could you study Selective Service in government?" asked a Johnson aide rhetorically. "You can imagine how young people would have reacted to a study of the draft from the Pentagon, even if it had said the exact same thing as the Marshall Commission [National Advisory Commission on Selective Service, 1966–67]." So the National Advisory Commission on Selective Service (1966–67) was not created because the Pentagon was considered incapable of generating a good draft reform proposal; Defense Secretary

McNamara had, in fact, already set forth new ideas, and the White House considered the Defense Department capable of doing the job. Rather, the White House hoped to take advantage of the commission's ability to communicate. The discount rate that would automatically be applied to proposals from the Pentagon by students, whose support was seen as important for the success of any new policy, was expected to be too high.

The preceding discussion of the suitability and use of commissions to remedy and compensate for the failings of bureaucracy has focused on situations in which the White House had a negative opinion of the performance or capabilities of an agency. Creating a commission in these cases was a means to avoid the normal channels and make an end run around the bureaucracy. All of the agencies in the Executive Branch are not, however, perpetually in the President's dog house. The only failing that some of them have is that they are not as popular with the public and the Congress as they are with the President. A desire by the President to rescue or support an agency can therefore be the reason for using a commission. The commission can increase the visibility of the threatened agency and emphasize the importance of its programs. The commissions to build support for the foreign aid program or to remove the cloud from over the head of the government's employment statistics collectors fit this mold.[71] The access of commissions to the media, their advantages as a communications source, and the perception of them as thorough and objective investigators make them well suited to be rehabilitators of agency reputations and salesmen of agency programs. These commissions can sell or protect those who cannot sell or protect themselves.

The need of the White House for innovative policy analysis and the inability of the bureaucracy to meet that need or to perform other tasks are the circumstances in which the capabilities of commissions are particularly useful. These circumstances are accentuated when the undertaking of a new federal responsibility is contemplated.[72] When the problem before a commission is likely to call for a broad extension of federal responsibility and a large new commitment of federal resources, commissions can play an important role. As one commission staff member noted, commissions can "transcend the normal political process in this ability to redefine responsibilities."

The need for innovative policy analysis is particularly acute when new federal responsibility is to be undertaken. No baseline of current federal policy exists as a starting point. The relationship of the new responsibility to existing federal responsibilities must be conceptualized. A philosophic as well as a practical rationale for this accretion of federal power must be offered. Policy guidelines for the new programs to carry out this responsibility, including methods of finance and administrative structures, are also required.

Commissions dealing with new federal responsibilities seem to be more extensively involved in problems of Executive Branch organization or reorganization than other commissions. For example, the President's Committee on Foreign Aid (1947) proposed the major outlines of the Economic Cooperation Administration, particularly specifying that it be kept separate from the Department of State.[73]

When an extension of federal responsibility is expected, the federal bureaucracy is generally even more limited than it is in dealing with changes in policy for already existing programs. To all of the bureaucratic limitations already discussed must be added the absence of any capability or location in the bureaucracy for analysis of the new responsibility. While many agencies would be willing to compete for control of a new jurisdiction, they lack the expertise to analyze the subject comprehensively. For example, there was no pool of federal experts on higher education in 1946 when the National Commission on Higher Education (1946-47) began a major foray by the federal government into this realm. By definition, a new responsibility exists at most only in embryonic form in the Executive Branch.

Because a credibility problem exists whenever the federal government advocates an extension of its own responsibility and power, the ability of commissions to persuade is important. Charges of self-aggrandizement and power-grabbing and suspicions of big government are apt to surface quickly. As a result of their prestige and legitimacy as disinterested and objective inquirers, commissions can place the call for new federal action in the context of the public interest or a national need. The President's Commission on Health Needs of the Nation (1951-52), for example, was in large part seen by the administration as being capable of combatting the charges of "socialized medicine" and the fears of those opposed to a far-reaching intrusion by the federal government into the doctor-patient relationship.[74]

A wide public must also be persuaded before an extension of federal responsibility is consented to. An extension of federal responsibility involves either a completely new governmental responsibility or a reallocation of governmental responsibilities from the state and local levels to the federal level. An example of the former would be the adoption of the Marshall Plan, in which the President's Committee on Foreign Aid (1947) played a key role. New federal responsibilities in the post-World War II era have much more commonly involved a transfer of power to the federal government from the states, as in education or law enforcement. In such cases, an extensive, diverse, and often skeptical if not hostile public, including most of the Congress, must be educated. Commissions can usually reach such a wide public with a message whose credibility will hopefully allay their fears and objections.

Finally, as a forum, commissions can begin the necessary persuasion by educating elite representatives of the affected interests, their own membership, concerning the problem.

Commissions have been active in various extensions of federal responsibility: to protecting the civil rights of individuals (President's Committee on Civil Rights, 1946–47); to aiding war-damaged and threatened countries through foreign aid (President's Committee on Foreign Aid, 1947); to supporting the expansion of higher education in the interests of national defense, and in general producing better citizens (National Commission on Higher Education, 1946–47, and President's Committee on Education Beyond High School, 1956–57); to providing aid for local law enforcement (President's Commission on Law Enforcement and Administration of Justice, 1965–67); to expanding the availability of health care through decreasing the financial burden of health costs on individuals and improving health care delivery systems (President's Commission on the Health Needs of the Nation, 1951–52, Commission on Heart Disease, Cancer, and Stroke, 1964, National Advisory Commission on Health Manpower, 1966–67, and National Advisory Commission on Health Facilities, 1967–68); and to broadly protecting consumers beyond the areas of food and drugs (National Commission on Product Safety, 1967–70). Changing the consensus that defines the areas of legitimate federal responsibility is one of the central problems of innovation in public policy. In this realm, commissions have been called upon to play a significant role. Approximately a quarter of them have been involved in the expansion of federal responsibilities, again with substantial overlap between this category and the preceding two.

Commissions have been primarily used as a technique for innovation in domestic politics rather than in foreign and security affairs. Only one, the Commission on National Goals (1960), dealt with basic issues of foreign policy. It, however, prepared only a summary presentation of the "conventional wisdom of the Eastern seaboard" on foreign policy. There was no attempt at a deeper analysis or rethinking of American policy in the modest six pages of its thirty-one-page report devoted to "Goals Abroad."[75] Only one commission dealt with a question of strategic military doctrine, the Air Policy Commission (1947–48). It examined the role of air power in national defense. The other commissions that have touched upon the military have been concerned with the recruitment of military manpower, the care and treatment of soldiers and veterans, military salaries, and the problems of discrimination faced by black soldiers.[76] These are all issues related to domestic and civilian concerns, rather than to the kind of military establishment we should have in terms of its defensive and offensive capabilities, and how it should be used as an instrument of national policy.

The very small number of commissions involved in problems of foreign policy and strategic doctrines reflects Executive Branch independence, combined with a general attitude of public "permissiveness" and congressional restraint toward executive action in this sphere during most of the period 1945–72. The traditional justification for executive predominance in foreign affairs because of its planning capability and access to better information and because of the need for speed, secrecy, and flexibility was compounded by the addition of nuclear missiles to the arsenals of the world.[77] With regard to public attitudes, William Caspary concludes that "American Public Opinion is characterized by a *strong* and *stable* 'permissive mood' toward international involvements. . . . [S]uch a mood provides a blank check for foreign policy adventures, not just a responsible support for international organization, genuine foreign assistance, and basic defense measures."[78]

While the role of Congress in foreign affairs has increased as America's foreign involvement has increased, Congress in the period 1945–72 played a "secondary" and limited role.[79] The Executive Branch possesses a high concentration of expertise in foreign affairs, has had relatively little need for extensive public or congressional persuasion on most issues, and of necessity makes most decisions in a nonpublic way. While it can be argued that this situation often leads to less than optimal decisions, it is nevertheless the case that, as it has been constituted, the foreign affairs policy process has relatively less use for the capabilities of commissions than does the domestic. Still, about a third of the commissions touched upon some concern in foreign or security affairs. This was true primarily under one of two circumstances.

First, because so many domestic problems have international or security implications, some commissions become involved in these matters as a corollary to their primary focus. For example, concern with foreign migratory laborers was part of the general problem of migrant labor, as international law enforcement and smuggling were part of the problem of narcotic and drug abuse, and the competitive advantages of foreign shipbuilders and the U.S. position in world trade were closely tied to the depressed state of the American shipbuilding industry.[80]

Second, commissions are called upon to deal with those aspects of foreign and security policy that the Congress concerns itself with. The Congress, of course, also comes to many problems with international ramifications through the primarily domestic nature of the problems.[81] However, the Congress, too, involves itself with some more purely international problems. These are usually in areas relating to the congressional power of the purse. The role of the Congress in appropriations has led it to feel particularly competent, and to be especially active in foreign aid and foreign economic policy.[82] Several commissions have dealt with foreign aid, and there have also been commissions dealing with foreign trade, foreign travel, and the balance of payments problem.[83] Where the Congress is active in foreign affairs or security affairs and the President faces resistance to his initiatives, commissions are called upon for their persuasive capabilities.[84] Given the Executive Branch resources in the State Department, Defense Department, and National Security Council, such commissions appear to be almost exclusively intended to be window-dressing persuaders rather than policy analysts. For example, the Presidential Study Commission on International Radio Broadcasting (1972–73) was clearly intended to help generate congressional support for Radio Free Europe and Radio Liberty. Congressional action in 1971–72 had "left the stations' futures in doubt," contrary to the policies of the Nixon Administration.[85]

The question remains: Why does not the White House just do the analysis and persuasion itself? In many cases, of course, it does, but in some ways commissions can be superior persuaders. This is true principally when the proposed solutions are likely to be discounted because of the government's lack of credibility and stature as a source. This advantage should not, however, be overrated. A substantial part of the visibility and prestige of a commission does, after all, derive from its status as a governmental body and from its connection to the presidency.

Nevertheless, assuming that commissions do have unique persuasive capabilities in some circumstances as compared to the White House, are they also superior to the White House as policy analysts? The ability of the White House to recruit staff and to have access to sources of data and expertise is at least as good as that of commissions, and probably superior in most cases. Because they are *ad hoc,* commissions have a capacity for work and for innovation that comes with being a "temporary system." However, the White House staff remains a sufficiently malleable instrument for the President to put aides in charge of *ad hoc* problems and to reshape its internal organization from time to time.[86] The real problem (in this period, 1945–72) was that though the White House was theoretically capable of doing the job of policy analysis, its staff was overwhelmed with routine program planning, administrative management, legislative liaison, political, and ceremonial tasks. There is simply no adequate institutional capability for innovation and "new thinking" on domestic policies in the White House.[87] Before the Domestic Council was created in July, 1970, there was no domestic policy analogue to the National Security Council.[88] In addition, "the original idea of the Domestic Council was that it would operate with a very thin staff that would sort out policy options for the President, letting the agencies do most of the research and groundwork," according to a Nixon White House aide. The Domestic Council was not intended to generate policy for the President, and the turbulence of the Watergate era and the transition to the Ford Administration have left its future unclear.

Thus the statement of the Brownlow Committee in 1937 that "The President needs help" remained true in the area of domestic policy planning through the end of Nixon's first term.[89] William D. Carey, senior consultant at Arthur D. Little, Inc., summarizes this problem as follows:

> The presidency is weak in *policy analysis.* It stands perched on a bottom-heavy administrative and operational system consisting of departments and agencies equipped with resources, clienteles, and historical baggage which continually threaten to outthink and outrun the tenuous policy management capabilities of the White House. In the main, the presidency is in the retail business when it comes to policy formulation; it reacts, responds, modifies, and tinkers with departmental policy and program thrusts, but it does not wholesale public policy in the sense of recasting priorities and evaluating the relationship of accrued commitments to long-term goals.[90]

For problems of domestic policy analysis, commissions have played the role of surrogate for the White House staff. Even if the White House were organized to provide policy analysis, the difficulties of institutionalizing a policy innovation role would remain.

A concluding note on perspective is in order. There may be a danger that the exclusive focus on the capabilities of commissions will lead to an overestimation of how widespread and important they are. The discussion above is limited to the characteristics and capabilities of commissions and the circumstances in which these seem to be most appropriately used. It excludes consideration of other means that might be used in the same circumstances. Other actors play major roles in circumstances calling for innovation. The limitations of the federal Executive Branch bureaucracy have been stressed, but it obviously plays a decisive role in normal program development. It is also very important in developing new programs that are corollaries or additions to established functions, and sometimes it is the breeding ground for broad new approaches and ideas. The Congress, on occasion, takes the lead in exploring and mapping new policy areas, as in the cases of the space program or auto safety. The other components of the "presidential advisory system" also make substantial contributions to the formulation and marketing of policy initiatives.[91] Interest groups and scholars in universities and private think tanks can also develop new public policy ideas and provide an important thrust for their adoption. There are no convenient yardsticks to measure the relative importance of these various actors in policy development and innovation. Commissions have a special competence for this. But they are not the only, or necessarily the most important, political actors with that competence.

CHAPTER FOUR

HOW DO PRESIDENTS CREATE COMMISSIONS?

TO UNDERSTAND how Presidents create commissions it is necessary to learn who can effectively communicate the idea of creating a commission to the President and by what authority (which is to say, with what funds) the President can act.

The evidence on who suggests having commissions is quite fragmentary. There are no case studies of the genesis of individual commissions from which generalizations can be drawn. So the discussion that follows is based on a variety of written comments and statements from interviews that provide at least a clue to the origin of the idea for about a third of the ninety-nine commissions. The nature of the evidence does not warrant generalizations about the relative frequency of the various sources of initiative. The sources will simply be enumerated and discussed. It is also particularly difficult to discover the lineage of an idea. The idea sources outlined below are, as far as could be determined, the most important, and those which have most directly brought the idea for a commission to the attention of the President. They are thus the final links in chains whose beginnings remain unknown and are perhaps undiscoverable.

The President is himself an active participant in the generation of ideas within the Executive Branch. He is not simply (and perhaps not at all) the locus upon which proposals, forces, and pressures are focused. The President proposes as well as disposes. The President was the source of the idea to have a commission on a number of occasions. Presidents Kennedy and Johnson seem to have been particularly active in this way. The President initiates the idea for a commission, as might be expected, in those substantive areas where he feels a particular competence or interest.

President Kennedy, for example, following his election in 1960, felt that the cost of the election and the process by which money was raised threatened to put officeholders in "moral hock" to contributors. He therefore proposed establishing the President's Commission on Campaign Costs

(1961–62) to study this problem and to formulate recommendations for dealing with it.[1]

President Johnson, probably because of his long legislative career, was particularly well-informed about and interested in the federal budget. He was important in generating the idea for the President's Commission on Budget Concepts (1967). One of President Johnson's staff observed,

> The Commission on Budget Concepts was created just because the public numbers were such an unrealistic representation to the American people. This was an interesting thing that Johnson did. There was no pressure for it. There was no pressure to change the budget concepts. We would get nothing out of it. It made our budget $200 billion rather than $150 billion. Johnson just thought that it was good for American government. To do something like this you needed a President who really understood the budget and appropriations, not someone who had been a military leader like Eisenhower. Johnson loved and understood the budget.

The Executive Office of the President and the rest of the federal Executive Branch are also often the source for a suggestion to have a commission. The staff in the White House sometimes suggest commissions. Philleo Nash and David Niles in the Truman White House, for example, were very active in advocating the creation of the President's Committee on Civil Rights (1946–47).[2] These aides saw the suggestion of a commission as a way to package and market a policy preference or commitment that they had. The seventeen presidential task forces created by President Nixon in 1969 (numbered 70–86 in appendix 2) were largely the result of an effort by the President's counsellor, Arthur Burns, to get ideas for recasting policy in a variety of areas in line with the philosophy of the new administration.[3] White House aides are not just neutral operatives but are often partisan advocates of different points of view.[4] They are also eager to advocate ideas that win the President's favor and help him to deal with substantive and political problems, as a way to increase their stature within the White House inner circle.

The other agencies within the Executive Office and the Executive Branch as a whole, when they suggest a commission, also see it as a vehicle for their policy preferences. For example, the institutional perspective of the Budget Bureau and its staff toward restricting expenditures were manifest in the proposal for the President's Commission on Veterans' Pensions (1955–56) which emanated from it.[5] A Budget Bureau staff member explained:

> I had tried to get a commission established on this subject [veterans' pensions] after World War II when the problem was what to do about the World War II veterans. . . . The idea got nowhere at the time. I kept the idea alive. During the Eisenhower Administration the World War I veterans were pushing for service-connected pensions in about

1953–54. I was enmeshed in getting the V.A. to make long-range projections of the costs to beat off this raid on the Treasury. I did the staff work leading up to the commission and drafted the executive order.

During the final years of the Johnson Administration there was a balance of payments problem. An interagency committee chaired by Vice President Humphrey was formed to examine the part of the problem caused by the fact that there were more American tourists going abroad than foreign tourists visiting the United States. This committee recommended what became the "Discover America" program, to encourage Americans to travel more extensively within the United States. However, explained a White House aide,

> [Secretary of the Treasury] Fowler was pissed off because he still had the balance of payments problem. All of these fine principles of freedom of movement didn't help his dollars and cents problems. So he prevailed on the President to appoint another task force on travel [Industry-Government Special Task Force on Travel, 1967–68]. . . . This was a more banking-oriented group. This was Fowler's way of making an end run around the free trade position of the task force. . . . Fowler made an end run to the White House because he was dissatisfied with the recommendations of the Humphrey task force.

Here again a commission was a means to advance the policy position of its advocate, this time from one of the departments.

Closely tied to the desire to push a particular policy is the aspiration, on the part of those who advocate commissions, to upgrade, expand, or save from extinction their agency or program. The National Security Resources Board (NSRB), for example, was created to plan mobilization for war and to plan policies for national readiness in case of war.[6] It had a troubled and turbulent history, with frequent reorganizations and changes in leadership.[7] When the United States became involved in the Korean War, the task of mobilization was vested in a new agency, the Office of Defense Mobilization. The NSRB was bypassed and effectively stripped of its mobilization function, partly because of its sorry state as an organization. Its budget and staff were drastically cut back.[8] W. Stuart Symington, chairman of the NSRB, recommended to President Truman that the President's Materials Policy Commission (1951–52) be created.[9] The mandate of the commission instructed it to study primarily the problem of readiness with regard to national security.

The NSRB's advocacy of the creation of the commission, and the commission's function of studying readiness from a national security point of view, can clearly be interpreted as an attempt by the NSRB to gain visibility and legitimacy for its own readiness function. The NSRB had lost its "glamour" function, mobilization. Its remaining function, continual planning for national readiness, was only vaguely understood and was generally a low-priority objective. These factors, combined with the weakness of the NSRB as an organization, meant that there was a high probability that the NSRB would soon become a bureaucratic derelict, if it was not abolished outright, unless it could upgrade its readiness function.[10]

Another example is the role of the Civil Rights Section of the Department of Justice in the creation of the President's Committee on Civil Rights (1946–47). In the immediate postwar period the demands for greater federal action in protecting civil rights were focused on the President and on the Civil Rights Section. The Civil Rights Section lacked a legislative mandate from which to work, and it also lacked the manpower to prepare legislation and to do a detailed study of the problem. So the Civil Rights Section was a prime advocate of a presidential committee to make recommendations for the legislation that would serve as the underpinning for a broader effort by them in protecting civil rights.[11]

The fact that the idea for a number of commissions has originated within the Executive Branch bolsters rather than contradicts the argument made in the previous chapter that commissions are created in part because of the deficiencies of the Executive Branch in intellectual orientation, capacity for policy analysis, and persuasive ability. It is generally high policy executives who advocate commissions. Such executives are more likely to be amenable to new ideas and change than their agency as a whole. Or the initiative comes from struggling agencies, like the Civil Rights Section or the NSRB, that recognize their own limitations. It may also be that those in the bureaucracy who sponsor the idea of a commission see it as a vehicle for the kinds of changes that a bureaucracy finds most congenial. That is, they hope that a commission may lead to policies which will make their job better or bigger or enable them to do a more effective job or to protect themselves.[12] Once the idea reaches the White House, it may be transformed there, through the broader perspective at that level, into a mechanism for much more extensive policy analysis. It may also be that a commission will take the ball, in the form of the mandate from the White House, and run much further with it in the direction of critical rethinking and reevaluation of basic policies than was intended by either the White House or the commission's advocates in the bureaucracy.

Interest groups or influential private citizens are the source of some suggestions for commissions. The NAACP was a major advocate of President Truman's Civil Rights Committee (1946–47).[13] Eunice Shriver, President Kennedy's sister, pushed for the creation of the Panel on Mental Retardation (1961–62). Mary Lasker, a well-known philanthropist in the health field, suggested that the Commission on Heart Disease, Cancer and Stroke (1964) be created. And John D. Rockefeller, III, was behind the creation of the Committee on Population and Family Planning (1968–69). With respect to the latter a White House aide recalled, "This committee was due to the relentless lobbying and intercession of John D. Rockefeller. He beat on the door about once a week on this." The motive of these individuals is primarily to further their own policy preferences or those of the organizations that they represent. Their major problem is gaining access to the White House and the President. It obviously helps to be a Rockefeller, the President's sister, or a friend of Mrs. Johnson, in the case of Mary Lasker, or to represent a group like the NAACP in whose constituency a new President felt weak and uncertain.[14]

Finally, the Congress is a significant source of initiatives for creating commissions, and initiatives have emanated from Congress in one of three ways. First, for example, the Congress created, by statute, at least two commissions that the President and the White House did not want. Despite the fact that they are classified as presidential advisory commissions, the initiative came from the Congress, and the President went along grudgingly.

One of these was the Commission on Marine Science, Engineering and Resources (1966–69). "The bill, S.944," said Senator Cotton on the floor, "is not part of the administration's program. In fact, it was opposed by every administration witness who testified before our committee, and by every administration agency which submitted written comments on it."[15] "I submit, Mr. Speaker," said Congressman Mosher, "that S.944 represents a very healthy example of congressional initiative in an area where Presidential initiative has been notably lacking."[16] The other commission for which the President lacked enthusiasm and which had its origins primarily in the Congress was the Commission on Obscenity and Pornography (1967–70). "We never wanted that one. It came out of Congress," said a Johnson White House aide.[17]

Second, several presidential advisory commissions have been created by Presidents when congressional studies were being discussed or appeared to be imminent. The threat of a congressional study taking away White House policy initiative seems to be an important prod inducing the President to create his own study commission. Illustrative of this situation is the case of the Air Policy Commission (1947–48). According to *Aviation Week,*

> A surprise Presidential Air Policy Commission began preliminary organizational work beating to the punch Congressional exponents of an Air Policy Board. . . . The President appointed his five man temporary body at the time when it appeared Congress was on the point of enacting a law establishing a 19-member board to perform approximately the same function.[18]

"This was an administration study to counter and contain the congressional study," explained a White House aide.

The desire by the President to head off congressional studies is further demonstrated by the fact that the congressmen who propose that Congress create a commission, or other congressmen, are often found on the presidential commission formed in response to this idea. Thus, the presidential study absorbs the congressional study by placing the advocates of the congressional study, or other congressmen, on the President's commission. Senator Harris, for example, introduced a bill to create a group to study the urban riots. He subsequently was appointed to the National Advisory Commission on Civil Disorders (Kerner Commission, 1967–68). With respect to the Missouri Basin Survey Commission (1952–53), President Truman noted, "The Survey Commission I am establishing . . . is similar to that which would be established under a joint resolution introduced last year by Senator Hennings and Congressman Magee of Missouri."[19] Senator Hennings was made a member and vice chairman of the commission. In both of these cases, no congressional study was conducted.

Third, the congressional initiative to have a commission may reach the President in the form of a direct personal suggestion from a congressman. The best example of this situation was the suggestion from Senator Vandenberg that a "non-partisan non-political committee of businessmen and experts" be created to study the Marshall Plan proposal.[20] Senator Vandenberg was a Republican from Michigan, the chairman of the Senate Foreign Relations Committee, and the key figure in postwar foreign policy bipartisanship. Senator Vandenberg felt strongly about the need for such a committee study and made its creation a precondition for his support of the Marshall Plan idea.[21] President Truman heeded this suggestion and created the President's Committee on Foreign Aid (Harriman Committee, 1947).

There are often multiple sources for the initiative to have a single commission. The President's Committee on Civil Rights (1946–47) is a good example. As was indicated above, the idea was advocated by Philleo Nash and David Niles within the White House, by the Civil Rights Section of the Justice Department, and by the NAACP and other civil rights leaders. It may be recalled that the Civil Rights Committee was presented in chapter 2 as an example of a commission for which the President had multiple goals. The crisis response and symbolic purposes of this commission responded to the pressure from the civil rights leaders. The policy analysis and window-dressing purposes reflected the desires of the Civil Rights Section and those on the White House staff who were interested in this problem. This suggests that the diversity of presidential goals for commissions reflects more than the presidential perspective—regarding each commission as a set of possibilities, some of which will be realized, depending upon how well the commission does its work and upon the political circumstances at the time it reports. The diversity of presidential goals also reflects the variety of expectations and demands held by the different political actors, each of whom advocates the same commission but from a different point of view.

In general, the President agrees to accept, on some occasions, the suggestion to have a commission, when it comes to him from one or several of the sources outlined above, because, from his perspective and in terms of his needs, a commission is seen as a useful and appropriate mechanism to accomplish one or more of his goals outlined in chapter 2. A commission is felt to be useful and appropriate because it has the special capabilities, described in chapter 3, which make it a particularly attractive choice in some circumstances.

In general, the process of search by which the White House comes upon the alternative of a commission shares many of the characteristics of "problemistic search" as described by Cyert and March.[22] "Problemistic search" has three characteristics: it is "motivated," "simple-minded," and "biased."[23]

Problemistic search is motivated "by a problem and is directed toward finding a solution to that problem."[24] In the context of the White House, "advisory commissions come about first and most often in response to a need for which there is no obvious solution," in the words of a Kennedy-Johnson aide. Problems flow in a steady stream to the White House, rising to flood proportion in periods of hardship or crisis. Programs that are not generating controversy are generally not reexamined to discover weaknesses and to consider improvements. Passive constituencies are usually not encouraged to reassess their subjective satisfaction. The White House does not make it a policy to "rattle the cages." Sleeping dogs and nonsqueaky wheels are left alone. The White House is activated by problems.

"Simple-minded search" is "(1) search in the neighborhood of the problem symptom and (2) search in the neighborhood of the current alternative."[25] In the case of White House search culminating in the establishment of a commission, the simple-minded search has usually already taken place and has failed to produce a satisfactory solution. A White House aide remarked, "The first thing the President asks when a problem comes up is, 'Don't we have a program that deals with that problem?' If there is no program, and no legislation or executive order that is readily available, then the President is frustrated, if he is an action President." This frustration and lack of a readily available solution pushes the search in the direction of somewhat more "complex" and "distant" alternatives. In the White House, this often takes the form of a search for a mechanism that will do the more extensive investigation and the necessary mobilization of political resources. The search thus turns to alternative mechanisms rather than to a greater effort aimed directly at the problem through broader and more intensive action by the White House staff. The basic reason for this is that the White House is not prepared to conduct extensive policy analysis.[26] The search for alternative mechanisms capable of policy analysis and useful as political resources is, however, also "simple-minded." In most cases the White House casts its net no more widely than the options presented by the "presidential advisory system," for example, Cabinet committees, the Council of Economic Advisers, interagency committees, White House task forces, or presidential advisory commissions.[27] Thus the search is generally limited to techniques which operate under the aegis of the White House. These are also all alternatives for which ample precedent exists. Commissions have been a fairly commonplace alternative within the White House, at least since the administration of Theodore Roosevelt, and, as was pointed out in chapter 2, they are now a routinely available option.[28] The search is rarely creative, in the sense of inventing a new technique. The White House preferences for matches of problems and advisory mechanisms vary, of course, with the type of problem and the circumstances surrounding it, and with the style of the administration in office.[29]

The "bias" of the search process does not appear to be a separate useful category beyond the biases outlined above in terms of the simple-mindedness of the process.

In addition to being "problemistic search," the search process by the White House that yields the option of commissions can also usefully be described as "mating search" rather than "prospecting search." A ". . . prospecting theory . . . assumes that the objects of search are passive elements distributed in some fashion throughout the environment. Alternatives and information about them are obtained as a result of deliberate activities directed toward that end. . . . [A] mating theory of search . . . [presumes that] not only are organizations looking for alternatives; alternatives are also looking for organizations."[30] Political actors on the White House staff and in the Executive Branch, the Congress, and the public, package the attempt to further their substantive, personal, and institutional interests in the form of a suggestion that a commission be created. The President and the White House are already aware of the same problem in most cases and are looking for a means to handle it. Or alternatively, the White House is not particularly aware of a problem and only becomes aware because the problem is being pressed upon them by the same people who are also suggesting that a commission be created. In either case, the White House search for a way to deal with a problem "mates" with the search by other political actors to obtain White House sponsorship for a commission that they see embodying their interests.

The White House perspective on the goals of a commission and that of the advocates of a commission are not necessarily congruent. It is hard to say whose perspective "wins" most often. On one hand, the President has the final say on the commission's mandate and appoints its members, thus pushing it beyond the narrow focus of its advocates. On the other hand, commissions are independent of White House control and tend to lose the broader presidential focus as they single-mindedly consider one problem or set of problems. Evidently the potential benefits are large enough and the probability of success is high enough for the advocates of commissions and for the White House, or for both at once, to keep the advocates continuing to advocate and the White House continuing to create commissions in steadily increasing numbers.

It should also be noted that those who press the suggestion for a commission on the White House are generally politically sophisticated and influential. They are not babes in the Washington woods. The evidence also indicates that their orientation is predominantly toward getting changes in policy rather than in preventing change. It is therefore unlikely that they would push for the creation, or allow themselves to be satisfied by the creation, of commissions, if this mechanism were in fact generally used by Presidents to avoid acting and were not effective in achieving changes in policy. These considerations thus support the argument that commissions are expected, primarily, to engage in policy analysis and mobilize political resources to achieve changes in federal policy.

The creation of commissions also involves a set of legal and constitutional questions. What are the instruments used to set up commissions? By what authority does the President appoint them? How does the President get funds for them? These are the kinds of questions that fifty years ago would have been the focus of an analysis of some aspect of the presidency.[31] At that time, the significance of legal and procedural considerations as determinates of the behavior of political actors was probably overrated. Today their significance is probably underrated in political analysis.[32]

As it turns out, the question of the President's authority to institute commissions is not a subject of much discussion or controversy. However, the question of how Presidents fund commissions is significant. It is significant because the Congress, with which the President periodically wages policy and institutional battles, has a grip on the purse strings. For over a hundred years the President and the Congress have waged an occasionally hot guerrilla war on the appropriations frontier over the ability of the President to fund *ad hoc* advisory bodies. In the final analysis, the President has come out on top because of the inability of Congress to match the inventiveness of the White House in evading congressional restrictions, and because of the inability or unwillingness of the Congress to cut too deeply into the flexibility and contingent essence of executive power, its "energy."[33]

Three kinds of instruments have been used to create commissions: statutes, executive orders, and announcements. An announcement can be a letter to the commission chairman that is made public, a message to the Congress, a speech, or a White House press release. These instruments vary in their specificity and comprehensiveness, from a simple statement of the subject of the study and the names of those who will undertake it to an elaborate statement of the questions the commission should (and should not) deal with, its membership, its staffing, administrative and funding arrangements, and its deadline.[34] As required by the definition of commissions, these instruments are publicly available documents at the time the commission is set up or soon thereafter. A total of nine commissions were instituted by statute, twenty-nine by executive order, and sixty-one by various kinds of announcements. The distribution of commissions created by each of these means through the five administrations is shown in table 1.

The choice of instruments for creating commissions clearly varies between administrations. This seems to be basically a matter of idiosyncratic administrative style having no particular policy or political implications.

There does seem to be some relationship between the "importance" of a commission and the kind of instrument used to authorize it. Important commissions, those which are widely publicized and which deal with broad and pressing questions of public policy, are more likely to be created by executive order or statute. Less important commissions are more likely to be created by some form of announcement. This is not, however, a very strong relationship. There are a number of important commissions that were chartered by announcement, for example, the President's Advisory Commission on Universal Training (1946–47), the President's Commission on Income Maintenance Programs (1968–69), and the President's Advisory Council on Executive Organization (1969–71). And several less important commissions were chartered by executive order, for example, the President's Communications Policy Board (1950–51) and the National Advisory Commission on Libraries (1966–68). There seems to be a closer match between commission importance and creation by executive order or statute during the Johnson Administration than during the other administrations. The general relationship between commission importance and authorization by statute or executive order probably reflects a desire within the White House to confer special

TABLE 1. Instruments Used to Create Commissions, by Administration

	Statute	Executive order	Announcement	Total
Truman	0 (0)	7 (41)	10 (59)	17 (100)
Eisenhower	1 (11)	2 (22)	6 (67)	9 (100)
Kennedy	0 (0)	4 (33)	8 (67)	12 (100)
Johnson	5 (18)	13 (46)	10 (36)	28 (100)
Nixon	3 (9)	3 (9)	27 (82)	33 (100)
Total	9 (9)	29 (29)	61 (62)	99 (100)

stature on those commissions called upon to deal with the most important problems.

Whether the President sets up a commission by executive order or by some form of announcement depends also on the means by which he plans to fund it. Commissions created by executive order are often funded from the Emergency Fund for the President or the Special Projects Fund. Those that are created by announcement are more likely to be funded through agency contributions or voluntary contributions from nongovernmental sources.[35] The feeling is probably that commissions drawing upon a regular appropriation, from one of the President's funds, need a more formal mandate than those that are going to have their funds scraped together from a variety of sources. It is also reasonable to assume that the President will be more willing to expend "his" funds on things that are important to him, such as the broad and pressing problems of public policy which commissions created by executive order tend to deal with.

No patterns were observed in the relationship between the creation of commissions and the great cyclical rhythms of American politics, presidential and congressional terms and elections, party conventions, the sessions of Congress, and the budgetary cycle in the Executive Branch and the Congress. The timing of commissions seems to be random. Perhaps no patterns emerge because a commission's official life begins with its public announcement, while the actual decision in the White House may precede that event by as much as a year. Also, since Presidents in general do not control the emergence of problems or crises, even if we knew the exact dates when commissions were decided upon, it is very unlikely that the dates would be related to any of the other basic political events.

By what authority does the President create *ad hoc* advisory commissions? The right of the Congress to inform itself, at least ostensibly for legislative purposes, through various kinds of investigations including *ad hoc* advisory bodies created by statute or resolution is well established.[36] There is therefore no question that the President may act under the authority of a statute authorizing him to appoint a commission which will advise him and the Congress.

However, this takes care of only nine of the ninety-nine commissions. The rest of them were created by either executive order or announcement. An executive order "is an exercise of the Executive power under Article II of the Constitution and must be based on authority derived from the Constitution or statute."[37] In the executive orders creating twenty-five of the twenty-nine commissions created by executive order, the only authority cited by the President was his authority "as President." In the other four cases of commissions created by executive order, this was supplemented by a general reference to the authority vested in him "as President of the United States by the

Constitution and statutes of the United States."[38] In no case was a specific statute or constitutional clause cited. No authority of any kind was cited in the case of the commissions created by some form of announcement. The only reason that any mention of an authority to create is contained in the executive orders is probably because it is standard form for executive orders to cite an authority.

It is easy to conceive of the President relying, with ample justification, on his constitutional duties to "take care that the laws be faithfully executed" or to "recommend to their [Congress's] consideration such measures as he shall judge necessary and expedient" as the basis for creating *ad hoc* advisory commissions.[39] However, such citations have not been viewed as necessary, because the President's right to create such bodies has not been seriously questioned or challenged. George Galloway, writing in 1931, stated that "there seems to be no question but that the President has full power to appoint as many commissions as he pleases."[40] This seems to be an accurate statement of the current state of affairs as well. Limits on presidential authority to create *ad hoc* advisory commissions are not an important constraint on the use of this advisory mechanism.

In 1842, a Representative Underwood of Kentucky proposed a resolution stating, in part, that it was ". . . the opinion of this House that the President has no rightful authority to appoint and commission officers to investigate abuses, or to procure information for the President to act upon."[41] The more prevalent congressional view is represented by Representative Wydler (R-N.Y.), speaking in 1970, who said:

> It seems to me that our main role in the Congress is not to try to second guess these agencies or the President in what committees or commissions they want to establish. They will make good ones and bad ones, I suppose, and that is a matter that will be very difficult for us to control; but it seems to me we have . . . very important areas where we are especially concerned. One is what money they spend on these commissions and how they spend it.[42]

Thus, while in the words of Theodore Roosevelt, "the Congress cannot prevent the President from seeking advice," and they have generally not questioned his authority to seek advice, his power to spend public money to support advisory commissions is another matter.[43] During the period 1945–72, there were on the books three provisions that were attempts by the Congress to limit the ability of Presidents to fund commissions and other temporary advisory and administrative bodies.

The first of these was passed in 1842, in response to President Tyler's commission which investigated corruption in the New York customshouse. (This commission also provoked Representative Underwood to offer the resolution quoted above.) The Congress opted for trying to control the

President's access to money rather than trying to define his authority. The 1842 provision states:

> No accounting or disbursing officer of the Government shall allow or pay any account or charge whatever, growing out of, or in any way connected with, any commission or inquiry, except courts-martial or courts of inquiry in the military or naval service of the United States, until special appropriations shall have been made by law to pay such accounts and charges.[44]

The second was an amendment to the Sundry Civil Service Appropriations Act, 1910, in reaction to the large number of *ad hoc* advisory commissions employed by President Theodore Roosevelt. This "Tawney Amendment" states:

> No part of the public moneys, or of any appropriation made by Congress, shall be used for the payment of compensation or expenses of any commission, council, board, or other similar body, or any members thereof, or for expenses in connection with any work or the results of any work or action of any commission, council, board, or other similar body, unless the creation of the same shall be or shall have been authorized by law; nor shall there be employed by detail, hereafter or heretofore made, or otherwise personal services from any executive department or other Government establishment in connection with any such commission, council, board, or other similar body.[45]

The third of these is the "Russell Amendment," another rider on an appropriations act, stimulated in this case by congressional ire over Franklin Roosevelt's freewheeling use of agencies created by executive order during the war, particularly the Fair Employment Practices Commission. It states, in part:

> After January 1, 1945, no part of any appropriation or fund made available by this or any other Act shall be allotted or made available to, or used to pay the expenses of, any agency or instrumentality including those established by Executive order after such agency or instrumentality has been in existence for more than one year, if the Congress has not appropriated any money specifically for such agency or instrumentality or specifically authorized the expenditure of funds for it.[46]

This veritable Maginot Line of barriers to funding commissions obviously did not, during the period under consideration, prevent Presidents from creating and somehow supporting the ninety-nine *ad hoc* presidential advisory commissions which are the subject of this study. Presidents have found, and in some cases been given by the Congress, means to evade these restrictions.[47]

The two most obvious ways to deal with the restrictions are to either comply with them or to interpret them in such a way as to make them less onerous. In the case of the nine commissions created by statute, their expenditures were authorized by the act creating them and appropriations were made through the normal appropriations process. In addition, statutory appropriations were sought for at least a dozen other commissions, thereby placing them in compliance with these provisions.[48]

The key clause in the Tawney Amendment requires that a commission be "authorized by law" before any public moneys can be expended for it. This restriction has been largely negated through the interpretation of that clause. Elmer Staats, Comptroller General of the United States, explained how the Tawney Amendment has been interpreted:

> Under the above statute [Tawney Amendment], it has been held by our Office, as well as the Attorney General, that the words "authorized by law" do not necessarily require that a committee be specifically provided for by statute. In other words, if the committee's task is related to an authorized function, then the committee is considered to be authorized by law.[49]

The Russell Amendment has proven a more thorny problem, since it does not require that a commission be authorized by law before money can be expended for it. This, as was seen above, is a very elusive criteria. Rather it requires that, regardless of the source of authority upon which a commission has been founded or how it was funded, any funds spent for it after it has been in existence for one year must be specifically authorized and appropriated for that commission. The Russell Amendment thus attempts to require that a legislative link be forged between *already existing* commissions and their funds. The Russell Amendment, however, has also been somewhat diluted through interpretation. Comptroller General Staats again explained:

> As a practical matter, if the expenses of the groups are justified in the budget presentations, this is regarded as being adequate for this purpose. When they say specific authorization by Congress, authorization by Congress is usually meant to be approval through the appropriation process if not through the regular legislative authorization process. In other words, it does not have to be specifically authorized by separate statute.[50]

A variety of other means, in addition to compliance and interpretation, also have been used to circumvent the Russell Amendment and the other legislative restrictions. The President has available to him two yearly appropriations which can be used "without regard to the provisions of law regulating the expenditures of Government funds or the employment of persons in the Government service."[51] These two funds are the Emergency Fund for the President and the Special Projects Fund. The Emergency Fund for the President was created in 1942 and has been continued every year since then.

The Special Projects Fund was created in 1955 and also has been continued since.[52] During most of their existence, the Special Projects Fund has been $1.5 million and the Emergency Fund $1 million per year, although during the war years (FY 1943–46 and 1951–54) the Emergency Fund was greatly increased.

Usually only in the mandates of commissions created by executive order has the source of their funding been explicitly set forth.[53] Fourteen of the twenty-nine commissions created by executive order cite either the Emergency Fund for the President or the Special Projects Fund as the source of their financing. In most of these cases the executive order specifically notes that the "payments [from the Emergency Fund for the President or Special Projects Fund] shall be made without regard to the provisions of (a) section 3681 of the Revised Statutes of the United States (31 U.S.C. 672) [the Act of 1842], (b) section 9 of the Act of March 4, 1909, 35 Stat. 1027 (31 U.S.C. 673) [the Tawney Amendment], and (c) such other laws as the President may hereafter specify."[54] A number of commissions created by executive order in which the source of funds is not specifically cited, or those created by announcement, have also, at least in part, been funded from one of the two presidential funds.[55] The three congressional restrictions would similarly not apply to them, even though these restrictions were not explicitly waived.

The two presidential funds have become quite stable, and they represent a secure source of money available to Presidents for commissions, as well as for other purposes, free from the three congressional restrictions. Congress, however, also clearly retains the power to cut the amounts available, to change the terms under which they are available, or to eliminate the two funds altogether. When a President faced a very hostile Congress, as Truman did the 80th Congress, the Emergency Fund for the President virtually dried up (fiscal years 1948 and 1949). It is noteworthy that during the calendar years 1948 and 1949, no commissions were created by President Truman. It is, however, also significant that even in this situation of hostility between President and Congress, the fund was not eliminated. The Congress has apparently been unwilling to eliminate the President's ability to act with flexibility and discretion to meet domestic and foreign problems by depriving him completely of these unrestricted sources of funds.[56]

Contributions from executive agencies whose concerns are touched upon by a commission are another source of funds for commissions. The Independent Offices Appropriation Act, 1946, provides:

> Appropriations of the executive departments and independent establishments of the Government shall be available for the expenses of committees, boards, or other interagency groups engaged in authorized activities of common interest to such departments and establishments and composed in whole or in part of representatives thereof.[57]

The subject of a commission must only be of "interest" to the agencies contributing, and the agency representatives need only form a "part" of the total commission membership. In the executive orders creating seven commissions, this act was cited as a source of funds for the commissions.[58] Agency contributions under the terms of this law have also been made to other commissions not created by executive order. In the opinion of Dwight Ink, Assistant Director of the Bureau of the Budget, "the effect of the Russell amendment was greatly limited by a 1945 act (31 U.S.C. 691)."[59] In some cases agency representatives have been appointed to commissions so that their agency could be tapped for funds to support a commission.

There also exists a substantial grey area in which research services, personnel on loan, office space, and money are provided by executive agencies to commissions which do not have agency representatives as members.[60] Without agency representatives, commissions do not qualify for agency contributions, under the 1945 act; but the transfer of agency resources is sometimes legitimized by making clear in the agency's budgetary presentation to Congress that some money will go to a commission.[61] Such agency contributions are often of substantial importance in making it possible for a commission to engage in policy analysis.[62]

Commission mandates often state, in various forms, that "each department and agency is directed, to the extent permitted by law and within the limits of available funds, to furnish information and assistance to the Commission."[63] It is most likely that calculations of the interests, stakes, and risks of the agencies determine the degree to which this kind of presidential command is honored, rather than the presence or absence of some specific legislative authorization. However, when such assistance is forthcoming, it again provides an important source of support for presidential commissions and another means to avoid congressional attempts to supervise commissions through legislation.

Statutes allow executive agencies, including the White House, to hire temporary experts and consultants and pay their expenses.[64] They furnish yet another source of money to support the work of commissions, including payment of fees, per diem, and travel expenses to commission members.

Finally, in addition to complying with or reinterpreting congressional restrictions on the funding of commissions, using the two presidential funds that are unrestricted, or relying on authorizations that allow spending for interagency committees and consultants, commissions have also been supported from private sources. The use of nongovernmental sources of support obviously avoids all of the restrictions that are tied to the expenditure of public funds. This nongovernmental support has been given in several forms. The most common is for interested groups and organizations to gather facts and do research for commissions without compensation.[65] They have also lent staff to commissions on a few occasions.[66] Unpaid volunteers have sometimes served as commission members.[67] On some occasions, when provisions have been made to pay commission members as consultants and to pay their expenses, the more wealthy members or those employed by organizations willing to assume the expenses do not collect the money due them, thereby releasing funds for other uses by the commission.[68] Foundations have made direct grants of money to support the work of commissions whose purposes they have found worthy. The most striking example is the National Commission on Goals (1960), which was entirely supported by foundation grants, although not at the level originally planned.[69] This appears, however, to have been the only commission completely supported by private funds. Others have had only some of their costs, or specific research projects, funded by a foundation.[70]

The use by the President of unpaid volunteers and funds from private sources raises constitutional questions about the limits of executive power and the ability of the President to evade congressional restraints exercised through the appropriation process.[71] With respect to commissions and other advisory mechanisms at least, this has not become a major issue. In fact, there have been no judicial decisions attempting to define the authority of the President to create or fund commissions. The President's ability to use voluntary services for advisory purposes has become a constitutional accretion by long practice and precedent, supporting President Theodore Roosevelt's dictum that "any future President can do as I have done, and ask disinterested men who desire to serve the people to give this service free to the people through these commissions."[72]

Many commissions, of course, obtain their resources from more than one source. For example, the President's Commission on Law Enforcement and Administration of Justice (1965–67) had statutory appropriations, but its mandate also makes clear that it was entitled to money from the President's Special Projects Fund and to payments to its members and consultants as temporary experts.[73] It also had substantial research contributions from a variety of governmental and nongovernmental sources.[74]

During the Johnson Administration, there was a greater reliance on funding through agency contributions under 31 U.S.C. 691 or by statutory appropriation than on funding through either the Emergency Fund for the President or the Special Projects Fund. This was apparently the President's preference, rather than a change in legislative-executive relations. A Johnson White House aide explained:

Johnson rarely used his discretionary funds to support commissions. He insisted on them being funded with contributions from the agencies. Each of them would be assessed to support a commission in their area. . . . He felt that he should return this money [in the two presidential funds] to Congress every year, that this somehow made him a frugal and wise man.

Most recently, in its attempts to control the use of presidential advisory commissions and other Executive Branch advisory bodies, Congress adopted the Federal Advisory Committee Act in September, 1972.[75] One basic thrust of this law is to establish guidelines for the Executive Branch in creating, administering, assigning tasks to, and responding to advisory bodies.[76] The Act also requires that the President submit a yearly report to the Congress giving detailed information about all advisory bodies. The intent seems to be to enable Congress to evaluate the use of advisory bodies more effectively, to encourage the termination of moribund advisory bodies, and to expose, and thereby eliminate, conflicts of interest of those serving on advisory bodies. The Act is aimed primarily at increasing the accountability of the Executive Branch for its use of advisory bodies. Attempts to control the use of advisory bodies through requiring congressional authorization for their creation or funding have yielded to more indirect, and perhaps more effective, accountability through full and systematic disclosure about them. It is still too early to assess the impact of this law as a constraint on the use of presidential advisory commissions.

In general, Congress has been unwilling or unable to limit the President's authority to create commissions. Its attempts to gain continuing supervision over presidential commissions or to restrict the President's ability to create them through their control of the purse strings have thus far also been largely unsuccessful. Part of Congress's lack of success is attributable to the ingenuity of the White House in employing a variety of means for supporting commissions. The Congress has also avoided reducing the President's capacity to act with flexibility in formulating domestic and foreign policies and in emergencies. In addition, generally amicable relations between the Congress and the President have prevailed during this period. While it has not been a continual honeymoon, and Congress has not gone along with all of the Presidents' programs, the mood of hostility that characterized the relations between President Truman and the 80th Congress has been the exception rather than the rule. Thus in the Congress there has usually not been a broad interest in the stringent application of existing congressional restrictions applicable to commissions or the creation of new ones.

Nevertheless, the Congress clearly has the ability to cut off the two unrestricted presidential funds, to modify the other legislation through which commissions have been funded, and to impose new restrictions. This power is not wholly latent; its exercise or the threat of it have been very real on occasion. The impact that this power can have is suggested by the correspondence between cuts in the Emergency Fund for the President during the 80th Congress and the fact that no commissions were created during those two years. The Russell Amendment was felt to be a real constraint by the White House staff in charge of setting up the President's Committee on Civil Rights (1946–47), by the President's Materials Policy Commission (1951–52), and by the President's Commission on Registration and Voting Participation (1963).[77] Fritz Morstein Marx, writing in 1952, said, "This restriction [the Russell Amendment] has erected a virtual compulsion to limit the tenure of Presidential advisory commissions to no more than one year."[78] Although Presidents have clearly not felt this "compulsion" too strongly, the Russell Amendment and the other legislative restrictions on the use of commissions are not dead, as witnessed by the questions raised during the 1970 hearings calling upon administration spokesmen to explain why these provisions of the law did not apply in various circumstances.[79] The money in the Emergency Fund for the President is for use by the President "for emergencies affecting the national interest, security or defense," and using this money for presidential commissions has often required some stretching of the language and has provoked critical comments in Congress.[80] The funds to continue the President's Committee on Education Beyond High School (1956–57) for the last half of 1957, until its reporting deadline, were eliminated on the floor of the House. They were later restored, but not before the committee was thrown into turmoil.[81] The President's Commission on Postal Organization (1967–68) had to scale down its consultant studies when Congress cut its appropriation.[82] The Congress clearly can be more than a paper tiger in this area.[83]

These instances of threatened or actual congressional action, the relatively small size of the President's unrestricted funds, and the need to scrape together funds from a variety of sources for commissions have probably made the White House less free in creating commissions than they might otherwise have been. It is impossible to say what the precise impact of the congressional actions and the *ad hoc* nature of commission financing has been in terms of the number of proposed commissions that were not created. These factors have probably accounted for some attrition among proposed commissions, and were the President to confront a hostile and determined Congress, advisory commissions could be drastically curtailed as a presidential option.

CHAPTER FIVE

ARE COMMISSIONS INDEPENDENT?

PRESIDENTIAL ADVISORY COMMISSIONS are independent. They are not packed or guided by the White House. What control there is by the White House is exercised through the choice of the political situation into which to launch the commission, the formulation of its task in its mandate, and the selection of its membership.

White House liaison with commissions is primarily to aid them in solving problems of government mechanics and to keep the White House informed of their progress, so that it can make use of the commission's work in program formulation and marketing, and, on rare occasions, so that it can prepare a defensive response to commissions whose recommendations the White House finds unpalatable. This liaison is not, however, for the purpose of controlling commissions.

The number of "runaway" commissions, the adequacy of commission budgets, their access to information, and the control by commissions over the recruitment of their staff are further indices of commission independence.

THE CONTEXT OF COMMISSIONS

The political circumstances at the time a commission is created are important determinants of what it will and can do. The parameters of the public debate about the commission's problem establish a set of expectations to which a commission must be responsive. Commissions must deal with issues as they are publicly defined. For example, the President's Advisory Commission on Universal Training (1946–47) was created at a time when President Truman had a strong commitment to the idea of universal military training and had already proposed legislation to the Congress. The commission necessarily took as its starting point a reexamination of the President's proposal which was the basis for the public debate about the issue. The issue of resources for defense was conceptualized by most people as the danger of exhausting fixed supplies, and the President's Materials Policy Commission (1951–52) had to deal with it in those terms in formulating its own approach to the problem. The public definition of an issue is usually explicitly reflected in a commission's mandate, but when this is not so, the definition is an implicit mandate. This source of control is probably used instinctively rather than consciously by the White House in establishing a commission.

COMMISSION MANDATES

The mandates of commissions, which take the several forms described in chapter 4, set out, with varying degrees of explicitness, the problems to be examined. The primary responsibility for drafting the mandate usually rests with the White House aide or the agency in whose area of substantive responsibility the commission is operating. Or it is drafted by the official or agency which advocated that the commission be created.[1] A draft mandate is often a supporting document accompanying the suggestion to create a commission. The draft mandate is often circulated to all agencies who have an interest in the commission's field. Final revisions are made by the top White House staff—for example, Joseph Califano during the later years of the Johnson Administration—and by the President. The drafting and approval of a mandate occurs simultaneously with the discussion of and decisions about commission membership, described below. The White House staff who were interviewed did not recall that the drafting of commission mandates was a particularly difficult task. The choice of the commission members was considered much more significant and exacting.

The commission mandate is interpreted to the commission in the charge made to the commission by the President or by one of his assistants. At the first meeting of many commissions, the President launches the enterprise. This is often a *pro forma* ceremony, with photographers and a brief statement by the President expressing his interest in the subject, his belief that it is important, and his appreciation to the members for their service.[2] The President's place is sometimes taken by one of his staff. This is usually the aide who has worked on the commission mandate and membership and who will often serve as its White House liaison during the tenure of the commission.[3]

While it is frequently *pro forma,* the charge to the commission can be used to express special interest in the problem, to lend particular urgency and importance to the commission's work, and to highlight particular parts of its mandate. For example, President Truman emphasized to the members of the President's Advisory Commission on Universal Training (1946–47) that they were intentionally called the Commission on Universal Training rather than the Commission on Universal *Military* Training because he wanted the judgment of the commission on the benefits and problems of training to be made in a broad context. President Johnson's remarks to the Commission on Heart Disease, Cancer and Stroke (1964) were characterized by a member of the commission who was present as an "impassioned statement" showing a "visible emotional commitment" by the President. This commission was also told that one of the "ground rules" for its inquiry was not to get into the questions of financing.[4]

The mandate of a commission as explicated and modified by the statements of the President and the White House staff are a commission's "terms of reference," which define the task the commission members and staff agree to undertake. Some modification occurs as the commission translates its mandate into specific guidelines for inquiry and as more is learned about the subject during the course of the commission's work. But the mandate sets directions and boundaries which control what the commission does. The mandate is also communicated to the public through the media, demonstrating to them presidential action and giving them a standard against which to measure the commission's performance.

APPOINTMENT OF MEMBERS: THE CRITERIA

The most important mechanism of White House control over commissions is the appointment of their members. Control is exercised by choosing individuals who share the general orientation of the White House toward a problem and who also fit the prevailing White House definition for "soundness."

Commissions are loosely packed. The members are screened to produce a group that is likely to favor the direction of presidential policy in the area or is at least open minded and not adamantly hostile to that direction. For example, a staff member of the President's Committee on Civil Rights (1946–47) described the members as follows: "All of the members were mildly left-of-center on civil rights. All of them were willing to support more government actions." An even more subtle kind of packing was used on another Truman commission, the President's Commission on the Health Needs of the Nation (1951–52). The White House aide who helped assemble the membership list recalled:

> Our rule was that for the key figures we wanted persons who had reached the pinnacle of success in the medical profession and had at some point taken on the A.M.A. [American Medical Association] and licked them. Many of these men were on the governing board of the A.M.A., but at some point they had arched their back and won but had not been kicked out.[5]

Thus in creating a commission, the White House has a general idea of the direction their recommendations will take. As a Johnson staff member observed, "To a degree, you have a sense of what a commission is going to come out with. If you have Kerner, Lindsay, Brooke, Abel, and Jenkins on a commission [National Advisory Commission on Civil Disorders, 1967–68], you know they are not going to say lynch blacks." While the White House often has an idea of the direction of a commission's recommendations from the composition of its membership, no evidence has been found to indicate that commission members are selected to be rubber stamps to a specific predetermined presidential policy or proposal.

Loose packing establishes a probable direction for commission recommendations. The criteria of "soundness" establishes the boundaries that limit how far a commission will go in any direction. It is an unarticulated assumption that all of those selected for membership on a commission will not be extremists. Commission members are drawn from the "Establishment" in the sense of having political and social beliefs that fall within the bounds of the existing consensus and of being drawn from the major institutions of American society: government, business, labor, the military, the churches, education, philanthropy, and the professions. These "sound" men and women will generally be supportive of the existing social order and will suggest ways of ameliorating its faults and reforming it but will not advocate radical or fundamental changes.

Presidents differ in their perceptions of soundness, but these differences are marginal variations in emphasis rather than basically different definitions of the pool from which commission members may be drawn. President Eisenhower's commissions, for example, had more businessmen and military men than those of the other Presidents. President Johnson, on the other hand, while by no means closing the door to businessmen or military men, seems to have had a greater penchant for choosing educators.

The tightness of the packing and the narrowness of the boundaries from within which commission members are selected are limited by the need to establish the legitimacy and credibility of the commission. In chapter 3 it was argued that the reputed competence, representativeness, and prestige of commission members are among the unique characteristics of commissions that enable them to serve the purposes for which Presidents create them. If a commission's recommendations are to be persuasive with the political actors whose consent is needed for authoritative action to be taken, the commission must at least be composed of knowledgeable members drawn from all of the major specialties and constituencies relevant to the commission's problem.[6] The fame, prestige, and status of these members will also add to the persuasiveness of a commission's recommendations and aid the dissemination of its message.

These are the qualities that commissions are reputed to have, and they are also the qualities that the White House seeks in selecting commission members. The competence of the members and the balance in their representativeness are the criteria most often mentioned by White House staff for selecting commission members.

A commission membership must include representatives of all sides of the major cleavages within the policy-making community and the attentive public on a given issue. This requirement for credibility thus dictates that the categories for the representational mix be different for different commissions. For example, particular care was taken to assure that the President's Commission on Campaign Costs (1961–62) was "truly bipartisan" and included representatives of "big money" and "small money" from each party. For the President's Committee on Civil Rights (1946–47), representation from the South and the inclusion of some black members were necessary to establish the committee's credibility. For the Commission on Heart Disease, Cancer and Stroke (1964) the major areas of professional specialization were the most important bases that had to be covered: heart disease, cancer (children's and adult's), stroke, practitioners, researchers (university and foundation), and rehabilitation.[7]

The usual criterion for selecting representatives of the relevant constituencies is that they have expressed positions that make them credible to the constituency from which they are drawn. At the same time, rabid or dogmatic partisans are avoided, so that the possibility of consensus will not be precluded. An alternate strategy is to select representatives from the relevant constituencies who are neutral or have taken no public position on the issue under consideration. This latter strategy was used in the selection of the members of the President's Commission on Income Maintenance Programs (1968–69) at the insistence of its chairman, Ben Heineman, who participated in the selection of the members. One of the commission staff explained:

> No one was on the commission who had a publicly known stand on the various proposals. The two economists Eckstein and Solow were distinguished economists but not noted for their special work in this field. There were a large number of other economists who had well-articulated ideas and plans in this area who were not chosen. There were to be no advocates for their own plans. . . . The norm established by Heineman was that this was to be a body of impartial experts who were not already committed to some position. . . . The commission [also] had a balance of business, labor, men, women, blacks, and academics.

In addition to the principle of making each commission representative in accordance with the peculiar nature of the problem it has to solve, a national demographic cross section is also sought. It is seen to be desirable to have men and women, blacks and whites, labor and business, members from all sections of the country, Democrats and Republicans, and Catholics, Protestants, and Jews. For all but the most technical and specialized commissions, such as the Special Board on Inquiry for Air Safety (1947), the President's Commission on a World's Fair (1959), or the President's Advisory Panel on Timber and the Environment (1971–73), some attempt at getting such a cross section is made. The more national a problem is, in terms of its importance and the broad impact any policies resulting from the recommendations of the commission will have, the more likely is the commission to be a national cross section. Such representation is particularly evident on the President's Advisory Commission on Universal Training (1946–47), the Commission on National Goals (1960), the President's Commission on Law Enforcement and Administration of Justice (1965–67), the President's Commission on Income Maintenance Programs (1968–69), and the President's Commission on an All-Volunteer Armed Force (1969–70). President Truman's Committee on Civil Rights was familiarly called the "Noah's Ark" commission among the White House and commission staffs "because there were two of everything," in the words of a Truman assistant. The committee had two women (one black, one white), two labor representatives (one AFL, one CIO), two blacks (one man, one woman), two Southerners (one man, one woman), two businessmen, and a Catholic, a Jewish, and a Protestant clergyman.

Assuming general agreement with the direction of administration policy by most members, and their basic soundness, the other criteria of selection, constituency representation, national representation, and competence, are overlapping. Once the decision is made on which bases must be covered and what kinds of substantive knowledge should be brought to bear, commission members are often sought to cover several categories at once. For example, Jeanne Noble, who was a member of the National Advisory Commission on Selective Service (1966–67) and the President's Committee on an All-Volunteer Armed Force (1969–70), is a woman, a black, and a professor of education. Her selection thus covered at least two national categories, blacks and women, and brought to the commission someone from the academic constituency as well as someone who could make a contribution from her specialty, education.

These categories overlap not only in being different facets or characteristics of the same person but also in that constituency representation and substantive knowledge are frequently identical. Thus Dr. Howard Rusk brought to the Commission on Heart Disease, Cancer and Stroke (1964) his knowledge as an eminent expert on rehabilitation, and at the same time represented the rehabilitation perspective or constituency. The calls to exclude "special interest" representatives from the consideration and formulation of policy reflects the erroneous view that detached and disinterested experts exist. The top people in any field are usually employed by partisans or are naturally partisans of the point of view represented by that field. Policy point of view is likely to coincide with the interests inherent in one's field of specialization.

Social workers, for example, are not likely to advise that welfare be reformed by increasing direct cash transfers at the cost of diminishing the casework approach. Denying a role to special interest representatives would exclude many of those who know most about the policies under consideration and many of those most directly affected by them.[8]

Obviously, also, the most eminent and well-known representative of each constituency or relevant body of knowledge is sought to increase the legitimacy and credibility of a commission. A Truman aide in charge of suggesting members for a commission remarked, "We wanted . . . not just people you would find under some bushel basket." A commission should be known to include not only all the relevant experts and representatives but also the "best" of them as roughly measured by their fame or the importance of their institutional position. Thus George Meany served on nine different commissions representing labor and Walter Reuther on three.[9]

The mixture is frequently leavened with a few "individuals with civic vision and a statesman's perspective," like John McCloy, John McCone, Marion Folsom, Milton Eisenhower, and James Killian, whose stature and breadth of experience puts them somewhat beyond constituency or categorical labels.[10] They are expected to bring the wisdom of the distinguished layman to bear and to guarantee the integrity of the commission. Because of the importance and delicacy of its assignment, the President's Commission on the Assassination of President Kennedy (1963–64) was composed primarily of recognized statesmen.

Also on every major commission there is usually at least one person whom the President knows personally, for example Samuel Rosenman, the Advisory Commission on Universal Training (1946–47), General Omar Bradley, the President's Commission on Veterans' Pensions (1955–56), Paul Porter, the President's Commission on Campaign Costs (1961–62), and George Reedy, the National Advisory Commission on Selective Service (1966–67). Such appointees are not cronies in the crass sense, since they are usually talented people with training, experience, and characteristics that qualify them for the commission in any case.[11] Nevertheless, a President may sometimes use a commission appointment to boost someone in whom he has an interest, or someone whom he has identified as a "bright young man" or a "comer."[12]

Finally, a minor consideration is the use of appointment to a commission as a way to reward someone to whom the President owes a political debt. Despite the general trend toward conversion in political currency from tangible rewards, jobs or contracts, to intangible rewards, recognition and prestige conferred by the chief executive, commissions are not used extensively as a source of patronage. No examples came to light of a commission member being appointed solely or even primarily as a payment for past services. Paying a political debt probably enters as a factor on an all-other-things-being-equal basis when the prospective commission member satisfies the requirements of being representative, competent, and prestigious. The citizen advisory bodies that are permanent appendages to the federal government and that have many members serving long and fixed terms are probably much more frequently used for patronage.[13]

Much of the discussion of various kinds of *ad hoc* advisory bodies, including commissions, in the nineteen-thirties and forties, focused on these bodies as a means to increase democratic participation in the big bureaucratic government, having wide discretionary authority, that was born during the New Deal and World War II. These bodies were seen as one means to decrease the dangers to citizen rights and to responsible government posed by the growth of such a government.[14] It should be clear that commissions are primarily a mechanism for broader elite participation in policy making and are only indirectly a channel through which the "public," in a broad sense, participates.

A Johnson White House aide compared assembling a commission membership to working a jigsaw puzzle: the commission must meet all the criteria determined to be relevant and yet stay within the size limitation decided upon for it. The following description of the membership of the National Advisory Commission on Health Manpower (1966–67) by a White House staff assistant closely involved in selecting the membership illustrates how the above criteria and considerations are employed and how they overlap with each other.

> He [an HEW official] knew an eminent establishment figure for the chairman. This was needed in this sensitive area. . . . A Republican like Irwin Miller from Indiana was an ideal chairman. We had to make sure that the A.M.A. [American Medical Association] would not blast us out of the water. Dwight Wilbur had been a vice-chairman of the A.M.A., so this served to neutralize them. Nelson and Ebert were the high-level medical education members. A major area of concern for the commission was increasing the capacity of the medical schools. Yerby is a Negro. You need a black on any presidential commission. Cain was the President's personal friend. He was also an eminent doctor at the Mayo Clinic. Either we put him on to please the President or the President suggested him in going over the list. I don't remember which. . . . Newton represented the Commonwealth Fund that had been concerned with education. He had also been president of the University of Colorado and mayor of Denver. So he also provided some political representation. Volker and Dent were to represent the South. Dent was from Dillard University and was a Negro. Kermit Gordon had been director of the Bureau of the Budget. He had the President's confidence. The President likes to know that on any commission there are one or two men with a high sense of political reality. Wilson was president of Xerox and a responsible business leader. Vail was the publisher of the *Cleveland Plain Dealer*. He had struck the President's fancy. The President was always on the lookout for able young men. He

was looking for good places to get Vail involved at the presidential level. Bunting represented women. Beirne represented labor, which you had to have since there were manpower questions involved. Odegaard was president of the University of Washington. . . . Nobody except Cain could be said to represent presidential cronyism. He had the virtue of being both a crony and an eminent physician.

It should be clear there are no hard and fast rules for the selection of commission members. The types of constituency representatives and substantive experts vary with the nature of the subject and the politics of the problem. The importance of having a national cross section seems to increase with the scope of the problem: a broader, more visible and national problem is likely to be examined by a commission on which sex, party, race, religion, occupation, and region are more obviously balanced. A personal relationship to the President is sometimes important but does not override other criteria. Patronage is an infrequently used and relatively unimportant criterion.

The requirements of credibility and legitimacy serve as very real and strong limits on the ability of the White House to pack a commission, because those who are to be persuaded by the commission, the attentive public and the policy community, especially the relevant committees and leaders in Congress, are not easily deceived. They know which are the relevant constituencies and who are the most eminent practitioners and scholars in each field. The people with whom a commission must be credible are good judges of its credibility. A collection of hacks and small fry will leave them unimpressed and probably resentful at the transparent attempt to dupe them.

APPOINTMENT OF MEMBERS: THE PROCESS

Given the above criteria and considerations for selecting commission members, the actual process of searching for names to fill the slots follows no rigid procedure. When a commission is suggested in the ways outlined in chapter 4, the suggestion is often accompanied by a proposed membership, and particularly a proposed chairman. The suggestion to establish the commission can then be sold in part by the attractiveness or appropriateness of the proposed members. For example, when the chairman of the National Security Resources Board, W. Stuart Symington, proposed that the President's Materials Policy Commission (1951–52) be created, he also suggested that William Paley be the chairman. Symington had in fact already been in contact with Paley as the prospective chairman.[15]

When the decision is made to go ahead with a commission, a White House aide is usually put in charge of formulating a list of members.[16] The President frequently makes suggestions on the criteria of selection he feels are most important for a given commission, the sources from which names should be solicited, and perhaps even a few specific names. For example, President

Johnson reportedly had Ben Heineman in mind to be chairman of the President's Commission on Income Maintenance Programs (1968–69) when he agreed to create it. The President's decision to appoint a commission is frequently tentative, contingent on the ability of his staff and those who are proposing the commission to come up with a membership and a mandate that he finds acceptable.[17]

Armed with the preliminary definition of the commission's task and the guidance given by the President, the White House aide begins soliciting names that will fit the President's criteria and the criteria he determines to be important in the composition of the commission. Generating the first long list of possible members is sometimes delegated by the top aide, who has had direct contact with the President, to an aide who is a specialist in the commission's area or, particularly during the Eisenhower Administration, to someone in the agency most directly concerned.

The usual process is for the staff man to sit down with a couple of other aides or with someone he knows from one of the agencies and to come up with, off the tops of their heads, a list of possible members and a list of people likely to be able to suggest members. The aide then begins calling around to the suggestors, whom he knows by acquaintance or reputation, getting suggestions for members from them and being referred to others who may have suggestions. Exploring the limbs of this information tree almost always involves contacting the agencies most concerned for suggestions.[18]

The suggestions for the membership of the National Advisory Commission on Health Manpower (1966–67) were solicited from the Department of Health, Education, and Welfare. The source of the suggestion for the commission is frequently contacted. For example, the Budget Bureau, which advocated the creation of the President's Commission on Veterans' Pensions (1955–56), was probably the source of the suggestion that General Omar Bradley be chairman of the commission.

In the office of the White House aide in charge of political appointments, such as Donald Dawson in the Truman Administration or Ralph Dungan in the Kennedy Administration, large files are maintained of people whose names have been recommended as potential appointees to federal positions or who have come to the attention of the White House because of the recognition they have received in some field. These files are usually consulted for suggestions, as are the files on various kinds of experts maintained by the Civil Service Commission. When the word seeps out that a commission is being constituted on some subject, names are sent to the White House by interested parties, and some self-promoting people volunteer. A constituency group may be asked to suggest names, particularly if its support is crucial to the success of the commission. The Republican National Committee, for example, was asked to submit a panel of names from which Republican members of the President's Commission on Campaign Costs (1961–62) could be chosen, since it was necessary that any reform in campaign financing have the support of both parties, and particularly that such a commission appointed by a Democratic President not be rejected out of hand by the Republicans.[19] The American Council on Education worked closely with the White House in selecting the members of the National Commission on Higher Education (1946–47). The lists of people who have served on previous commissions or task forces, who have held positions in previous administrations, or who have appeared at congressional hearings in the relevant area are often combed for candidates or for the names of people who might suggest candidates. Thus, former cabinet members often turn up on commissions.

The long list of proposed members is reduced by working out the jigsaw puzzle, given the criteria relevant to a commission, the size limitation, the preferences expressed by the President, and the preferences the President is anticipated to have by his staff. The proposed list is worked over by a top aide if the initial search was delegated, then the list is given to the President for his approval. President Johnson, according to one White House aide, "paid meticulous attention to the appointment of all presidential groups." He would frequently cross off or add names and check the list out with people whose judgment on a particular issue he trusted and respected. Depending on the commission, the attention to the appointment of commission members by other Presidents has varied from similar deep involvement to *pro forma* approval. It is at this point in the process, as well as at the time of original presidential approval and suggestions, that the names of people the President knows personally or has an interest in are most likely to be added. For example, according to a White House assistant, "President Kennedy added Vorys' name to the list [for the President's Commission on Campaign Costs, 1961–62]. He was conservative as hell but the President respected him. Kennedy had served in the House with him and may have served on the same committee with him." In one case, that of the President's Commission on a World's Fair (1959), all three of the members were "personal friends" and "personal selections" of the President.

Sometime during the process, when the list of names has been narrowed down, it is cleared through the White House political appointments office to make sure that the bitter enemy of some senator is not being appointed or that some other political liability of a candidate is not being overlooked.[20]

Particular attention is always paid to the selection of the chairman, since he is the one "who has to carry the ball a long way." He will be the public symbol of the commission, and his name will often be used as a shorthand way to refer to the commission (e.g., Warren Commission, and Kerner Commission). He will be the commission member who is most frequently called on to testify in Congress, give speeches, appear on television, and write articles about the work of the commission. On him will rest the primary responsibility for making sure that the commission produces a report within the time allotted to it and that the commission reaches a consensus on a set of recommendations. President Johnson personally selected Chief Justice Earl Warren to be the chairman of the President's Commission on the Assassination of President Kennedy (1963–64).[21]

Often, the chairman is consulted on the choice of the other members, once he has been chosen. This varies from clearing the final membership with him, as a courtesy, to having him actively participate in the process of generating names and making up a list. The participation of Ben Heineman in the selection of the other members of the President's Commission on Income Maintenance Programs (1968–69) was mentioned above. Senator Paul Douglas made suggestions concerning the composition of the National Commission on Urban Problems (1967–68) of which he was chairman.[22] The chairman of President Truman's Commission on the Health Needs of the Nation (1951–52), Dr. Paul Magnuson, worked with the White House staff in selecting the other members of the commission.[23]

In the case of the President's Committee on Foreign Aid (1947), according to a high official in the Truman Administration,

> The President talked to Senator Vandenberg in advance before appointing the committee and showed a list to him. Senator Vandenberg thought that there ought to be one or two more men of bipartisan national prominence. Owen Young and Senator LaFollette were added in response to Senator Vandenberg's concern.

Since the primary purpose of the committee, which was suggested by Senator Vandenberg, was to remove any lingering doubts from the Senator's mind about the wisdom of the Marshall Plan and to help him convince other skeptical senators, President Truman consulted with him in this case.

One potential problem in the appointment of the members of commissions is getting them to agree to serve. As a Kennedy aide put it, "Once you get the list of people, you have to get the people to say yes." The calls to prospective members are usually made by the White House staff, although President Johnson personally extended the invitations to the members of the President's Commission on the Assassination of President Kennedy (1963–64) and the National Advisory Commission on Civil Disorders (1967–68). The unanimous testimony of the White House aides who commented on this subject in interviews is that only very rarely is the invitation to serve on a commission turned down.[24] The main reason why so few invitations are refused is, in the words of a member of several commissions, that "You just don't say no to the President of the United States."[25] President Johnson's application of his famous "treatment" to Chief Justice Warren illustrates well the persuasiveness of the call from the White House. President Johnson writes:

> I said [to Warren] I didn't care . . . how opposed he was to this assignment [as chairman of the President's Commission on the Assassination of President Kennedy]. When the country is confronted with threatening divisions and suspicions, I said, and its foundation is being rocked, and the President of the United States says that you are the only man who can handle the matter, you won't say "no" will you?"
> He swallowed hard and said, "No, sir."[26]

A more serious problem in the recruitment of commission members is that "almost an established class of commissioners who are tapped repeatedly for service" has developed.[27] A Johnson assistant described the problem:

> There is a problem that the same damn names turn up time after time. It is hard as the devil to find new people. There was a lot of talk about finding that bright young man in Iowa in the Kennedy Administration. They didn't find him. There is really sort of a liberal house establishment. The same people keep turning up on the same problems. You have a deuce of a time trying to reach out to get outside of the major cities. Too often the selection is from among people like George Ball, the Bundy brothers, Heineman, and John Gardner. They are all good people, but it's hard to get beyond them.

The danger of this situation is that the loss of freshness and variety in commission memberships will foster a "ho-hum-those-guys-again" attitude in the public, reducing the commission's persuasiveness and impact.

Several White House staff members pointed out the importance of the top staff members of a commission in getting the commission's job done and in determining the substantive direction of its recommendations. There has been no extensive or systematic attempt to guide the staffing of commissions to further White House control or influence over them, however. When staff are suggested by the White House, it is usually as a way to help a commission, without any clear political thinking behind it, and the White House suggestions are always subject to the agreement of the commission chairman and sometimes the full commission.[28] Staffing is controlled by the commissions, and it will be discussed in the next chapter.

WHITE HOUSE LIAISON WITH COMMISSIONS

A suspicion appears to exist that, through their contacts with the commission members and staff, the White House staff controls, manipulates, or influences the substantive recommendations of commissions. This suspicion seems to be unfounded. The following comments by White House and commission staff members are representative of their view that such manipulation does not and cannot occur.

White House staff:

> Then once they were set up we let them alone. . . . The White House kept hands off the committee. (Truman aide with reference to the President's Committee on Civil Rights, 1946–47.)
> After we set it up, we didn't touch them again. . . . There were no pressures on the commission. . . . We didn't dare touch them, although we may have wanted to. (Truman aide with reference to the President's Commission on the Health Needs of the Nation, 1951–52.)
> Not only can't you control them [commissions], but you have no defenses against them. (Eisenhower aide.)
> You can't guide the results [of commissions]. (Eisenhower aide.)
> If you get these people with prestige and stature, they are going to want to reach their own conclusions and not be led down some primrose lane. (Kennedy-Johnson aide.)
> When you establish a commission, there is little you can do but grin and bear it. (Johnson aide.)

Commission staff:

> There was no attempt by the White House to shape the outcome of this commission. There was no influence or pressure of any kind. (President's Advisory Commission on Universal Training, 1946–47.)
> There was no political intervention. (President's Commission on Veterans' Pensions, 1955–56.)
> There was no influence from the White House. (Commission on National Goals, 1960.)
> There was no White House interference. (Commission on Heart Disease, Cancer and Stroke, 1964.)
> They never interfered in our work or pushed us. They never tried to influence our work. There was no guidance from the White House. (National Advisory Commission on Selective Service, 1966–67.)

With respect to the National Commission on the Causes and Prevention of Violence, which was created by President Johnson but reported during the Nixon Administration, its chairman, Milton Eisenhower, notes that President Nixon "was most cooperative . . . in leaving us free to reach our own conclusions. . . ."[29]

Two things are particularly significant about these statements. First, most of them were made with reference to commissions that dealt with important, visible, and politically sensitive issues: civil rights, universal military training, health insurance, veterans' pensions, and selective service. If influence was exerted anywhere it would be expected on these issues, yet the testimony indicates that this was not the case. Second, these statements were made by people who would know political influence and manipulation if they saw it.

All of the statements quoted above, by the commission staffs, are from men who had long experience at high levels in the Executive Branch of the federal government. One member of the staff of the President's Committee on Civil Rights (1946–47) was struck not by the presence of close liaison with the White House, but by its absence. It seemed to him that the White House was being "politically irresponsible," since the committee "could have exploded in his [President Truman's] face." The only reported instance of an attempt by the White House to influence a commission is that the White House "tried to head off some things" and "tried to get a positive note on Johnson's programs included" in the report of the National Advisory Commission on Civil Disorders (1967–68). It is the rare exception, and it failed.

The reality of White House liaison with commissions is quite different from the image of White House operatives prowling through commission offices, buttonholing commission members and staff, and prodding or bludgeoning commissions to follow the path chosen by the White House. Usually each commission has some White House assistant designated as their point of contact with the White House. This is frequently the aide who had the responsibility for doing the staff work on the commission membership and mandate, and he is likely to have some knowledge of the problem on which the commission is working.

Most of the contacts between the White House and a commission are offers of assistance or more frequently calls for assistance from the commission to help deal with "mechanical problems." The White House acts as an ombudsman for this new temporary organization in dealing with the permanent federal bureaucracy. They may suggest staff members, help the commission formulate its budget, find money, locate office space, or intercede with federal agencies to get data and other forms of cooperation requested by the commission.[30] A member of the staff of the President's Citizen Advisers on the Mutual Security Program (1956–57) related the following example of handling one "mechanical problem" through the White House:

> I remember one problem that we had. At our first meeting Admiral Radford was coming over. It occurred to me that no one on the commission had security clearance. It would have been bad if someone had asked the Admiral a question and he said he couldn't answer because the commissioners hadn't received clearance. Some of them who didn't understand these rules about clearance might have been upset and got up and left saying, "If you don't trust us, why did you appoint us for this job?" Fairless [chairman of the commission] went to Sherman Adams, and he got them all interim clearance, and then they were all cleared. I don't think they every knew anything about it.

The second major purpose of liaison between the White House and commissions is to keep the White House informed on the progress of the commission. There are several reasons why the White House wants to keep "abreast of what is going on" in a commission. First, they want to make sure that the job is getting done, that the commission is conducting its inquiry, is not bogged down by administrative problems, has not reached a stalemate, and is on the way to producing its report. Assistance is offered if a commission has hit some snag where the White House can help. They are concerned to learn when a commission will complete its report, and particularly if it will be finished by its deadline. Knowing when the report will be completed allows the White House to plan for its reception and release to mesh with its program planning and public relations on the problem the commission is studying.

The White House is also interested in being informed on "where the commission is coming out" substantively.[31] White House aides act as "bird dogs" or keep their "antennae out" for the direction of a commission's substantive recommendations, again so that they can plan to use the commission product in their policy formulation and salesmanship. If an issue is very hot when a commission begins its work or becomes so during the life of the commission, the White House may be eager to benefit from it before it completes its work, to use its findings in a speech, a message to Congress, or a legislative proposal. For example, the White House felt they were "in the crunch" on health manpower after the passage of Medicare. An aide in contact with the National Advisory Commission on Health Manpower (1966–67) remarked, "We were anxious for the spin-off from the commission [before it completed its final report]."[32]

Staff monitoring of the work of commissions also serves to warn the President of "unforeseen backfiring" or recommendations that will be "an embarrassment to the President." The response by the White House to a "runaway" commission is almost entirely defensive. The defensive reaction consists in scheduling the release of the report to minimize its exposure (the Friday after Thanksgiving was suggested as ideal for this purpose), not harnessing the media resources of the White House behind it, preparing statements in reaction to the report or preparing to go underground on the subject of the report, and scheduling or staging other events to compete with the release of the report and hopefully "blanket" it and push it onto page 75 next to the obituaries and corn prices.[33] The White House feels powerless to change the recommendations of a commission.[34] The comment of a Johnson aide was that "all you can do is be embarrassed. . . . There is no way the President can order them [a commission] to do anything."

The White House elicits the information it wants from commissions by informal contacts with the commission members and staff, by visits to commission meetings, and by interim, progress, or preliminary reports scheduled into the commission mandate, requested by the White House, or volunteered by the commission. The flow of substantive information from a commission to the White House was accurately characterized by a presidential assistant as a "one-way street." Suggestions from the White House on substantive policy recommendations do not seem to be transmitted to commissions.[35]

The frequency of White House contacts with commissions varies a great deal. Although almost every commission has a liaison at least formally designated for it, the extent of contact varies from "none whatsoever," to "very little," to "regular," to "very close." Much of the variation is accounted for by the interest of the President in the commission and by the importance and urgency of the subject being considered by the commission. A Johnson aide remarked, "What monitoring there is is a function of the interest of the President. The staff take their cues from him on how much attention to pay to a commission." Much of the liaison with commissions is *ad hoc* or on a "fire alarm" or crisis basis. If there is a leak to the press from a commission, a crisis on the commission, external events that suddenly make the commission's work more important, or an awakening of presidential or White House interest in the commission's area, close contact will be established with the commission for a time. Thus for all except those commissions dealing with problems of the highest priority or having the strongest interest for the President, watching by the White House is done with periodic bursts of attention that usually fade after a short time. Only a very few are closely and systematically watched. What minimal regular watching of commissions there is is largely a reflection of the need of White House aides to keep generally informed. A Johnson aide explained, "A White House aide needs a response if the President should ask, 'What the hell is this group doing?' He has to be able at least to say, 'They're coming along well and on schedule.' "

Why is the White House limited to being an ombudsman for commissions, keeping informed about what they are doing, and preparing supportive or defensive responses to their work? Why can the White House not control them? There are several reasons:

1. For the great majority of commissions, there is no clear idea in the White House of what course of action they favor. The primary reason for creating most commissions is to explore and analyze alternate courses of action and to reach a consensus on one. The White House wants the independent judgment of the commission on the policy problem. They are looking for the "new ideas" that a commission can provide. An Eisenhower aide said, "If you try to guide a commission, it destroys the purpose of having one." The White House may have some idea of where they do not want to go, and those suggestions that are made to commissions are probably made to head off undesirable conclusions rather than to guide commissions to predetermined ones. Thus, even if a mechanism for steering commissions existed, the White House would not be interested in steering, and if it were interested,

it would be hard to steer a commission if it had no clear idea of where it wanted it to go.

2. If the President is to get full benefit from a commission, for his purposes of policy analysis and window dressing, the commission must be credible. Besides having to be representative, competent, and prestigious, a credible commission must be independent and objective. The reputed integrity and prestige of the commission members is one important guarantee of commission independence. Lack of interference from the White House is another necessary guarantee of a commission's credibility. White House fingerprints on the commission report or attempts to suppress the report are likely to be discovered, and will defeat the purpose in creating the commission or will increase the damage from a report that turns out badly from the White House point of view. Not interfering with a commission "is the way to get a strong enough report to be helpful," said a Truman aide. The press and the Congress are generally alert watchdogs who will detect and expose any discontinuities between commission image and commission reality.[36]

3. Even if the White House knew where it wanted to go and was willing to risk damage to the commission's credibility by trying to influence it, the members and staff generally take seriously the role of disinterested seekers after truth and the public interest. They do not see themselves as servants of the President's purposes, other than the publicly stated purpose of every commission, to collect and review information, engage in analysis, and make recommendations. They will blow the whistle if there is White House interference. "Magnuson [chairman of the President's Commission on the Health Needs of the Nation, 1951–52] wouldn't have brooked any interference if we had tried," remarked a Truman aide. "No one could control that unguidable missile, General Clay [chairman of the President's Committee to Strengthen the Security of the Free World, 1962–63]," observed a Kennedy aide. Commission members often, in fact, believe that they bear a "commission," with the connotation of independence that that word has. A member of two commissions created during the Johnson Administration said, "Commission members really do feel like commissioners." The people who are appointed to commissions, people with reputations for expertness and high prestige, are likely to be independent. Many of them are also likely to be suspicious of "politics" and "political influence." A White House staff member recounted the following incident:

> Dr. Graham [a member of the President's Commission on the Health Needs of the Nation, 1951–52] said [at the presentation of the report to the President], "Mr. President, when I was asked to be on this commission, I expected that there would be pressures on us. But the fact that I signed the report and that I am here today indicates that there were none."

4. Even if the White House were willing to violate the expectations of commission members, they generally have no hold over them. Nationally prestigious constituency representatives and experts are usually not buyable with any of the coins of presidential politics, except perhaps in rare circumstances by a presidential entreaty framed in terms of the national interest and the public good. A member of two commissions who also had White House experience remarked, "You would be surprised to see how few of the men on the . . . [two commissions] were dependent on the federal government *per se.* I think in general very few men on presidential commissions need to look to the federal government for their bread and butter."

5. Finally, even if the White House knew where it wanted a commission to go, were willing to risk damaging the commission's credibility, were willing to ignore the expectations of commission members, and could in fact get leverage on the members, they usually would have neither the resources nor the inclination to do the job. They lack the inclination, because the White House staff as a rule believes, with the commission members, that the study should be done independently of the White House and that it is not legitimate to try to influence it. A member of the Kennedy-Johnson White House staff recalled his experience with one commission:

> I came to some of their meetings mostly to observe and not to contribute. I didn't contribute because it was not my bag. I was not a member of the commission, and I thought it would not be appropriate to tell them what I believed or what I believed that the President believed, especially on such a politically delicate subject.

The White House also lacks the time and manpower to closely monitor or to try to influence a commission.[37] The following statements by White House staff members make the point quite well. A Johnson aide: "The White House is the busiest place on earth. No one has time to manipulate a commission." A second Johnson aide: "My impression is that Presidents usually set up commissions and then forget about them. . . . The President probably isn't aware of the commission again until about a month before it reports." An Eisenhower aide: "I think that they [commissions] do pretty much tend to be forgotten after they are created. No one pays much attention to something that isn't going to report for one or two years. There are too many more immediate problems." Most commissions are quickly crowded off into a far corner of White House concerns, and by the time they reemerge into the consciousness of the White House staff, shortly before they report, it is too late to do anything but prepare a response. Commissions are more often forgotten and neglected than pressured or closely watched.

If the White House staff does not control commissions directly, it might be suspected that control is exercised indirectly through the administration officials or the President's men who are appointed to commissions. This also does not appear to be the case.

Twenty-four of the commissions had at least one Executive Branch official among their members, and several commissions had interagency advisory committees attached to them. While the officials on commissions tend naturally to be somewhat defensive and protective about their own agencies and may put a damper on the criticism and the suggested revisions of existing programs that can be included in commission reports, no evidence was found that they speak for the White House or are a channel for the expression of the views of the White House. Such officials are placed on commissions because they represent a legitimate interest, those in the federal government who are dealing with the commission's problem, and they usually know a great deal about the problem. They can therefore make a contribution to the commission and add to its strength. Reports signed by Executive Branch officials are likely to have an easier time when reviewed within the Executive Branch and to be more persuasive to the members of Congress who have positive working relationships with the agencies from which the officials are drawn. Some agency officials, particularly Cabinet members, are named to commissions as a way to associate their departments with the enterprise. Many of them rarely attend commission meetings but are represented by junior officials instead. Their formal membership on the commission gives the commission a claim on money, staff, and information from the department.[38]

The interagency advisory committees attached to commissions seem to be even less active than the Executive Branch members of commissions, and to function almost exclusively as a point of access for the commission to the agencies represented on the committee. A member of the staff of the National Commission on Technology, Automation, and Economic Progress (1964–66) explained the role of its Interagency Advisory Committee:

> To my knowledge they never met as a group. They were drawn upon by the staff. We would call them and tell them that they were members of the committee. They were then more accessible and willing to help. The committee was a way of making these people more available and accessible to the commission staff.

The cronies, friends, and acquaintances of Presidents and the men in whom the President takes a personal interest who are appointed to commissions have been characterized by Elizabeth Drew as "White House 'plant [s]' " who represent the point of view of the President on the commission.[39] The evidence indicates that they do not serve as a pipeline for White House influence on commissions. In fact, one member of a commission dealing with a sensitive issue who knew President Kennedy offered to speak for the President and was turned down. The President did not have any views he wanted pushed, and he wanted the benefit of the commission's analysis.

These members serve two purposes on commissions other than the one suggested by Drew. First, they are often part of the White House information network, to keep track of how the commission is progressing and where it is coming out. A Johnson aide remarked, "We would try to put somebody on the commission as a member to keep us well informed." There is no evidence that their communication with the White House is not one-way, as that between commission members and staff and the White House has been. Of course, these members may be more candid with the White House, and more sensitive to the kind of information the White House wants in order to use and respond to a commission report effectively.

Second, presidential friends on commissions serve as a familiar yardstick giving the President a quick way to reach a preliminary evaluation of a commission report. An official with extensive experience in the Executive Branch during the Truman, Kennedy, and Johnson administrations explained:

> Johnson always wanted someone that he knew on a commission. Most people misunderstand this. They think he is trying to dictate the results of the commission's work. But this isn't true. He wants someone whom he trusts and has confidence in on the commission so that he knows it [the report] has been massaged by this person before it gets to him. Johnson wanted to be able to say, "If . . . [x] was on that commission and he didn't dissent from the report, then I can be confident that it's sound and doesn't contain any big traps." This is true of all Presidents and is probably why Truman had Rosenman on the military training commission [President's Advisory Commission on Universal Training, 1946–47].

OTHER INDICES OF COMMISSION INDEPENDENCE

Another indicator of the independence of commissions and of the inability of the White House to control them is the number of commissions that "turn around and bite you in the ass" as one White House staff member put it. A substantial minority of commissions issue reports which are an embarrassment and a liability to the President. White House aides are particularly sensitive to the risk that a commission will "backfire" or be a "runaway," since "the White House aide who was supposed to keep in touch with it gets his block knocked off" even though there is very little he can do to prevent such an outcome. Describing the risks and dangers of commissions brings forth some of their most vivid language:

> You have to be prepared to eat what they come out with if it isn't to your liking. (Truman aide.)
> Sometimes they can sneak up and belt you on the blind side. If the report is something the President doesn't agree with, it provides perfect ammunition, especially for the Congress. . . . As one of my congres-

sional friends used to say, they dig up more snakes than you can kill. (Eisenhower aide.)

Sometimes they come up with shocking things. . . . These groups do their own thinking. If you enlist the time and energy of a group of able men, sometimes you are surprised by the result. (Kennedy-Johnson aide.)

When you appoint a commission, you are marrying a porcupine, and it's going to be hard to make love with. They are liable if not likely to give you recommendations that are political turkeys. You have to accept a 60–40 chance that you will be saddled with something and may end up on the hook with the opposition party. . . . If you appoint a commission with a spectrum of members, you are equipping your potential enemies with poison darts. (Nixon aide.)

Prominent examples of commissions that have been characterized as "runaways" are the President's Advisory Committee on a National Highway Program (1954–55), the President's Committee to Strengthen the Security of the Free World (1962–63), the National Commission on Urban Problems (1967–68), the National Advisory Commission on Civil Disorders (1967–68), the Commission on Obscenity and Pornography (1967–70), and the President's Commission on Campus Unrest (1970).[40] If a commission is to be of use to the President as a policy analyst and a political salesman, it must be credible, and if it is to be credible, the risks of its becoming a runaway must be and are borne.[41]

The commission staff who were queried all agreed that the amount of money available to them was adequate, and three reported turning unused money back at the completion of their commission's work.[42] The independence of commissions and their ability to examine the problems set before them is not jeopardized by a lack of money. However, the funding arrangements for some commissions are very *ad hoc,* and funds come from a variety of sources, as described in chapter 4. This sometimes means that a commission staff spends a lot of time piecing together financial support and is distracted from the commission's mission.

The independence of commissions and their capacity to carry out their mandate have not been hindered, either, by the denial of access to information in the Executive Branch. Federal agencies have, for the most part, been very cooperative and provided commissions with the information they requested.[43] In the few cases where cooperation was not forthcoming, the White House has actively intervened in behalf of the commission to secure for it the desired information.[44]

A good summary on the independence of commissions is provided by Lloyd Cutler, executive director of the National Commission on the Causes and Prevention of Violence (1968–69). Speaking of this commission, he says:

> . . . I think that certainly this commission developed an independence of thought and really an independence of being directed or influenced

by those who had appointed it. That was very considerable [*sic*]. I think it was in part because almost any entity develops a life and spirit of its own, because members of the commission are not really beholden, most of them, to the appointing authority for anything in particular, and they get to believe in what they are doing and their own value. And then I think we were granted a good deal of independence both by Mr. Johnson and, especially, by Mr. Nixon.[45]

There appears to be very little muck to rake on the subject of the independence of commissions. Broad boundaries are established for them by the political context into which they are put, by their mandates, and by the soundness of their members. Commissions are pointed in the general direction of administration policy by the selection of their members. But they are not packed, and they are not manipulated through White House liaison, through White House control of their staffing or their access to money and information, or through the presence of federal officials and presidential friends among their membership. The requirements of credibility preclude packing and interference, and the number of runaway commissions demonstrates the independence of commissions and the risk the White House accepts in creating them.

CHAPTER SIX

HOW DO COMMISSIONS WORK?

MOST COMMISSIONS face a formidable set of tasks. They must reach findings about a controversial and complex social problem and make recommendations for solving the problem. This involves translating their mandate into operational terms, recruiting a staff, and undertaking data gathering and research. The findings and recommendations must be agreed to by at least a majority, and, if possible, by all of the commission members, who have been selected in part for their representativeness of diverse constituencies and who usually have had no previous experience in working with each other as a group. Their findings and recommendations must be stated in a written document that through some kind of analysis relates the findings to the recommendations and relates both of these to the problems posed to the commission. All of this must be accomplished within the time limit imposed by the President. An investigation of how commissions go about accomplishing these tasks is the major thrust of this chapter. In particular, it will focus on the nature of the inquiry undertaken by commissions, the respective roles of the staff and the commission members in the writing of the reports, the means used to reach agreement among the members, and the kinds of findings and recommendations most frequently made by commissions.

DEFINING THE TASK

The first important task facing a commission is to define the problem it is examining. This usually involves deciding how a general problem should be broken down into a set of more specific and manageable problems. Frequently this is seen to be "obvious" or "self evident from the mandate."[1]

In some cases, however, explicit choices on the mission of the commission are made. The President's Committee on Civil Rights (1946–47) decided not to construct a "balance sheet" evaluating the "extent to which civil rights have been achieved," and it therefore focused on the "bad side of the

96

record."[2] The committee also decided not to become involved in identifying "specific instances of wrong doing" and to focus on the problems in general policy terms. The President's Commission on the Status of Women (1961–62) decided "not to delve into the psychology of women and the anthropological approach."[3]

This initial conceptualization of the problem rarely evokes a great deal of debate or controversy within the commission. The decisions are usually made by the top staff in consultation with the chairman and other key commission members and routinely approved by the whole commission at one of its early meetings.[4] On some of the smaller commissions, such as the President's Advisory Commission on Universal Training (1946–47) or the Air Policy Commission (1947–48), the commission as a whole participated more actively in deciding how to define the issues. Definition of issues generally provokes little controversy, because the most knowledgeable and interested commission members are actively involved, and because the other members often do not yet know enough about the subject to have objections or offer alternatives.

For some commissions the focus of the inquiry shifts or evolves during the course of the commission's work. The President's Commission on Law Enforcement and Administration of Justice (1965–67) added organized crime, juvenile delinquency, narcotics and drug abuse, drunkenness, and science and technology to its original list of central concerns—police, courts, corrections, and assessment of crime.[5] The President's Materials Policy Commission (1951–52) decided in the course of its work to shift emphasis from the "supply and demand situations for various commodities to the broader implications of the materials problem," and it abandoned its comparison of the raw materials positions of the United States and Russia.[6]

CONDUCTING AN INQUIRY

Commissions usually cast their nets broadly and solicit information from everyone who might know something about their problem. For example, the President's Water Resources Policy Commission (1950) sent letters of inquiry to every state governor, every state attorney general, every state agricultural experiment station, the presidents of 80 universities and colleges, and 750 other public and private agencies.[7] More focused inquiry is undertaken through contacts with government agencies closely involved with whatever the problem may be, such as the Office of Economic Opportunity and the Department of Health, Education and Welfare, in the case of the President's Commission on Income Maintenance Programs (1968–69), or the Departments of Interior and Commerce, in the case of the National Commission on Materials Policy (1970–73).

Experts in the field are contacted and frequently hired as staff or consultants. For example, Professor William Dillingham, who had written *Federal Aid to Veterans, 1917–41,* was hired full time by the President's Commission on Veterans' Pensions (1955–56), and Kenneth Dolbeare and James Davis, political scientists at the University of Wisconsin who were completing their book *Little Groups of Neighbors: The Selective Service System,* served as consultants to the National Advisory Commission on Selective Service (1966–67).[8]

Commissions often hold extensive hearings at which those who are interested are invited to testify.[9] The hearings are usually public and are often held in several regions of the country where the problem is particularly acute or where there are important constituencies related to the problem. The President's Commission on Migratory Labor (1950–51), for example, held twelve public hearings, mostly in the South and West, at which "representatives of farmers, growers, processors, employees, labor organizations, officers of Federal, State, and local governments, social workers, health authorities, educational leaders, religious groups, and numbers of migrant workers themselves" were heard.[10]

Commission members undertake field inspections. Four members of the President's Advisory Commission on Universal Training (1946–47) visited Fort Knox to study the Army's UMT Experimental Unit, members of the Commission on American Shipbuilding (1970–73) went to American, European and Japanese shipyards, and members of the National Advisory Commission on Civil Disorders (1967–68) travelled to the ghettoes where several of the riots had occurred.[11] Contracts are also let to research firms like the Battelle Institute or Arthur D. Little, Inc.[12]

The inquiries of commissions are broad, in the sense of not overlooking any source of public or private information, experience, or judgment about a problem. They explore thoroughly the state of the problem-solving art in their field. Amassing all of this substantive and political information serves several purposes or functions for the commission.

First, and most important, it serves as the basis for the process of analysis and judgment undertaken by the commissions, which is discussed below.

Second, it establishes the scientific legitimacy of the commission. As explained in chapter 3, one of the reasons why commission recommendations are accepted as authoritative is that they are reached in accord with the public's conception of how decisions should be made. One element of this public ideal for legitimate decision making is that there be extensive factual inquiry supporting the conclusions reached. While the inquiries by commissions are not scientific or rational-comprehensive for all of the reasons outlined below, they do satisfy the lesser public definition of science and research by gathering all of the available data.[13] Employing expert consultants, letting research contracts, and holding special conferences and consultations with experts serve to satisfy the somewhat stricter standards of the professionals in the field. Usually an attempt is made to co-opt every expert who might challenge a commission's scientific credibility, by giving them all an input.

Third, broad solicitation of information and views establishes the political legitimacy of a commission, the other major element in the legitimacy of a commission's decision making. In giving all interested parties their day in court, the inquiry establishes that the commission is fair and democratic.[14]

Fourth, the wide-ranging inquiry of commissions, particularly through public hearings and field inspections, directly furthers the achievement of some of the President's goals in creating the commission and some of the commission's own goals. By publicizing a problem and establishing their own scientific and political legitimacy, commissions are enhanced as policy-marketing devices for the President, and they accomplish some immediate public education as well as increasing their prospects for having a long-range educational effect. When commissions are a response to a crisis, their public visibility also demonstrates government action and concern.

From the commission's point of view, establishing their visibility and legitimacy helps to attain those goals they usually share with the President, educating the public and selling their proposals. It also increases the leverage of the commission with the President, whose support is crucial if its recommendations are to be implemented.

Fifth, a thorough inquiry, particularly if it involves extensive participation by the commission members, helps commissions to attain internal integration. Travelling together and holding hearings, discussions, and meetings at which information is gathered builds a foundation of shared knowledge and experience, practice in working together, and *esprit de corps* that serves a commission well when the time comes to reach decisions on findings and recommendations.[15]

"We reviewed and synthesized what we got elsewhere," remarked a member of the staff of the President's Advisory Commission on Universal Training (1946–47). Members of the staffs of other commissions agreed with the substance of this statement as a description of the research undertaken by commission staffs.[16] Some commissions have been known for the innovative "research" they undertook. The studies by the President's Commission on Veterans' Pensions (1955–56) of the social and economic status and the attitudes of veterans and non-veterans, the studies of the characteristics of local draft board members, of classifications and reclassifications, and of the decision making by local draft boards and appeals boards by the National Advisory Commission on Selective Service (1966–67), and the survey of unreported crime by the President's Commission on Law Enforcement and

Administration of Justice (1965–67) are important examples of this type of research. In these and other cases commissions have succeeded in making important but basically straightforward new findings of fact.[17]

These commissions and commissions in general do not, however, undertake research in the sense of scientifically testing hypotheses related to the causes of social phenomena or the consequences of adopting alternate public policies. Where such research has been attempted, as in the assessment of the "harm" that results from exposing people to explicit sexual material (Commission on Obscenity and Pornography, 1967–70), the results have not been satisfactory.[18] William Hamilton notes that the President's Materials Policy Commission (1951–52) "never did succeed in establishing the existence of shortages," although the existence or imminent threat of such shortages was one of the central findings from which many of the commission's recommendations followed.[19]

Commission recommendations are implicitly statements about the future. For example, the recommendation of the National Advisory Commission on Selective Service (1966–67) that the composition of local draft boards "should represent all elements of the public they serve" says, in effect, that if this is done, the Selective Service System will be fairer, more legitimate, and more effective.[20] This statement about the future is 1) based on a future state of affairs different from the current state of affairs, the commission's recommendations having been implemented; 2) made with respect to complex social phenomena, the relation of citizens to the system for compulsory induction into the armed forces; and 3) to be evaluated on the basis of subjective and imprecise criteria of performance or fairness, legitimacy, and effectiveness. It necessarily carries with it, at best, a low and uncertain probability. Commissions can rarely if ever demonstrate that there is a high probability that their recommendations will produce the state of affairs they are intended to produce.

There are several reasons why commissions are neither social-scientific nor rational-comprehensive in their approach.[21] First, commissions operate under severe time constraints which affect their capacity for scientific research and rational-comprehensive choice. The average commission lasts 11.6 months. Roughly half of this time is available for data gathering and research; the rest is occupied by initial organization and staff recruitment, analysis of the research and data by the staff and the commission members, commission decision making on findings and recommendations, and writing the report. Six months for the average commission is hardly time enough to engage in extensive research, or even to attempt to gather data not already available. The two longest commissions, with three-year tenures, had about two years to conduct their inquiries, only a modestly sufficient period for extensive research and, of course, inadequate for any studies of long-term phenomena.

Roland Renne, a member of the President's Water Resources Policy Commission (1950), remarked, "Obviously the short time available to the Commission before its report is due precludes any possibility of conducting extensive new research or studies."[22] Other commentators on commissions have also noted the time pressures facing commissions and the limitation this imposes on their ability to conduct research.[23]

Second, while commissions are not in general starved for funds, they rarely have enough to undertake broad, basic social science research or to make rational-comprehensive choices.[24] A member of the staff of the President's Commission on Law Enforcement and Administration of Justice (1965–67), which by commission standards was very well funded by both Congress and the President, reported that the approximately $400,000 which the commission's surveys cost, "would have been too great a strain and too big a chunk out of the commission's budget." These surveys were funded instead, in large part, through the Office of Law Enforcement Assistance.[25] Thus one of the commissions with the best access to government funds could not afford, out of its own budget, to gather extensive basic data, to say nothing of supporting broad fundamental research.

Most meaningful research on the feasibility and consequences of public policies is done by government-funded pilot programs, since only the government has the resources and the authority to undertake such experiments. Even these programs are frequently hindered by having too little time because of impatience for results, inadequate funding, and compromises in the face of reality that leave their results far short of scientific certainty.[26] Commissions are not unaware of the limitations placed upon them by a lack of time and resources, and they frequently couch their recommendations in terms of suggested pilot programs or topics and directions for research.[27]

Third, the full-time professional staffs of commissions are frequently not oriented toward rational-comprehensive decision making or scientific inquiry. They are most often lawyers and middle-level substantive experts from the federal government. Their training and professional experience incline them toward a method of problem solving that proceeds by collecting the available data and analyzing it in terms of making pragmatic adjustments and modifications in the existing programs and approaches. A rational-comprehensive or hypothesis-experiment investigation is foreign to them.[28] Much the same can be said for most of the commission members. Social scientists are often engaged by commissions as consultants and sometimes as staff, as in the case mentioned above of Davis and Dolbeare on the staff of the National Advisory Commission on Selective Service (1966–67), or of Lloyd Ohlin, a professor of sociology at Columbia University, on the staff of the President's Commission on Law Enforcement and Administration of Justice (1965–67). These are exceptions, however, and commissions frequently find it difficult to recruit academic social scientists because they cannot easily obtain extended leaves on short notice and because the career payoffs of full-time work on a commission are much lower for them than for lawyers and government experts.[29] For the latter, service on a commission is a prestigious step to a presidential platform within the political and policy community from which they are drawn, rather than just an interesting hiatus or detour into politics and public service.

Fourth, even with unlimited time and resources, commission inquiry would be limited by the fact that it is not an investigation of bacteria in cultures but of people in society. People in a country like the United States will not submit their lives to anything approaching the conditions required for a valid scientific inquiry related to an important question of public policy. James Q. Wilson provides a graphic example of what such a social science experiment would require:

> A more revealing experiment [than the laboratory experiments of the Commission on Obscenity and Pornography, 1967–70] would be to compare the attitudes and behavior of a group of children, reared in a community with easy and frequent access to erotica . . . to those of a group, carefully matched in all other respects, reared in a community with no access, or only occasional and furtive access, to the obscene . . . . Obviously, such an experiment would have to last over many years–perhaps two generations, in order to control for prior parental attitudes–and the subjects would have to be carefully monitored to insure that experimental conditions were not violated by, for example, moving to another town or taking frequent trips to New York City to patronize the book stores on 42nd Street.[30]

Fifth, the questions posed to commissions frequently call for an assessment of a broad and important event or process in which a large number of complex, interrelated, and usually ill-defined variables are involved.[31] The National Advisory Commission on Civil Disorders (1967–68), for example, was asked by President Johnson to find out "Why riots occur in some cities and do not occur in others?" and "Why one man breaks the law, while another, living in the same circumstances, does not?"[32] The answers of social scientists to such questions are likely to be inconclusive and to consist largely of a laundry list of "factors" rather than precise statements about the relationships between the variables. This was indeed the case in the report of the Civil Disorders Commission. With respect to the first question cited above, the commission reported, "We have been unable to identify constant patterns in all aspects of civil disorders. We have found that they are unusual, irregular, complex, and, in the present state of knowledge, unpredictable social processes."[33] On the question of rioters and non-rioters, the commission only noted some differences in the "characteristics" and "attitudes" between the two groups but did not draw any definite conclusions.[34] Lipsky and Olson conclude that "riot commissions [including the National Advisory Commission on Civil Disorders] are inherently incapable of providing sophisticated answers to the most important questions relating to riots."[35]

Sixth, the broadest and most basic patterns of social behavior and attitudes are the most important variables to understand in social science. Yet they are variables that do not vary. In the short run they are constants and therefore very difficult to evaluate. Research that cannot effectively take into account large but indeterminate factors has the unreality of a map of a military campaign that portrays the entire landscape as a giant table top, and each division as of equal weight regardless of its morale, training, or experience. These variables also constitute the assumptions and conceptual "paradigm" that guide and circumscribe inquiry rather than being the subject of inquiry. Isaiah Berlin observes:

> In part ... we are immersed and submerged in a medium that, precisely to the degree to which we inevitably take it for granted as part of ourselves, we do not and cannot observe as if from the outside; cannot identify, measure and seek to manipulate; cannot even be wholly aware of, inasmuch as it enters too intimately into all our experience, is itself too closely interwoven with all that we are and do to be lifted out of the flow (it *is* the flow) and observed with scientific detachment, as an object.[36]

In sum the fourth, fifth, and sixth arguments just outlined indicate that when it comes to dealing with the most profound problems of public policy, social scientists cannot be scientists.

Seventh, while the above exposition of the limitations on the success of commissions as social scientists assumes that the questions posed to them are, in theory at least, capable of being answered by social science techniques, in fact, many of the most fundamental questions are scientifically unanswerable. Questions such as What is the nature of a citizen's obligation to serve in the armed forces? (National Advisory Commission on Selective Service, 1966–67) and What are the obligations of government to its citizens who have served in the armed forces? (President's Commission on Veterans' Pensions, 1955–56) call for moral choices from among theories of obligation, citizenship, and the nature of man and the state. They are not questions that can be "scientifically" answered even in theory.[37]

That commissions cannot be rational-comprehensive decision makers or scientists is something that they themselves frequently learn only by experience. Philip Coombs, executive director of the President's Materials Policy Commission (1951–52), in January, 1951, prepared a five-phase schedule for development of the commission's work that visualized basically such a process. Seven months later he circulated a memo among the staff arguing that they could not afford "certainty" or "completeness" and that they would have to live with uncertainty and write a report in which all the problems were not treated in the manner they merited.[38]

The fact that commissions are not highly skilled social science research teams or rational-comprehensive decision makers does not condemn them to arriving at their findings and recommendations with the aid of a ouija board or tarot cards. Commissions engage in policy analysis. They make rational and informed judgments about the questions of public policy before them based on the extensive inquiry they normally undertake. Commission members bring to bear the facts they collect, along with their values and political knowledge.[39] The typical organization of a chapter of a commission report—presentation of data and findings, examination of alternative proposals, criticism of existing programs, analysis and generalization based on the findings, and recommendations by the commission—is representative of the general process by which most recommendations are arrived at.

In many cases the findings clearly point to what recommendations should be made. For example, the President's Commission on Migratory Labor (1950–51) found a trend toward employing more farm workers per year for fewer days apiece, and it therefore recommended that "no special measures be adopted to increase the number of alien contract laborers."[40] The President's Commission on Law Enforcement and Administration of Justice (1967–68) learned that a major problem facing the police was an inadequate number of radio frequencies, and it recommended that "frequencies should be shared through the development of larger and more integrated police mobile radio networks."[41]

In other cases, the move from findings and evidence to recommendations is a leap, albeit a rational leap. The National Advisory Commission on Civil Disorders (1967–68), for example, found that ghetto residents in riot cities felt that their most intense grievances were police practices, unemployment, and inadequate housing, and it recommended extensive programs aimed at ameliorating the conditions identified as grievances. However, there was no conclusive evidence that rioters engaged in their behavior because of the grievances they felt, or that ameliorating the grievance-producing conditions would have prevented the riots or would prevent future riots, although there are reasonable grounds for believing that this might be the case.[42]

In some cases commissions generalize on the basis of limited pilot programs. For example, the President's Advisory Commission on Universal Training (1946–47) drew on the experience of the UMT Experimental Unit at Fort Knox in suggesting a program for universal training and in assessing the probable effects of such training on the physical and mental health of the trainees.[43] The President's Commission on Law Enforcement and Administration of Justice (1965–67) relied heavily on the experience of the Vera Institute bail project in making its bail reform recommendations.[44]

Commissions also reason by analogy to foreign experience in dealing with similar problems. The Commission on Obscenity and Pornography (1967–70) used the experience of Denmark to instruct it about the relation between the availability of erotic material and sex crimes, and the President's Commission on an All-Volunteer Armed Force (1969–70) reviewed the experience of foreign nations with voluntary military service.[45]

Commissions use the information they gather to reject policy options that appear to have failed in the past.[46] Commission analysis narrows the scope of uncertainty and circumscribes the area for choice and judgment. While the inquiry undertaken by commissions is not scientific and only rarely unearths previously unknown facts, their analysis frequently does result in bringing more relevant information to bear more systematically on public policy problems than has been done before. This analysis does produce a significant amount of new thinking about problems. Policy analysis appears to be the most significant technique used by commissions in making most of their decisions.[47] Hamilton notes, with respect to the President's Materials Policy Commission, "The records of the commission from beginning to end showed that everyone connected with it was sincerely interested in finding, especially through rigorous analytical procedures, the facts which would indicate the proper course of action."[48] A member of the staff of the Air Policy Commission (1947–48) remarked, "From what I observed, an effort was made [by the members] to be as objective as possible and to reach the best answers in the time available." The weight of the evidence and the persuasiveness of the arguments put forth are the major determinants of what a commission recommends. Commissions use their capacity for policy analysis, described in chapter 3, to reach their decisions. Commissions give the President their informed judgments, not scientific certitude. This is all that can be expected of them and all that the President asks of them.

Policy analysis is never complete or conclusive, and it is always open to dispute. It is therefore to be expected that the analysis of commissions will be frequently subject to challenge. James Q. Wilson, for example, argues that the conclusions of the National Commission on the Causes and Prevention of Violence (1968–69), based on its analysis of existing studies related to the harmfulness of television violence, are a "hasty and unsupported acceptance of the most farfetched interpretations of the aggression experiments."[49] On the other hand, criticisms of commissions for their failure to prove or demonstrate the validity of their conclusions are beside the point, since neither commissions nor any other policy analysts can hope to be scientists in any strict sense.

As policy analysts, commissions in general are probably superior to the two other major agencies of policy analysis employed by the federal government, Executive Branch staff studies and congressional committee hearings and reports. Their ability to make sustained, systematic, well-informed, and expert analyses was discussed in chapter 3. In contrast to that of Executive Branch staffs, the energy of commissions is not siphoned off by the press of operational problems, and their perspectives are not warped by the need to carry out program responsibilities and defend and justify their performance.[50]

The inquiries undertaken by congressional committees frequently lack a unified or clear focus. The jurisdictional lines of congressional committees frequently fragment their efforts. A congressional inquiry is also often an adversary process and is more easily diverted by the short-run exigencies of partisan politics, and it usually lacks the physical and intellectual resources available to commissions in time, money, staff, and data. A congressional committee staff study is frequently a loose compendium of documents with only a thin overlay of explication and discussion, comparing very unfavorably to the intellectual depth and rigor of commission reports, which are themselves on the whole of only medium depth.[51] Generally, the process of inquiry and analysis undertaken by commissions is the same as that employed by other government and nongovernment actors when faced with important public policy questions, except that in general commissions tend to be capable of doing, and in fact do, better.

One major qualification must be offered to the above description of the data gathering and analysis undertaken by commissions. The description implies that all of the questions before a commission are open and unresolved until all the data are collected and analyzed. In fact, some questions are resolved before all the facts are in, quite early in the life of the commission. Thus the process of data gathering and analysis proceeds on two simultaneous and parallel tracks. On one track, options are being solicited and evidence gathered and weighed on the open questions. On the other track, data are being assembled and analysis done which justifies, builds a case for, and backstops the decisions that have already been reached.[52] Often the questions that are settled early are the most basic questions facing the commissions. These "threshold questions" are settled early for several reasons:[53]

1. The evidence may be so clear and overwhelming that little time is needed to reach a decision. It was almost a truism to the members of the President's Commission on Income Maintenance Programs (1968–69) that the existing complex of programs to deal with poverty were a failure and that they needed to be fundamentally altered, and the focus of the commission was on devising a replacement.

2. Resolving these questions may be necessary before any other questions can be dealt with. The National Advisory Commission on Civil Disorders (1967–68) could not direct its efforts toward gathering data on ghetto conditions and the attitudes of ghetto residents and begin considering pro-

grams for changing those conditions until it was decided that the riots were caused by the existence of those conditions and the response of ghetto residents to them. If riots were caused instead by agitators and conspirators, an entirely different set of subsidiary questions from those pursued by the commission would have required answers.[54] Similarly, the President's Materials Policy Commission (1951–52) could not consider how to use resources more effectively because of impending shortages until it decided whether or not shortages were impending.

3. The preferences and ideology of the commission members may lead them to close basic questions. The President's Civil Rights Committee (1946–47) assumed from the beginning that strong federal action was necessary across the board to deal with civil rights problems, rather than a reliance on gradual changes in public attitudes followed by incremental changes in government policy. A member of the committee staff recalled, "All of them [the committee members] were committed against gradualism from the beginning. There was a sense of indignation, outrage, and urgency."[55]

4. The gateway questions that channel the direction of commission inquiry are also often the most difficult questions faced by commissions, because they are so broad and fundamental. Therefore there is little hope of settling them definitively, and a tendency exists for commissions to pass over them with easy assumptions and prejudices and move on to questions that can be more satisfactorily pursued. Epstein, for example, argues that the difficulty perceived by the members of the President's Commission on the Assassination of President Kennedy (1963–64) "of proving a negative to a certainty" on the question of whether there was more than one assassin is one reason why it undertook only a "limited and relatively superficial" investigation of this question. Instead, the commission answered the question in terms of the assumptions of the members about the benefits to the national interest of discrediting the argument that there might have been more than one assassin.[56]

RECRUITING THE STAFF

The professional staffs for commissions are largely drawn from the federal government. They are usually substantive experts loaned from the agencies working in the commission's area of concern.[57] For example, Michael March, technical adviser to the President's Commission on Veterans' Pensions (1955–56), had long experience in the Budget Bureau, dealing with veterans legislation. In an interview, one of these experts was aptly characterized as an "ambitious bureaucrat with analytic skills." Those staff members who do not come from the government are recruited from universities, industry, research companies, and private law practice. The members of the staff from outside of government are also substantive experts. The exceptions on the staff who are not experts are those hired primarily because of their administrative ability, like Bradley Patterson, executive director of the National Advisory Commission on Selective Service (1966–67), and writers like Robert Rice, who worked for three presidential commissions.[58] The staff recruited from outside of government frequently has had experience working in the federal government. Thus the professional staffs are composed almost entirely of substantive experts with government experience. They are all people who have been dealing with the problem on a pragmatic, governmental policy level rather than armchair theorists or basic researchers only.

The most obvious and the most important criterion used in selecting the staff is their knowledge relevant to the work of the commission. However, many of the criteria for choosing commission members apply, in lesser degree, in choosing the staff. To add to the scientific legitimacy and persuasiveness of a commission, an attempt is made to get the best and the best known experts to serve on the staff or at least to be associated with the commission as consultants or advisers. It is hard to define the point at which an expert is sufficiently eminent to be considered for commission membership, and when his eminence makes him a primary target for staff recruitment. Seniority is probably the most significant dividing line: the older experts who are probably more widely known outside their fields are likely to be chosen as commission members over their junior colleagues who may be their equals in technical proficiency and reputation within their disciplines or professions.

An attempt is made to establish the objectivity and independence of the staff in the eyes of the outside world by introducing some representativeness into the staff—by not relying too heavily on personnel from any one source, especially not from one agency known to have a particular point of view on the problems before the commission. One member of the staff of a commission dealing with sensitive minority problems remarked, "I had the advantage of not being from the Justice Department or from a minority group, so that I was thought to be relatively unbiased."

To help establish the political credibility of a commission and to purge it of any suspicion of working in an ivory tower, a premium is also placed on experts who have some experience in or ties to the important constituencies that the commission must deal with. For example, in congressional hearings, the chairman of the President's Materials Policy Commission was called on to establish, and did establish, that many members of the commission staff were engineers and had a "practical background" and "experience in the field of natural resources."[59] Michael March, technical adviser to the President's Commission on Veterans' Pensions (1955–56) stated in congressional hearings:

Basically, two guidelines were established early in the recruiting. . . . The first of those guidelines was that we obtain the best qualified staff and consultants that possibly could be obtained. . . . Now, the second guideline laid down was that, if possible, we would take a veteran for the job rather than a nonveteran, on the theory that the man who was responsible for conducting factfinding in any of these vitally important areas, should have as down-to-earth a view of the needs of veterans as possible.[60]

The process of recruiting the commission staff relies very heavily on personal acquaintance and contact, much more so than that of recruiting commission members, for whom a more systematic search is made.

The first and most important staff member sought is the executive director. In all of the cases (14) on which information was found on the recruitment of executive directors, the candidate was known personally either by someone in the White House or by someone in the agency advocating the creation of the commission, who recommended him to the commission chairman, or was known by the commission chairman or commission members. For example, Francis Brown, executive director of the National Commission on Higher Education (1946–47), and George Zook, the commission chairman, were both from the American Council on Education.[61] Robert K. Carr, executive director of the President's Committee on Civil Rights (1946–47), was well known in the Justice Department, one of the advocates of creating the committee, since he had just finished a book on the Civil Rights Section of the Department.[62] Carr also knew commission member John Dickey, president of Dartmouth College, where Carr was a faculty member.

The commission chairman makes the decision on hiring the executive director often with the concurrence of the rest of the commission.[63] If it is a small commission, the rest of the staff are usually recruited by the executive director, sometimes with the active participation of the chairman. The other staff are also usually people known by the executive director or by members of the commission.[64] On larger commissions, the executive director chooses the top staff, who in turn find their staffs through the same network of personal contacts. Only one case came to light of a senior staff member of a commission hearing about the formation of a commission and applying for a job without knowing either a commission member or a member of the staff who was already hired. The personal grapevines into the policy community of the commission chairman and executive director are the way by which commission staff are sought.[65]

The major problem faced by commissions in recruiting staff is their inability to get all of the highly qualified people they seek.[66] Government agencies are not eager to give up their best people, since they need them to mind the shop. The difficulty is partly remedied by the willingness of innovation-minded young turks within the agencies to make themselves available for commissions. Academics are frequently unwilling or find it impossible to leave their permanent positions.[67] While commissions generally succeed in gathering a staff of high quality, it is often a time-consuming process that delays their substantive work.[68] The late arrival and early departure of key staff people because of prior commitments also result in some discontinuity and confusion in staff work.[69]

WRITING THE REPORT

Following the data-gathering process and in some cases paralleling it, a commission report is produced. Reports vary in length from the three-page letter to the President from the President's Commission on a World's Fair (1959) to the six volumes of the National Commission on Higher Education (1946–47) or the five volumes of the President's Materials Policy Commission (1951–52). Many of the reports include volumes of technical reports, task force studies, and transcripts of hearings.

Producing a report generally follows one of three patterns. A common pattern is for the data to be gathered and reviewed by specialized subcommittees or panels of the commission. Each subcommittee has staff members assigned to it. The staff produces draft position papers, which are reviewed and revised by the subcommittee, and recommendations are then made to the full commission. The full commission reviews the subcommittee products, makes revisions, directs redrafting to be done, and finally gives its approval to a report it finds acceptable. This pattern seems most characteristic of the commissions which have been given the most time for their work, which have enough members to make a division of labor feasible, and which have a broad mandate requiring specialization on various subtopics.

A second pattern frequently followed is identical to the first, except that detailed consideration of the data and preliminary drafts is not done by subcommittees. All review and revision is done by the commission acting as a committee of the whole. This pattern seems most characteristic of commissions that are shorter-term and smaller and have more sharply focused mandates.

The third and least-frequent pattern is for commissions to take stands on issues or decide policy questions in the absence of written drafts, which are then produced in conformity to the decisions of the commission. This was the pattern followed by the President's Commission on Immigration and Naturalization (1952–53) when it was very pressed for time at the conclusion of the Truman Administration.

These three are general patterns only. There is frequently specialization by commission members that is not formalized into a subcommittee structure, and, as noted above, a commission may reach its various decisions at different times. Staff drafts are also produced in light of what the drift, tone, or sense of the commission seems to be on an issue in the absence of any formal decisions by the commission.

In writing the commission report a key role is played by the executive director of the commission staff. On him rests the primary responsibility for managing the mechanics of the process: scheduling hearings, conferences, consultations, trips, and meetings; getting hearing transcripts produced; arranging for office space; hiring staff and assigning research tasks; finding money; getting studies and drafts from contractors, consultants, and staff in time for consideration by the commission; drafting and editing the report; and arranging for printing, release, and publicity of the report. In general, it is his responsibility, as well as the commission chairman's, to see that the job gets done, that the process is structured so that by the commission's deadline a document is produced that contains findings and recommendations supported by persuasive and lucid arguments reflecting the views of the commission members and bearing on the questions posed in the commission's mandate.

On many commissions, some goal displacement occurs.[70] The executive director becomes preoccupied with producing a report and getting the job done rather than with the task of producing the best answers to the questions and problems posed in the commission's mandate.[71] The intellectual task of analyzing policy problems is replaced by the concrete and political tasks of getting the commission to agree on something and getting that agreement embodied in a printed volume. This is not surprising, given the fact that many commissions have deadlines that fall relatively soon after they are created.

The frequently heard statement that staffs write the reports of commissions is literally quite correct. Most of the words in every commission report are set on paper by members of the commission staff, or represent the efforts of commission consultants or contractors. The implication of this statement that therefore commission reports predominantly reflect the views and judgments of staffs rather than commission members is, however, incorrect. The dominant and decisive influence on the content and tone of commission reports is exercised by the commission members.[72] Commission members have the decisive influence for the following reasons and in the following ways:

1. Commissions hold frequent meetings, providing opportunity for members to become thoroughly acquainted with the problem, assess the work of the staff, and reach their own judgments on the findings and recommendations of the commission. Evidence with respect to twenty-five commissions indicates that the full commission meets on the average of once every month or two for two or three days each time. Thus a commission of average length (11.6 months) would have from two weeks to a month of full commission

meetings.[73] In addition to the time spent in full sessions of the commission, individual members, groups of members, or sometimes the full commission meet in subcommittees and panels, hold hearings, and undertake field trips and inspections. For example, the President's Commission on Heart Disease, Cancer and Stroke (1964) reported having only five one-day sessions of the full commission during its nine-month life. Fifty-one meetings were held by its various subcommittees, however.[74] Commission members also spend time reading and reviewing studies and drafts that are circulated to them between meetings, and some commission members spend extended periods of time working at the commission office. For example, William Paley, chairman of the President's Materials Policy Commission (1951–52), actually moved to Washington to supervise personally the work of the commission, and Edward Mason and Eric Hodgins, members of the commission, also spent months in Washington with the commission.[75]

The shorter commissions tend to meet more frequently and for longer periods, so that they spend almost as much time in session as the longer commissions. There are usually one or two initial meetings with the President or their White House liaison and to reach decisions on the program of work, the method of operation, and staffing. There then is a period of relatively few meetings of the full commission, while studies are prepared, data are gathered, the subcommittees meet, and hearings are held. This is followed by more frequent and longer meetings, as the full commission makes decisions on its findings and recommendations and reviews drafts of the report.

The members of commissions are not excluded from commission work and then paraded in at the end to skim over the reports. In fact, conscious efforts are frequently made by the staff director and chairman to increase the participation and involvement of the commission members.

2. The attendance of commission members at commission meetings is generally very good. Estimates by commission staff members of the average attendance at full meetings of the commissions ranged from one-half to four-fifths attendance.[76] The President's Commission on Heart Disease, Cancer and Stroke (1964), for which a precise statement on attendance is available, reported that on the average, 83 per cent of its members were in attendance at meetings of the full commission.[77] The attendance at subcommittee and panel meetings and hearings seems also, in general, to be quite good.[78] No commission staff member or commission member reported that poor attendance was a significant problem on his commission.

The two main reasons for absences by commission members seem to be overcommitment and illness, rather than lack of interest. For example, Franklin D. Roosevelt, Jr., resigned from the National Commission on Higher Education (1946–47) and Henry Ford II from the Air Policy Commission

(1947–48) because of the pressures of other commitments.[79] George Meany, who served on nine commissions, is notorious for his poor attendance at commission meetings.[80]

Prestigious commission members are often elderly and subject to illness. Illness or age, for example, reduced the participation of William Donovan in the work of the President's Commission on Veterans' Pensions (1955–56), of Learned Hand, the Commission on National Goals (1960), of V. O. Key, the President's Commission on Campaign Costs (1961–62), and of Roy Wilkins, the President's Commission on an All-Volunteer Armed Force (1969–70). Eleanor Roosevelt, chairman of the President's Commission on the Status of Women (1961–62), died during the course of the commission's work, as have several other commission members.[81]

3. Not only are commission members physically present in large numbers at meetings, but a large proportion of those who attend are active in the debates and deliberations and put forth a strong effort in the work of the commission.[82] A frequently heard description of the activity of the commission members is, "They worked." Members of a variety of commissions were characterized as "very active," "extremely dedicated," "very committed," "very serious," "involved," and "very interested." It was reported of several commissions that the final draft of the commission report was read aloud word for word in the commission meeting.

4. Commission members are not only active participants in the work of commissions, they are also effective participants. They shape the report in line with their assessment of the facts and their policy judgments and preferences. They are effective in part because of their interest and involvement in the work of the commission, which means that they generally become well informed about the substance of the commission's work. They are also effective because they have knowledge and experience relevant to the commission's problem and because they are generally strong-minded and intelligent.

The effectiveness of the commission members is indicated by the number of times that they require drafts of the commission report or chapters of it to be done over. A member of the staff of the National Commission on Technology, Automation and Economic Progress (1964–66) recalled, "The report went through fourteen bloody drafts, and I mean bloody. You couldn't recognize the relation between the first two drafts and the final report. This indicates the impact that the commissioners had." This may be an extreme case, but many other staff members also reported that several drafts were required to satisfy commission members.[83] Staff drafts have been rejected either because they failed to express lucidly and persuasively the position of the commission, because they failed to reflect the policy decisions of the commission, or because the commission disagreed with them if decisions had not yet been reached. A member of the staff of the President's Commission on Income Maintenance Programs (1968–69) recalled the following example:

> It [the first draft of the report] had a lot of redistributive bite. This draft went to the commissioners in the summer. Notes came back asking what the hell was going on and using words like "socialism." They said they had agreed to a negative income tax in principle, but they objected to the redistributive tone. The draft had to be completely revised to take account of the objections of the conservatives to the redistributive definition of the issue and to the tone.

As noted above, the commission chairman is usually quite active, frequently with the participation of all or some of the members and at least with their concurrence, in selecting the top staff of the commission, defining the commission's mandate, reaching decisions on the techniques for data gathering and the types of studies to be undertaken, and in making decisions on the threshhold questions, all of which determine the direction of the inquiry and circumscribe the field within which the final findings and recommendations will lie.

5. The effectiveness of the commission members in putting their stamp on the report is also evidenced by the numerous reports of vigorous and extended debates among the commission members over important and controversial recommendations. Such debate, for example, occurred over the recommendations dealing with the oil depletion allowance on the President's Materials Policy Commission (1951–52), the tax credits for campaign contributions and the use of federal appropriations for campaign costs on the President's Commission on Campaign Costs (1961–62), the equal rights amendment on the President's Commission on the Status of Women (1961–62), and student deferments and conscientious objection on the National Advisory Commission on Selective Service (1966–67).[84]

In general, the recommendations of commissions represent the collective judgments of at least a majority of the membership. One can also identify specific recommendations with a point of view predominantly advocated by one commission member, again indicating the influence of the members. For example, the recommendations of the President's Committee on Civil Rights (1946–47) dealing with disclosure reflect the interest of Morris Ernst, and the recommendations to organize regional development on the basis of the Federal Reserve Districts was the idea of Robert Ryan on the National Commission on Technology, Automation and Economic Progress (1964–66). Eric Hodgins, a member of the President's Materials Policy Commission, had a staff and his own volume of the report dealing with technology.[85]

Although the effectiveness of commission members was occasionally evaluated negatively, such as "they [two commission members] didn't measure up to the knowledge and strengths they had," or "she was always asleep during the meetings," or "he gave the impression of being lazy," the following general comments are much more typical: "What is in the report was reviewed and argued over word by word by subgroups and by the full commission. This was not a nominal group." "The commission would really get into the substance of the drafts." "The commission members were not just figureheads."

Only one case came to light where, because of unusual circumstances, there was not an opportunity for the entire commission to review the final version of the report. According to a member of the committee and a member of the staff, the final report of the President's Committee on Foreign Aid (1947) "was issued without final approval because [Senator] Vandenberg was demanding it before he would begin hearings [on the Marshall Plan]." The subcommittees of the committee had all reached agreement on their reports, and the members "approved in principle" what was in the final report, but it was issued "without a formal vote on it by the full committee" and without "final clearance." The final report was produced by "an inner group" of committee members and staff. "It was touch and go whether members would stay stuck. At least one or two were inclined to dissent from some part of the report. However, given the immediate favorable response and praise it received in the press, they did not."

6. Commissions as a whole do not usually immerse themselves deeply in the "pick and shovel work" of making studies and gathering data, except through their participation in hearings and field inspections. Most of the impact of commission members comes through their consideration of staff-gathered data and staff-produced position papers and drafts, in their homework between commission meetings, in the subcommittees and panels of the commission, and in the sessions of the full commission. However, it should be clear from the discussion above that individual commissioners may, and do, intervene, and can be active at any and all stages of a commission's work in everything from recruiting staff to closely supervising the research work.

Some commission members are also active in a staff-like capacity. Leland Olds, a member of the President's Water Resources Policy Commission (1950), and Eric Hodgins, a member of the President's Materials Policy Commission (1951–52), were on the payrolls of their commissions as staff members. Olds was, in effect, staff director.[86] Other commission members have worked on drafting sections of reports or have submitted memoranda on particular questions before the commission.[87] For example, James McCrocklin submitted a memorandum outlining a draft lottery plan to the National Commission on Selective Service (1966–67), and Kingman Brewster prepared a paper on student deferments for the same commission. In preparing the final report, commission members have on several occasions drafted the most important sections of the report, those that set out a basic philosophical orientation, as well as drafting other sections. For example, the ringing rhetoric of the "Introduction" of the report of the National Advisory Commission on Civil Disorders (1967–68) was largely the product of John Lindsay, a commission member, and his staff.[88]

7. Further evidence that commission members have the decisive influence on the content of commission reports is that the drafts produced by the staff are written not only to be in agreement with the decisions taken by the commission but also in anticipation of what will be accepted and approved by the commission. Staff members quickly learn the views of the "sensitive commissioners" whom they have to "worry about" on various issues, and they write accordingly. A member of the President's Committee to Strengthen the Security of the Free World (1962–63) explained that the first draft of the committee report was written by the staff director, and then the member added, "Of course, he wrote a first draft of the type he thought the commission would accept."

8. The dominance of the commission members in shaping the recommendations and findings of commissions is sometimes challenged by members of the staff who are strong advocates of particular policies. Many staff members welcome the opportunity to work for a commission because, in part at least, they look upon it as a vehicle for advancing their own views. There also tend to be generational and ideological differences between commission members and staff. The staff is usually younger and more apt to favor large-scale, far-reaching, and rapid action by government to ameliorate social problems, in contrast to the perspective of the commission members, who are older and usually, at least at first, oriented toward more moderate and gradual change.

The partisan perspectives of members of the staff and the general differences in orientation sometimes lead to conflicts between members of the commission and the staff and to suspicions by commission members that the staff is presenting biased and distorted analyses.[89] This source of tension and threat to the independent decision-making ability of commission members is reduced in several ways.

First, in many cases the conflict is nonexistent because commission members and staff sometimes share the same perspective. More important, staff members often define their role not as partisans but as neutral "tool[s] and the agent[s] of the entire commission." For example, the executive director of an important commission during the Truman Administration said, "I never indicated how I felt about the subject. . . . I felt my job was to force the best possible intellectual process but not to influence that process. I bent over backwards to stay away from exerting influence." He also remarked that he was sure that none of the commission members knew what his position was on the major issue before the commission and that, in fact, he was personally opposed to the recommendation of the commission on that issue.

Second, the differences between the perspectives of the staff and the members tend to narrow as they undergo a common educational experience during the course of the commission's work. Not only are the views of commission members often broadened and liberalized, but those of the staff are often moderated and tempered.[90]

Third, particularly on the commissions dealing with controversial subjects and having large staffs, there are partisan staff representing differing and conflicting points of view. This diversity and conflict within the staff protects the commission members from being led down any one path by a unified staff front presenting only one alternative to them. Such staff conflicts, for example, were reported on the President's Materials Policy Commission (1951–52), the President's Commission on Veterans' Pensions (1955–56), the National Advisory Commission on Civil Disorders (1967–68), and the President's Commission on Income Maintenance Programs (1968–69).[91]

Fourth, commission members have access to information, proposals, and ideas outside of the channels controlled by the staff, in particular their own personal contacts, experience, and knowledge. For example, a member of the staff of the National Advisory Commission on Selective Service (1966–67) said, "The commission met on Friday and Saturday. On Saturday, General Shoup would sometimes say that he wanted to make a personal report. He had been down in Georgetown drinking with students on Friday night and talking to them about the draft, and wanted to report."

Fifth, the need to establish the scientific and political legitimacy of a commission, recognized by both the members and the staff, also mitigates the danger that the choice of witnesses, consultants, and staff will be stacked to represent only one point of view.

Finally, the neutral-servant-of-the-commission role definition seems to be most frequently characteristic of the top staff members of commissions. Strong partisans are found more often among the middle-level experts on the professional staff. The top staff people who control the day-to-day workings of the commission thus can assure that the commission is exposed to all the available policy alternatives, and they rein in the staff who continue to advocate their own policies after the commission has reached a decision.

A number of commission staff members expressed surprise, when they were interviewed, at how much effort was put forth by the members of their commissions and how the members actively determined the content of the reports. They singled out their commissions as the exceptions and contrasted them with their stereotype of the "normal" commission in which members show up only at the conclusion of the work, to ratify a staff document. The evidence indicates that the "exceptions" are more typical than the "normal" commissions. One commission staff member remarked, "I think the report closely reflected the views of the commissioners."[92] This view seems to hold true for commission reports in general.

REACHING DECISIONS

The great majority of commission decisions are unanimous, and do not seem to be decided at all in the usual sense of conscious choices from among a number of alternatives. A consensus on many findings and recommendations emerges in the course of the commission's inquiry, and when the time comes to decide, the choice seems self-evident, and all that is needed is for someone to capture and express the common point of view. Thus it is common to be told that it was "not much trouble," "not a problem," or "not difficult" to reach a consensus.[93] A member of the staff of the President's Advisory Commission on Universal Training (1946–47) remarked, "A fairly wide consensus on the need for the program [of universal military training] had developed over the months." This consensus that develops on the basic questions is a result of the preselection of the members, and of the common educational experience of the commission members which modifies their preconceptions and prejudices and leads them to a common ground. "You would be surprised how many minds became unset during the course of the commission's work," remarked one commission member.[94] The movement of a diverse commission to a common point of view is also commented on by William Byrne, executive director of the President's Commission on Campus Unrest (1970):

> I can assure you . . . that when I first looked at the nine people who made up this Commission and listened to them talk at their first two meetings, I was convinced that these people were never going to agree to anything. They were all from different backgrounds and different political beliefs, but when they were confronted with having to come up with some solutions to grave social problems, within ten weeks the nine of them were able to sit down and were able to agree on every word in 537 pages discussing these problems.[95]

Where a clear consensus does not emerge from the commission's inquiry, because of the different perspectives and values of the members based in large part on their backgrounds in diverse clientele groups, the search for agreement proceeds by long debates and discussions in which more information is brought to bear and bargaining among the commission takes place. This bargaining takes one of several forms.

When recommendations have been expressed in concrete numerical amounts that can be disaggregated, bargaining may occur over incremental differences between the preferences of commission members who disagree. More frequently, however, commission recommendations are expressed in terms of policy statements that cannot as easily be expanded and contracted to find a statement for which a consensus exists. In these more common cases, bargaining on policy recommendations takes the form of debate on nuances in language.[96] There is give and take and compromise among the members.[97]

In some cases when a member is not convinced by the point of view that is dominant among the members, he will go along because he does not believe that the subject is important enough to fight over or dissent about. In other cases, he may give in on one recommendation, on the understanding that others will give in to him on other recommendations. One commission member explained, "This [agreement to a recommendation] represented a surrender on my part to get equivalent surrenders on the part of other members on other recommendations. . . . I got modifications on a number of other recommendations." On the other hand, the rest of the commission will sometimes give in to one or a few members who have a particular "hobby-horse," in return for their going along with the rest of the report or with some other recommendations.[98]

The important point is that the overwhelming majority of commission recommendations are the expression of a unanimous consensus among the commission members, and in a great many cases all of the recommendations of an entire report will be unanimously agreed to.

Often the commission consensus is arrived at by a "sense of the meeting," rather than by successive votes on different formulations until unanimity is achieved or unanimous agreement is seen to be impossible. According to the sense of the meeting technique, members speak as the voice of the group addressing the question before them.[99] When one of these voices elicits no objections or further discussion, the statement is recorded and the commission moves on to the next question. A staff member or writer will often sit in on commission discussions and try to capture and express the consensus in a draft that is then presented to a future meeting of the commission for its approval. Votes are sometimes taken as a formality to ratify the commission consensus. Of course, on some commissions there are issues upon which unanimity cannot be reached, and the recommendations of the commission come down to a question of the number of votes commanded by rival positions. In a few cases opinion on major issues has been very closely divided, as on the question of how to achieve a more market-oriented agriculture (the National Advisory Commission on Food and Fiber, 1965–67) and the question of student deferments (the National Advisory Commission on Selective Service, 1966–67). Where there is disagreement, it is usually that of only one or a few members dissenting from a large majority.

There are two other factors not yet mentioned which lead most commissions to reach unanimous decisions. One is the great pressure for consensus and unanimity, coming most often from the White House, the commission chairman, and the executive director of the staff. They believe, quite correctly, that the impact of the report and its chances for implementation will be greatly diminished if the group is divided.[100] Thus to the natural desire to reach agreement is added a very practical and compelling political reason for doing so. Given the importance of unanimity, the threat of a minority report is a potent bargaining lever in the decision making of commissions.

The other factor results from their intense work together for an extended period as an *ad hoc* body dealing with an important question of public policy. A sense of camaraderie and commission *esprit de corps* frequently develops among the commission members and staff.[101] A striking example is related by one of the staff of the President's Citizen Advisers on the Mutual Security Program (1956–57). He recalls walking along with Benjamin Fairless, president of U.S. Steel and chairman of the commission, and John L. Lewis, president of the United Mine Workers and a member of the commission. Fairless and Lewis were laughing about what a picture they made walking arm in arm, since they had been bitter antagonists when the Mine Workers were organizing the "captive mines" controlled by the steel companies and helping to organize the steel industry as a whole. Other commission staff noted how the members "worked well together," "interacted very successfully," and that "there was surprisingly little back biting among the members."[102] Two commissions were reported to have held reunions many years after they completed their work. The usually amicable personal relations among the members and the development of a sense of group identity facilitate the process of reaching agreement and keep disagreements from becoming too heated and bitter.

In addition to consensus by natural coalescence, consensus by bargaining, and majority-rule votes, commission decisions are made by reciprocity. When commissions have specialized subcommittees, the preliminary recommendations of the subcommittees are often accepted by the full commission with only a minimum of scrutiny to assure consistency with other recommendations and conformity to the general philosophy adopted by the commission. In the absence of subcommittees, individual commission members active in the work of the commission and expert in some aspect of the commission's work, or who make themselves expert in the course of the work, are often deferred to on their subject by other members and exert a great influence on the recommendations. One consequence of this reciprocity between specialized subcommittees or expert commissioners is that a commission report sometimes "turns out to be a rosary of a report rather than a holistic reasonable treatment," in the words of a member of the staff of the Commission on Heart Disease, Cancer and Stroke (1964).

A unanimous consensus, frequently reached by bargaining in a large group, is obviously sometimes purchased at the price of "watering down," "fudging," "fuzzing up," "waffling," and "superb ambiguous language" on the most controversial recommendations.[103] While this provides some support for homilies about committee products, what is more surprising is how little watering down there is and on how few issues. The characteristics of commissions, described in chapter 3 and above, that make them good policy analysts, and the active and effective participation of commission members, result in recommendations that are generally more specific, focused, and direct than those of other committees. The common clichés describe the least-common-denominator compromises that are characteristic of interagency committees to which the members come with set positions from which they are frequently forbidden to deviate. These committees are not like commissions, on which the members are detached from their clientele group or not even representatives of a clientele, and where they engage in an inquiry and interact over many months before reaching decisions.

ROLES OF COMMISSION MEMBERS

Another way to look at the activity and impact of commission members is to discuss the various roles that they adopt in the work of a commission. The first and most obvious distinction in roles is between the active and the passive. The passive members are either those who do not attend commission meetings or who attend but do not actively participate. Examples of members with poor attendance and some of the major reasons for it are given above. As discussed there, the level of attendance and activity of commission members is generally quite high.

Among the active members (and among the passive members as well, when final actions on commission recommendations are taken) there are basically two perspectives on the problem before the commission. The first is the statesman's perspective, where the member tries to look at the problem in terms of some concept of the public interest.[104] The second is the perspective of the constituency representative, who views problems primarily in terms of their impact on the clientele from which he is drawn. A labor leader remarked, for example, "When I serve [on a commission], I do so as an individual citizen, but always with the thought of labor's viewpoint, of course. . . . I just sit as a member and discuss the report, in particular how it affects the workers."

The statesman's perspective seems to predominate. It predominates first because some members are recruited for their reputations as distinguished statesmen or because they are not known to have strong views on the commission's subject.[105] It tends to be dominant also because of the breadth of the education received by the members while on the commission; because of the tenor of their assignment from the President, which emphasizes objectivity, impartiality, and nonpartisanship in an inquiry which will result in policy recommendations that will serve the national interest; and because the unique environment of commissions as temporary organizations tends to stimulate open-mindedness and a willingness to entertain ideas that are novel to the members. On one commission it was reported that business members supported positions contrary to the perceived interests of their industry, and even defended those positions publicly after the commission had completed its work. Naturally, members are most prone to act as constituency representatives on those recommendations most directly affecting their constituents, and to become statesmen with respect to other recommendations. Of course it is also very common for those acting as constituency representatives to claim that if the interest of their constituency is served, then the broader public interest will also be served.

A fraction of the active members, often between a quarter and a half, can be classified as leaders, influentials, or "bellwethers." Among these, there are two kinds of roles played, those of social leader and task leader.[106] Social leaders exert their primary influence in engineering bargains and compromises, helping to build consensus, cooling bitter arguments, and maintaining amicable personal relations among the members. A member of the President's Commission on Campaign Costs (1961–62) described the role of fellow member Paul Porter: "Porter was the expediter and compromiser. He is very affable. He is willing to take the half-loaf or even the quarter-loaf or eighth-loaf. He was a bridge influence."

The task leader, on the other hand, asserts himself in analyzing the problem before the commission. He is immersed in the substantive work, asking challenging questions, formulating policy proposals, and vigorously and persuasively advocating positions he believes to be correct. The task leaders on commissions greatly outnumber the social leaders, and commission members were frequently described as playing this role by those interviewed. Among the task leaders there are those whose influence is "across the board" on all the issues before the commission and those whose leadership is exerted on only a few issues. For example, Edward Mason, a member of the President's Materials Policy Commission (1951–52) was characterized as the "leading light" and "dominant force" on the report as a whole, while Harold Swift, a member of the National Commission on Higher Education (1946–47), "spoke up on trustee matters." Naturally, commission members who see themselves as constituency representatives would be most likely to be specialized task leaders, and commissions which have specialized subcommittees would encourage the adoption of specialized task leadership roles.

The commission chairmen were always described as very active in the work of the commissions and most frequently appear to be social leaders rather than task leaders. Chairmen of various commissions were described as "benign," the "resident boy scout," "the great rationalizer," "a nice guy," "a compromiser," and "a grandfather figure." On the substantive issues before commissions, the chairmen ususally do not push their own points of view, and they display "a lot of flexibility on what . . . [is] said in the report."[107]

The chairmen generally do play another important role, in addition to attempting to bring the group into agreement and to maintain an amicable relationship among the members. They are preoccupied, much like the executive director, with getting the job done, with producing a book, the report, within the allotted time. Commission chairmen want to produce a "good report" in the sense that it is a "high quality piece of intellectual and analytic work" and that it is, if possible, unanimous.[108]

In this role of report-producer, the chairmen do many of the things that the executive directors are doing: select and schedule witnesses, hire staff, maintain liaison with the White House and federal agencies, oversee the staff studies and consultant work, and manage the mechanics of printing and distributing the report.

In contrast to the executive director, however, the chairman presides at the commission meetings. This gives him a position from which to exercise social leadership, and it also permits him to expedite and facilitate the process. The chairmen were reported to be "fair," "judicious," and effective presiding officers. The role of the chairman is most often primarily political, producing agreement, and administrative, producing a report, rather than substantive. Thus referring to a commission by the name of its chairman—the Warren Commission (the President's Commission on the Assassination of President Kennedy, 1963–64), the Kerner Commission (the National Advisory Commission on Civil Disorders, 1967–68), or the Scranton Commission (the President's Commission on Campus Unrest, 1970)—should be viewed in most cases as a journalistic expedient to avoid using the awkward official names of commissions and to personalize the news, rather than as a reflection of the impact of the chairman on the substance of the commission report.

TRENDS IN COMMISSIONS AS INSTITUTIONS

No significant pattern of development or change in the institutional form of commissions could be found in the course of this survey. A commission in 1945–46 was basically the same as a commission in 1971–72. In particular, commissions have not been institutionalized since 1945. They are not routinely considered the most appropriate way to handle certain classes of problems, although they are routinely considered an available option.[109] They have not become standardized in their format, and routine procedures for setting up and following commissions have not evolved.[110] Although an earlier commission will sometimes serve as a model for a later one, each one has been, in fact, very much *ad hoc*.[111] Commissions have been a flexible option available to Presidents.

While commissions have not undergone significant changes as institutions and have not become institutionalized, three trends are observable over the period 1945–72. As evidenced by tables 2, 3, and 4, commissions, in general, became more frequent, larger in their memberships, and longer.

The increasing frequency with which commissions have been created may reflect a growing recognition by Presidents of their utility as policy analysts and for winning acceptance for innovative domestic policies. Or it may be a reflection of the fact that setting up a commission is now a standard available option. This place in the array of White House techniques would also have been achieved by past demonstrations of success. The growth in the number of commissions may also be corollary to the general expansion of the domestic functions of the federal government in response to the increasing demands and expectations focused on the federal government in general and the President in particular. Or finally, the steady growth of the federal bureaucracy, and of the new tasks undertaken by the federal government, may have increased the need to use a mechanism to bypass the established agencies in the search for new ideas and to examine the performance of existing programs.[112]

The trend toward more members on commissions may reflect the demands for representation on commissions by more constituencies, as commissions are recognized to have an important influence on the formulation of domestic policy. Or it may be a function of the growing numbers of politicized interests participating in domestic politics; that is, there are more interests demanding to be represented on commissions as well as more interests to be represented.

TABLE 2. Frequency of Commissions, by Administration

	Truman	Eisenhower	Kennedy	Johnson	Nixon (1st term)	Overall
No. of commissions	17	9	12	28	33	99
No. of commissions per year	2.5	1.1	4.2	5.4	8.3	3.6

TABLE 3. Number of Members per Commission, by Administration

	Truman	Eisenhower	Kennedy	Johnson	Nixon (1st term)	Overall
Mean	9.2	12.1	12.0	15.7	13.6	13.3
Median	7	8	10.5	15.5	13	12

The trend toward longer commission life may reflect a general recognition that problems have become substantively and politically more complex and difficult to analyze, as the federal government has taken on new functions and grown in size and as the number of politicized interests has increased. These problems require more time to study them successfully and to reach agreement on findings and recommendations. The increasing size of commissions may also require them to spend more time to get organized and to reach agreement. There does not appear to be any good explanation for the deviance of the Eisenhower Administration from this trend.[113]

There also seems to be some variation in the number, subject, and organization of commissions that reflects the style and concerns of the Presidents who created them. For example, President Truman's concern to avoid a postwar reaction against the New Deal and to revive domestic liberalism is reflected in his commissions on civil rights, higher education, health care, and water resources policy. The postwar problems of recovery, reconversion, and the cold war are manifest in his commissions on foreign aid, universal military training, merchant marine, air policy, and materials policy. By contrast, President Kennedy chose to use commissions primarily on subjects that were at the time only second-level domestic policy concerns, such as mental retardation, the status of women, narcotic and drug abuse, and public higher education in the District of Columbia.

President Eisenhower created the fewest commissions per year, and this may reflect his disinclination to engage in domestic policy innovation. It may also reflect his administrative style, preferring to rely on the established agencies of government and on intragovernmental mechanisms, such as interagency committees, for advice, instead of on *ad hoc* bodies with large contingents of "outsiders." The Johnson Administration had a large number

TABLE 4. Duration of Commissions in Months, by Administration

	Truman	Eisenhower	Kennedy	Johnson	Nixon (1st term)	Overall
Mean	8.7	7.1	12.5	15.1	11	11.6
Median	8	5	11	14.5	6	9.5

of commissions per year, also perhaps reflecting the style of the President. A Johnson aide remarked, "Johnson had the feeling that you could never ignore an issue. You had to do something about it. On some issues, you couldn't do much more than appoint a commission."

President Nixon appointed the largest number of commissions per year. The contrast between the number of commissions created by Presidents Eisenhower and Nixon, the two Republicans included in this study, may point to an important difference in their concepts of the presidency. It is probably fair to characterize both of them as ideologically conservative in the context of American politics. President Eisenhower had a more passive or "Whig" view of the presidency, however, not attempting to build and assert presidential power to achieve his ideological preferences. President Nixon, on the other hand, had an activist view of the presidency, expanding and using presidential power to achieve his goals. The large number of Nixon commissions can be interpreted as part of his effort to use the presidency to reorient and redirect federal policy to achieve his objectives. Thus the number of commissions a President creates may be an index of presidential activism rather than of presidential ideology.

President Johnson appointed the only commissions with a primarily Southern focus in their subject areas and membership: the National Advisory Commission on Food and Fiber (1965–67) and the National Advisory Commission on Rural Poverty (1966–67). President Truman's personal interests and background can be seen in the Missouri Basin Survey Commission (1952–53).

President Johnson integrated commissions more closely with task forces, interagency committees, and citizen advisory councils than did other Presidents, and preferred to fund commissions with agency contributions rather than with the discretionary funds available to the President.[114]

THE CONTENTS OF THE REPORTS

It is difficult to characterize what commissions find and what they recommend because there have been so many, and because most of them made many findings and recommendations in a wide variety of frequently very-technical fields. However, some general observations can be offered.

1. The findings of commissions usually exhibit what can be called the Perils of Pauline syndrome. It is almost always found that the situation the commission is examining is serious, grave, and even immoral, but most of all, "a crisis." The nation, or whoever or whatever the commission is examining, rests on the brink; it is the eleventh hour, and the situation is critical. The situation has not yet plunged over the edge, however, and the possibility of rescue and salvation remain open.[115] So the grimness of the findings is

always combined with a ray of hope and a touch of optimism about the future.

2. Standing pat, doing nothing, is rejected as a response. Action, doing something, is always seen as both possible and desirable. Commissions display a "can do" mentality, and there are a number of explanations for this. First, the freshness and newness of the commission environment stimulates the enthusiasm and optimism of the members and the staff. Second, the commission members are likely to want to justify the confidence that the President has shown in them and to not want to dash the hopes that have been aroused by the creation of the commission. They are also likely to want to justify the expenditure of public money and the contributions from many public and private agencies and individuals whose help they solicit. The only feasible way to satisfy these expectations is to recommend a "positive" program, some kind of action, rather than being negative by arguing that nothing can be done. Third, the commission members are men and women who are successes in the institutions of society; they are "doers" not given to musings about the limits of man and his institutions.

When taken together, the dire situation painted by commission findings, the tone of optimism, and the emphasis on action are reminiscent of Marshall Foch's message to Marshall Joffre: "My center is giving way, my right is in retreat, situation excellent. I am attacking."

3. The action that is recommended is almost always to be action by the federal government. This is not surprising, since a recommendation of private action or nonfederal government action would not meet the needs of the number-one constituent of commissions, the President. Commissions are created not because a problem exists in the abstract but because the President has a problem, expectations and demands for action are focused on him, and creating a commission is a way for him to deal with the demands or to learn how to deal with them. Furthermore, commissions are agencies of the federal government dealing with a problem identified by the federal government, and they have a staff either drawn from the federal government or with past experience in it, and members who have also frequently had experience in the federal government or are federal officials. Thus, the alternatives presented to commissions and those most seriously considered and embodied in recommendations are likely to be heavily weighted toward suggestions for federal action.

4. The solutions to the problem are not found to lie in extreme or radical action by the federal government. Although the situation is a crisis, the social, economic, and governmental systems are found to be basically sound. The recruitment of commission members from the established institutions of society and the fact that commissions are institutions of the government accounts for this rejection, often implicit, of basic and fundamental change.

5. A dominant characteristic of commission recommendations is the ubiquity of comparative adjectives: more, better, further, greater, or larger. Thus many recommentations begin with current policies as a baseline and suggest that the problem will be solved if more of the same is done and if it is done better. Specific suggestions on how much more and how the job can be done better are frequently offered. Thus many recommendations are basically ameliorative, proposing incremental and marginal changes in the status quo.

6. Another dominant characteristic of recommendations for federal action is the frequent appearance of "new." Commissions often recommend that the federal government undertake new responsibilities or that it meet its existing responsibilities through new programs. These innovative recommendations of commissions are usually new only in the limited sense of not being current policy rather than in the sense of being truly original. They are also primarily reformist rather than radical. The limited scope of recommended innovation and the tendency of commissions to recommend adjustments in the status quo are, of course, corollaries to their exclusion of radical and extreme alternatives from consideration.

7. Commissions often engage in political exhortation, calling upon government to make a greater "commitment," exhibit more "leadership," or elevate the problem at hand to a "higher priority." Commissions engage in exhortation when the problem is so broad that they can do little else, given their time and resources, or when they cannot find or agree on any more specific recommendations.

8. At a more specific level, commissions often recommend that current programs be better coordinated and that reorganization be undertaken to achieve this coordination, that the government's commitment be made visible in the form of a new agency, or that a new responsibility or a new program be undertaken. They often recommend more research and pilot programs, as they discover the limits of the state of the art and of their own capacities as investigators. They also recommend that permanent advisory mechanisms be created in the field, to channel the new information from research into government and to maintain the innovative thrust of the commission.[116]

Commissions do not recommend radical or revolutionary solutions, and much of what they recommend might be considered by many to be old hat and a collection of tired clichés. However, this should not obscure the fact that many of their recommendations represent substantial departures in policy when viewed in the context of the normal pace of change and the range of live policy alternatives within the federal government. There is also the real possibility that they may be right; that no matter how tired or old hat the suggestions are, they may still be the most effective for dealing with the problem.

CHAPTER SEVEN

WHAT HAS BEEN
THE IMPACT
OF COMMISSIONS?

WHEN ONE ADMITS to working on a study of presidential advisory commissions, a typical response is summed up by the rhetorical question, "Do they *ever* do *anything?*" Art Buchwald presents an example of this state of mind in the following scenario on the fate of commission reports:

> This is a government of reports and studies. . . . Just by chance I discovered the secret burial grounds of reports and studies made by presidential commissions. . . . Mr. Gottfried Snellenbach has been caretaker of the burial area for government reports since the Harding administration. . . .
>
> "We've got some of the great reports of all times buried here," Mr. Snellenbach said. "We've got reports that cost $20 million, and we've got reports that cost $2,000, but in the end they all wind up here, buried 6 feet under."
>
> "Sir, what kind of reports are resting here?"
>
> "It might be better to ask what kind of reports aren't buried here. We have reports on violence, studies on blacks, students, unemployment, the economy, the Communist threat, housing, health care, law and order. You name it, and we've buried it."
>
> "How does a report find its final resting spot in this setting?"
>
> "Well, as you know, the President is always appointing a commission to study something or other, and after the study they're supposed to hand in a report. Now, lots of times the President has no intention of paying any attention to the report, and it's dead before it's ever written. Other times someone on the President's staff reads a report handed in by a commission and says, 'This stuff is dynamite. We have to kill it.'
>
> "In some cases the President says, 'Let's release this report to the press and then bury it.' Occasionally a report will just die of heartbreak because nobody pays any attention to it.
>
> "In any case, after the report is dead, it has to be buried, because if you're President you don't want someone finding it at a later date and using it against you."[1]

In a less tongue-in-cheek vein, Elizabeth Drew sets out the rules for "How to Handle the Report" of a presidential advisory commission. Her view is that commissions are formed either to delay action or to recommend to the President that which he already wants to do. However, some commissions, she concedes, go beyond these limits. In these cases acceptance of the report is delayed, its release is played down, it is denounced, or it is ignored. In sum, commissions either delay action, reinforce a predetermined course of action, or have no impact at all.[2]

More serious critics point to the fact that there have been commissions dealing with the problems of poverty, crime, racism, and urban decay, and yet these problems remain acute and the commission recommendations unimplemented. In opening his 1971 hearings on presidential commissions, Senator Edward Kennedy of Massachusetts remarked:

> It seems as though most Presidential commissions are merely so many Jiminy Crickets chirping in the ears of deaf Presidents, deaf officials, deaf Congressmen, and perhaps a deaf public. They could be the nation's conscience, spurring us on to do what we know ought to be done, showing us the way, strengthening our determination to build a just and peaceful and productive society.
> But all too often we reject them, or ignore them, or forget them.[3]

On the other hand, a social scientist with experience working with several commissions remarked (somewhat facetiously), "Well, there was a commission created to study the urban riots and there have been no more big urban riots, and a commission was created following the assassinations in 1968 and there have been no more political assassinations. If you believe in correlations at all, there must be something there."

STANDARDS FOR EVALUATING COMMISSION IMPACT

The logic of the arguments made by the social scientist quoted above would require that an assessment of the impact of a commission be made by comparing the status of the problem that the commission examined before the commission was created and again at some time after the commission issued its report. If the problem was ameliorated by the designated time after the commission had reported, then the commission would be counted a success; if the problem was unchanged or worse, then the commission would be marked a failure.

This is not a satisfactory criterion for analyzing the impact of commissions. It has been argued at length above that the primary presidential purposes for commissions are to engage in innovative policy analysis and to persuade others to adopt their recommendations, that commissions have a unique ability to perform these tasks, and that commissions almost universally operate free from White House direction or interference. Therefore, two more-appropriate standards by which to assess the impact of commissions are (1) the changes in government policy that have occurred as a consequence of their findings and recommendations, and (2) the degree to which Presidents have adopted and supported their findings and recommendations. These are the most relevant and important standards, given the purposes for which commissions are established. Thus, if there is a correspondence between a commission's recommendations and changes in government policy, or if the President advocates the commission's point of view (particularly if these developments are accompanied by evidence linking the commission to the changes or the President's views), then the commission will be judged to have had some impact.

If the world then fails to change as a result of these new government policies or the presidential commitment, this may indicate one of several things: (1) that the problem cannot be solved by presidential or government actions (It is useful to recall a couplet by Samuel Johnson, "How small of all that human hearts endure/ That part which laws or kings can cause or cure."); (2) that the problem is soluble but that full commitment to and full adoption of the commission recommendations which would have solved it were not forthcoming; (3) that while a full commitment was made, the government was ineffective in implementing it; or (4) that even with full commitment to and effective implementation of the commission's recommendations dealing with a soluble problem, the recommendations may simply be wrong.

On the other hand, commissions may have little direct impact on government policies, as was the case with the National Advisory Commission on Civil Disorders (1967–68), the National Commission on the Causes and Prevention of Violence (1968–69), and the President's Commission on Campus Unrest (1970). Yet the immediate problems that these three commissions were called upon to deal with—urban riots, political assassinations, and campus unrest—have abated. This phenomenon reminds us that there are other mechanisms of social change besides commissions in particular and government in general. There are also substantial zones of ignorance in which there are no good explanations for why things happen. The phenomenon also suggests that commissions may leave their impression in ways other than through short-run adoption of their recommendations by the President or as government policy.

The evidence to be presented will bear on the question of whether commission reports are "ignored" and "buried." This will be followed by a discussion of what other impact commissions have had in addition to their direct effect upon presidential or government policy making. The broader questions of the limits of government power and the correctness or incorrectness, as solutions, of commission recommendations and the government actions taken to implement them are beyond the scope of this study. To examine ninety-nine sets of problems to determine if they could have been solved by government and to discover what the ideal solutions might have been compared to what commissions recommended and what government did would be a mammoth if not impossible undertaking. The aspirations of this study are more modest, and it should also be made clear that some effective commissions (having presidential support or producing changes in government policy) may have led to ineffective action (not producing amelioration of the problem).

COMMISSIONS, PRESIDENTIAL SUPPORT, AND POLICY CHANGE

Table 5 presents schematically the presidential and governmental action that was taken in response to the report of each commission.[4] A presidential response is any action taken on the authority of the President, and it includes statements, messages, the introduction of administration legislation, and administrative action taken by the President or within the Executive Branch (columns I, II, III, and IV in table 5). Government action is action by the federal government, including administrative action and legislation that is passed (columns IV and V in table 5). These two categories overlap, in that administrative actions are included in both. The table was assembled from a systematic survey of the *Public Papers of the Presidents,* 1945–72, the *Weekly Compilation of Presidential Documents,* 1965–July, 1974, and the three volumes of *Congress and the Nation,* for evidence of the contributions of commissions to presidential or governmental actions. These sources were supplemented with scattered data from personal interviews and a variety of secondary sources. Insofar as the table is biased, it probably underrepresents the effect of commissions, since it does not systematically take into account increases in budgetary requests and appropriations for already existing programs, made as a consequence of commission findings and recommendations, and it does not include those contributions to policy formulation that were left unmentioned in the three sources because they occurred at a low level within the bureaucracy, the White House chose not to call attention to them, or for some other reason.

Before proceeding to summarize and analyze the data presented by table 5, an explanation of the categories used in it is in order. A "statement" is a presidential statement endorsing, drawing upon, or commenting on the work of a commission, usually with a mention of the commission by name. A mark in this column, as in all of the others, may indicate more than one response of the type designated by the column. Each of the marks in the columns also indicates an affirmative or supportive response to the commission. There were only three cases that came to light of a President explicitly rejecting findings and recommendations of commissions.[5] A "message" is a presidential message to the Congress. "Message 1" indicates the use of a commission's findings or advocacy of its recommendations in *part* of a message. "Message 2" indicates that a *full* message was devoted to this purpose or to the issues upon which the commission focused. In both of these cases the commission is also usually cited by name. "Administrative action," "legislation introduced," and "legislation adopted" are self-explanatory. For these columns "1" indicates that the administrative action taken, legislation introduced, or legislation adopted was based on a *minor* or less-important recommendation of the commission; "2" that a *significant* recommendation was included; and "3" that an *important* recommendation was included.

Three things should be made clear about these judgments. First, they are obviously subjective and therefore are open to challenge. If they are in error, it should be on the side of conservatism rather than overgenerosity in attributing an impact to commissions.

Second, the rating of a commission's recommendation as minor, significant, or important when implemented by an administrative action or legislation or included in proposed legislation refers to its status among the recommendations of the commission and not to its general status as a question of public policy. Thus the National Advisory Commission on Libraries (1966–68) had its most important recommendation, that a permanent federal advisory and coordinating body be set up to deal with libraries, implemented by legislation. This was, however, hardly a public policy decision of first importance. Nevertheless, an important commission recommendation is usually an important question of public policy. This is, for example, most obviously true with respect to the important recommendations of the President's Commission on Income Maintenance Programs (1968–69) or the President's Commission on an All-Volunteer Armed Force (1969–70).

Third, even if a commission receives the maximum favorable response in terms of the categories in table 5, it does not mean that the commission has had all or even most of its package of recommendations implemented. Such a standard of expectation would be too exacting and unrealistic. Commissions are, after all, advisory bodies and must compete with other sources of initiative, as well as struggle for priority for their problem areas. Most commission members and staff and White House staff members who were interviewed judged a commission to be a success if some of its most significant or important recommendations were adopted. Some had even more lenient standards. Furthermore, since many commission recommendations are general calls to action and exhortations for greater commitment with respect to broad social problems, it would be difficult in many cases to determine when, if ever, all of a commission's recommendations had been adopted.

In appendix 3, the statements, messages, legislation introduced, administrative actions, and legislation presented in summary form in table 5 are cited

TABLE 5. Responses to Commission Recommendations

	Commission	Presidential response						Government response						VI Presidential support	VII Government action
		I State-ment	II Message		III Legislation introduced			IV Adminis-trative action			V Legis-lation				
			1	2	1	2	3	1	2	3	1	2	3		
1	Medical Services													0	0
2	Higher Education	x	x		x		x(C)						x	1	3
3	Universal Training			x			x							3	0
4	Civil Rights	x	x	x	x			x						3	3
5	Merchant Marine	x	x	x			x			x				3	3
6	Air Safety									x				3	3
7	Foreign Aid	x		x			x						x	1	3
8	Air Policy	x					x(C)						x	3	3
9	Water Policy	x		x						x				3	3
10	Communications								x					2	2
11	Migratory Labor	x	x	x			x		x				x	3	3
12	Veterans' Hosp.													0	0
13	Materials Policy	x		x				x						2	1
14	Health Needs	x		x										2	0
15	Missouri Basin		x											1	0
16	Airports	x	x			x				x		x		2	3
17	Immigration	x	x	x						x				2	0
18	Internat'l Info.	x								x				3	3
19	Housing		x				x						x	3	3
20	Highways	x	x				x						x	3	3
21	Vets Pensions	x				x	x					x		3	3
22	Ed. beyond H.S.		x			x	x(C)					x		2	2
23	Mutual Security	x		x			x						x	3	3

24	Military Assist.	x		x		x				2	2
25	World's Fair						x			3	0
26	Goals									0	0
27	Retardation	x	x	x		x		x		3	3
28	Campaign Costs	x	x	x			x		x	3	1
29	Employment Stats.						x	x		3	3
30	Status of Women	x				x			x	2	2
31	Pay	x		x		x			x	3	3
32	Pennsylvania Ave.	x					x			3	3
33	Armed Forces Op.	x					x			3	3
34	Foreign Aid	x		x		x		x		3	3
35	Drug Abuse	x	x			x		x		3	3
36	Voting	x			x	x		x		3	3
37	Higher Ed. in D.C.	x	x	x		x		x		3	3
38	Sale of Securities	x	x	x		x		x		3	3
39	Warren	x			x		x			3	3
40	Heart, Cancer	x	x			x		x		3	3
41	Automation					x(C)				1	0
42	Pay			x		x		x		3	3
43	East-West Trade	x				x				3	0
44	Patents	x	x	x		x				3	0
45	Crime in D.C.	x	x	x		x	x	x		3	3
46	Crime	x	x	x		x		x		3	3
47	Food and Fiber	x		x		x				1	0
48	Health Manpower	x						x		3	3
49	Careers	x					x			3	3
50	Marine Science		x			x	x	x		3	3
51	Draft	x	x			x	x	x		3	3
52	Libraries							x		3	3
53	Rural Poverty									0	0
54	Urban Problems			x		x	x	x		3	3

Continued

TABLE 5, *continued*

| | Presidential response | | | | | | Government response | | | | | | | |
| | I | II Message | | III Legislation introduced | | | IV Administrative action | | | V Legislation | | | VI Presidential | VII Government |
Commission	Statement	1	2	1	2	3	1	2	3	1	2	3	support	action
55 Budget Concepts			x						x				3	3
56 Postal Organ.	x	x	x			x						x	3	3
57 Housing	x	x				x		x				x	3	3
58 Civil Disorders	x		x			x		x				x	3	3
59 Obscenity													0	0
60 Health Facilities	x												1	0
61 Travel	x		x			x	x						3	1
62 Product Safety			x			x	x					x	3	3
63 Income Maintenance													0	0
64 Human Rights Year	x												1	0
65 Violence					x								2	0
66 Population			x		x						x		2	2
67 All-Volunteer	x		x			x(C)			x			x	3	3
68 Exec. Organization		x	x			x			x			x	3	3
69 Internat'l Dev.	x		x										2	0
70 Business Tax									x				3	3
71 Small Business			x			x		x				x	3	3
72 Model Cities													0	0

No.	Topic											
73	Rural Dev.							x(C)		x	0	3
74	Women										0	0
75	Higher Ed.										0	0
76	Science Policy										0	0
77	Housing										0	0
78	Aging						x				0	1
79	Oceanography	x						x(C)		x	3	3
80	Phys. Handicapped										0	0
81	Economic Growth	x		x					x		2	2
82	Prisoners										0	0
83	Urban Renewal										0	0
84	Highway Safety										0	0
85	Air Pollution										0	0
86	Ment. Handicapped										0	0
87	School Finance	x		x							1	0
88	Nonpublic Ed.		x		x						3	1
89	Internat'l Trade	x	x	x		x			x		2	3
90	Campus Unrest	x		x			x				1	2
91	Financial Reg.	x	x	x							3	1
92	United Nations	x	x	x			x			x	3	3
93	Fed. Statistics										0	0
94	Shipbuilding										0	0
95	Materials Policy										0	0
96	Workmen's Comp.	x		x(C)	x						1	1
97	Timber	x				x					2	2
98	Health Ed.		x			x					3	3
99	Internat'l Radio	x		x						x	3	3

more fully by categories corresponding to those used in the table. The appendix also indicates in which statements and messages specific reference was made to the commission in question.[6]

Presidents have issued a total of eighty-nine statements in response to commissions and used their findings or advocated their recommendations in parts of forty messages and in fifty separate messages to the Congress.[7] The statements were made with respect to fifty-one different commissions, the parts of messages with respect to twenty-six commissions, and the separate messages with respect to thirty-six commissions. Legislation was introduced to implement recommendations of fifty commissions, and administrative action was taken to implement recommendations of forty commissions.[8] In sum, for seventy-seven of the ninety-nine commissions, one or more of the above types of supportive and affirmative response from the Presidents have been discovered. This establishes that in the overwhelming majority of cases Presidents do respond in some positive way to commissions. This is, however, not as astounding as it may seem at first glance, because all that it really says is that for 78 per cent of the commissions, the President on at least one occasion found some nice words to say about the commission and its work. The real question is how many commissions received various levels of support. To answer that question, the following crude scale of public presidential commission support is offered:

0 none: no affirmative response
1 minimal: *only* statement or message (1), or legislation introduced (1), or administrative action (1)
2 substantial: *at least* message (2), or legislation introduced (2), or administrative action (2)
3 major: *at least* legislation introduced (3), or administrative action (3)

The score for each commission is indicated in column VI of table 5. The number of commissions receiving each of these levels of support is summarized in table 6.

TABLE 6. Public Presidential Support of
Commission Recommendations

Level of presidential support	N	Per cent of all commissions
0	22	22
1	10	10
2	14	14
3	53	54
Total	99	100

Thus 53 per cent of the commissions received major public support from the President, which means that at least one of the important recommendations of each of these commissions was introduced as legislation by the administration or implemented by administrative action. Sixty-eight per cent of the commissions received either substantial or major public support from the President.[9]

Changes in governmental policy are defined as the implementation of commission recommendations by administrative action or the passage of legislation. Less concrete, although often no less important, changes in policy can also of course occur in the absence of the kind of formal authoritative action that is used as a measure here. These kinds of policy changes are not assessed here.

Sixty-four commissions evoked some authoritative response from the federal government.[10] A scale, similar to the one described above, of the levels of authoritative action follows:

0 none: no authoritative action
1 minimal: *at least* administrative action (1) or legislation passed (1)
2 substantial: *at least* administrative action (2) or legislation passed (2)
3 major: *at least* administrative action (3) or legislation passed (3)

This score for each commission is indicated in column VII of table 5. The number of commissions whose recommendations received each of the levels of authoritative action is summarized in table 7.

Thus 54 per cent of the commissions had at least one of their important recommendations implemented by administrative action or legislation and 68 per cent had at least one important or significant recommendation implemented.[11] In sum, about two-thirds of the commissions have received at least some substantial implementation for their recommendations, about seven in ten some strong public support from the President, and about eight in ten some kind of favorable response from the President. Commission reports are not routinely ignored or buried by Presidents. Their recommendations are

TABLE 7. Government Action in Response
to Commission Recommendations

Level of government action	N	Per cent of all commissions
0	35	35
1	6	6
2	8	8
3	50	51
Total	99	100

very often a substantial element in proposed or actually accomplished changes in federal policy. These findings are made even more significant by the fact that not all commissions are intended to engage in policy analysis and political salesmanship and that commission recommendations have other, indirect, consequences in addition to their effect on presidential and governmental policy, narrowly conceived.

Before we turn to the impact of those commissions not intended for policy analysis and window dressing, and to other consequences of all commissions, one other topic remains to be discussed: the extent to which the efforts of commissions are responsible for any correspondence between the policies supported by the President and adopted by the government and the commission recommendations themselves.

There are two easy ways to handle this topic. The first is to say that the causal link between the commission recommendations and the governmental response is established first by the fact that the commission recommendations preceded the response and were in many cases identical or similar to it. Indeed, the presidential messages and statements recommending action and the statements made commenting on the actions taken often credit the commission involved with an important role in generating and formulating the proposals that were enacted.

While this is significant evidence, it can be discounted somewhat by the fact that it is common form in politics to acknowledge the many fathers of a successful innovation. Credit is frequently given to commissions and other individuals and advisory bodies who have reported before the government has acted, recommending action similar to that taken. It is also reasonable to assume that Presidents look for opportunities to give favorable mention to commissions, if at all possible, since their members are prominent people who have often contributed a great deal of time and work to the commissions. Attributing influence to them for the action taken is one way of rewarding them for serving on the commission. Thus the attribution of significant influence to commissions by the President does not prove that they had such influence or that the same governmental actions would not have been taken had the commissions never existed.

The second easy response is that it is impossible to determine the causal impact of commissions with any certainty, and that while this is undoubtedly a relevant topic, it cannot be pursued fruitfully. Political science in its analysis of public policy formation is not an experimental science. The clock cannot be turned back and the policy process be rerun with the commission factored out to see if the results would be different.

These easy responses are not, however, fully satisfactory. While certainty is unattainable in the attribution of influence to commissions, reasonable judgments can surely be made. Such judgments could be based on careful, detailed case studies of the process of policy development and enactment for each of the ninety-nine commissions, or at least a sizeable sample of them. Unfortunately, no such case studies examining the links between commission recommendations and authoritative government actions exist in the literature of political science, and they have not been undertaken here. Were such case studies to be written, the major problem would be to assess how important the fact was that by creating the commission, the President, in most cases, indicated a commitment to action in the field. Thus it is difficult to evaluate how much of a commission's success is attributable to the existence of a presidential commitment of which the commission is evidence, and how much is attributable to the independent work of the commission in fleshing-out, articulating, and marketing policies to implement that commitment. [12] The increasing frequency with which commissions were created in the sixties and early seventies by Presidents Kennedy, Johnson, and Nixon supports the view that in the judgment of those who chose to create them, they have had an impact.

That this impact has been toward promoting innovation and change is supported by the following arguments. First, it should be evident that the legislation and administrative actions with which commissions are associated, presented in appendix 3, represent, in most cases, innovative federal action. They frequently involve the recognition of new responsibilities by the federal government, for example civil rights and foreign aid; the expansion of existing responsibilities, as in product safety; the adoption of new approaches to meeting established responsibilities, for example civil commitment of addicts and a pay commission and legislative veto arrangement to deal with federal salaries; the recasting of institutional arrangements and procedures, as in the cases of the Post Office, the Budget, and the Domestic Council; and changes in policy based on more technical and expert information, for example in air safety and timber harvesting. Since commissions have been associated with these policies, what impact they have had has been in these innovative directions.

Second, more commissions per year were created by the Presidents with a reputation for commitment to innovation in domestic policy—Truman, Kennedy, Johnson, and Nixon—than by the President reputed to have had much less commitment in this direction—Eisenhower. Assuming that Presidents choose means adapted to their purposes, this fact also points in the direction of the generalization that the primary impact of commissions has been toward innovation.

Third, as pointed out in chapter 4, those who advocate that commissions be created are generally politically sophisticated, influential people with an interest in innovation in federal policy, and it is unlikely that they would allow themselves to be satisfied by the creation of an ineffective institution.

There do not appear to be any commissions for which it can be said, with a high level of confidence, that if the commission had not existed, a major policy would not have been enacted. There are a substantial number of commissions which clearly had an important influence on the actions that were taken in conformity to their recommendations, for example, the President's Committee on Civil Rights (1946–47), the President's Commission on Veterans' Pensions (1955–56), the President's Commission on Law Enforcement and Administration of Justice (1965–67), the President's Commission on Budget Concepts (1967), and the President's Advisory Council on Executive Organization (1969–71).

One can also point to a number of commissions whose recommendations were acted upon for reasons almost wholly independent of the work of the commissions. For example, the National Defense Education Act, providing extensive federal financial aid to students in higher education, was much more a reaction to the launching of the Russian sputnik than to the efforts of the President's Committee on Education Beyond High School (1956–57). Similarly, the civil rights movement of the early sixties and the Johnson landslide of 1964 were the tidal wave on which the Voting Rights Act of 1965 and the 24th Amendment rode, and the President's Commission on Registration and Voting Participation (1963) added very little.

On balance, the best judgment that can be made with the available evidence is that commissions, overall, have had a significant marginal impact on the course of public policy in the period 1945–68. That is, if no commissions had been created in this period, the general course of public policy would not have been altered in any major way but would have been altered in innumerable lesser ways. This is not an inconsequential impact, since specific provisions of legislative and administrative actions which are not of major importance in the grand scheme are indeed very significant to the large groups of people upon whose lives they will directly bear.[13] Commissions have also played a role in accelerating the adoption of some major initiatives, which is important to making the government responsive to the needs of the citizenry.

Commissions are not a panacea for achieving innovation in federal policy. But then no other available political institutions can readily transform indifference into commitment and sharp disagreement into consensus on social problems. Neither are commissions a sham; they have made important independent contributions in substantive proposals, facilitated consensus building, and helped to persuade other political actors to agree with their proposals.

In terms of the presidential goals for commissions outlined in chapter 2, the levels of presidential support discussed above can be taken as a measure of the degree to which the policy analysis goal reaches fruition. The average presidential-support scores for the commissions whose primary purpose was judged to be policy analysis seems to be about the same as the average score for commissions in general. This suggests that while the dominant purpose for a commission seems to have some influence on its final outcome, it is probably more accurate to view (as was done in chapter 2) each commission as a set of possibilities. Which of these possibilities is realized depends on how the commission does its job and on the political circumstances into which it launches its completed report. These factors will be discussed in detail in the following chapter.

The high frequency with which Presidents refer to the findings and recommendations of commissions in various statements and messages (cited in appendix 3) indicates the common use of commissions for window dressing. The frequent references to commission reports by administration witnesses testifying before Congress and the appearance of commission members and staff as witnesses at congressional hearings dealing with the substantive issues of the reports also indicate the use of commissions for window dressing. [14] The degree of authoritative government action in response to commission recommendations, discussed above, is a rough measure of the success of commissions as effective political salesmen for policy proposals. Again, the average score for all commissions and the average score for those commissions identified as having window dressing as an important purpose seem to be almost identical. The same observation made above with respect to the commissions created for policy analysis also applies in this case.

Thus, commissions created primarily to serve the two most frequent presidential purposes, policy analysis and window dressing, have been successful in seeing these goals accomplished. Yet they do not seem to be notably more successful in these areas than commissions in general, suggesting either that the investigation of purposes needs to be refined, after more extensive research, or that purpose is not the decisive determinant of the impact a commission will have. The latter possibility indicates that the multiple and tentative nature of presidential purposes for commissions must be further emphasized.

COMMISSIONS AND CRISES

A prominent member of several commissions remarked that "Sometimes the appointment of a commission is an accomplishment in itself." That is, for those commissions created to respond to a crisis or to defer or avoid action on an issue, the primary impact of the commission comes when it is appointed rather than when it reports. There are no measures of the degree to which commissions created in response to crises succeeded in quieting public anxieties and satisfying the expectations of presidential action. The only evidence that can be offered on this score is the observation that they continue to be used to deal with crises and are even more frequently proposed. A lot of people who are supposed to have sensitive political antennae at least believe that they are effective. Despite the widespread criticism of the National Advisory Commission on Civil Disorders (1967–68) and the National Commission on the Causes and Prevention of Violence (1968–69), President Nixon created, in June, 1970, a Commission on Campus Unrest.[15] As might be expected, the crisis commissions appear to have lower scores of presidential support and governmental action than the average scores for commissions in general, and some of these commissions have been judged by commentators not to have been effective in promoting changes in government policy.[16]

Only one commission seems to have been a complete success in smothering further discussion of an issue. This was the Committee to Study Means of Establishing a Public-Private Mechanism for Providing Funds for Overseas Activities, established by President Johnson in 1967.[17] The committee was created in response to the public controversy generated by the discovery of funding links between the Central Intelligence Agency and the National Student Association and other private groups. The success of the committee in sidetracking the embarrassing public debate until it had died is indicated by the fact that the committee never issued a final report (and is therefore not listed in appendix 2). The public debate quieted during the life of the committee and with the announcement by the President that he had ordered such funding to cease.[18] In all other cases, the issue to which the commission addressed itself was still alive when the commission reported, at least to the extent that the report could not be withheld from public circulation, assuming there may at times have been a desire to do so. The publication of all of the other reports also, of course, indicates the independence of commissions from White House control. Even if an issue had receded from public view sufficiently for there to be a wish in the White House not to have its report made public, thereby rekindling interest in a touchy problem, the commission nonetheless reported.

However, in the overwhelming majority of cases there was White House interest in drawing public attention to the problem with which the commission dealt and in using the report of the commission as the basis for executive actions and proposals and as a tool of persuasion. In the internal policy-making process of the White House, commission reports perform, on many occasions, important services. They provide a competent technical and substantive analysis of competing policy proposals which, it was argued in chapter 3, the White House is generally unable to do. This provides the White House with a substantive baseline, an excellent working paper, from which to proceed in formulating its actions and recommendations.

In the areas of conflict caused by uncertainty or by differences in values and preferences, the kind of consensus that a commission has reached or the nature of the divisions where consensus was not reached provide the White House with a reading of the political winds with respect to the problem. The same function is performed by the White House evaluation of the reactions of various publics to the report. From these the White House gains a political baseline, an assessment of the political world, from which to proceed.

Finally, the work of commissions defines the way in which further substantive analysis, political persuasion, coalition building, and public debate can proceed. The President's Commission on Law Enforcement and Administration of Justice (1965–67), for example, set the structure of the debate on federal efforts to combat crime in terms of the mechanisms by which and the purposes for which federal money should be made available to state and local law enforcement authorities.

Given the existence of a minimum level of felt need, the push for action on a problem by the White House requires that the White House have a proposal, an assessment of the political forces, and a definition of the problem and its remedy in terms of which "politics" can proceed. Commission reports are one technique available to the White House for reaching this point. Commission reports in this respect often serve for the White House in policy making a function analogous to that which the President's Budget and State of the Union messages serve for the Congress.[19] They fix a series of points and their relative magnitude in the policy universe, which need not be and often are not accepted in both the cases of the White House and the Congress, but which provide a starting place from which decisions can be reached.

Commissions are not a means for avoiding issues, since in most cases the White House does not want them to serve that purpose, and even if it did, it could not control their reporting, the content of their reports, or even their access to the public. On the latter point, the reports of the National Advisory Commission on Civil Disorders (1967–68), the Commission on Obscenity and Pornography (1967–70), and the President's Commission on Campus Unrest (1970), all of which were received very coolly by the White House, have not languished in obscurity on a dusty shelf. In fact, the broad circulation of their views has probably been aided by the notoriety they gained from being largely disowned by the President.

COMMISSIONS AS EDUCATORS

Commissions are also intended by the President to play a part in educating the public. Again, no measures of their success in this realm are available. Changes in public attitudes reflected in public opinion polls are not very useful, because factors other than commission reports cannot all be identified or held constant, even if it could be assumed that the questions asked by polls were specific enough to permit some connection to be seen between the questions and the commission reports.

The educational impact of commissions is felt in four directions: general public education, education of government actors, use within the professional community, and education of commission members.

1. General public education is separable into two categories, agenda setting and concept articulation or error corrections. Commissions have helped to place broad new issues on the national agenda, to elevate them to the level of legitimate and pressing matters about which government should take affirmative action. Thus various commissions were spoken of in interviews as "a benchmark," "a landmark," and "a turning point."

The President's Committee on Civil Rights (1946–47) is a prime example of agenda setting. It stirred public awareness of the problem of civil rights primarily in terms of the legal barriers to equality, and it gained currency for the term "civil rights." Coretta Scott King characterizes the creation of the committee and its report as "one of the first steps toward racial justice."[20] Writing in 1948, James and Nancy Wechsler evaluated the impact of the report:

> "The fact of the Committee report remains a major fact of contemporary life. . . . Release of the report precipitated a reaction which is evident throughout this autumn's political wars. It stirred a national debate. . . . In any balance-sheet, the controversy provoked by the civil-rights report must be recorded as a notable advance."[21]

A national debate over the role of the federal government in higher education and whether higher education should be available to everyone with a capacity to profit from it was begun by the National Commission on Higher Education (1946–47).[22] A college textbook, *Education for Democracy: The Debate Over the Report of the President's Commission on Higher Education,* was published four years after the commission reported.[23] It is an indicator of the broad interest generated by this issue and of the role of the commission in stimulating the debate.

With the perspective of over twenty-five years since the Civil Rights and Higher Education commissions reported, it is clear that these issues did become national concerns and that the federal government and the nation responded to them.[24] It may also be suggested that the National Advisory Commission on Civil Disorders (1967–68) legitimized the issue of "racism" (in contrast to discrimination or segregation).[25] Judging from the experience of the past, it is too early to know whether this and other broad social issues recently examined by commissions, obscenity or violence for example, have achieved a solid place on the national agenda.

Other commissions have aimed messages at the public which were not designed to raise broad new issues, but rather to promote new perspectives on old issues or to correct pervasive misperceptions about areas of public policy. The President's Commission on Veterans' Pensions (1955—56) attempted to articulate a philosophy defining the responsibilities of government toward veterans and guiding the discharge of those responsibilities. The most controversial tenet of this philosophy, representing a break with the dominant outlook expressed by veterans' groups, was: "Military service in time of war is an obligation of citizenship and should not be considered inherently a basis for future Government benefits."[26] While the Pension Commission's philosophy did not become the new public orthodoxy on the subject, it did establish a well-argued and well-supported "other side" in the debate over veterans' benefits.[27]

One commission that tried to correct what was believed to be a pervasive error in public beliefs was the National Commission on Technology, Automation and Economic Progress (1964—66). In the early sixties, it was widely believed that automation would destroy *work*, that fewer man-hours of labor would be needed in the future to produce a steadily increasing amount of goods and services, and that widespread unemployment would therefore result. A verse of the union song "Automation," written in 1960, goes:

> I walked all around, all round, up and down
> And across the factory.
> I watched all the buttons and the bells and
> the lights—
> It was a mystery to me.
> I hollered, "Frank, Hank, Ike, Mike, Roy, Ray,
> Bill and Fred and Pete!"
> And a great big mechanical voice boomed out:
> "All your buddies are obsolete."[28]

The commission argued that automation, and technological change in general, do not destroy work but simply eliminate specific kinds of *jobs* while increasing the demand for workers with other skills; thus there need be no general net loss of work.[29] In the late sixties the fears of unemployment caused by automation seemed to have eroded, in part because of the permeation of the commission's arguments, particularly through the labor unions. In the discussion of automation in the 1968 *AFL-CIO Platform Proposals,* technological change is admitted to be "inevitable and usually desirable," in contrast to the mournful message of the song quoted above.[30]

2. All public education, of course, affects the thinking of government actors, and the window-dressing impact of commissions, discussed above, is one measure of the efficacy of commissions in educating government actors to accept their findings and recommendations. There are some commissions,

however, whose influence is largely confined to the government actors in a specialized policy arena and is not reflected in any government actions or overt changes in policy. Their impact is to change the intellectual perspective within the government.

The President's Materials Policy Commission (Paley Commission, 1951–52), for example, injected the "Paley approach" into thinking within the government about public policy for resources.[31] It "put intellectual weapons in the hands of supporters of its point of view," in the words of one of its staff. A member of the staff explained:

> It [the commission] was particularly important in reorienting thinking away from the perspective of professional resource people who saw resources in terms of their uniqueness, and toward an economist's perspective of seeing resources in terms of substitutions and trade-offs rather than absolute limits. It was influential in setting the way to think about and talk about the problem.

Two members of the commission staff and one executive serving in the Interior Department spoke of the "intellectual impact" of the report and its importance in "reorienting thinking," particularly within the Executive Branch. One of them also spoke of it as "a seminar on resources for second- and third-level people in the government." Resources for the Future, a nonprofit research corporation supported by the Ford Foundation which was founded shortly after the commission reported and which had as its first major activity a citizen's conference on resources based mainly on the commission's report, continues to embody the commission's perspective in much of its research work.[32]

Another commission, the President's Citizen Advisers on the Mutual Security Program (1956–57), had a similar impact, helping to turn the focus of government thinking about foreign aid toward long-term loans of development capital to the new, underdeveloped nations of Asia and Africa.[33] Also, the linking of urban and rural poverty in policy analysis and the consideration given to the problem of optimum population distribution by the government may reflect the work of the National Advisory Commission on Rural Poverty (1966–67). A member of the commission staff recalled, "Part of the myth we were trying to explode was that rural poverty was a self-contained problem. We wanted to show that it was linked to poverty in general and therefore that broad-range solutions had to be proposed."

The educational impact of commissions within government sometimes occurs through their ability to make it safer for congressmen and federal executives to openly discuss or advocate a proposal that has been sanctioned by such an "august group."

3. Many commission reports have had an important influence within the nongovernmental professional and intellectual circles concerned with the

problems that the commissions have examined. They have served as "intellectual milestones," summarizing the current state of thinking on the problems, gathering and presenting important data for the first time, providing a tool for teaching about the subjects, and stimulating further research and discussion.

Poverty Amid Plenty, the report of the President's Commission on Income Maintenance Programs (1968–69) summarized the public policy alternatives for dealing with poverty. A staff member of the commission, commenting on the impact of the report, said:

> Non-experts in various fields who were, however, professionals, academics, lawyers, and businessmen, were brought into a discussion of the technical solutions and problems. The report was a contribution to bringing the proposals out of obscurity. It may be a document to which people will refer. It brought together a lot of information. . . . The Commission codified and culminated a movement toward the income maintenance approach.[34]

The reports of the President's Commission on Law Enforcement and Administration of Justice (1965–67), the National Advisory Commission on Selective Service (1966–67), and the President's Commission on School Finance (1970–72), as well as many others, collected and put into accessible form important data. For example, the comparison of the social and economic status of veterans and non-veterans and the survey of the attitudes of veterans on the question of whether they felt they had been handicapped in civilian pursuits because of military service were significant contributions by the President's Commission on Veterans' Pensions (1955–56).[35]

These reports have become sourcebooks for other commentators and analysts. According to Lloyd Cutler, executive director of the National Commission on the Causes and Prevention of Violence (1968–69), "You might even say . . . that we created a new field of scholarship that had not existed before . . . [F]ew of them [scholars] had written anything from the vantage point of violence . . . and we did create a literature in that field . . . that did not exist before."[36]

In addition to collecting data and making it available, commissions have introduced concepts and terms into use in the professional and academic community: "civil rights" and the "Paley approach" mentioned above, for instance, or "urban renewal" in the case of the Advisory Committee on Government Housing Policies and Programs (1953).[37] James Vorenberg, executive director of the President's Commission on Law Enforcement and Administration of Justice (1965–67), believes that the commission had a lasting and widespread effect in propagating the concept of law enforcement as a system. The commission report contains a flow chart illustrating the interrelations of the components of the system. "Now," says Vorenberg, "you see that chart in virtually every police manual, every criminal law text."[38]

Numerous commission reports have been used as reading materials in college courses, and occasionally in secondary schools. It was found, from interviews, that such use was made of the reports of the National Commission on Higher Education (1946–47), the President's Committee on Civil Rights (1946–47), the President's Materials Policy Commission (1951–52), the Commission on National Goals (1960), the National Commission on Technology, Automation and Economic Progress (1964–66), the President's Commission on Law Enforcement and Administration of Justice (1965–67), the National Advisory Commission on Rural Poverty (1966–67), and the National Advisory Commission on Civil Disorders (1967–68). Otto Kerner, chairman of the Civil Disorders Commission, expressed the view that the commission "report has aroused nation-wide interest . . . stimulated a wide-spread discussion, . . . engendered strong reactions . . . [and] it is being used as a text book throughout the United States."[39]

In addition to the university channel, commission reports have reached the professional and intellectual strata, as well as a broader public, through distribution and use as educational tools by interest groups and other organizations sympathetic to the commission point of view. Milton Eisenhower, chairman of the National Commission on the Causes and Prevention of Violence (1968–69), for example, said:

> I am glad to say that three great national organizations—Urban Coalition, the American Jewish Committee, and the National Council on Crime and Delinquency with chapters all over this country—are using both the Kerner [National Advisory Commission on Civil Disorders] and Eisenhower reports . . . as their basic working educational documents. . . .[40]

The impact of commission reports upon various specialized publics as well as upon the public as a whole has been increased through the availability in the 1960s of commercial paperback editions of some of the most important reports. Commercial editions have two advantages over government editions in reaching the public. First, they are usually available sooner and are thus available when interest is high, right after a commission has officially reported to the President. Second, the extensive marketing and distribution resources of commercial publishers place the reports in bookstores, drugstores, bus stations, and supermarkets across the country.[41] Milton Eisenhower, chairman of the National Commission on the Causes and Prevention of Violence (1968–69), estimated that two million copies of the commission's report were circulated in the United States, of which one and three-quarters million were in commercial editions.[42]

By gathering data, summarizing current thinking and promoting discussion, commissions have often stimulated scholars and commentators to undertake further research and analysis. "The biggest effect the report had," said a staff member of the National Advisory Commission on Rural Poverty (1966–67), "was the research that is now being done through the land grant institutions in their departments of agricultural economics and rural sociology."

4. Finally, serving on a commission is frequently an educational experience for commission members: not education in the worst sense, indoctrination, but usually rather education in the best sense of increasing substantive and political information, heightening analytic skills in dealing with the problem, and broadening perspective. A commission member is exposed to a variety of points of view and a great deal of information through hearings, investigatory trips, conferences, written statements by interested persons, the research of the commission staff and consultants, as well as through the views expressed by fellow commission members. This education has resulted in some major "conversions" among commission members who emerged from their experience "changed men." Sundquist describes one such process of education and conversion:

> When Devereux Josephs assembled his Committee on Education Beyond High School, in 1956, most of the members were predisposed against any massive federal financial intervention in the field of higher education. Enlargement of the federal government and its budget had no more inherent appeal to them than to any other group of Eisenhower appointees.
> But when they finished their work, a year later, they recommended— by at least a "substantial consensus"—grants by the federal government for construction of classrooms, laboratories, libraries, and other facilities at colleges and universities throughout the country.
> What converted them? Those who participated in the committee's work answer simply: "the facts." . . . [T]he committee projected the figures on college enrollment and translated them into costs. . . . Then they appraised the potential support from all sources. . . . After making maximum allowance for increases in support from all these sources, they found a gap remained, and only one additional source of funds could be identified—federal aid.
> "Josephs started out being quite negative to the idea of federal aid," recalls one participant. "His conversion took place in the committee meetings in front of all the other members. When he swung over, so did the other members who were open-minded.[43]

Trips and hearings in which commission members directly encounter a social problem—"rubbing genteel noses in the muck," as one author characterized it—have been particularly effective as educational experiences for commission members.[44] A member of the staff of the President's Commission on Immigration and Naturalization (1952) recounted the following incident:

> At the key meeting on this question [of nationality quotas], he [a commission member] said, "When I came into this commission, I thought that this was a white nation and a northern European nation and should stay that way. But as I listened to the testimony, I decided that if the United States tried to remain that way in a world that is two-thirds non-white and non-northern European it would go down the drain. I spent many prayerful hours and decided that unless we abolished the national origins quotas this country would go down the drain."

A similar impact on the thinking of some commission members was reported to have resulted from the hearings of the National Commission on Urban Problems (1967–68), the National Advisory Commission on Civil Disorders (1967–68), and the President's Commission on Income Maintenance Programs (1968–69).[45]

The education of commission members has several important consequences. Most obviously, it means that the commission member who helps to shape the findings and recommendations of the commission is often not the same person who received the call from the White House. Thus a commission report in most cases is not a least common denominator factored from the preexisting positions of the commission members as constituency representatives. In many cases, the recommendations represent a consensus that is a departure from the beliefs of commission members before they came to the commission and at variance with the views of the constituencies from which they are drawn. Of course, ample room for disagreement remains, on a variety of philosophical, temperamental, and political grounds; some commission members are intransigent in their views, and some agreements are reached only by bargaining and trading. The remarkable thing, however, is the extent to which commission members do change their minds and their positions as a result of their commission education, and do agree on recommendations that often defy the predictions made by political observers when the commission was created. Such observers conceive of the commission process in terms of a simple mechanistic pluralism, which is far from the reality of the experience, in most cases.

The usual consequence of the commission education seems to be that more "conservative" commission members gain an appreciation of the seriousness of a problem and become more willing to entertain innovative policies and more extensive government intervention, as in the case of the President's Committee on Education Beyond High School (1956–57) described above. In addition to this "liberalizing" effect, the education of commission members has a generally moderating influence on the often strongly held and sharply divergent views that commission members bring with them. The education of commission members thus accounts in part for the frequency with which commission reports are unanimous or contain only a few minority or dissenting opinions. A staff member of the National Commission on Rural Poverty (1966–67) remarked, "They [commission members] saw at first hand what the experiences of the rural poor were. I think this is the reason why we had so few [dissenting] footnotes [in the report]."[46] There are also, of course, political reasons which place a premium on commission unanimity, the main one being that a unanimous report will have more impact on the President and be more useful to him as a persuasive resource than a report that is split on its major recommendations.[47]

As a result of their education, commission members often become strongly interested in the subject of the commission beyond the duration of the commission. Morris Cooke, chairman of the President's Water Resources Policy Commission (1950), led the commission to exceed its presidential mandate and to formulate its own draft "Water Resources Act of 1951." This draft was circulated within the Executive Branch along with the commission's report, and when action was not forthcoming, Cooke was able to reestablish contact with the other members of the commission and gain their consent to making the draft public a year later.[48] Many commission members have testified before Congress, written articles, and given speeches and lectures explaining and advocating the points of view expressed by their commissions.

If the President adopts all or part of the recommendations of a commission, he has available to him zealous supporters who are prestigious representatives from significant constituencies, and the prospects for successful adoption of the proposed policy will be increased. Thus by educating the commission members, the commission serves to mobilize elite interest in its problem and elite support for presidentially sponsored action to deal with the problem beyond the support the President gains by having their names on the commission report.

On the other hand, there are risks incurred by the President in allowing these elite representatives to become educated, interested, and in many cases deeply committed to their policy areas. If he should fail to press for adoption of a commission's recommendations, he may be assailed by its members, whose personal prestige has been augmented by their service on the commission which has qualified them all as "experts" in the field, and who have also come to share some of the prestige and visibility of the presidential office by their membership on a presidential commission.

The impact of commissions as policy analysts as seen in the presidential support they receive, their impact as policy salesmen as seen in the government actions taken to implement their recommendations, and their role as educators indicate that in the process of policy formulation and enactment the impact of commissions is not limited to any one stage. Some of them sow seeds in the public mind which are harvested a decade or more later, others formulate policy recommendations after the ideas have germinated elsewhere, and still others are thrown into the final weeks of a legislative battle.

OTHER EFFECTS OF COMMISSIONS

In addition to that influence which corresponds to the purposes for which they were created, the focus of the discussion above, commissions have also had an impact in other areas. They have influenced the actions and policies of state and local governments. The President's Commission on Law Enforcement and Administration of Justice (1965–67) stimulated states and local governments to undertake criminal justice planning (even before the federal act was passed making such planning a condition for receiving federal funds), and many of its recommendations concerning police procedures and practices were put into effect on the local level.[49] Similarly, the report of the National Advisory Commission on Civil Disorders (1967–68) led to changes in local law enforcement and National Guard philosophy and procedures for dealing with civil disturbances.[50] William Scranton, who served on the President's Advisory Panel on Insurance in Riot-Affected Areas, a subgroup of the Civil Disorders Commission, reports that "now over 35 states have put into being what we suggested in the way of a system of insurance."[51]

Commission recommendations have also served as a rallying point for opposition to the President, or as a club with which to politically beat the President and his program. For example, President Johnson's Administration was found wanting when its performance was measured against the recommendations of the National Advisory Commission on Civil Disorders (1967–68). The Urban Coalition observed that in the year after the commission reported, not "even a serious start toward the changes in national priorities, programs and institutions advocated by the Commission" had been made.[52]

A variation of this theme is the ability of commissions in some cases to force the President to advocate positions that he does not favor. A prestigious commission in a controversial area often cannot be repudiated by the President. He must either go along with it or disown his own specially selected expert and prestigious advisers and have their report become the foundation for opposition to him

The President's Advisory Committee on a National Highway Program (1954–55), for example, recommended a bond-financing arrangement for the proposed interstate highway system. Before reporting to the President, the committee's chairman, Lucius Clay, made public speeches describing and advocating the plan, and even criticizing President Eisenhower's pay-as-you-go tax plan for highway financing. Clay drummed up considerable support for the committee's plan. The end result was that "by the time President Eisenhower officially received the Clay report . . . he had little choice but to accept the Clay proposals. To repudiate the Clay report would be to repudiate the support Clay had received from the highway user groups, the Governors Conference's Special Highway Committee and other interested groups." [53]

President Kennedy was confronted with a report from the Committee to Strengthen the Security of the Free World (1962–63) which advocated cuts in the foreign aid program while defending the program in principle. Representative Otto Passman, the archfoe of foreign aid, praised the report and contrasted it to the work of similar commissions whose only role had been, he said, to "strengthen the hand of the Executive with Congress and the public . . . [and] to 'bail-out' foreign aid." [54] It was decided within the Administration not to reject the report, so that General Clay, the committee's chairman, could testify for the program, and because rejecting the report might push Clay into Passman's camp. [55] Thus President Kennedy cut his foreign aid request in line with the committee's recommendation and succeeded in getting Clay to defend the aid program vigorously. However, in Congress the President's cut was accepted and further cuts were made, adding up to the largest cut in the history of the foreign aid program, and new restrictions were added to the program. [56]

Finally, it can at least be speculated that commissions may affect the general level of support for national political institutions, apart from their impact on policy in various substantive areas. Because they provide a public image of influence in government policy making by expert and representative people from the public who solicit information and opinions broadly before arriving at carefully deliberated and justified recommendations, their frequent use may have raised the general level of public support for the national government. The same result may also come from articulation by commissions of symbolic reassurances to alienated or frustrated segments of the populace. Former Attorney General Katzenbach, for example, said, "Statements by the Kerner Commission [National Advisory Commission on Civil Disorders, 1967–68] like 'white racism' are extremely important. They help restore the confidence of the black community in the integrity of Government and public institutions." [57] Joseph Rhodes, a member of the President's Commission on Campus Unrest (1970), remarked, "I think it is important to consider that our Commission had a very positive, soothing and effective impact on this climate of extreme tension and anxiety in the country through its open hearings and its many investigations." [58]

Conversely, because their recommendations are often not fully and rapidly implemented, commissions may breed cynicism and disappointment among those who expect immediate and complete adoption of the recommendations of such eminent, objective, learned, and representative bodies. [59] For example, Lloyd Cutler, executive director of the National Commission on the Causes and Prevention of Violence (1968–69), observed, "[O]ne of the scholars we consulted when we were organizing our work suggested, and I think not entirely in jest, that we should have a task force on violence that results from the frustrations that build up in people who read these excellent Commission reports and then find that none of the recommendations was carried out."[60] The reader is left to judge for himself the merits of these interpretations, since no persuasive evidence has been found to support either one.

CHAPTER EIGHT

WHY DO COMMISSIONS SUCCEED OR FAIL?

PRESIDENTIAL ADVISORY COMMISSIONS in general have enjoyed a good measure of success in having their recommendations supported by the President and adopted as government policy. This chapter pursues the topic, begun in the last chapter, of the link between the recommendations of commissions and the actions of the President and the changes in government policy. The last chapter examined the nature and magnitude of the commission's effect in this linkage. This chapter will discuss the conditions which strengthen or attenuate that effect.

An appreciation for two basic facts is central to an understanding of the situation in which the recommendations of a commission exist. First, the recommendations are only advisory. As an educational device, commissions may have an indirect effect on decisions by changing the attitudes of people in the government and in the public, and thereby perhaps altering their behavior. But no changes in government policy will occur on the authority of a commission alone. As one Truman aide remarked, "These reports are not self-executing."

Second, the reports and recommendations of a commission are orphans. The completion of the report and the termination of the commission are synonymous. In some cases, the commission continues for a short time as a skeleton staff writing thank-you letters to those who testified before it or packing the commission's records for deposit in the National Archives. But for all practical purposes, commissions literally cease to exist. A commission report becomes an "inanimate object" once the commission has concluded its work. Thus the crucial problems that must be solved, if a report is to lead to government action, is how to maintain "continuing leverage" once the commission has disbanded, and how to gain this leverage over those who have the authority to act on the recommendations.

PRESIDENTIAL SUPPORT

If they are to be implemented, commission reports must rely primarily on the support of the President. Support by the President, in general, is the most efficacious means to attain innovative changes in policy. The President and his subordinates have the power to implement some commission recommendations. Numerous examples of administrative actions taken in conformity with the recommendations of commissions can be found in appendix 3.

The President is also the primary source of legislative initiative. His legislative program is the major item on the congressional agenda. Only in a few cases was the legislative implementation of a commission report generated in the Congress. The usual pattern, in general and with respect to legislation to implement commission recommendations, is that the President proposes and the Congress accepts or rejects.

The President not only proposes most important and innovative legislation, but his proposals have a good chance of being adopted. There is a strong relationship between the score for legislation proposed by the President and the score for the legislation passed by the Congress (in table 5, chapter 7). Of the fifty-one cases where legislation proposed primarily on the initiative of the President was discovered, Congress enacted legislation having the same score as the proposed legislation in forty cases (79 per cent). In one case, legislation having a smaller score was enacted, and in only ten cases was there no legislation passed in response to a presidential initiative. These statistics are merely suggestive, since they do not do justice to the complexity and subtlety of the legislative-executive process, and they relate subjective scores based on incomplete data. In particular, they probably underestimate the attrition undergone by presidential proposals once they reach Congress. If the President makes five proposals (score 3) and the Congress passes one of them (score 3), the scores are identical, even though 80 per cent of the President's recommendations were not adopted. Furthermore, a presidential proposal may be defeated several times before being finally enacted, yet those two scores will also be identical. Nevertheless, these statistics tend to confirm the well-established generalization that the President is the most important and efficacious source of legislative initiative.

The testimony in a number of interviews also affirms this view. The following comments by two White House aides are illustrative: What is done to respond to a commission report "depends wholly on the President. If he wants something to happen, then it will happen, if not, then nothing will happen." Implementation of commission reports is "totally reliant on the executive branch. . . . They [commissions] must rely on the personal interest of the President."

Because of his authority as chief executive and because of his pivotal role in the initiation of legislation, the President is clearly the most important and effective commission supporter. He is also the most likely to be favorably disposed toward commission recommendations. All commission members are presidential appointees, and in most cases commissions have been created on the President's authority and he has given them their mandates and resources.[1] Within the constraints to establish the legitimacy and credibility of a commission, a commission is tailored to the President's purposes when it is launched. It is his adviser and it reports to him.[2]

The national constituency and national perspective of the President and his institutional position as chief executive of the federal government also generally mean that he is more sensitive to new national problems and more willing to entertain proposals for new solutions through federal action. Thus he is likely to be amenable to the proposals of commissions, which generally advocate changes in federal policy in the direction of more extensive federal action.

It was seen in the preceding chapter that, in general, commission enjoy a high level of presidential support.[3] There has been substantial variation in the amount of that support, however. The President's Commission on Law Enforcement and Administration of Justice (1965–67) had its report used in six presidential messages and ten presidential statements, but the report of the National Advisory Commission on Rural Poverty (1966–67) was greeted by a stony silence.[4] Given that the commission will be seeking the support of the President and that he will be predisposed to give it, what factors determine whether or not it will indeed be forthcoming? What circumstances make it likely that the President's support, once given, will be effective in gaining congressional assent?

The problem that the commission dealt with must still be a live issue when the commission reports, if its recommendations are to receive the support of the President. No problem, no support. Irrelevancy was the fate of the National Commission on Technology, Automation and Economic Progress (1964–66). Howard Bowen, the commission chairman, explained the situation and his wistful hope for the future:

> Since the establishment of the Commission in 1964, conditions have changed. Unemployment has been reduced, inflation threatens, and we are at war. At the moment, the problems that loomed large in 1964 have receded into the background. But when peace returns, these same problems will reappear and the recommendations of the Commission will again be timely and relevant.[5]

Two members of the commission staff were more specific. "Unemployment had gone down. Johnson was not interested. The problem had gone away." "There was very definitely a sense of having been made irrelevant by events."

The President cannot support a commission's recommendations if he has no support to give. When he is no longer in office, a lame duck, discredited, or fully occupied with problems of a higher priority than those the commission treated, he has little or no support to give to a commission or his support is of little value.

Commissions which report to a President who did not appoint them or which report shortly before a change in administrations so that action will have to be taken by a new administration have less chance of being supported by the President than those which report earlier. A new President usually wants to put his own distinctive stamp on a legislative program and set his own tone for the new administration. He is not interested in tying up the loose ends from the previous administration. This is particularly true in three of the four presidential transitions falling within the studied period, transitions which included a change of party as well as a new man in office (Truman-Eisenhower, Eisenhower-Kennedy, and Johnson-Nixon). In such a situation, it is even more likely that the new President will seek to distinguish himself from his predecessor, particularly in domestic policy. Thus the President's Commission on the Health Needs of the Nation (1951–52) and the President's Commission on Immigration and Naturalization (1952), both of which reported shortly before the end of the Truman Administration, were not supported or their recommendations acted upon during the Eisenhower Administration. Similarly, the Nixon Administration did not respond favorably to the reports of the Commission on Obscenity and Pornography (1967–70), the President's Commission on Income Maintenance Programs (1968–69), or the National Commission on the Causes and Prevention of Violence (1968–69), all of which came into being during the Johnson Administration but issued their reports during the Nixon Administration. However, under the Nixon Administration there has been legislative or administrative follow-up to the Commission on Marine Science, Engineering and Resources (1966–69), the National Advisory Commission on Selective Service (1966–67), the National Advisory Commission on Libraries (1966–68), the President's Commission on Postal Organization (1967–68), the National Commission on Product Safety (1967–70), and the Committee on Population and Family Planning (1968–69), showing considerably more carryover from the Johnson Administration to the Nixon Administration than there was from the Truman Administration to the Eisenhower Administration. The report of the National Commission on Goals (1960) was the only Eisenhower legacy to the Kennedy Administration, and its report did not call for specific policy changes.

The important exception to this rule was the transition between the Kennedy and Johnson Administrations. This was a transition within the same party, but more important, it happened while the nation was in trauma, after the assassination of President Kennedy. President Johnson responded to the tragedy by stressing the theme of continuity during his first year in office. "Let us continue," he said in his first major address.[6] One manifestation of this continuity was the presidential support and implementation received by the six commissions created by President Kennedy which reported during the Johnson Administration.[7]

In the case of each of the three transitions by election (Truman-Eisenhower, Eisenhower-Kennedy, and Johnson-Nixon), it was known for some time before the election that the President would not, or in the case of Eisenhower, could not, run for reelection. President Truman announced that he would not run in late March, 1952, and President Johnson in late March, 1968. Commissions reporting during the lame-duck period find that the support of the President is not a very powerful engine to move their recommendations. The President's Materials Policy Commission (1951–52) issued its report in June, 1952, after President Truman had declared his intention not to run again. President Truman had high praise for the report, transmitted it to Congress, and began a process of review within the Executive Branch conducted by the National Security Resources Board and the Bureau of the Budget.[8] No action was taken during the remaining months of the Truman Administration, the commission's recommendations dropped from sight as live policy options, and the National Security Resources Board was abolished early in the Eisenhower Administration. A member of the commission staff remarked:

> If there was a general lesson for commissions, it is that they should not be formed during the last two years of an administration. This one was a lame duck. Thus its substantive impact in legislative and administrative changes was very small because of the change in administrations. . . . This was true even though Paley [the commission chairman] was a strong man for Eisenhower and had good relations with him.

Similarly, the recommendations of the President's Commission on Postal Organization (1967–68) languished during the final months of the Johnson Administration. They were resurrected and substantially implemented by President Nixon as measures to respond to the postal strike in 1970.

The President will have little political capital to expend on behalf of a commission's recommendations if he is discredited. President Truman, for example, was assailed by a variety of problems in 1951 and 1952; an unpopular war, inflation, the internal security issue, the revelations of corruption in government highlighted by the 1951 Kefauver hearings, the controversy surrounding the firing of General MacArthur, and the steel seizure crisis of the spring and summer of 1952. President Truman's popularity registered an all-time low of 26 per cent approval in the spring of 1952. The political muscle available to President Johnson had deteriorated in his final two years in office because of the Vietnam war, the failure of the War on Poverty to live up to its promises, and the "credibility gap."

Finally, the availability of presidential support is affected by the press of other issues and crises which may crowd a commission's recommendations off the President's list of priorities. For example, the Korean war began in June, 1950, midway in the life of the President's Water Resources Policy Commission. Public attention to the publication of the commission's report on December 11, 1950, was diverted by the proclamation of a national emergency only a few days later. The war, particularly in 1950 when it was going badly for this country, distracted public attention from all domestic problems. The priority of domestic reforms in general and those dealing with water resources in particular was diminished by the war. President Truman, for example, noted in his Annual Budget Message in January, 1951, "Although long-range improvement of our river basins is essential for the continued economic strength of the country, in the fiscal year 1952 we must emphasize those aspects of the programs which primarily support the national defense."[9] A year later he said, "Pre-Korea plans for development of our land and water resources have been modified to reflect the urgent needs of the defense emergency."[10]

Domestic programs also declined in priority during the later years of the Johnson Administration, despite the promise of "guns and butter," as the Vietnam war absorbed the attention and energies of the White House.

The unavailability of presidential support and its inefficacy if given were most noticeable in the last year of both the Truman and Johnson administrations. In 1952 and 1968, both of these Presidents were lame ducks, both had suffered severe erosion of their political support, and both were preoccupied by war crises which pushed domestic innovation onto the back burner. The cumulative impact of all three factors produced a pattern of nonsupport and ineffective support in these two last years. Table 5 in chapter 7 indicates that the commissions reporting in these two years received, in general, less presidential support than those reporting in other years, and that when presidential support was given, it seems to have been less effective in achieving changes in government policy. The President's Materials Policy Commission (1951–52), the President's Commission on the Health Needs of the Nation (1951–52), the Missouri Basin Survey Commission (1952–53), the President's Airport Commission (1952), and the President's Commission on Immigration and Naturalization (1952–53) reported between January 1, 1952, and January 20, 1953. They had an average presidential support score of 1.8, compared to an average score of 1.9 for all commissions during the Truman Administration, and they had an average government action score of 0.6, compared to an average score of 1.7 for all commissions during the Truman Administration. The National Advisory Commission on Libraries (1966–68), the National Commission on Urban Problems (1967–68), the President's Commission on Postal Organization (1967–68), the President's Committee on Urban Housing (1967–68), the National Advisory Commission on Civil Disorders (1967–68), the National Advisory Commission on Health Facilities (1967–68), the Industry-Government Special Task Force on Travel (1967–68), and the Committee on Population and Family Planning (1968–69) reported between January 1, 1968, and January 20, 1969. The average scores for presidential support and government action for these commissions are about the same as the average scores for all commissions during the Johnson Administration, because the National Advisory Commission on Libraries (1967–68), the President's Commission on Postal Organization (1967–68), and the Committee on Population and Family Planning (1968–69) had important recommendations enacted during the Nixon Administration. The point is that for these three commissions, as well as for the National Advisory Commission on Health Facilities (1967–68) and the Industry-Government Special Task Force on Travel (1967–68), no government action implementing their reports was discovered for the last year of the Johnson Administration.

The commissions created during President Nixon's first term received, on the average, less presidential support and less implementation by government action than the commissions created during the other four administrations covered in this study.[11] This can be explained by some general factors related to the Nixon administration as well as by some specific problems faced by the large group of task forces created in 1969.

With respect to the Nixon administration in general, it is the most recent administration under study. Thus action may still be taken on recommendations of the Nixon commissions, improving their record of success. More important, of the four activist Presidents included in this study (Truman, Kennedy, Johnson, and Nixon), only Nixon's administration confronted, during its entire tenure, a Congress controlled by the opposition party. Therefore, the generally lower level of receptivity of the Democratic Congress to the initiatives of the Republican administration may be reflected in less willingness to take legislative action implementing the recommendations of the Nixon commissions. This is particularly evident, for example, in the congressional rejection of the Nixon proposals for massive Cabinet reorganization following from the recommendations of the President's Advisory Council on Executive Organization (1969–71). The problem of legislative-executive tension in the Nixon administration was also aggravated by the poor congressional relations of the Nixon White House. Finally, beginning in 1973, the preoccupation of the Nixon administration with the Watergate scandal diverted it from domestic policy initiatives and eroded the influence it might have exerted on behalf of commission recommendations.

The seventeen task forces created by President Nixon in 1969 (numbered 70–86 in appendix 2) have by far the poorest record of presidential support and of adoption of their recommendations as government policy. In fact, these task forces account for well over two-thirds of all of the commissions receiving a score of 0 in presidential support, and over half of those receiving 0 in government action.

These task forces were created at the initiative of White House counselor Arthur Burns, as a means to reorient the policies of the federal government and bring them in line with the goals of the new administration. The major reason for their lack of success was that they faced a situation analagous to that of commissions reporting under a President who has not created them. By the time most of them reported or were having their reports reviewed for implementation, Burns had left the White House to assume the chairmanship of the Federal Reserve Board. Thus most of the reports languished in unfriendly or indifferent hands in the White House, in the absence of the powerful White House aide who had initiated them. The chairman of one of these task forces remarked, "The truth is that the Administration didn't give a damn about the report. . . . After Burns left the White House, no one cared about the task force."

The 1969 task forces also faced two other problems in achieving implementation. First, such a large pack of them were created over such a short period of time that they had relatively little public visibility. They lacked the uniqueness that assures most presidential commissions of some public notice and an expectation that there will be some response to their reports. Second, a very short deadline of a few months was imposed on them. Therefore their reports are, in general, quite brief and lack the full and thorough presentation based on staff work, hearings, field trips, and consultant studies that characterizes most commission reports. They are statements of recommendations which are thin in building a case to support the recommendations. These reports did not present a compelling substantive argument for the implementation of their recommendations.

If a commission's problem is still live and if the President has support to give, there are several other factors which determine whether or not the support is given. Presidents most obviously will not support commission recommendations that they do not agree with. There are rare exceptions to this generalization, such as President Eisenhower's support for the recommendations of the President's Advisory Committee on a National Highway Program (1954–55) and President Kennedy's acceptance of the foreign aid cuts advocated by the President's Committee to Strengthen the Security of the Free World (1962–63).[12]

No instances were discovered in which the President disagreed with a commission because he felt that its findings of fact were in error. Presidential disagreement has been premised on differences in normative assumptions, policy preferences, or judgments concerning the importance and priority of a problem. President Nixon, for example, characterized the report of the Commission on Obscenity and Pornography as "morally bankrupt" because he assumed that the answer to the question "Is pornography harmful?" was a resounding "Yes." The commission, on the other hand, following the literal words of its mandate, regarded the question as open, and it marshalled data which led it to the opposite conclusion.[13]

In contrast, President Eisenhower's response to the report of the President's Citizen Advisers on the Mutual Security Program (1956–57) is reported to have been "Yes, this is the way I feel." It received a high level of support from the President.

In addition to supporting those reports that they agree with, Presidents also support reports of those commissions in which they have an interest. For example, a member of the President's Commission on Campaign Costs (1961–62) explained what he perceived as the minimal support given the commission by President Kennedy:

> I would hypothesize . . . [that] the Commission was never in the main-stream of the President's interest. His view of political parties and politics was conditioned by his Massachusetts experience where the process is wretched and the subject of constant improvisation. He was of the school of thought that believed that one used politics and one ought to reform it, but there was nothing final that could be done to it since it was always fluid and changing. He was not willing to use much personal credit for the Commission's recommendations.[14]

Presidents have not been notably self-critical or humble and contrite in response to criticism of their stewardship. They are therefore likely to disagree with and not support those commission reports which criticize their administrations. A member of the staff of the National Commission on Goals (1960), a pet project of President Eisenhower's, said, concerning the poor reception of the report: "Perhaps Eisenhower was miffed at the report. There was a lot in it that was critical of what had gone on in the fifties and by implication therefore critical of the Eisenhower Administration. Eisenhower did nothing to call attention to the report." The less-than-enthusiastic response by the White House to the report of the National Commission on Urban Problems (1967–68) was also attributed, in part, to its criticism of the Johnson Administration.[15]

The documentation of the gravity of any social problem is in a sense an implied criticism of the performance of the administration in office. All reports which document such facts are not, however, rejected for this reason. The boundary of acceptable criticism is a real but hazy one. Criticism that is sweeping and unmitigated by some praise and good marks, or that is overly explicit in comparing administration promises to performance or in pointing out specific failures in execution, seems to be beyond the pale. More generalized breast-beating over the failures in the past to give adequate attention to a problem seems to be acceptable. A focus on what can and should be done in the future rather than on assigning blame for the failures of the past is likely to make a report more acceptable to the President.

The political utility of a commission report and its recommendations is another major determinant of the support it will receive from the President. Political feasibility, the likelihood that commission recommendations, if supported, will be able to muster the agreement necessary from other actors to achieve action, is the most important aspect of political utility. A President's judgment on political feasibility tends to overlap with his feelings about the values and preferences expressed by the commission. "Do I like it?" and "Will it go?" are questions that are often not separated in the White House. In part, this overlap reflects a feeling by the President that if the report is not acceptable to him, then it is also not likely to be acceptable to the others whose agreement is needed. There is some justification for this feeling, since the President is elected by a national constituency at least in part because his values and preferences are preferred by a majority to those of his opponents.

In assessing political feasibility, the President and his advisers reach a political judgment about the various recommendations of a commission. Do they ask for too little or too much? Is the time ripe to press for their adoption? Will pressing for adoption hurt the chances of other more urgent initiatives? These kinds of considerations determined the decision not to support the recommendations of the National Advisory Commission on Rural Poverty (1966–67). A key Johnson White House aide explained:

> When the report came out, we were enormously concerned about the numbers in it. It would have scared the hell out of Congress. We had the model cities program, education programs, medicare, and job training [already before Congress]. There were people in Congress who thought that we wanted to spend everything in sight.

A member of the commission staff similarly recalled that "the OEO budget was in bad condition and it was not a good time to turn the report loose. . . . The report was criticized by White House sources because it asked that so much be done."

The political utility to the President of a commission report is greatly diminished if the report is seriously divided on its major recommendations.[16] Part of its value to the President lies in the fact that it represents the consensus of a prestigious, representative, and expert body on a single course of action. A commission which has the two halves of its membership on opposite sides of an important policy question is not half as useful as a unanimous commission. Its worth is zero as an instrument for persuasion, since the halves cancel each other out. A Truman aide remarked, "[David] Niles [another Truman aide] was concerned that there should be no dissents, that the report [of the President's Committee on Civil Rights] should be unanimous whatever they decided." The committee was, however, almost evenly split on one question, whether nondiscrimination by builders should be made a condition for federal financial assistance to them. No mention of this proposal was made in the President's messages and speeches responding to the report.[17] The National Advisory Commission on Food and Fiber (1965–67) was split on one of its major recommendations. The commission received only minimal support from the President, and it failed in its role as an agent for change in government farm-support policy.[18]

The utility of a commission report to the President is also enhanced if it is intellectually rigorous and coherent in the presentation of its findings and in the argument for its recommendations; if it is lucidly and persuasively written; and if it is produced in an attractive format which includes eye-catching pictures, charts, and other illustrations. A member of the President's Committee on Foreign Aid (1947) felt that a large part of the committee's success in getting a favorable response from the President, Congress, and the general public was due to "the extraordinary clarity of mind and ability to express complex economic questions in a comprehensible way . . . of Dick Bissell [the executive director of the committee who did much of the drafting of its report]."

OTHER SOURCES OF SUPPORT

When presidential support is lacking, other sources of support for commissions are not likely to produce action to implement commission recommendations. The institutional perspectives and interests of Congress and the federal bureaucracy frequently make them cool to the idea of supporting the recommendations of presidential commissions. Congressmen, and particularly congressional leaders, have a strong desire to maintain the integrity and independence of the Congress. Commission reports are on occasion picked up in the Congress after being shelved by the President, because there is an interest in their substantive findings and recommendations or because doing so presents an opportunity to harrass and embarrass the President. However, a resort to White House rejects as grist for the congressional mill demonstrates the feebleness of Congress in generating its own alternatives and highlights its role as reactor to the President. Thus when President Johnson expressed little interest in or support for the report of the National Commission on Technology, Automation and Economic Progress (1964–66), a commission staff member reported that "behind the scenes we tried to get the Senate Labor

Committee to hold hearings on the report. But there was no interest." This
was the case even though the commission was created by legislation which
had been approved by the Senate Labor Committee, and it had among its top
staff two former members of the committee staff.[19]

The President's Commission on Income Maintenance Programs (1968–69)
was not supported by President Nixon. A member of the commission staff
reported, "In January, 1970, Heineman [the commission chairman] and
Harris [the commission executive director] gave a briefing to DSG [Demo-
cratic Study Group, a group of liberal House Democrats]. They were trying to
generate interest in it [the commission report] as a Democratic alternative
[to President Nixon's Family Assistance Plan]. DSG, however, did not treat
the report as a resource."

The federal Executive Branch is also likely to regard the recommendations
of commissions with suspicion. Commissions are one means used by the
President to bypass the federal bureaucracy. They are a technique for generating policy analysis and options outside of the normal channels. When commissions fail to receive the support of the President, the bureaucracy is more
likely to applaud the vanquishing of the usurpers than to rally in their
defense. The unsympathetic treatment that commission reports often receive
when reviewed by Executive Branch agencies (described below) supports the
interpretation that there is a basic conflict of institutional interests between
commissions and line agencies.

Executive Branch agencies, also, cannot sponsor major initiatives in policy
contrary to the wishes of the White House. The role of Congress in formulating major policy initiatives is severely restricted, and limited primarily to
prodding the President to action. Thus the strategic position of the President
in the policy-making process also precludes an extensive role for the federal
bureaucracy or the Congress when the President is opposed to a commission
report, even if the Congress and the federal bureaucracy are partisans of the
report, which they are not likely to be. Interest groups which favor commission reports must also depend primarily upon strategies aimed at eliciting the
support of the White House.

The picture should not be overdrawn, however. Things do happen in the
national policy arena without the support of the President and on occasion
contrary to his wishes. However, the dominant pattern since World War II is
that innovation and change in domestic policies do not occur without at least
the tacit consent of the President, and his active support very significantly
boosts the prospects for change. Therefore the prospects for commission
reports getting effective support from sources outside the presidency are slim.
As one commission staff member observed, "Presidential commission reports
really have no home other than the President."

In several interviews, it was suggested that more congressmen be placed on commissions so that the reports would have more "friends in Congress." A number of commissions have had congressional members.[20] Their success does not seem to have been greater than that of commissions in general. More congressmen on commissions might marginally improve the prospects of recommendations which were accepted by the President and proposed to the Congress as legislation. However, more congressmen on commissions is unlikely to change basically the congressional suspicion of these "presidential" bodies, and is therefore not apt to be of much help in cases where the President does not support the commission report. Having more congressmen on commissions will also, of course, not substantially improve the capacity of Congress to become a more active source of domestic policy initiative, even if they should be favorably inclined toward the reports.

EXECUTIVE BRANCH REVIEW

The commission report transmitted to the White House is often a document of several hundred pages containing an analysis of complex and technical problems and making a number of recommendations, as many as one hundred, in some cases. These are often supplemented by several volumes of staff studies, technical papers, task force reports, and transcripts of hearings. What to do about it is the question. Three types of responses are needed. First, political policy judgments on the recommendations of the commission are needed. Second, there is a need for drafting of legislative proposals, administrative orders, and messages based on the recommendations that are accepted. This is necessary because most commissions frame their recommendations in terms of statements of policy rather than in terms of specific legislative or administrative language. Third, the legislative and administrative proposals must be reviewed to attain coordination and consistency with other proposals and with ongoing programs.

The discussion of the determinants of presidential support touched on only the most important actor in these three areas and implied that his choices were based on his individual judgment. In fact, the processes by which these choices are made extend far beyond the President, and the decisions to grant or withhold presidential support engage many more actors than the President himself. The President has neither the time nor the expertise to review thoroughly all of a commission's recommendations, to judge their policy implications and technical viability, and to assess their political feasibility. In this process of policy judgment, drafting, and review lie substantial opportunities for the erosion and side-tracking of commission recommendations. To illustrate, the "normal" process will be described, followed by a case study of this normal process for one commission. An analysis of the constraints imposed by this normal process on full implementation of commission reports will then be followed by a discussion of the techniques that have been used to short-circuit this process, when there is strong White House support for a report.

A commission report is not a surprise package handed to the President at a public ceremony transmitting the report to him. The report has often been completed for several weeks, and the President and his staff have had an opportunity to make a preliminary assessment of it while it was at the printer or while they were waiting for a suitable time to schedule the public ceremony. The White House has also been informed through interim reports from the commission, its own liaison with the commission, and anything the Washington rumor mill has generated about the recommendations and tone of the report. At this point it is decided to play down the report, to play up the report, or to be neutrally positive—that is, to express gratitude to the commission for its labors, and generalized interest in the problem area, but to make no commitments in general or specific. Those commission reports that do not receive presidential support generally wash out at this preliminary White House assessment stage, and their reports are played down in the manner described in chapter 5. Most commission reports, however, receive either the positive or neutral stamp, and there is a public presentation to the President, with suitable remarks by him, followed by a briefing and question-and-answer session for the press.

Some commissions evoke such a favorable response or deal with problems of such high priority that their findings and recommendations are almost immediately incorporated into messages, legislative proposals, and administrative actions. This was the case, for example, with the report of the President's Committee on Foreign Aid (1947) and with many of the major recommendations of the President's Commission on Law Enforcement and Administration of Justice (1965–67). In at least one case, the President's Committee on Urban Housing (1967–68), the findings and recommendations of the commission were incorporated into a message and legislative proposals before the commission made its final report.[21]

In most cases, however, a process of consultation, discussion, and analysis is initiated to determine for which recommendations action should be taken or sought. In the case of the President's Committee on Civil Rights (1946–47) this took the form of a spirited debate within the Cabinet and the White House staff, both of which were split on the wisdom of strong advocacy of the report by the President. In the White House, Clark Clifford championed the report, while John Steelman led the opposition. President Truman came down for vigorous support of the report.[22]

Often the agency most directly concerned with a commission's recommendations has been designated to act as the "spearhead agency" in conducting an evaluation of the Commission report. For example, the National Security

Resources Board was instructed to organize a "task force recruited from various Government agencies to study the detailed recommendations of the President's Materials Policy Commission and to give . . . [the President], within no more than sixty days, suggestions for carrying them out."[23] In other cases the Bureau of the Budget (since 1970 the Office of Management and Budget) has fanned out the report to the departments and agencies, particularly if the recommendations had large budgetary implications. A plethora of interagency committees and intraagency task forces come into being to handle a major report, to make agency recommendations on it, to bring those recommendations together, to iron out differences between agencies, and to make recommendations to the President. The President and his staff then decide on the recommendations. During the Eisenhower Administration, the Cabinet played a major role in making decisions on the initial response to a report and on the response to agency recommendations.

For those recommendations upon which the President has decided to act and which require legislation or administrative orders, drafting is undertaken. The drafting is usually done by experts from the agencies, by draftsmen from the Bureau of the Budget, in the White House office of the President's counsel, or by some combination of these. The initial circulation of the report often generates suggestions for specific language that should be incorporated in legislation, or administrative orders giving the draftsmen a starting place. On some occasions the White House will express its judgment on the recommendations of a commission in general terms and leave the decision on what action is appropriate and the task of drafting entirely to the agencies concerned. It will review the agencies' work only as it reaches the White House as part of the agencies' yearly package of legislative proposals and periodic proposals for administrative changes that require White House approval. Following drafting, the draft legislative act or the draft administrative orders are again reviewed by the affected agencies to assure their consistency with existing programs, statutes, and regulations, with the clearance ususally conducted by either the Bureau of the Budget or the agency most concerned. Finally, the legislation is sent to Congress or the administrative action is taken.

How the normal process of the Executive Branch can result in the erosion and sidetracking of a commission's recommendations is illustrated in the following brief case study. This is an atypical example because of the extreme obstacles faced by the report, but it serves admirably to highlight the perils that may be encountered as a commission report wends its way through the bureaucratic labyrinth. It should be pointed out before beginning that this case study will focus on the activities of the central agency in the Executive Office of the President charged with formulating a concrete response to this commission, that is, the Bureau of the Budget, and those of the one department most deeply involved in this substantive area, the Department of the Interior. Thus this case study represents only one slice of the process.

The President's Water Resources Policy Commission issued its general report, *A Water Policy for the American People,* on December 11, 1950. The commission made over seventy recommendations, the general thrust of which was that water resource use and development must be tied to general national objectives, that there must be unified responsibility for planning in this area, that planning must be done in terms of multipurpose river basin develop-ments, that there must be increased popular participation in the planning and implementation of developments, and that modifications must be made in project evaluation, cost allocation, and repayment standards and procedures. Almost all of these recommendations went counter to existing practice and challenged the interests of someone in the Executive Branch, the Congress, or the public.[24]

Shortly after the publication of the commission report, the President delegated the task of supervising the review of the report and its recommen-dations to the Budget Bureau.[25] For this review, the Budget Bureau set up an Interagency Water Policy Review Committee composed of representatives of the Departments of Agriculture, Commerce, and Interior, the Federal Power Commission, the Federal Security Agency, the Tennessee Valley Authority, the Army Corps of Engineers, and the Budget Bureau itself. This Interagency Review Committee was supported by a sizeable network of subcommittees, each with responsibility for some subgroup of the commission's recommenda-tions. The elaborateness and complexity of this review mechanism were noteworthy even in the federal government, where touching all the bases is a way of life.

The agency representatives and Budget Bureau officers reviewed the com-mission report and solicited the views of other interested governmental agencies, as well as those of concerned private groups. This process of soliciting the views of all concerned agencies lasted through most of 1951. Then, from November, 1951, to February, 1952, the Interagency Review Committee prepared about forty long review papers stating its conclusions on different groups of recommendations and laying out areas of disagreement where they existed.[26] Based on these review papers and other materials they had received, the Budget Bureau prepared a draft "Water Resources Policy Act of 1952." This draft was sent to the agencies for comment on February 20, 1952. Thus fifteen months had elapsed before the first draft Act emerged from the Budget Bureau.

The Budget Bureau, which has a Treasury-guarding bias and its own institu-tional interests to preserve, may not have been overly eager to get a legislative proposal to the President. The length and complexity of the review procedure established by the Budget Bureau at least allows for the possibility that the

Budget Bureau was hostile to the report rather than a servant of the President's policies.[27]

After about two months, the agencies responded to the Budget Bureau draft, pointing out various "shortcomings" in the draft Act and offering "constructive criticisms" that would help in "perfecting the bill." Translated from the euphemistic jargon of the government, this meant that some of them would not buy the draft Act even though it had been preceded by the elaborate consultative and review process under the Interagency Water Policy Review Committee in which they had participated.

The Budget Bureau put some pressure on the agencies to speed consideration of this draft Act so that it could be sent to Congress, and one agency complained of "the short time allotted for the review of this proposed legislation."[28] The Budget Bureau revised the draft Act, incorporating those suggestions it found to be "consistent with the general objectives of the draft."[29] The second draft Act was transmitted to the agencies on May 29, 1952, with the warning that "this draft is the last which will be available for agency comment prior to submission of the recommendations to the President."[30] Noting the continued interest of the President and the possibility of congressional adjournment in the near future, the Budget Bureau required that review of the second draft of the "Water Resources Policy Act of 1952" be completed by June 11, 1952, less than two weeks away, and that suggested revisions be confined to "specific rewording of the provisions of the Act," rather than being general analyses and critiques of its policy.[31]

The agencies again complained about the "hasty and incomplete" review and continued to express a variety of objections to the Act, including continued reservations about its basic policy. Despite its "last chance" warning of May 29, 1952, the Budget Bureau was unable or unwilling to recommend legislation to the President for submission to Congress.

Having failed to breach the walls of resistance on this front, the Budget Bureau abandoned the attempt to achieve agreement on a legislative draft, and opened a second front. On August 8, 1952, it circulated to the agencies a draft Budget Circular which would put into effect, by administrative action binding on all executive agencies, new standards of project design and evaluation, including some aspects of the commission recommendations and of the Budget Bureau's drafts of the "Water Resources Policy Act of 1952." Again there were objections from the agencies, based in part on policy disagreements and in part on the alleged inappropriateness of a Budget Circular as a means to change policy. Legislation was asserted to be the only proper way to establish new policies in this area, a contention which, when combined with the Budget Bureau's inability or unwillingness to produce such legislation for the President, added up to a call for no changes of policy in this area.[32] The Budget Bureau submitted a second draft of this circular to the agencies on Nobember 3, 1952, and it was met with similar objections.[33] Finally, on December 31, 1952, over two years after the commission had issued its report, the Budget Bureau took authoritative action in issuing Budget Circular No. A-47, despite unresolved agency objections to it.

The Department of the Interior was a very active participant in the review of the commission report. On December 29, 1950, shortly after the publication of the report, the Secretary of Interior, Oscar L. Chapman, set up a task force within the department to analyze and comment on the recommendations contained in the report. In specific, its mandate was:

> (1) To prepare . . . an analysis of the effect each recommendation in the report, if adopted, would have on the work of the Department.
> (2) To recommend the position which the Department should take with respect to each recommendation.
> (3) To determine which of the recommendations, if satisfactory to the affected Bureau and the Department, might be effectuated by (a) Secretarial Order or (b) Executive Order.
> (4) To develop data for use in the preparation of testimony which representatives of the Department will present at hearings on legislation growing out of the Commission's report.
> (5) To point out cases, if any, where the recommendations of the report are in conflict or vague and to propose a departmental interpretation of such recommendations.[34]

The task force was composed of twenty-two members representing the various subdivisions of the Department of Interior. Seven other interested officials from the department also attended the task force's meetings. Between December 29, 1950, and April 24, 1951, this task force met as a body over fifty times. The meetings were devoted to a chapter-by-chapter analysis and commentary on the commission report and to the reworking of its own report. Eight chapters of the commission report were reserved for discussion by the task force as a whole, having been designated of "general interest." The eleven other chapters were subjected to preliminary discussion by "working groups" composed of task force members interested in the more narrowly focused and specialized chapters of the report. These working groups brought to the full task force drafts of comments on their particular chapters, which would then be discussed by the full task force.[35] One can safely assume that the task force and working group members were also supported by substantial staff work in their own bureaus, services, offices, or administrations. The task force report, as transmitted by the Secretary to the Budget Bureau, was two hundred pages long.

Concurrently with the work of the Department of Interior's task force and extending beyond the life of the task force, representatives of the department were actively participating in the Interagency Water Policy Review Committee and its subcommittees established by the Budget Bureau. The department's representatives had available to them the proceedings and conclusions of the department's task force, in making their contribution to the two score review papers produced by the Interagency Committee before its termination in February, 1952.

This represents in outline the activity of the Department of Interior in the first review given the commission report. A similar procedure of analysis, review, drafting, and clearance of commentaries was followed in reaction to the February 20, 1952, and the May 29, 1952, drafts of the "Water Resources Policy Act of 1952" and to the August 8, 1952, and the November 3, 1952, drafts of Budget Circular No. A-47. Documents were dispatched to the Budget Bureau in response to each of these drafts, expressing the department's agreements, concurrences, reservations, objections, and criticisms. These documents did not involve as much work as the original review had, since much of the groundwork had been done by the task force and was reusable. The essential point is that the same thorough canvassing procedure and opportunity for substantive review of new proposals in the drafts existed each time, although it was not formalized in a task force each time.

The Department of Interior's response to the commission report and to the subsequent Budget Bureau drafts was probably the most comprehensive and detailed of any federal agency, since in the words of Assistant Secretary Warne, "the recommendations in the recently issued report of the President's Water Resources Policy Commission affect this Department more than any other department in the Government."[36] The Interior Department's response was however only a larger version of, and not basically different from, the response of other federal agencies whose interests the commission recommendations and the Budget Bureau drafts touched. The Interior Department's response is also probably generally typical of the reaction of federal agencies to substantial intrusions into their bailiwicks by the recommendations of any presidential advisory commission—typical not in the sense of being for or against the substantive recommendations (Interior was on the whole favorably inclined toward much of the commission report), but rather in the elaborateness and complexity of the process of evaluation and review.

The result, the response of the Executive Branch to the work of the commission, that greeted the incoming Eisenhower Administration in January, 1953, was Budget Circular No. A-47 and the Budget Bureau draft "Water Resources Policy Act of 1952." After over two years of work within the Executive Branch, the President was still unable to send a bill to Congress. President Truman finally resorted, on his last day in office, to the gesture of sending a "Special Message to the Congress on the Nation's Land and Water Resources," which included a number of proposals based on the recommendations of the commission.[37]

In this case there was (1) an exhaustive and comprehensive review of the commission report by Executive Branch agencies, (2) a President who had a long-standing interest in the field, made it a major point in his domestic program, and retained, after the commission had disbanded, an interest in and commitment to getting legislation based on its report,[38] and (3) a commission which took unusual action in preparing and later releasing with presidential backing its own legislative draft, and which had several active, influential, and concerned members who continued to lobby in behalf of the commission's recommendations.[39] Yet no legislation reached Congress before the end of the Truman Administration. One observer who knows the field of water resources well and was one of the government officials involved in reviewing the commission report summed up the end result of the Executive Branch activity outlined above with a gesture holding his thumb and index finger about a half inch apart.

The scant output from the commission report was due in part to some strong factors peculiar to this case. First, there was particularly strong and effective resistance by public agencies and private groups in the field of water resources to any restructuring and reorientation.[40] Second, the Korean war began during the tenure of the commission, in June, 1950, lowering the priority of domestic reforms. Third, what little ability President Truman had to push his domestic program forward in wartime was sapped by a host of other problems which beset him in 1951 and 1952.

However, the important lessons to be drawn from this study deal with the constraints on implementation of a commission's recommendations inherent in the process of review in the Executive Branch that has been described above. Commission reports come to less than is generally hoped for partly because of the opportunities and advantages possessed by those opposed to change (which commission reports generally advocate) in this Executive Branch review process. The advantages possessed by the opponents of change derive from three aspects of this process: (1) the length of time the process often takes, (2) the comprehensiveness of the process, and (3) the need to rely on the President and the White House as the primary advocates and defenders of a commission's recommendations.

1. More than a year elapsed between the release of the commission report and the circulation of the first draft "Water Resources Policy Act of 1952" from the Budget Bureau. There are two consequences of such a long review that are inimical to implementation of a commission's recommendations.

First, a long period of internal government review dissipates the original force of a commission report. The interest in and awareness of a problem in the Congress and among the public, stimulated by the statements of the President on receiving the report and by the articles and commentary in newspapers, weekly news magazines, and other media, decline as nothing further is heard for many long months. The attention of politicians and others attentive to the issues is drawn away by the rush of events.

Second, this long hiatus between making a report public and submitting legislation to Congress permits those opposed to changes in the status quo to organize more extensively and to make their opposition felt during the review process and during any subsequent periods of congressional consideration. It may be argued that those in favor of change enjoy a similar opportunity to mobilize and assert themselves. However, menacing established relationships and threatening to deprive people of what they already have are usually a more powerful impetus to political action than are speculative promises of future gains. In general, the stakes are likely to appear higher and attitudes to be more intense among those who stand to lose what they have than among those with the possibility of gaining what they do not have. Thus time is usually on the side of defenders of the status quo.[41]

2. The process of review of the Water Resources Policy Commission report was comprehensive, in the sense that all federal agencies having any substantial interest in the report's recommendations were consulted in the initial review of the report, and these agencies were repeatedly and systematically canvassed as succeeding drafts of legislative proposals and Budget Circulars were produced. Thus there were many points of access, both in terms of the number of participants and the number of sequential and repetitive stages in the review. The well-organized are most likely to be able to avail themselves of opportunities for access in the decision-making process. Since the opponents of change are likely to be better organized, as indicated above, they are therefore likely to be more able to make themselves heard effectively in this process.[42]

More important, however, the Executive Branch participants in this process represent all those who formulate and administer existing policies in the area of a commission's concern. Since most commissions advocate innovation or change, these Executive Branch participants are likely to oppose many of a commission's basic recommendations. It was argued in chapter 3 that one of the capabilities that presidential advisory commissions have is that of providing the President with an instrument for formulating and advocating those changes which are unlikely to emerge through the normal processes of the Executive Branch. However, the weight of established clearance procedures and the need for Executive Branch expertise in review and drafting tend to negate this capability. The review and clearance procedures involve all those whose inability to produce analysis and proposals desired by the President led to the creation of the commission in the first place, and whose interests are most likely to be threatened by the commission's report. The agencies involved in the review, or at least a good part of them, are obviously usually lacking in enthusiasm for full and rapid implementation of the commission's recommendations and are likely to seek to temper them and water them down. An official in the Department of Health, Education, and Welfare, commenting on the President's Task Force on Higher Education (1969–70), remarked, "This was a White House initiative, but it had nothing to do with the guys who were in the pit on higher education policy making."

In addition, the federal agencies who are reviewing a commission report are likely to have settled and symbiotic relations with the established interest groups in the area, who will also often be those most resistant to innovations and disruptions in the status quo. Thus, besides the advantages interest groups opposed to the recommendations have by reason of the length of the review process and their superior organization, they have easy access to the review process through open and sympathetic channels between themselves and the agencies conducting the review.

3. The success of a report often depends on the exercise of presidential persuasion within this process in which the cards are often stacked against a favorable response. The success of the report therefore depends on its continued strong claim on the President's resources for persuasion and on the existence of such resources to put a claim on. In the case of the President's Water Resources Policy Commission, despite President Truman's strong and continued interest in water resources, the claim of the commission on his resources was downgraded by other competing claims, particularly those arising from the Korean war. In addition, the total fund of President Truman's resources upon which claims could be placed declined significantly in 1951–52, as he suffered from domestic political problems and became a lame-duck President.

The main point of the preceding is that the normal process of Executive Branch review provides substantial opportunity for those hostile to a commission's report to effectively kill or whittle down the recommendations that they find objectionable.[43] Mike Gorman, a member of the staff of the President's Commission on the Health Needs of the Nation (1951–52), summed up the problem well: "[W]hen you try to look for where some reports are, some faceless guy has it in some faceless office. That is the weakness of the Presidential commission."[44] Of course, the opportunities for bureaucratic sabotage, when used, do not always result in success for the opponents of commission recommendations. Nor is the Executive Branch review process always hostile territory. Some reports have been greeted with warm approval by at least some agencies and established interest groups.

In addition the White House has employed a number of short circuits to assure reports a more sympathetic hearing in the Executive Branch. These are stratagems to overcome the limits of the White House policy management outreach encountered when reports are dispatched to the bureaucracy for review.[45] They are also means for the White House to avoid being confronted with agency recommendations hostile to a commission report, recommendations backed by the legitimacy of the agency's statutory responsibility in some field, by its expertise, and by the support of its presidentially appointed executives. Such agency recommendations can only be overrideen at a substantial cost to the President in terms of the politics of the Executive Branch.

When a commission report is first reviewed, to make policy decisions on its recommendations, the White House role can be expanded to absorb the review by agencies. If the report is of particular interest to the President or the dangers in the Executive Branch are obvious, a White House staff man may be put in charge of analyzing the report. A Johnson White House aide remarked:

> Theoretically, reports were supposed to go to the White House, then be circulated to the affected agencies for comment, and then be returned to the White House. But basically, the White House worked them over and made recommendations to the President.

In this situation, agency opinions are sought, but the priorities and preferences of the White House are a much stronger influence in the evaluation of the report.

The White House usually is clearly aware of the likelihood of Executive Branch opposition to a commission report, and it can use this situation to kill recommendations it opposes, simply by letting the agencies review them. This occurred in the review of one part of the recommendations of the National Advisory Commission on Selective Service (1966–67). A member of the commission staff explained:

> The President didn't buy the commission's reorganization proposal. He waffled on that. He set up an internal interagency committee composed of [General] Hershey [director of the Selective Service System], Defense, and Bureau of the Budget which in turn set up a staff committee and had an executive director, some old guy from Defense. Selective Service dominated the staff. They had them by where the hair is short. They wrote an internal report saying it couldn't be done.[46]

Task forces were frequently used during the Johnson Administration. Over a hundred of these usually secret advisory groups, having at least some members from outside of the Executive Branch, were appointed in the years 1964–68.[47] Many were created to engage in policy analysis and idea generation and were thus in a number of ways similar to commissions. They dealt with a wide variety of topics, such as child development, meat inspection, water pollution, and new towns.

Another large group of the task forces were created to make specific recommendations for legislation and administrative actions, to help generate the President's program rather than to analyze problems. Among this group, several were set up specifically to undertake the review of presidential commission reports, and several others considered commission reports, as well as proposals from other sources, in producing legislative recommendations for a broad policy area such as education or health. Because such task forces include experts from outside of the Executive Branch and because they operate under the auspices of the White House, their review of commission reports is another way in which the perils of Executive Branch review can be avoided. A member of a task force on crime created in 1967 explained the operation and purposes of that task force:

> [Joseph] Califano, [White House aide], called me up a few months after the Crime Commission [the President's Advisory Commission on Law Enforcement and Administration of Justice, 1965–67] had issued its report. One message and bill had been sent up to the Congress. This bill eventually became the Safe Streets Act. But the nine volumes of the report just sat there. No one knew what to do with them—what to do next—what was important or unimportant. The President was interested in doing something on crime, and there was great public interest also. Califano wanted . . . a task force to make specific recommendations for legislation and administrative actions. We were to report by December so that our recommendations could be incorporated in the State of the Union Message. . . . Our mandate was clear. We were to be an operational group. We were to look for ideas and programs beginning with the Crime Commission reports, but not limited to them. Our report turned out to be the President's crime message. . . . Johnson used task forces to respond to commission reports. He didn't trust the agencies. He felt that either they would tell him that nothing could be done, or send him warmed over proposals that they had had in their desks for the last twenty years. They [the White House] took our report and sent it around to the agencies, HUD, HEW, and Justice. But the report was submitted in December and it was to be used for the State of the Union Address. So the agencies didn't have much time to react to it. Our work was done in isolation from the agencies. They were consulted but not involved in the work of the task force. The President didn't give the agencies much chance.

One of the major problems encountered by this task force was the presence of a key executive from the Justice Department among its members. His presence resulted in the tempering of recommendations dealing with reorganization of the Justice Department, thus providing a hint of the erosion that might have occurred had the commission report been reviewed exclusively by Justice and other agencies rather than by the task force.

In the process of clearing draft legislation and administrative orders, the normal channels in the Executive Branch can also be short-circuited by the White House inserting itself in the process. There are variations in the degree of White House participation at the clearance stage, as there are at the review stage. Legislation from a commission report that emerged from the White House, in contrast to the normal flow of legislation that came "welling up" from the departments, was always treated by the Budget Bureau in undertaking clearance "on a case by case basis," according to a Truman aide. "They gave it custom-made treatment," he said. White House liaison with the clearance operation and the imposition of deadlines from the White House are somewhat more intensive efforts to assure that too much is not lost from the White House point of view. Clearance of legislation by the White House itself is a guarantee of sympathetic treatment. During the Kennedy and Johnson administrations, White House clearance was given with increasing frequency to important legislation, often including legislation to implement the recommendations of commissions.[48]

In addition to these techniques for constructing institutional by-passes to the executive review, drafting, and clearance procedures, the intensity of presidential interest and commitment to a course of action favored by a commission is an important aid in navigating the process successfully. In the case study of the President's Water Resources Policy Commission, the presidential commitment was there and was sufficient to keep the commission recommendations alive within the Executive Branch for two years, but the President's ability to back up that commitment steadily declined, and the commission's recommendations were drastically whittled down.

OTHER DETERMINANTS OF SUCCESS

A commission which manages to mobilize the support of a politically strong President in behalf of its recommendations and which manages to avoid the pitfalls in the Executive Branch process through which its recommendations are translated into action documents is still not guaranteed that its recommendations will become government policy. In the case of legislative proposals, it obviously is important that Congress be favorably disposed. While presidential support makes favorable congressional action more likely, it does not make it a certainty. President Truman, for example, was a strong advocate of universal military training, but the legislation based on and supported by the recommendations of the Advisory Commission on Universal Training (1946–47) "fizzled out" in the face of opposition in Congress. President Johnson gave strong support to legislation for liberalized trade with communist countries, in line with the recommendations of the Special Presidential Committee on U.S. Trade Relations with Eastern European Countries and the U.S.S.R. (1965), but congressional hostility again prevented passage of the legislation.[49]

A strong interest group which becomes aroused in opposition to legislation can also help to prevent its enactment. Legislation was submitted to implement the reccommendations of the President's Commission on Campaign Costs (1961–62), during the Kennedy Administration. White House support was not overwhelming, and the Congress was not very favorably disposed toward reform in campaign financing, but any chances for the legislation were crushed by the opposition of the labor unions. A White House aide explained:

> We turned it [the commission report] into a legislative mechanism. . . . We got it sent up. Then the shit hit the fan. The union boys and especially the UAW descended on poor Larry O'Brien [the White House staff member in charge of congressional relations] . . . . Neil Staebler [a member of the commission] had in fact touched base with Vic Reuther [of the UAW], I think. So we were surprised by the reaction. They were very hot and there were charges of bad faith. It was understandable that they liked things the way they were. They thought that they were broadening the base of political support [through their solicitation of campaign contributions from union members, and that therefore legislation for this purpose was not needed]. They had their hands on the spigot. There was a big, big, big ruckus. Finally tempers were cooled down and the accusations of bad faith were dropped. But it was understood that they would oppose it on the Hill. It didn't go anywhere.

If a commission's recommendations lose supporters within the Executive Branch, this can also decrease their chances of success in Congress. Robert Patterson, "who had been the strongest civilian advocate of universal training" as Secretary of War, left for private life. James Forrestal was Secretary of Defense of the new unified Department when implementation of the report of the Advisory Commission on Universal Training (1946–47) was being sought by President Truman. Forrestal was a Navy man, and the Navy had always been lukewarm to the idea of universal military training, since they never had had to rely on conscription to get their manpower. Forrestal shared the Navy skepticism. Thus the legislation to implement the recommendations of the commission lost one of its most important supporters, one who might have helped to overcome congressional opposition, and the legislation was not passed. Along the same lines, the "discontinuity at Justice" when Attorney General Katzenbach, who was also chairman of the President's Commission on Law Enforcement and Administration of Justice (1965–67), moved to the State Department, resulted in the loss by the commission of some of its impact, when its chairman was no longer in the position of being a major participant in implementation.

Commission reports do not make their mark on a *tabula rasa* in their area of concern. They launch their reports into an ongoing debate in which there are usually established positions in various parts of the government, the professional community, and the public at large. Thus reports exist in a context of supportive and antagonistic initiatives in the same field, and they stand upon the shoulders or are haunted by the ghosts of previous efforts to deal with the problem. Commissions may intensify debate, make people more aware of it, or enlarge the number of participants in it, but they do not begin it. Whether a commission will prevail in the debate and have its definition of the situation accepted as authoritative and its recommendations acted upon depends, in addition to the considerations outlined above, on who its allies and enemies in the debate are. The probability of success is increased if a commission is supported by initiatives from other prestigious and influential sources.

For example, in addition to creating the President's Committee on Foreign Aid (1947) to assess and, it was hoped, support the Marshall Plan proposal, President Truman ordered two other studies to be undertaken within the federal government, one under the direction of Secretary of Interior Krug and one by the Council of Economic Advisers. Congressman Herter also headed a select committee of the House of Representatives which travelled to Europe to study the recovery problem and the best means to deal with it. Besides that, the Committee on European Economic Cooperation, composed of representatives of the European nations, studied the Marshall proposal and made an assessment of European needs. All five of these studies were in basic agreement on the broad questions of European needs, the wisdom of the United States providing aid, and the capacity of this country to supply the aid without serious economic disruption. From the point of view of the President's Committee on Foreign Aid, the prospect that its recommendations would be adopted was significantly enhanced by the fact that it was swimming with this tide rather than against it. A Truman aide remarked that the Committee on Foreign Aid was "a beautifully articulated part of a grand strategy."[50]

In contrast, shortly after President Johnson established the National Advisory Commission on Selective Service (1966–67), Congressman L. Mendel Rivers (D–S.C.), chairman of the House Armed Services Committee, set up an advisory panel of distinguished citizens headed by General Mark Clark. The Clark Panel recommended that the Selective Service System be retained without major changes. The commission recommended substantial reforms. Those recommendations of the commission that were incorporated by the President into his legislative recommendations on the draft met defeat in the Congress the first time they were sent up.[51] It is doubtful that the Clark Panel persuaded many congressmen, but it did give them a way to avoid confronting the arguments of the commission. If there are competing groups of "experts" of roughly equal status and legitimacy, a legislator can follow his natural inclinations and point to the group that agrees with him, to support his position. If there is only one group which does not agree with him, its analysis and recommendations must be more directly confronted and opposition to its recommendations must be more fully justified. The dominant mood in Congress in 1967 did not favor draft reform, and the Clark Panel headed off some of the immediate educational impact of the commission report in the Congress.[52]

A set of initiatives supporting the thrust of a commission's recommendations can be orchestrated from the White House, once more pointing to the importance of presidential support. For example, to follow up on the work of the Panel on Mental Retardation (1961–62), a permanent citizen advisory council, the President's Committee on Mental Retardation, was created, and the President called the White House Conference on Mental Retardation. The case of the President's Committee on Foreign Aid (1947) described above is another example.

COMMISSION EFFORTS IN THEIR OWN BEHALF

Assuming that the above discussion outlines the major determinants of and constraints on implementation of commission recommendations, what can a commission do to increase its chances of success? Commissions are not the "armed prophets" who Machiavelli says will rarely fail as innovators. They cannot "compel," but they are not wholly unarmed either.[53] There are several things that commissions can do to maintain leverage and to help forge links between their recommendations and government action. A commission can be most effective in serving its own cause in those aspects of its work over which it exercises some direct control—its report and its activities to publicize and promote the report after it has been transmitted to the President.

One of the most important things a commission can do is to do its job well. A report of high quality, lucidly written and tightly argued, is likely to be persuasive in the White House and elsewhere. The power of forcefully presented ideas is a major weapon possessed by a commission. Government actors basically want to do what is right, what is in the public interest. Within broad limits, they are willing to be persuaded by strong analysis and findings.

Most major commissions hire professional writers and often photographers, layout consultants, and graphic artists, to increase the readability, persuasiveness, and attractiveness of their reports. A member of the staff of the National Advisory Commission on Rural Poverty (1966–67) felt that the impact of the commission report had been diminished because it contained too many recommendations and too much detail. Commissions can and do pay a great deal of attention to the literary and artistic merits of their reports.

Another aspect of a commission doing its job well is making sure that it touches all bases in arriving at its findings and recommendations. A commission can make certain that it will not be vulnerable to discrediting for failure to consult all of those who have an interest in or knowledge of its area of concern. Most commissions are scrupulous in soliciting written statements or personal testimony from all conceivably relevant sources.[54] The possible consequences of not doing so were illustrated above in the case of labor's reaction to the report of the President's Commission on Campaign Costs (1961–62).

Commissions can and do act in some ways to increase the acceptability and political utility of their reports to the President. They obviously have very little control over when they will report, since most of them have a fixed deadline, and those that do not usually have the release of their report scheduled by the White House or determined by the completion of their work. Commissions can do nothing to prevent the President who created them from being discredited, distracted by other problems, or thrown out of office, or to prevent the problem they are considering from declining in importance. Successful commissions, however, avoid strident criticism of the administration and strive mightily to have a unanimous report. Martha Derthick, a member of the President's Commission on Campus Unrest (1970), remarked, "Unanimity is perceived to be the first condition of effectiveness."[55]

Do commissions tailor their recommendations according to their reading of the political winds? In a very basic sense the answer is yes. Commission members are chosen because they have risen to a place of prominence and prestige in the institutions of American society. It is almost impossible to conceive of them making utopian recommendations, or recommendations that diverge in any basic way from dominant values and established institutions. They are sound, reasonable, and practical people whose training, experience, and inclinations restrain them within the existing paradigm. Thus political realism is implicit and powerful in all their deliberations. On the other hand, commissions seem to pay relatively little explicit attention to weighing and assessing the short-term political situation, the calculus of political feasibility over the period during which the commission's recommendations will be under consideration. Such factors are not entirely ignored. Some of the discussion over the dollar amount of the income maintenance floor among the members of the President's Commission on Income Maintenance Programs (1968–69) was reported to be in terms of what the President and the Congress would be likely to accept. A member of the staff of the President's Commission on the Status of Women (1961–62) recalled:

> They [the commission] felt for political reasons that they couldn't study abortions and they couldn't advocate family planning. They thought it was the better part of valor to avoid these issues since they would have vitiated the usefulness of the really constructive recommendations that the Commission made.[56]

However, narrowly political considerations are usually muted in the deliberations of commissions, sometimes with the result that their reports receive a chilly reception from the White House. This weakness (if indeed it is a weakness) is largely inherent in the nature of commissions as institutions. It was argued in chapter 3 that commissions have a unique capability for innovative policy analysis in large part because they are "temporary systems." As temporary systems they can focus intensive efforts on the problems they must deal with, and because they are detached from existing programs and institutions and free from most boundary and maintenance problems, they can entertain new and unorthodox proposals. In fact, they generally do put forth intensive effort and entertain such proposals.[57] The result is that while commissions often share the President's perspective on the issue they are studying, that is, a national perspective and a focus on solutions by federal action, they usually do not share the President's perspective on the relation of their issue to other issues. Their recommendations are not forced to compete with proposals dealing with other problems. Given the single-issue focus of commissions, it is quite understandable that they lack the President's sense of legislative priorities and budgetary constraints, and consequently that they sometimes make recommendations that are not feasible in these presidential terms. President Eisenhower said, for example, with regard to the Gaither report:

> The Gaither Report contained certain useful distillations of data and some interesting suggestions, but the entire report could not be accepted as a master blueprint for action. The President, unlike a panel which concentrates on a single problem, must always strive to see the totality of the national and international situation. He must take into account conflicting purposes, responding to legitimate needs but assigning priorities and keeping plans and costs within bounds.[58]

An added consequence of the fact that commissions are temporary systems is that they develop norms within the group that support inquiry, speculation, and experimentation. The atmosphere of intellectual *engagement* sometimes leads commission members and staff to feel that they are *deciding* what should be done based on their research and debates, rather than that they are *recommending* a course of action to the President. This also results in some recommendations which from the President's perspective lack political feasibility.

The White House, however, usually does not encourage commissions to weigh immediate political prospects in making their recommendations; in fact, they often strongly discourage it. One reason is, in the words of a Johnson aide, "We thought we were better at it." More important, one of the primary benefits the White House hopes to derive from most commissions is a fresh look at a problem, and new ideas. That this look occasionally results in unfeasible recommendations that may be an embarrassment is a price they seem willing to bear. From the White House perspective, most commissions are viewed as agents of change, and they are not expected to bat a thousand in the short-run feasibility of their proposals.[59]

Securing presidential support is their primary objective, but commissions also try to maintain some continuing leverage while their recommendations are under consideration in the Executive Branch and the Congress. They cannot assure themselves of a friendly Congress or a sympathetic bureaucracy, and they must rely primarily on those levers which they can control. The quality of their analysis and recommendations is again, of course, an important consideration. The trick is for them to make their case forcefully without waving red flags that will arouse and mobilize strong opposition in the Congress or the bureaucracy.

The ability of a commission to gain and keep the attention of the relevant policy community helps it maintain influence during the process of implementation. Assuming that the report is persuasive and attractively packaged, commissions have undertaken a variety of activities to achieve favorable exposure. The hearings and public inspection trips of a commission during its lifetime help to generate public awareness and interest. The timing and staging of the release of the report are planned for maximum effectiveness. Reporters are often given prepublication copies and summaries of the report to help familiarize them with it, background briefings are held, and a date for release is chosen with front-page coverage in mind. In planning and executing all these endeavors the White House staff works closely with the commission and exercises substantial control, so that the impact on the media at the time of release is only partially controlled by the commission itself.[60]

Some commissions seek to achieve continuing public exposure by not releasing all the sections or volumes of their reports, or their separate task force reports, at once. They release them, instead, one by one, and get fresh and continuing coverage. The National Commission on the Causes and Prevention of Violence (1968–69) used this strategy. In the words of its executive director, Lloyd Cutler,

> The Violence Commission's findings of fact probably reached a larger public audience than those of any prior commission. While the Kerner [National Advisory Commission on Civil Disorders, 1967–68] report sold well over 2 million copies, its important findings and conclusions were summarized in the press and electronic media only once—at the time the report was first published. Our Commission deliberately adopted a different tactic, publishing each topical segment of our final report—and each of our task force reports—seriatim as it was completed. As a result, the Commission's successive releases became front page newspaper stories and television stories throughout the country on approximately 20 separate occasions. One each occasion a summarized text of the findings, running to several thousand words, appeared in leading newspapers such as the New York Times and the Washington Post. We also conducted numerous television press conferences and

permitted both the press and the television cameras to cover our 8 weeks of public hearings.[61]

As described in chapter 7, rapidly available commercial paperback editions of commission reports were arranged for by several commissions in the 1960's. This meant that the reports were available when interest was high, following the first media coverage of the release of the report, and that the reports were distributed more widely than they otherwise would have been. The Commission on National Goals (1960) set aside part of its budget to subsidize a commercial publication of its report in order to keep the price down and make the report more accessible to the public.

To assure that the target audience is reached, many commissions distribute free copies of their reports. A member of the staff of the President's Commission on Law Enforcement and Administration of Justice (1965–67) explained:

> The Commission did a massive free mailing. The report was sent to mayors, police chiefs, legislators, and judges. We also assembled lists of criminologists from the directories of the psychological and sociological associations and got up other lists and sent these people the report. Some funds were reserved for distribution of the report.[62]

The skillful and sustained efforts of commission members in speeches, written articles, press conferences, television interviews, and congressional hearings can also be a source of continuing leverage for a commission. For example, a member of the President's Committee on Foreign Aid (1947) attributed much of the favorable impact of the committee report on the public and the Congress to the efforts of Senator LaFollette, who was also a member of the committee:

> He [LaFollette] did an excellent job in making presentations to different committees. He could put things in a politically understandable manner. There was a press conference when the report first came out. . . . It was the first report that all the reporters understood. They asked a number of good questions, and there was a good interchange. The favorable public reaction was due to that. . . . One of the reasons for the success of the report . . . [was] the very practical presentation with political understanding of the answers people wanted to hear.

The discussion in this chapter has focused on the determinants of commission impact in terms of getting authoritative government action to implement commission recommendations. In the absence of any presidential support or government action, commissions may still have an educational impact. The educational impact will, of course, be enhanced if presidential support is forthcoming, even if Congress or the federal bureaucracy is unresponsive.

In concluding this chapter, the operation of some of the variables that determine commission success or failure can be illustrated by briefly examining the responses by the government and the President to the National Advisory Commission on Civil Disorders (Kerner Commission, 1967–68). Various commentators have concluded that the commission was a failure both in the quality of its analysis of urban riots and in the presidential and government responses to its report.[63] The reasons for the failure of this and similar commissions to provide satisfactory answers to broad and basic questions of public policy were discussed in detail in chapter 6. Let us focus here on the reasons for the failure of the commission to receive a more favorable response from the government and the President.

First, however, it should be noted that the commission was not an unmitigated failure. It was effective in several ways:

1. Legislation was passed (Title XI, "Urban Property Protection and Reinsurance," Housing and Urban Development Act of 1968, PL 90-448, 82 Stat. 476) to implement the recommendations of the President's Advisory Panel on Insurance in Riot-Affected Areas, which was a subunit of the commission.

2. Police and National Guard procedures for dealing with civil disorders have been modified to reflect the recommendations of the commission. Law-enforcement officials are probably better trained, more disciplined and restrained, and aided by better planning and intelligence in their handling of civil disorders as a result of the commission's work.[64]

3. There has probably been an incremental acceleration in the adoption and funding of programs to deal with urban problems.[65]

4. The commission's findings and conclusions have been broadly disseminated through the appearances of commission members at congressional hearings, on radio and television, and at a large number of public meetings, and through the widespread use of the commission report in university courses and as a resource by commentators on public policy, interest groups, and government officials.[66] This has probably resulted in the commission's having an important educational impact.[67] Specifically, as a result of the commission, it is likely that more attention has been focused on urban social and economic problems in general, that the issue of racism has been introduced into the national dialogue, and that the social-causes-of-riots theory has been established as a strong alternative to the conspiracy or agitator theories.

While the commission was not a total failure, and in table 5 of chapter 7 it is scored as having the highest degree of presidential support and government action on the basis of the urban property insurance legislation that was introduced and passed, President Johnson gave only a minimal and lukewarm response to this important commission. He made only one press conference statement on the report, in response to a direct question, and made a couple of passing references to it in speeches.[68] There has not been implementation of most of the commission's recommendations through legislation, administrative action, or increased funding for existing programs. There are several reasons for the lack of government action and the cool response by President Johnson:

1. President Johnson's political capital and his capacity to support domestic innovation were seriously eroded by the Vietnam war, the failures of the War on Poverty, and the "credibility gap." He became a lame-duck President less than a month after the commission issued its report. The commission reported too late even to be included in the formulation and presentation of the regular budget and legislative program that were sent to the Congress during the final year of the Johnson Administration. Within less than a year after the commission issued its report, there was a change in administrations with a change in party control of the presidency. The commission's executive director, David Ginsburg, observed, "There is a tendency to forget that this report was published in March 1968, 60 days after Tet and 30 days before an eligible President decided not to seek reelection."[69] Thus the President who created the commission, and on whom it primarily had to rely for support if its recommendations were to be implemented, was distracted, discredited, and very soon out of office. This is probably the most important reason why more was not done to implement the commission's recommendations.

2. The total package of the commission's recommendations was judged in the White House to be unrealistic, and possibly counterproductive if supported, given the political situation at the time. President Johnson explained:

> The commission called for a substantially increased outlay of resources, doubling or tripling each ongoing program. The Bureau of the Budget estimated that the recommendations would cost in the vicinity of $30 billion, in addition to the $30 billion plus already in the budget for the poor.
> That was the problem—money. At the moment I received the report I was having one of the toughest fights of my life, trying to persuade Congress to pass the 10 per cent tax surcharge without imposing deep cuts in our most critical Great Society programs. I will never understand how the commission expected me to get this same Congress to turn 180 degrees overnight and appropriate an additional $30 billion for the same programs that it was demanding I cut by $6 billion. This would have required a miracle. . . . I would have been delighted to have had an appropriation of an additional $30 billion to solve the problems of our cities, but I knew that was unrealistic. Setting such an unattainable goal could easily have produced a negative reaction that in turn might have endangered funds for the many invaluable programs we had fought so long to establish and were trying so hard to strengthen and expand. . . . With the tax bill hanging by such slender threads, I knew that any call for increased spending would give my opponents the excuse they sought to call me a reckless spender and kill the tax bill. . . . It was a risk we could not afford.[70]

Thus the higher priority placed on a tax increase to support the Vietnam War and the fear that supporting the "unrealistic" recommendations of the commission report would jeopardize funding for existing Great Society programs convinced President Johnson to withhold enthusiastic public support from the commission.

3. President Johnson is reported to have felt that he, as President, could not give a blanket endorsement and strong public support to the commission report because of some of the rhetoric it contained. In particular the statement in the commission report, "Our Nation is moving toward two societies, one black, one white—separate and unequal,"[71] reportedly troubled the President. A White House aide remarked:

> He [Johnson] felt strongly about the self-fulfilling nature of prophesies like that. That was the reason for our ambiguous response to this report. I was at meetings where Johnson was praising the report in glowing terms. And I was at other meetings where he said, "Why the hell did they say that?"

4. President Johnson was also reported to have been miffed by the fact that the commission's criticism of past government policies and programs, including those of his Administration, was not combined with any positive words on the Administration's domestic program. Acknowledgement of the past efforts of the Administration, or at least crediting it with good faith, would have, of course, been personally satisfying to the President, and it would have been potentially useful in selling the Administration's domestic program to the Congress.

Thus the commission's influence on government policy was tied to the fortunes of President Johnson, which were at their nadir in the months after the commission issued its report. The commission failed to elicit strong symbolic support from the President because he judged that this would be harmful to his legislative goals, because he was concerned about the impact of the commission's rhetoric, and because he was displeased with the unrelieved criticism of his Administration.

The high volatility of all of the considerations outlined in this case and in this chapter as a whole tends to confirm the view expressed in chapters 2 and 7 that the White House sees each commission, when it is created, as a set of possibilities. Which, if any, of the possibilities is realized depends for the most part on the political context into which fortune casts the commission report and on the skill with which the commission does its job.

It should be clear that it is impossible to reduce the determinants of commission success to an equation having a finite number of variables with fixed weights and relations to each other, or even to codify a series of rules.

An overview of ninety-nine commissions created during a twenty-seven-year period and the nature of American politics in general permits only the general guidelines offered above. One generalization stands out in its certainty and importance, however: the vigorous support of a sympathetic and strong President is the most valuable asset a commission can have.

CHAPTER NINE

AN OVERVIEW

CONCLUSIONS

IT IS WIDELY BELIEVED that Presidents create commissions to avoid problems and that they respond to their reports with indifference and inaction. The evidence from this study of ninety-nine commissions operating over a period of more than twenty-five years under five Presidents suggests that this is not the case. Indeed, precisely the opposite conclusions are supported by the facts. During the years investigated, Presidents created commissions primarily to make independent policy analyses and to provide window dressing for presidential initiatives. Commission reports were usually not ignored by Presidents. Typically, they received presidential support and were very often an important contribution to proposed or implemented changes in federal policy. Commissions also had a broad and significant impact as educators of the general public, government officials, the professional community, and their own members.

Most commissions are formed because the President wants to act but is not sure how, or is not sure that important segments of public opinion, Congressional leadership, or Executive Branch agencies are ready to support him. Usually he can decide for himself when he wants to set up a commission. Occasionally, however, events force his hand—a crisis occurs in which demands for action are focused on the President and for which he has no ready response. In such circumstances, he sometimes sets up a commission partly to respond to the public demand that something be done and partly to help him formulate his own response.

In general, it has been the reports of these "crisis-induced" commissions that have received less than full presidential support—the National Advisory Commission on Civil Disorders (1967–68), the National Commission on the Causes and Prevention of Violence (1968–69), and the President's Commission on Campus Unrest (1970) come to mind. It is primarily upon the modest response of Presidents to the very visible reports of commissions such as these that the bad public image of commissions rests. Even here, however, the

193

194 PRESIDENTIAL ADVISORY COMMISSIONS

extent to which Presidents ignored the advice they got has been exaggerated, and the usefulness of these commissions as public educators has been overlooked.

Since the relatively meager presidential response to these commissions has been politically damaging to the Presidents and since it has cast a shadow over the general responsiveness of Presidents to commissions, it is important to understand that the reasons for the failure of these commissions may be inherent in the nature of crises and of commissions as institutions. When a crisis leads a President to appoint a commission that is supposed to tell him how to prevent urban riots, political assassinations, or campus disorders, he is almost certainly going to be disappointed. Such commissions will invariably not give him much practical advice on how to avoid such tragedies but will, instead, tell him that he ought to improve those basic social conditions that are seen to be the underlying causes of the crisis events. This almost inevitably happens, because of the kind of activist and socially conscious members and staff appointed to such commissions and because of the broad scope of the inquiry they undertake.

A President may indeed want to enlarge civil rights, end poverty, banish racism from America, instill in the nation a new sense of purpose, and do all of the other things recommended by these commissions. Their broad and sweeping recommendations, however, tend to lack both concreteness and political feasibility. The commissions call for basic changes in national direction and for large-scale new legislative programs and executive actions reminiscent of Franklin Roosevelt's "Hundred Days," but by the time of their reports the sense of crisis which spawned them has abated, if indeed it ever existed with sufficient intensity to support the implementation of their recommendations. The President will be operating in the normal context of gradual and incremental political change. The commission report will tell the President what in general should be done in the future, but it will tell him very little about what he can do next week or next month, and it will provide him with very little that can be incorporated in a legislative package that has any prospects for acceptance in the short run.

The consequences for the President are that although he may agree with the sentiments expressed by the commission, he will be politically capable of only a modest effort along the lines they have suggested and will have very little that is new and practical to draw upon from them. In a very short time he will be pilloried in the comparison between the broad social changes and programs recommended by the commission and the modest results he will be able to show, even with the best will and a maximum effort on his part (which is not likely to be forthcoming, since Presidents do not make large expenditures of their political capital in hopeless fights). The blame for any repetition of the crisis which led to the creation of the commission will also

be laid on the President's doorstep, since he "failed" to act on the recommendations of his own advisory commission.

These consequences of creating commissions in crises which have broad
social causes suggest that to avoid political wounds and to preserve the utility
of commissions as political devices, Presidents should not, in general, appoint
commissions to respond to such events. Commissions are best used in situations where a President *wants* to do something about the problem and at the
same time *can* do something about it.

If Presidents do create commissions to deal with crises, the models provided
by two successful crisis commissions, the President's Airport Commission
(1952) and the Commission on the Assassination of President Kennedy
(Warren Commission, 1963–64), should be followed. The President's Airport
Commission (1952) was called upon to deal with a crisis, airplanes crashing
into neighborhoods near airports, which could be handled without major
changes in existing institutions and through the application of available
technology and skills. This crisis did not raise fundamental social questions,
and the recommendations from the commission were within the power of the
President to carry out.

The crisis that led to the creation of the Warren Commission (1963–64),
the assassination of President Kennedy, could have been interpreted in terms
of the basic social questions that were raised after the assassinations of
Senator Robert Kennedy and Dr. Martin Luther King, Jr., in the case of the
National Commission on the Causes and Prevention of Violence (1968–69).
However, the Warren Commission's mandate and the selection of its members
and staff were designed to limit the commission to a specific fact-finding
task: to discover what happened in the assassination of the President and in
the subsequent murder of Lee Harvey Oswald. The Warren Commission's
report certainly was controversial. This was largely due, however, to acci-
dental features of the situation—the alleged assassin was dead and could not
be questioned, the commission had to prove a "negative fact" (that nobody
else killed the President), and there was a widespread public predisposition to
believe in conspiracies. Nevertheless, from the President's point of view, the
commission did not saddle him with recommendations for an unattainable
program and by implication place blame on him for any future assassinations
if he should fail to implement the program rapidly.

If a President is particularly altruistic and willing to bear intense political
heat in order to put before the nation an extensive social program that will
not reach fruition for a decade or two (for instance, that of President
Truman's Committee on Civil Rights, 1946–47, the recommendations of
which were implemented in the 1960's), then he can create commissions in
crisis having broad social causes. However, barring this circumstance, Presidents would be well advised either not to appoint commissions in crises or to

do so only if the crisis problem is most likely to call for recommendations that will be within the power of the President to implement; otherwise, to limit them to a narrow fact-finding role.

In addition to the determinations made about the presidential purposes for commissions and their responsiveness to commission recommendations, the other major finding of this study is that as institutions, commissions have unique characteristics which enable them to engage in policy analysis and to be persuasive salesmen of their recommendations. In the period studied, their talents were most frequently called upon when the problem confronted by the President required extensive rethinking which the federal bureaucracy was thought incapable of doing. This was particularly true when an increase in federal responsibility was contemplated.

The creation of commissions is usually suggested to the Presidents by policy entrepreneurs in and out of government who see them as mechanisms for achieving innovation and change. Though the President's authority to appoint commissions has not been seriously challenged, the Congress has attempted, thus far unsuccessfully, to exercise supervision over them through its power of the purse and the imposition of reporting requirements on the President.

Commissions are independent. Through the selection of the members and the formulation of commission mandates, Presidents establish only general boundaries and directions. Commissions are not directly or indirectly guided or manipulated by the White House during their tenure. White House liaison with commissions is to assist them in dealing with mechanical problems and to keep the White House informed on the timing and substance of the reports.

In their inquiries, commissions extensively and thoroughly canvass for available information and summarized the state of the art of dealing with the problems they were confronting. They make rational and informed judgments about problems of public policy. But they are not and cannot be rigorous social scientists. Decisive influence on commissions is exercised by the members and not by the staff. The commission members are active and effective in shaping the contents of commission reports. The great majority of commission decisions are reached by a unanimous consensus, often without the need for formal votes or for extensive bargaining among the members. Commissions generally claim that the problems they have examined are serious but not insoluble, and that they should be dealt with by federal government action that is innovative and reformist rather than radical.

The major determinant of commission success in seeing their recommendations implemented is their ability to elicit the support of the President. Thus, changes in administration or erosion of a President's ability to sponsor domestic innovation are major threats to the success of commissions. Support from Congress or the federal bureaucracy is less likely to be either forthcoming or effective. The process of Executive Branch review provides a substantial opportunity for those hostile to commissions to sidetrack their recommendations. The White House frequently short-circuits this process through its more active participation and through the use of task forces for reviewing reports. The prospects for commission success are also increased if there are other initiatives supporting the direction of their recommendations and if commissions produce unanimous reports of high quality, establish their scientific and political legitimacy, and avoid strident criticism of the administration and completely unrealistic recommendations.

COMMISSION REFORMS

Proposals for reforming and improving the operation of presidential commissions and for increasing the impact of their reports and recommendations have been made from time to time. The most recent extensive proposal has come from Senator Edward M. Kennedy (D–Mass.) as an outgrowth of hearings on presidential responsiveness to commissions, held by the Senate Judiciary Committee's Subcommittee on Administrative Practices and Procedures, which Senator Kennedy chairs. The Kennedy proposal, as outlined in the 1971 hearings, is the following. After a commission issues its final report:

1. The President designates a Cabinet member to be responsible for implementation of the report;

2. This Cabinet member issues a public report within one month of his implementation of the report;

3. After six months, the Cabinet member makes a more detailed public report indicating whether the report is accepted or rejected and why;

4. After a year, the commission reconvenes to question the Cabinet member on implementation of the report;

5. The Cabinet member issues a final report on implementation of the commission report after two years.

This proposed procedure is modeled after British practice in responding to the reports of Royal Commissions.[1]

This proposal is founded on the erroneous belief that Presidents have not in general been responsive to the reports of commissions. That belief is largely based on the modest presidential response to the recent highly visible crisis commissions, which was discussed above.

The obvious thrust of the Kennedy proposal is toward compelling, institutionalizing, and formalizing responses of the Executive Branch to the recommendations of commissions. It is unlikely that the Congress, by legislation, can compel the President to respond. There is most certainly no way to compel a President to respond in an other than perfunctory and *pro forma* manner if he finds that to be to his interest and convenience.

If a way is found to compel the President to respond to commissions, along the lines suggested by the Kennedy proposal, this is likely to be damaging to the institution of commissions. Such damage to commissions would be unfortunate, since commissions have played an effective and constructive role in innovation and reform in federal policies in the direction of making them more responsive to social needs.

The damage would be done because compelling the President to respond would increase the risk to him of embarrassment, criticism, or being put on a spot that he does not want to be on. The result is likely to be that:

1. Presidents would create only public commissions to deal with noncontroversial and safe subjects;

2. Presidents would place greater reliance on secret task forces and other nonpublic advisory mechanisms to deal with controversial and sensitive subjects;

3. If commissions were created to deal with sensitive subjects, the White House would be much more likely to pack them with safe members;

4. If commissions were created to deal with sensitive subjects, there would be a much greater temptation and incentive for the White House to attempt to control and guide them in their line of inquiry and their recommendations.

In short, the Kennedy proposal is either futile or harmful. It is also based on an inappropriate analogy between British and American politics. It is the special quality of English political institutions and English political life which enables the procedures embodied in the Kennedy proposal to work successfully there. To transplant English procedures for responding to royal commission reports to the United States would be to graft on the English form without its substance, since American politics is not and is unlikely to become like English politics in the ways that make the English procedures work successfully.

The 1972 Federal Advisory Committee Act, which in the Senate was a product of the Government Operations Committee rather than the Kennedy Judiciary Subcommittee, contains a provision which is a very modest version of the Kennedy proposal.[2] Section 6(b) of the Act states:

> Within one year after a Presidential advisory committee has submitted a public report to the President, the President or his delegate shall make a report to the Congress stating either his proposals for action or his reasons for inaction, with respect to the recommendations contained in the public report.

Thus far, this provision seems to fall into the category of a futile rather than a harmful congressional effort to compel Presidents to respond to the reports of their advisory commissions.

If the Congress is indeed serious about increasing the responsiveness of the federal government to the reports of presidential commissions, their efforts would be most fruitfully directed toward creating a mechanism in the Congress to evaluate more systematically and closely the reports of the major commissions, rather than tinkering with the Executive Branch. One idea for such a congressional mechanism is to have a permanent Joint Committee on Social Problems. This committee would have a membership either appointed in the way joint committees are appointed now or, to give it more stature, appointed by the Speaker of the House and the President *pro tem* of the Senate. The committee would have one unique element. Its membership would be renewed to respond to each major commission report. The membership would thus include those with skills, experience, and interests relevant to the specific commission report, and they would have the legitimacy and visibility of serving only to consider that one report.

To improve the operation of commissions, it has been suggested that a "permanent committee secretariat" be created to provide commissions with administrative (and perhaps professional) staff services.[3] This proposal also seems likely to be more damaging than helpful to commissions. While this "reform" would certainly result in commissions being more quickly and efficiently organized, it is also likely to result in less organizational flexibility for commissions, as organization becomes the responsibility of a permanent staff cadre. There would also be a danger that the independence of commissions would be compromised by removing from the members the power to choose their own staff, and by compelling them to accept a staff with which they might not feel personally or professionally compatible and which might have its own bureaucratic point of view (for example, that expenditures should be held down, if this staff were permanently housed in the Office of Management and Budget).

Mention was made earlier of the need for more regular and secure means to finance commissions, and of the danger of having the same people repeat as members of more than one commission.[4]

In the foreseeable future, Presidents are likely to need expert policy analysis independent of the federal bureaucracy, and support for domestic policies by prestigious members of the public having recognized competence and representing important constituencies. Thus commissions as advisory mechanisms that uniquely combine the capacities for analysis and persuasion will remain a prominent feature of presidential policy making, as a proven technique to facilitate and stimulate presidential action. Writing in 1949, Clinton Rossiter expressed the judgment that the practice of creating presidential advisory commissions "would continue unabated."[5] At present, there appears to be no reason to disagree with him.

REFERENCE MATTER

INTERVIEWS AND INTERVIEWING

A MAJOR PORTION of the data for this study was gathered in personal interviews. Seventy-four interviews with sixty-five people were conducted, four by phone, the rest in person. Most were between a half hour and an hour in length. Those interviewed included thirty commission staff members. The executive directors of twelve commissions were among the commission staff interviewed, and almost all of the other commission staff interviewed were senior professional staff members. Twelve commission members, who served on commissions a total of twenty-six times, were interviewed. The commission staff and the commission members interviewed served on thirty-four different commissions. Eighteen White House staff members, including at least three from each of the five administrations, were also interviewed. A number of others who were neither commission staff, commission members, or White House staff were also interviewed because of their knowledge of specific commissions or of the topic in general.

A set of general questions reflecting the major topics covered in this study was used as the basis for the interviews. The questions were tailored, of course, to fit the subject of the interview. For example, the interviews with White House staff members concentrated on the topics of presidential purposes, the process of deciding to create a commission, appointing commission members, White House liaison with commissions, and the responses to commission reports. For each interview a set of question relating to the unique, interesting, or significant aspects of the particular commission or of the interviewee's role was also prepared. An attempt was made, usually successfully, to make the interviews more like conversations than interrogations. Therefore the prepared questions were often not followed closely, and they served more as preparation for the interview than as a format for it. In general, the wisdom and guidance on interviewing techniques of Professor James Q. Wilson of Harvard University and of Lewis A. Dexter in *Elite and*

203

Specialized Interviewing (Evanston, Ill.: Northwestern University Press, 1970) were relied on.

All of the interviews were conducted on an off-the-record basis. Notes were taken during the interviews, and the conversations were reconstructed as fully as possible as soon as possible afterward.

PRESIDENTIAL ADVISORY COMMISSIONS

TRUMAN ADMINISTRATION (April 12, 1945–Jan. 20, 1953)

1 President's Committee on Integration of the Medical Services of the Government; announced by the President Dec. 12, 1945; report released June 18, 1946; Harold W. Dodds, Chairman; *Report to the President of the United States by the Committee on Integration of the Medical Services of the Government* (press release, June 18, 1946, 9 pp.).

2 National Commission on Higher Education; letter from the President July 13, 1946; report transmitted Dec. 11, 1947; George F. Zook, Chairman; *Higher Education for American Democracy*, 6 vols. (Washington, D.C.: Government Printing Office, 1947).

3 President's Advisory Commission on Universal Training; White House announcement Nov. 20, 1946; report dated June 1, 1947; Karl T. Compton, Chairman; *Program for National Security* (Washington, D.C.: Government Printing Office, 1947).

4 President's Committee on Civil Rights; Executive Order No. 9808, Dec. 5, 1947; report released Oct. 29, 1947; Charles E. Wilson, Chairman; *To Secure These Rights* (Washington, D.C.: Government Printing Office, 1947).

5 Advisory Committee on the Merchant Marine; Letter to the members March 11, 1947; report made public Nov. 15, 1947; K. T. Keller, Chairman; *Report of the President's Advisory Committee on Merchant Marine* (Washington, D.C.: Government Printing Office, 1947).

6 Special Board of Inquiry for Air Safety; letter appointing members, June 15, 1947; final report dated Dec. 29, 1947; James M. Landis, Chairman; *Report to the President of the U.S.* (Washington, D.C.: Government Printing Office, 1947).

7 President's Committee on Foreign Aid; press release June 22, 1947; report dated Nov. 7, 1947; W. Averell Harriman, Chairman; *European Recovery and American Aid* (Washington, D.C.: Government Printing Office, 1947).

8 Air Policy Commission; letter appointing members, July 18, 1947; report made public Jan. 13, 1948; Thomas K. Finletter, Chairman; *Survival in the Air Age* (Washington, D.C.: Government Printing Office, 1948).

9 President's Water Resources Policy Commission; Executive Order No. 10095, Jan. 3, 1950; report dated Dec. 11, 1950; Morris L. Cooke, Chairman; *A Water Policy for the American People, General Report* (Washington, D.C.: Government Printing Office, 1950).

10 President's Communications Policy Board; Executive Order No. 10110, Feb. 17, 1950; report dated Feb. 16, 1951; Irvin Stewart, Chairman; *Telecommunications, Program for Progress* (Washington, D.C.: Government Printing Office, 1951).

11 President's Commission on Migratory Labor; Executive Order No. 10129, June 3, 1950; report dated March 26, 1951; Maurice T. Van Hecke, Chairman; *Migratory Labor in American Agriculture* (Washington, D.C.: Government Printing Office, 1951).

12 Committee to Review Veterans Hospitals; presidential statement June 5, 1950; report transmitted Sept. 22, 1950; Howard A. Rusk, Chairman; *Report to the President on Veterans' Medical Services* (Washington, D.C.: Government Printing Office, 1950).

13 President's Materials Policy Commission; letter to the Chairman Jan. 22, 1951; report dated June 2, 1952; William S. Paley, Chairman; *Resources For Freedom: A Report to the President,* 5 vols. (Washington, D.C.: Government Printing Office, 1952).

14 President's Commission on the Health Needs of the Nation; Executive Order No. 10317, Dec. 29, 1951; report released Dec. 18, 1952; Paul B. Magnuson, Chairman; *Building America's Health,* 5 vols. (Washington, D.C.: Government Printing Office, 1952).

15 Missouri Basin Survey Commission; Executive Order No. 10318, Jan. 3, 1952; report dated Jan. 12, 1953; James E. Lawrence, Chairman; *Missouri, Land and Water* (Washington, D.C.: Government Printing Office, 1953).

16 President's Airport Commission; letter to Chairman Feb. 20, 1952; report dated May 16, 1952; James H. Doolittle, Chairman; *The Airport and Its Neighbors* (Washington, D.C.: Government Printing Office, 1952).

17 President's Commission on Immigration and Naturalization; Executive Order No. 10392, Sept. 4, 1952; report released Jan. 1, 1953; Philip

B. Perlman, Chairman; *Whom We Shall Welcome* (Washington, D.C.: Government Printing Office, 1952).

EISENHOWER ADMINISTRATION (Jan. 20, 1953–Jan. 20, 1961)

18 President's Committee on International Information Activities; statement by the President Jan. 26, 1953; report released July 8, 1953; William H. Jackson, Chairman; summary of report appears as White House press release, July 8, 1953 and also in *Department of State Bulletin*, vol. 29 (July 29, 1953).

19 Advisory Committee on Government Housing Policies and Programs; Executive Order No. 10486, Sept. 12, 1953; report issued Dec., 1953; Albert M. Cole, Chairman; *Recommendations and Report* (Washington, D.C.: Government Printing Office, 1953).

20 President's Advisory Committee on a National Highway Program; White House announcement Aug. 7, 1954; report dated Jan., 1955; Lucius D. Clay, Chairman; *Ten-year National Highway Program* (Washington, D.C.: Government Printing Office, 1955).

21 President's Commission on Veterans' Pensions; Executive Order No. 10588, Jan. 14, 1955; report dated April, 1956; Omar N. Bradley, Chairman; *Findings and Recommendations, Veterans' Benefits in the United States* (Washington, D.C.: Government Printing Office, 1956).

22 President's Committee on Education Beyond High School; PL 84-813, July 26, 1956; final report dated July, 1957; Devereux C. Josephs, Chairman; *Second Report to the President* (Washington, D.C.: Government Printing Office, 1957). This was the final report of the committee.

23 President's Citizen Advisers on the Mutual Security Program; letter from the President Sept. 22, 1956; report dated March 1, 1957; Benjamin Fairless, Chairman; *Report to the President by the President's Citizen Advisers on the Mutual Security Program* (Washington, D.C.: Government Printing Office, 1957).

24 President's Committee to Study the United States Military Assistance Program; letter from the President Nov. 24, 1958; final report transmitted to Congress Aug. 20, 1959; William H. Draper, Jr., Chairman; *Composite Report of the President's Committee to Study Military Assistance Program,* 2 vols. (Washington, D.C.: Government Printing Office, 1959).

25 President's Commission on a World's Fair; appointed by the President Oct. 10, 1959; report issued Oct. 29, 1959; Harry A. Bullis, Chairman; report was issued as a White House press release Oct. 29, 1959.

26 Commission on National Goals; White House announcement Feb. 3,

1960; report released Nov. 16, 1960; Henry M. Wriston, Chairman; *Goals for Americans* (Englewood Cliffs, N.J.: Prentice-Hall, 1960).

KENNEDY ADMINISTRATION (Jan. 20, 1961–Nov. 22, 1963)

27 Panel on Mental Retardation; appointed by the President Oct. 17, 1961; report released Oct. 16, 1962; Leonard W. Mayo, Chairman; *A Proposed Program for National Action to Combat Mental Retardation* (Washington, D.C.: Government Printing Office, 1962).

28 President's Commission on Campaign Costs; Executive Order No. 10974, Nov. 8, 1961; report made public April 18, 1962; Alexander Heard, Chairman; *Financing Presidential Campaigns* (Washington, D.C.: Government Printing Office, 1962).

29 President's Committee to Appraise Employment and Unemployment Statistics; statement by the President Nov. 10, 1961; report dated Sept. 27, 1962; Robert A. Gordon, Chairman; *Measuring Employment and Unemployment* (Washington, D.C.: Government Printing Office, 1962).

30 President's Commission on the Status of Women; Executive Order No. 10980, Dec. 14, 1961; final report presented to the President Oct. 11, 1962; Eleanor Roosevelt, Chairman; *American Women* (Washington, D.C.: Government Printing Office, 1963).

31 President's Advisory Panel on Federal Salary Systems; White House announcement Dec. 28, 1961; final report dated Aug. 16, 1963; Clarence B. Randall, Chairman; *Final Report* (Washington, D.C.: Government Printing Office, 1963).

32 President's Council on Pennsylvania Avenue; appointed by the President June 1, 1962; report made public April, 1964; Nathaniel A. Owings, Chairman; *Pennsylvania Avenue* (Washington, D.C.: Government Printing Office, 1964).

33 Committee on Equal Opportunity in the Armed Forces; letter from the President June 24, 1962; final report released Dec. 28, 1964; Gerhard A. Gesell, Chairman; *Initial Report: Equality of Treatment and Opportunity for Negro Military Personnel Stationed within the U.S.* (mimeographed, 1963); *Final Report: Military Personnel Stationed Overseas and Participation in the National Guard* (mimeographed, 1964).

34 President's Committee to Strengthen the Security of the Free World; White House announcement Dec. 10, 1962; report released March 22, 1963; Lucius D. Clay, Chairman; *The Scope and Distribution of U.S. Military and Economic Assistance* (Washington, D.C.: Government Printing Office, 1963).

35 President's Advisory Commission on Narcotic and Drug Abuse; Executive

Order No. 11076, Jan. 15, 1963; final report released Jan. 24, 1964; E. Barrett Prettyman, Chairman; *Final Report* (Washington, D.C.: Government Printing Office, 1963).

36 President's Commission on Registration and Voting Participation; Executive Order No. 11100, March 30, 1963; final report released Dec., 1963; Richard M. Scammon, Chairman; *Report of the President's Commission on Registration and Voting Participation* (Washington, D.C.: Government Printing Office, 1963).

37 Committee on Public Higher Education in the District of Columbia; White House announcement Sept. 23, 1963; report released June, 1964; Francis S. Chase, Chairman; *Report to the President, Public Higher Education in the District of Columbia* (Washington, D.C.: Government Printing Office, 1964).

38 Task Force to Promote Overseas Sale of Securities of U.S. Companies; White House announcement Oct. 2, 1963; report dated April 27, 1964; Henry H. Fowler, Chairman; *Report to the President of the U.S.* (Washington, D.C.: Government Printing Office, 1964).

JOHNSON ADMINISTRATION (Nov. 22, 1963–Jan. 20, 1969)

39 President's Commission on the Assassination of President Kennedy; Executive Order No. 11130, Nov. 29, 1963; report released Sept., 1964; Earl Warren, Chairman; *Report* (Washington, D.C.: Government Printing Office, 1964).

40 Commission on Heart Disease, Cancer and Stroke; announced by the President March 7, 1964; report presented to the President Dec. 9, 1964; Michael E. DeBakey, Chairman; *National Program to Conquer Heart Disease, Cancer, and Stroke* (Washington, D.C.: Government Printing Office, 1965).

41 National Commission on Technology, Automation and Economic Progress; PL 88–444, Aug. 19, 1964; report transmitted to the President Jan. 29, 1966; Howard R. Bowen, Chairman; *Technology and the American Economy* (Washington, D.C.: Government Printing Office, 1966).

42 President's Special Panel on Federal Salaries; announced by the President Jan. 28, 1965; report dated April 15, 1965; Marion B. Folson, Chairman; *Report* (House Doc. 170, 89th Cong., 1st Sess., 1965).

43 Special Presidential Committee on U.S. Trade Relation with Eastern European Countries and the U.S.S.R.; announced by the President Feb. 16, 1965; report released May 6, 1965; J. Irwin Miller, Chairman; *Report to the President* (Washington, D.C.: Government Printing Office, 1965).

44 President's Commission on the Patent System; Executive Order No.

11215, April 8, 1965; report dated Nov. 17, 1966; Harry H. Ranson and Simon H. Rifkind, Co-chairmen; *To Promote Progress of Useful Arts in an Age of Exploding Technology* (Washington, D.C.: Government Printing Office, 1966).

45 President's Commission on Crime in the District of Columbia; Executive Order No. 11234, July 16, 1965; report dated Dec. 15, 1966; Herbert J. Miller, Chairman; *Report of the President's Commission on Crime in the District of Columbia* (Washington, D.C.: Government Printing Office, 1966).

46 President's Commission on Law Enforcement and Administration of Justice; Executive Order No. 11236, July 23, 1965; report dated Feb., 1967; Nicholas Katzenbach, Chairman; *The Challenge of Crime in a Free Society* (Washington, D.C.: Government Printing Office, 1967).

47 National Advisory Commission on Food and Fiber; Executive Order No. 11256, Nov. 4, 1965; report dated July, 1967; Sherwood O. Berg, Chairman; *Food and Fiber for the Future* (Washington, D.C.: Government Printing Office, 1967).

48 National Advisory Commission on Health Manpower; Executive Order No. 11279, May 7, 1966; report dated Nov. 30, 1967; J. Irwin Miller, Chairman; *Report of the National Advisory Commission on Health Manpower* (Washington, D.C.: Government Printing Office, 1967).

49 Presidential Task Force on Career Advancement; announced by the President May 11, 1966; report released spring 1967; John W. Macy, Jr., Chairman; *Investment for Tomorrow* (Washington, D.C.: Government Printing Office, 1967).

50 Commission on Marine Science, Engineering and Resources; PL 89-454, June 17, 1966; report submitted Jan. 11, 1969; Julius A. Stratton, Chairman; *Our Nation and the Sea: Plan for National Action* (Washington, D.C.: Government Printing Office, 1969).

51 National Advisory Commission on Selective Service; Executive Order No. 11289, July 2, 1966; report transmitted to the President Feb., 1967; Burké Marshall, Chairman; *In Pursuit of Equity: Who Serves When Not All Serve?* (Washington, D.C.: Government Printing Office, 1967).

52 National Advisory Commission on Libraries: Executive Order No. 11301, Sept. 2, 1966; report transmitted to the President Oct. 3, 1968; Douglas M. Knight, Chairman; *Library Services for the Nation's Needs: Toward Fulfillment of a National Policy* (Bethesda, Md.: Educational Resources Information Center, 1968).

53 National Advisory Commission on Rural Poverty; Executive Order No. 11306, Sept. 27, 1966; report dated Sept., 1967; Edward T. Breathitt, Chairman; *The People Left Behind* (Washington, D.C.: Government Printing Office, 1967).

54 National Commission on Urban Problems; announced by the President, acting under authority of Sec. 301 of Housing and Urban Development Act of 1965, PL 89-117, Jan. 12, 1967; report issued Dec., 1968; Paul H. Douglas, Chairman; *Building the American City* (Washington, D.C.: Government Printing Office, 1968).

55 President's Commission on Budget Concepts; announced by the President March 3, 1967; report dated Oct. 10, 1967; David M. Kennedy, Chairman; *Report of the President's Commission on Budget Concepts* (Washington, D.C.: Government Printing Office, 1967).

56 President's Commission on Postal Organization; Executive Order No. 11341, April 8, 1967; report dated June, 1968; Frederick R. Kappel, Chairman; *Towards Postal Excellence* (Washington, D.C.: Government Printing Office, 1968).

57 President's Committee on Urban Housing; presidential directive June 3, 1967; report issued Jan. 1, 1969; Edgar F. Kaiser, Chairman; *A Decent Home* (Washington, D.C.: Government Printing Office, 1969).

*58 National Advisory Commission on Civil Disorders; Executive Order No. 11365, July 29, 1967; report dated March 1, 1968; Otto Kerner, Chairman; *Report of the National Advisory Commission on Civil Disorders* (Washington, D.C.: Government Printing Office, 1968).

59 Commission on Obscenity and Pronography; PL 90-100, Oct. 3, 1967; report released Sept. 30, 1970; William D. Lockhart, Chairman; *The Report of the Commission on Obscenity and Pornography* (Washington, D.C.: Government Printing Office, 1970).

60 National Advisory Commission on Health Facilities; appointed by the President Oct. 6, 1967; report issued Dec., 1968; Boisfeuillet Jones, Chairman; *Report to the President* (Washington, D.C.: Government Printing Office, 1968).

61 Industry-Government Special Task Force on Travel; appointed by the President Nov. 16, 1967; report issued Feb., 1968; Robert M. Mc-Kinney, Chairman; *Report to the President of the U.S.* (Washington, D.C.: Government Printing Office, 1968).

62 National Commission on Product Safety; PL 90-146, Nov. 20, 1967; report dated June, 1970; Arnold Elkind, Chairman; *Final Report of the National Commission on Product Safety* (Washington, D.C.: Government Printing Office, 1970).

63 President's Commission on Income Maintenance Programs; presidential directive Jan. 2, 1968; report dated Nov. 12, 1969; Ben W. Heine-

*The President's Advisory Panel on Insurance in Riot-Affected Areas (announced August 10, 1967) is not listed as a separate commission, since it was a specialized sub-unit of the National Advisory Commission on Civil Disorders and its findings and recommendations were incorporated in the report of that commission, as well as being issued separately.

man, Chairman; *Poverty Amid Plenty: The American Paradox* (Washington, D.C.: Government Printing Office, 1969).

64 President's Commission for the Observance of Human Rights Year, 1968; Executive Order No. 11394, Jan. 20, 1968; final report transmitted to the President April 29, 1969; W. Averell Harriman, Chairman; *To Continue Action for Human Rights, Final Report* (Washington, D.C.: Government Printing Office, 1969).

65 National Commission on the Causes and Prevention of Violence; Executive Order No. 11412, June 10, 1968; report transmitted to the President Dec. 10, 1969; Milton Eisenhower, Chairman; *To Establish Justice, To Insure Domestic Tranquility* (Washington, D.C.: Government Printing Office, 1969).

66 Committee on Population and Family Planning; announced by the President July 16, 1968; report transmitted to the President Jan. 7, 1969; Wilbur J. Cohen and John D. Rockefeller, III, Co-chairmen; *Population and Family Planning: Transition from Concern to Action* (Washington, D.C.: Government Printing Office, 1968).

NIXON ADMINISTRATION, FIRST TERM (Jan. 20, 1969–Jan. 20, 1973)

67 President's Commission on an All-Volunteer Armed Force; announced by the President March 27, 1969; report submitted Feb. 20, 1970; Thomas S. Gates, Chairman; *Report* (Washington, D.C.: Government Printing Office, 1970).

68 President's Advisory Council on Executive Organization; announced by the President April 5, 1969; termination announced May 7, 1971; Roy Ash, Chairman; *Memoranda for the President of the United States: Establishment of a Department of Natural Resources; Organization for Social and Economic Programs* (160 pp., processed Feb. 5, 1971); *A New Regulatory Framework* (Washington, D.C.: Government Printing Office, 1971).

69 Presidential Task Force on International Development; announced in presidential message to Congress May 28, 1969; report submitted March 4, 1970; Rudolph A. Peterson, Chairman; *U.S. Foreign Assistance in the 1970s: A New Approach* (Washington, D.C.: Government Printing Office, 1970).

70 President's Task Force on Business Taxation; announced by the President Sept. 22, 1969; report dated Sept., 1970; John H. Alexander, Chairman; *Business Taxation* (Washington, D.C.: Government Printing Office, 1970).

71 President's Task Force on Improving the Prospects of Small Business; announced by the President Sept. 24, 1969; report presented Dec. 1,

1969; J. Wilson Newman, Chairman; *Improving the Prospects of Small Business* (Washington, D.C.: Government Printing Office, 1970).

72 President's Task Force on Model Cities; announced by the President Sept. 24, 1969; report transmitted Dec. 16, 1969; Edward C. Banfield, Chairman; *Model Cities: A Step Towards the New Federalism* (Washington, D.C.: Government Printing Office, 1970).

73 President's Task Force on Rural Development; announced by the President Sept. 29, 1969; report transmitted Jan. 12, 1970; Mrs. Haven Smith, Chairman; *A New Life for the Country* (Washington, D.C.: Government Printing Office, 1970).

74 President's Task Force on Women's Rights and Responsibilities; announced by the President Oct. 1, 1969; report submitted Dec. 15, 1969; Virginia R. Allan, Chairman; *A Matter of Simple Justice* (Washington, D.C.: Government Printing Office, 1970).

75 President's Task Force on Higher Education; announced by the President Oct. 6, 1969; report submitted Jan. 15, 1970; James M. Hester, Chairman; *Priorities in Higher Education* (Washington, D.C.: Government Printing Office, 1970).

76 President's Task Force on Science Policy; announced by the President Oct. 6, 1969; report presented Dec. 10, 1969; Ruben F. Mettler, Chairman; *Science and Technology; Tools for Progress* (Washington, D.C.: Government Printing Office, 1970).

77 President's Task Force on Low Income Housing; announced by the President Oct. 10, 1969; report submitted Jan. 15, 1970; Raymond J. Saulnier, Chairman; *Toward Better Housing for Low Income Families* (Washington, D.C.: Government Printing Office, 1970).

78 President's Task Force on the Aging; announced by the President Oct. 10, 1969; report presented Feb. 20, 1970; Garson Meyer, Chairman; *Toward a Brighter Future for the Elderly* (Washington, D.C.: Government Printing Office, 1970).

79 President's Task Force on Oceanography; announced by the President Oct. 10, 1969; report submitted Dec. 18, 1969; James H. Wakelin, Jr., Chairman; *Mobilizing to Use the Seas* (Washington, D.C.: Government Printing Office, 1970).

80 President's Task Force on the Physically Handicapped; announced by the President Oct. 15, 1969; report transmitted Feb. 10, 1970; Ralph E. DeForest, Chairman; *A National Effort for the Physically Handicapped* (Washington, D.C.: Government Printing Office, 1970).

81 President's Task Force on Economic Growth; announced by the President Oct. 15, 1969; report submitted Jan. 9, 1970; Neil H. Jacoby,

Chairman; *Policies for American Economic Progress in the Seventies* (Washington, D.C.: Government Printing Office, 1970).

82 President's Task Force on Prisoner Rehabilitation; announced by the President Oct. 16, 1969; report submitted Jan. 27, 1970; John M. Briley, Chairman; *The Criminal Offender–What Should Be Done?* (Washington, D.C.: Government Printing Office, 1970).

83 President's Task Force on Urban Renewal; announced by the President Oct. 17, 1969; report submitted Jan. 12, 1970; Miles L. Colean, Chairman; *Urban Renewal: One Tool Among Many* (Washington, D.C.: Government Printing Office, 1970).

84 President's Task Force on Highway Safety; announced by the President Oct. 23, 1969; report submitted Dec., 1969; Franklin M. Kreml, Chairman; *Mobility Without Mayhem* (Washington, D.C.: Government Printing Office, 1970).

85 President's Task Force on Air Pollution; announced by the President Nov. 18, 1969; report submitted June 9, 1970; Arie Jan Haagen-Smit, Chairman; *Cleaner Air for the Nation* (Washington, D.C.: Government Printing Office, 1970).

86 President's Task Force on the Mentally Handicapped; announced by the President Dec. 18, 1969; report submitted May 28, 1970; Jeannette Rockefeller, Chairman; *Action Against Mental Disability* (Washington, D.C.: Government Printing Office, 1970).

87 President's Commission on School Finance; Executive Order No. 11513, March 3, 1970; final report submitted March 3, 1972; Neil H. McElroy, Chairman; *Schools, People, & Money: The Need for Educational Reform* (Washington, D.C.: Government Printing Office, 1972).

*88 President's Panel on Nonpublic Education; announced by the President April 21, 1970; report submitted April 14, 1972; Clarence Walton, Chairman; *Nonpublic Education and the Public Good* (Washington, D.C.: Government Printing Office, 1972).

89 Commission on International Trade and Investment Policy; appointment of members announced by the President May 21, 1970; report dated July, 1971; Albert L. Williams, Chairman; *United States International Economic Policy in an Interdependent World* (Washington, D.C.: Government Printing Office, 1971).

90 President's Commission on Campus Unrest; Executive Order of June 13,

---

*Although the President's Panel on Nonpublic Education was technically a sub-unit of the President's Commission on School Finance, it is listed as a separate commission because its findings and recommendations were issued separately and were neither approved by the parent commission nor incorporated in its report.

1970; report transmitted Sept. 26, 1970; William W. Scranton, Chairman; *Report* (Washington, D.C.: Government Printing Office, 1970).

91 President's Commission on Financial Structure and Regulation; appointment of members announced by the President June 16, 1970; report submitted Dec. 22, 1972; Reed O. Hunt, Chairman; *Report* (Washington, D.C.: Government Printing Office, 1972).

92 President's Commission for the Observance of the Twenty-fifth Anniversary of the United Nations; Executive Order No. 11546, July 9, 1970; report submitted April 26, 1971; Henry Cabot Lodge, Chairman; *Report* (Washington, D.C.: Government Printing Office, 1971).

93 President's Commission on Federal Statistics; announced by the President August 12, 1970; report submitted Sept. 25, 1971; W. Allen Wallis, Chairman; *Federal Statistics* (Washington, D.C.: Government Printing Office, 1971).

94 Commission on American Shipbuilding; PL 91-464, October 21, 1970; report submitted Oct. 19, 1973; Albert G. Mumma, Chairman; *Report* (Washington, D.C.: Government Printing Office, 1973).

95 National Commission on Materials Policy; PL 91-512, Oct. 26, 1970; report transmitted June 27, 1973; Jerome L. Klaff, Chairman; *Material Needs and the Environment Today and Tomorrow* (Washington, D.C.: Government Printing Office, 1973).

96 National Commission on State Workmen's Compensation Laws; PL 91-596, Dec. 29, 1970; report submitted July 31, 1972; John F. Burton, Jr., Chairman; *Report* (Washington, D.C.: Government Printing Office, 1972).

97 President's Advisory Panel on Timber and the Environment; appointment of members announced by the President Sept. 2, 1971; report submitted April 30, 1973; Fred A. Seaton, Chairman; *Report* (Washington, D.C.: Government Printing Office, 1973).

98 President's Committee on Health Education; appointment of chairman announced Dec. 29, 1971; report presented Sept. 25, 1973; R. Heath Larry, Chairman; *Report* (Washington, D.C.: Department of Health, Education, and Welfare; Health Services and Mental Health Administration, n.d.).

99 Presidential Study Commission on International Radio Broadcasting; announced by the President August 10, 1972; report submitted Feb. 5, 1973; Milton S. Eisenhower, Chairman; *The Right to Know* (Washington, D.C.: Government Printing Office, 1973).

RESPONSES TO THE RECOMMENDATIONS OF COMMISSIONS

1 President's Committee on Integration of the Medical Services of the Government (1945-46)

Statement, *"Letter to the Director Bureau of the Budget Concerning Integration of Federal Medical Services," White House press release, June 18, 1946, rejects one of the major recommendations and defers action on the second.

2 National Commission on Higher Education (1946-47)

Statement, "Address at Rollins Park College, Winter Park, Florida," March 8, 1949, *Truman Papers, 1949,* Item 51, p. 167, mentions broadening of higher education opportunities and federal scholarships.

Message (1), "Special Message to the Congress: The President's Economic Report," January 7, 1949, *Truman Papers, 1949,* Item 5, p. 26, mentions broadening of higher education opportunities and federal scholarships.

Proposed legislation (1), $1 million item requested in budget for studies, including one on "means of providing additional opportunities for capable young people who could not otherwise afford a college or a university education." "Annual Budget Message to the Congress: Fiscal Year 1950," January 10, 1949, *Truman Papers, 1949,* Item 8, p. 71.

Legislation (3), Housing Act of 1950, Title IV, "Housing for Educational Institutions," PL 81-475, 64 Stat. 77, authorizes grants-in-aid and loan fund for use by higher education institutions to construct student and faculty housing.

3 President's Advisory Commission on Universal Training (1946-47)

*Commission specifically mentioned

Message (2), *"Letter to the President of the Senate and to the Speaker of the House Transmitting Report of the Advisory Commission on Universal Training," June 4, 1947, *Truman Papers, 1947,* Item 106, p. 262.

Proposed legislation (3), *"Following June–July 1947 hearings, . . . the House Armed Services Committee July 26 reported a bill (HR 4278) to establish a National Security Training Corps along the lines proposed by the Compton Commission [President's Advisory Commission on Universal Training]. Congress recessed the same day . . . and no further action was taken on UMT in 1947." The Selective Service Act of 1948 did not include UMT, and the Universal Military Training and Service Act of 1951 provided only for drawing up a plan for UMT. *Congress and the Nation, 1945–64* (Washington, D.C.: Congressional Quarterly Service, 1965), pp. 250–66.

4 President's Committee on Civil Rights (1946–47)

Statement, *a) "Address in Harlem, New York, upon Receiving the Franklin Roosevelt Award," October 29, 1948, *Truman Papers, 1948,* Item 265, pp. 923–25.

*b) "Commencement Address at Howard University," June 13, 1952, *Truman Papers, 1952,* Item 169, pp. 420–24.

Message (2), *"Special Message to the Congress on Civil Rights," February 2, 1948, *Truman Papers, 1948,* Item 20, pp. 121–26.

Administrative action (1), a) special training for FBI agents in the civil rights field.

2) investigation by the Secretary of the Army of the status of civil rights in the Panama Canal Zone. Both of these administrative actions were announced in "Special Message to the Congress on Civil Rights," February 2, 1948, *Truman Papers, 1948,* Item 20, pp. 125–26.

Administrative action (3), a) Executive Order No. 9980, July 26, 1948, fair employment practices in the federal government.

b) Executive Order No. 9981, July 26, 1948, establishes President's Committee on Equality of Treatment in the Armed Forces.

c) Executive Order No. 10308, December 3, 1951, to obtain compliance with the nondiscrimination provisions of federal contracts and create Committee on Government Contract Compliance.

Legislation (1), PL 80-886, 62 Stat. 1231, July 2, 1948, deals with evacuation claims of Japanese-Americans.

5 Advisory Committee on the Merchant Marine (1947)

Statement, *a) "The President's News Conference on the Budget," January 10, 1948, *Truman Papers, 1948,* Item 4, p. 17.

b) "Statement by the President Making Public the Report of the Advisory Committee on Merchant Marine," November 15, 1947, *Truman Papers, 1947,* Item 223, pp. 491–92. These two statements imply a rejection by the President of a greatly expanded and accelerated shipbuilding program.

Message (2), *a) "Message to the Congress Transmitting Reorganization Plan 6 of 1949: United States Maritime Commission," June 20, 1949, *Truman Papers, 1949,* Item 133, pp. 319–21.

*b) "Special Message to the Congress Transmitting Reorganization Plan 21 of 1950," March 13, 1950, *Truman Papers, 1950,* Item 76, pp. 223–27; reorganization of the United States Maritime Commission.

Legislation (3), a) Reorganization Plan 6 of 1949, 63 Stat. 1069, effective August 20, 1949.

b) Reorganization Plan 21 of 1950, 64 Stat. 1273, effective May 24, 1950.

6 Special Board of Inquiry for Air Safety (1947)

Administrative action (3). The actions taken by the Civil Aeronautics Administration, Civil Aeronautics Board, and other federal agencies, in response to the large number of technical recommendations of the commission, are outlined in chapter 1 of Special Board of Inquiry on Air Safety, *Final Report to the President of the United States* (Washington, D.C.: Government Printing Office, 1947).

7 President's Committee on Foreign Aid (1947)

Statement, *"Statement by the President Making Public a Report 'European Recovery and American Aid,' " November 8, 1947, *Truman Papers, 1947,* Item 219, pp. 485–86.

Message (2), *"Special Message to the Congress on the Marshall Plan," December 19, 1947, *Truman Papers, 1947,* Item 238, pp. 515–29.

Legislation (3), Economic Cooperation Act of 1948, PL 80-472, 62 Stat. 137, Marshall Plan.

8 Air Policy Commission (1947–48)

Statement, *"Statement by the President upon Making Public the Report of the Air Policy Commission," January 13, 1948, *Truman Papers, 1948,* Item 7, p. 61.

Legislation (3). The Supplemental National Defense Appropriation Act, 1948, PL 80-547, 62 Stat. 258, added $3.2 billion to the fiscal 1949 budget to start a seventy-group Air Force program which was opposed by President Truman, who did, however, sign the Act. *Congress and the Nation, 1945–64,* pp. 251–53.

9 President's Water Resources Policy Commission (1950)

Statement, *a) "Statement by the President Making Public a Report by the Water Resources Policy Commission," December 17, 1950, *Truman Papers, 1950,* Item 306, p. 748.

*b) "Letter to Department and Agency Heads on the Report of the Water Resources Policy Commission," March 14, 1951, *Truman Papers, 1951,* Item 55, p. 185.

*c) "Address in Arkansas at the Dedication of the Norfolk and Bull Shoals Dams," July 2, 1952, *Truman Papers, 1952,* Item 194, pp. 459–60.

Message (1), *a) "Annual Budget Message to the Congress: Fiscal Year, 1952," January 5, 1951, *Truman Papers, 1951,* Item 13, p. 85.

*b) "Annual Budget Message to Congress: Fiscal Year, 1953," January 21, 1952, *Truman Papers, 1952,* Item 18, p. 89.

Message (2), *"Special Message to the Congress on the Nation's Land and Water Resources," January 19, 1953, *Truman Papers, 1952,* Item 388, pp. 1208–15.

Administrative action (3), Budget Circular No. A-47, December 31, 1952, criteria for water resources project design and evaluation.

10 President's Communications Policy Board (1950–51)

Administrative action (2), Telecommunications Planning Committee announced in a White House press release, August 28, 1952.

11 President's Commission on Migratory Labor (1950–51)

Statement, *"Statement by the President on Making Public the Report of the Commission on Migratory Labor," April 7, 1951, *Truman Papers, 1951,* Item 75, pp. 220–21.

Message (1) a) "Annual Budget Message to the Congress: Fiscal Year 1953," January 21, 1952, *Truman Papers, 1952,* Item 18, pp. 94–95.

*b) "Annual Budget Message to the Congress: Fiscal Year 1954," January 9, 1953, *Truman Papers, 1952,* Item 367, p. 1151.

Message (2) *"Special Message to the Congress on the Employment of Agricultural Workers from Mexico," July 13, 1951, *Truman Papers, 1951,* Item 154, pp. 389–393.

Proposed legislation (1), S. 3300 to establish Federal Committee on Migratory Labor not passed. *Congress and the Nation, 1945–64,* p. 749.

Administrative action (2), Department of Labor enforcement upgraded. "Annual Budget Message to the Congress: Fiscal Year 1953," January 21, 1952, *Truman Papers, 1952,* Item 18, pp. 94–95.

Legislation (3), PL 82-283, 66 Stat. 26, March 20, 1952, Anti-Wetback Law.

12 Committee to Review Veterans Hospitals (1950)

13 President's Materials Policy Commission (1951—52)

Statement, *a) "Letter in Response to Report of the President's Materials Policy Commission," June 23, 1952, *Truman Papers*, 1952, Item 179, pp. 438—39.

*b) "Statement by the President on the Report of the President's Materials Policy Commission," July 1, 1952, *Truman Papers, 1952*, Item 192, pp. 454—55.

*c) "Letter to Chairman, National Security Resources Board, Concerning the Report of the President's Materials Policy Commission," December 22, 1952, *Truman Papers, 1952*, Item 355, pp. 1096—97.

Message (2), *"Letter to the President of the Senate and to the Speaker of the House Transmitting Report of the President's Materials Policy Commission," July 1, 1952, *Truman Papers, 1952*, Item 192, pp. 455—56.

Administrative action (1). National Security Resources Board was directed "to undertake a continuing review of the entire materials situation" and to organize a review of the commission report. Budget Bureau was also directed to review the report. "Statement by the President on the Report of the President's Materials Policy Commission," July 1, 1952, *Truman Papers*, 1952, Item 191, pp. 454—55.

14 President's Commission on the Health Needs of the Nation (1951—52)

Statement, *"Statement by the President on the Report of the Commission on the Health Needs of the Nation," December 18, 1952, *Truman Papers, 1952*, Item 352, p. 1087.

Message (2), *"Special Message to the Congress Transmitting Volume One of the Report of the President's Commission on the Health Needs of the Nation," January 9, 1953, *Truman Papers, 1952*, Item 369, p. 1166.

15 Missouri Basin Survey Commission (1952—53)

Message (1), *"Annual Budget Message to the Congress: Fiscal Year 1954," January 9, 1953, *Truman Papers, 1952*, Item 367, pp. 1147—48.

16 President's Airport Commission (1952)

Statement, *"Letter to the Chairman, Air Coordinating Committee, Transmitting Report of the Airport Commission," June 5, 1952, *Truman Papers, 1952*, Item 155, pp. 399—400.

Message (1), "Annual Budget Message to the Congress: Fiscal Year 1954," January 9, 1953, *Truman Papers, 1952*, Item 367, p. 1144. Recommends new obligational authority for federal assistance for airport construction.

Administrative action (3). "On September 3, 1952, the White House issued a statement on the implementation of the Commission's recommendations. The statement noted that the Air Coordinating Committee had devised a plan for dividing up the many recommendations of the Doolittle Commission so that each phase of the problem could be dealt with by the agency concerned. The statement announced that the President had that day sent letters to the Secretary of Defense, the Secretary of Commerce, the Postmaster General, and the Chairman of the Civil Aeronautics Board asking them to begin immediately to place into effect the Commission's recommendations." "Letter to the Chairman, Air Coordinating Committee, Transmitting Report of the Airport Commission," June 5, 1952, *Truman Papers, 1952,* Item 155, p. 400 (note).

Legislation (2), Departments of State, Justice, and Commerce Appropriations Act, 1954, PL 83-195, 67 Stat. 367, August 5, 1953, includes a new appropriation for "planning and developing a national system of aids to air navigation and air traffice control." traffice control."

17 President's Commission on Immigration and Naturalization (1952–53)

Statement, *"Statement by the President on Report 'Whom We Shall Welcome' by Commission on Immigration and Naturalization," January 5, 1953, *Truman Papers, 1952,* Item 364, pp. 1112–13.

Message (1), *"Annual Budget Message to the Congress: Fiscal Year 1954," January 9, 1953, *Truman Papers, 1952,* Item 367, p. 1163.

Message (2), *"Special Message to the Congress Transmitting Report of the President's Commission on Immigration and Naturalization," January 13, 1953, *Truman Papers, 1952,* Item 373, pp. 1169–70.

18 President's Committee on International Information Activities (1953)

Statement, *"The President's News Conference of July 8, 1953," *Eisenhower Papers, 1953,* Item 128, p. 472.

Administrative action (3). a) "The Committee recommended, among other things, . . . the establishment within the National Security Council of an Operations Coordinating Board. Such a board was established on September 3, 1953, by Executive Order 10483." "The President's News Conference of July 8, 1953," *Eisenhower Papers, 1953,* Item 128, p. 472 (note).

b) "Directive Approved by the President for the Guidance of the United States Information Agency," October 28, 1953, *Eisenhower Papers, 1953,* Item 231, p. 728. A note states that the directive reflects "the concepts of the President's Committee on International Information Activities."

19 Advisory Committee on Government Housing Policies and Programs (1953)

Message (1), *"Annual Budget Message to the Congress: Fiscal Year

1955," January 21, 1954, *Eisenhower Papers, 1954,* Item 14, p. 146.

Message (2), *a) "Special Message to the Congress on Housing," January 25, 1954, *Eisenhower Papers, 1954,* Item 17, pp. 193–201.

    b) "Special Message to the Congress Transmitting Reorganization Plan 2 of 1954 Relating to the Reconstruction Finance Corporation," April 29, 1954, *Eisenhower Papers, 1954,* Item 95, p. 444.

Legislation (3), a) Housing Act of 1954, PL 83-560, 68 Stat. 590. See *Congress and the Nation, 1945–64,* p. 485.

    b) Reorganization Plan 2 of 1954, 68 Stat. 1280, Reconstruction Finance Corporation.

20 President's Advisory Committee on a National Highway Program (1954–55)

Statement, *a) "President's News Conference of May 4, 1955," *Eisenhower Papers, 1955,* Item 90, p. 465.

    *b) "President's News Conference of June 29, 1955," *Eisenhower Papers, 1955,* Item 146, p. 656.

    *c) "President's News Conference of August 4, 1955," *Eisenhower Papers, 1955,* Item 185, p. 765.

Message (1), *"Annual Budget Message to the Congress for Fiscal Year 1957," January 16, 1956, *Eisenhower Papers, 1956,* Item 12, p. 139.

Message (2), *"Special Message to the Congress Regarding a National Highway Program," February 22, 1955, *Eisenhower Papers, 1955,* Item 39, pp. 275–80.

Legislation (3), Federal Aid Highway Act of 1956, PL 84-627, 70 Stat. 374. This Act created the greatly expanded interstate highway system, but with a method of financing markedly different from that recommended by the committee and reluctantly supported by the President. See Ronald Kahn, "The Politics of Roads: National Highway Legislation in 1955–56" (Master's thesis, University of Chicago, 1967), pp. 88–90.

21 President's Commission on Veterans' Pensions (1955–56)

Statement, *"Letter to James A. Sheehan, Associate Editor, National Tribune, on the Government's Veterans Program," October 24, 1956, *Eisenhower Papers, 1956,* Item 267, pp. 1003–4.

Administrative action (1), "Our administrative recommendations led the V.A. to create an advisory council. It did not turn out to be what we wanted." Statement by a member of the commission staff.

Legislation (2), Servicemen's and Veterans' Survivor Benefits Act, PL 84-881, 70 Stat. 857, August 1, 1956.

Legislation (3), Veterans' Pension Act of 1959, PL 86-211, 73 Stat. 432, a needs pension with a sliding income scale. Also, in line with the wishes of the President and the recommendations of the commission, no service pension for World War I veterans was passed. See *Congress and the Nation, 1945–64*, pp. 1337–38 and 1351–55; and Gilbert Y. Steiner, *The State of Welfare* (Washington, D.C.: The Brookings Institution, 1971), chapter 7.

22 President's Committee on Education Beyond High School (1956–57)

Message (1), "Special Message to the Congress on Education," January 27, 1958, *Eisenhower Papers, 1958*, Item 24, p. 131.

Message (2), *"Special Message to the Congress on Federal Aid to Education," January 28, 1957, *Eisenhower Papers, 1957*, Item 19, pp. 91–92.

Proposed legislation (3). Senator Clark in 1958 introduced a bill for federal aid for college construction patterned on the recommendations of the committee. James L. Sundquist, *Politics and Policy: The Eisenhower, Kennedy, and Johnson Years* (Washington, D.C.: The Brookings Institution, 1968), p. 197.

Legislation (2), National Defense Education Act of 1958, PL 85-864, 72 Stat. 1580. The committee was only a minor part of the background of this Act. *Congress and the Nation, 1945–64*, pp. 1200, 1208.

23 President's Citizen Advisers on the Mutual Security Program (1956–57)

Statement, *a) "President's News Conference of March 7, 1957," *Eisenhower Papers*, 1957, Item 45, pp. 176, 185.

*b) "President's News Conference of March 13, 1957," *Eisenhower Papers, 1957*, Item 50, pp. 196–97.

Legislation (3), Mutual Security Act, 1957, PL 85-114, 71 Stat. 355, provided for longer authorization and more flexibility as recommended by the commission and the President.

24 President's Committee to Study the United States Military Assistance Program (1958–59)

Statement, *a) "Letter to William H. Draper, Jr., Regarding the Second Interim Report of the President's Committee to Study the U.S. Military Assistance Program," June 24, 1959, *Eisenhower Papers, 1959*, Item 137, pp. 474–75.

*b) "President's News Conference of July 8, 1959," *Eisenhower Papers, 1959*, Item 154, p. 513.

Message (2), *a) "Letter to the President of the Senate and to the Speaker of the House of Representatives on the Recommendations of the Committee to Study the U.S. Military Assistance Program," April 29, 1959, *Eisenhower Papers, 1959*, Item 90, pp. 355–57.

*b) "Letter to the President of the Senate and to the Speaker of the House of Representatives Transmitting Report 'The Organization and Administration of the Military Assistance Program,'" June 24, 1959, *Eisenhower Papers, 1959,* Item 136, pp. 473–74.

*c) "Letter to the President of the Senate and to the Speaker of the House of Representatives Transmitting Report 'Economic Assistance: Programs and Administration,'" July 23, 1959, *Eisenhower Papers,* 1959, Item 170, pp. 548–49.

*d) "Letter to the President of the Senate and to the Speaker of the House of Representatives Transmitting the Final Report of the President's Committee to Study the U.S. Military Assistance Program," August 20, 1959, *Eisenhower Papers, 1959,* Item 183, pp. 587–88.

Administrative action (2), Some administrative changes were made in the assistance program in line with the recommendations of the committee. "Letter to William H. Draper, Jr., Regarding Second Interim Report of the President's Committee to Study the U.S. Military Assistance Program," June 24, 1959, *Eisenhower Papers, 1959,* Item 137, pp. 474–75; and "Letter to the President of the Senate and to the Speaker of the House of Representatives Transmitting the Final Report of the President's Committee to Study the U.S. Military Assitance Program," August 20, 1959, *Eisenhower Papers, 1959,* Item 183, pp. 587–88.

25 President's Commission on a World's Fair (1959)

Administrative action (3). The President accepted the recommendation of the commission that New York be the site preferred by the federal government for the World's Fair. Charles Sawyer, *Concerns of a Conservative Democrat* (Carbondale: University of Southern Illinois Press, 1968), pp. 317–20. Sawyer was a member of the commission.

26 Commission on National Goals (1960)

27 Panel on Mental Retardation (1961–62)

Statement, *a) Letter to State Governors Announcing a Conference on Mental Retardation," July 24, 1963, *Kennedy Papers, 1963,* Item 313, p. 598.

*b) "Letter to Dr. Stafford L. Warren at the Opening of the White House Conference on Mental Retardation," September 19, 1963, *Kennedy Papers, 1963,* Item 364, p. 692.

Message (2), *"Special Message to the Congress on Mental Illness and Mental Retardation," February 5, 1963, *Kennedy Papers, 1963,* Item 50, pp. 132–33.

Administrative action (2), White House Conference on Mental Retardation, September 19–20, 1963.

Legislation (3), a) Maternal and Child Health and Mental Retardation Planning Act, PL 88-156, 77 Stat. 273, October 24, 1963.

b) Act for the Construction of Mental Retardation Facilities and Community Mental Health Centers, PL 88-164, 77 Stat. 282, October 31, 1963.

28 President's Commission on Campaign Costs (1961–62)

Statement, *"President's News Conference of April 18, 1962," *Kennedy Papers, 1962,* Item 152, p. 332.

Message (2), *a) "Letter to the President of the Senate and to the Speaker of the House Transmitting Bills to Carry Out Recommendations of the Commission on Campaign Costs," May 29, 1962, *Kennedy Papers, 1962,* Item 219, pp. 444–46.

*b) "Letter to the President of the Senate and to the Speaker of the House Transmitting Bills to Carry Out Recommendations of the Commission on Campaign Costs," April 30, 1963, *Kennedy Papers, 1963,* Item 151, pp. 356–58.

Proposed legislation (3), A system of tax incentives for political contributions, repeal of federal limits on receipts and expenditures of interstate political committees and on the amounts individuals can contribute to such committees, a system of disclosure and publicity of campaign contributions, a Registry of Election Finance to publicize and report the contribution data, temporary suspension of the "equal time" legislation for the 1964 election, and authorization of the Post Office to make change-of-address records available to political parties were proposed. See the two messages cited above.

Legislation (1), Presidential Transition Act of 1963, PL 88-277, 78 Stat. 153, March 7, 1964, provided for financing presidential transitions as recommended by the commission.

29 President's Committee to Appraise Employment and Unemployment Statistics (1961–62)

Administrative action (3). "It [the committee report] was implemented in the main. The presentation [of the statistics] was revised so as to give a more complete and intelligible report. . . . We suggested that an inventory of job vacancies be attempted. We were uncertain about the feasibility of such an undertaking. It was tried and found not to be feasible. We recommended changing the definition of unemployment—that was implemented. We recommended a different grouping of age brackets to more effectively take account of teenagers—that was implemented. Virtually all of our recommendations were carried out." Interview statement by a member of the committee.

30 President's Commission on the Status of Women (1961–62)

Statement, *a) "Letter to Mrs. Eleanor Roosevelt on Receiving Report by the Commission on the Status of Women," August 26, 1962, *Kennedy Papers, 1962,* Item 347, p. 644.

*b) "Remarks at Presentation of the Final Report of the President's Commission on the Status of Women," October 11, 1963, *Kennedy Papers, 1963,* Item 409, pp. 780–81.

Administrative action (2), Executive Order No. 11126, November 1, 1963, creating Interdepartmental Committee on the Status of Women and Citizens Advisory Council on the Status of Women.

31 President's Advisory Panel on Federal Salary Systems (1961–63)

Statement, *a) "Remarks Upon Signing the Postal Service and Federal Employees Salary Act of 1962," October 11, 1962, *Kennedy Papers, 1962,* Item 447, pp. 756–57.

*b) "Remarks Upon Signing the Uniformed Services Pay Raise Bill," October 2, 1963, *Kennedy Papers, 1963,* Item 396, p. 757.

Message (2), "Special Message on Federal Pay Reform," February 20, 1962, *Kennedy Papers, 1962,* Item 55, pp. 145–49.

Legislation (3), a) Postal Service and Federal Employees Salary Act of 1962, PL 87-783, 76 Stat. 832.

b) Uniformed Services Pay Act of 1963, PL 88-132, 77 Stat. 210.

c) PL 88-426, which includes Federal Employees Salary Act of 1964, Federal Legislative Salary Act of 1964, Federal Executive Salary Act of 1964, and Federal Judicial Salary Act of 1964, 78 Stat. 400. The most important aspects of this legislation were the establishment of the principle of "comparability" between federal and private sector salaries and the raising of congressional salaries, which served as a *de facto* ceiling on Executive Branch salaries.

32 President's Council on Pennsylvania Avenue (1962–64)

Statement, *a) "President's News Conference of June 2, 1964," *Johnson Papers,* 1963–64, Item 379, p. 738.

*b) "Recorded Remarks After Further Study of the Report of the Council on Pennsylvania Avenue," October 23, 1964, *Johnson Papers, 1963–64,* Item 700, pp. 1405–6.

Administrative action (3), The council's recommendations became the basis for the administration's plan for Pennsylvania Avenue and were implemented to a limited extent, but congressional opposition to full funding has prevented complete implementation. "Hill Stirs on Pennsylvania Ave. Plan," *The Washington Post,* August 20,

1970, pp. B1, B3. President Johnson designated Pennsylvania Avenue a National Historic Site in September, 1965. "Letter to the President of the Senate and to the Speaker of the House on the Pennsylvania Avenue National Historic Site," September 30, 1965, *Johnson Papers, 1965,* Item 538, pp. 1027–28.

33 Committee on Equal Opportunity in the Armed Forces (1962–64)

Statement, *a) "Letter to the Secretary of Defense and to the Chairman, Committee on Equal Opportunity in the Armed Forces, in Response to the Committee's Report," June 22, 1963, *Kennedy Papers, 1963,* Item 251, pp. 495–96.

*b) "Letter to Secretary McNamara Transmitting Final Report of the President's Committee on Equal Opportunity in the Armed Forces," December 28, 1964, *Johnson Papers, 1963–64,* Item 816, p. 1669.

Administrative action (3). The defense Department ordered base commanders to protect the civil rights of servicemen on base and off base and allowed them, upon approval of their civilian Secretary, to declare segregated housing and other establishments off limits to all military personnel. *Congress and the Nation, 1945–64,* p. 1635; and Ruth P. Morgan, *The President and Civil Rights: Policy Making by Executive Order* (New York: St. Martin's Press, 1970), p. 26.

34 President's Committee to Strengthen the Security of the Free World (1962–63)

Statement, *"Letter to General Clay in Response to a Report on U.S. Military and Economic Assistance Programs," March 24, 1963, *Kennedy Papers, 1963,* Item 111, p. 288.

Message (2), *"Special Message to the Congress on the Free World Defense and Assistance Programs," April 2, 1963, *Kennedy Papers, 1963,* Item 118, pp. 294–303.

Legislation (3), Foreign Aid and Related Agencies Appropriation Act, 1964, PL 88-258, 77 Stat. 857. The President accepted the cuts recommended by the committee and Congress cut still more. Foreign aid was cut by the largest percentage since the program began, by 33.8 per cent, from $4.8 billion to $3 billion.

35 President's Advisory Commission on Narcotic and Drug Abuse (1963–64)

Statement, *a) "Letter to the Chairman in Response to the Interim Report of the President's Advisory Commission on Narcotic and Drug Abuse," April 4, 1963, *Kennedy Papers, 1963,* Item 121, p. 312.

*b) "Letter to Judge Prettyman in Response to Report of the

President's Advisory Commission on Narcotic and Drug Abuse,"
January 28, 1964, *Johnson Papers, 1963–64,* Item 159, pp.
246–47.

*c) "Statement by the President on Narcotic and Drug Abuse,"
July 15, 1964, *Johnson Papers, 1963–64,* Item 458, p. 860.

Message (1), *a) "Special Message to the Congress on the Nation's
Health," February 10, 1964, *Johnson Papers, 1963–64,* Item 179,
p. 283.

*b) "Special Message to the Congress on Law Enforcement and the
Administration of Justice," March 8, 1965, *Johnson Papers, 1965,*
Item 102, pp. 266–67.

Administrative action (3). President ordered that the "full power of the
Federal Government" be brought to bear to end illegal drug traffic,
prevent drug abuse, and rehabilitate addicts, and designated a White
House Liaison to implement the directive. "Statement by the President on Narcotic and Drug Abuse," July 15, 1964, *Johnson Papers,
1963–64,* Item 458, p. 860. "Addendum to the Testimony of Dr.
Roger O. Egeberg" in "Presidential Commissions," *Hearings before
the Subcommittee on Administrative Practice and Procedure of the
Senate Committee on the Judiciary,* 92d Cong., 1st Sess. (1971),
pp. 346–49 outlines in detail the specific administrative actions
taken to implement the commission's recommendations. Dr. Egeberg was a member of the commission.

Legislation (3), a) Drug Abuse Control Amendments of 1965, PL
89-74, 79 Stat. 226, extended federal control to barbiturates,
amphetamines, and hallucinogenic drugs.

b) Narcotic Addict Rehabilitation Act of 1966, PL 89-793, 80 Stat.
1438, provides for civil commitment of addicts. See, also, *Hearings*
(1971), for additional legislative implementation (pp. 346–49).

36 President's Commission on Registration and Voting Participation (1963)

Statement, *a) "Remarks upon Accepting Report of the Commission
on Registration and Voting Participation," December 20, 1963,
Johnson Papers, 1963–64, Item 57, p. 73.

*b) "Statement by the President on Voter Registration in the
District of Columbia," January 30, 1964, *Johnson Papers,
1963–64,* Item 167, p. 252.

Administrative action (1). The report was transmitted to the governors by the President, and they were encouraged to establish state
commissions to review their registration and voting laws. "Remarks
Upon Accepting Report of the Commission on Registration and
Voting Participation," December 20, 1963, *Johnson Papers,
1963–64,* Item 57, p. 73.

Legislation (3), a) 24th Amendment, January 28, 1964, poll tax.
b) Voting Rights Act of 1965, PL 89-110, 79 Stat. 437. The
commission's recommendations concerning poll taxes, literacy
tests, and the removal of other barriers to registration were probably only a minor force in the passage of both of the above.

37 Committee on Public Higher Education in the District of Columbia
(1963–64)

Statement, *a) "Statement by the President upon Accepting Report
of the Committee on Public Higher Education in the District of
Columbia," July 12, 1964, *Johnson Papers, 1963–64,* Item 457, p.
859.

*b) "Statement by the President upon Signing the District of
Columbia Public Education Act," November 7, 1966, *Johnson
Papers, 1966,* Item 586, p. 1345.

Message (1), *"Special Message to the Congress on the Needs of the
Nation's Capital," February 15, 1965, *Johnson Papers, 1965,* Item
70, pp. 187–88.

Message (2), *"Letter to the President of the Senate and to the
Speaker of the House Transmitting Bill to Establish Colleges in the
District of Columbia," March 18, 1965, *Johnson Papers, 1965,*
Item 111, p. 294.

Legislation (3), District of Columbia Public Education Act, PL
89-791, 80 Stat. 426, establishes Federal City College and Washington Technical Institute.

38 Task Force to Promote Overseas Sale of Securities of U.S. Companies
(1963–64)

Statement, *a) "Remarks in Response to a Task Force Report on the
Balance of Payments Problem," April 27, 1964, *Johnson Papers,
1963–64,* Item 296, pp. 569–71.

*b) "Statement by the President upon Signing the Foreign Invest-
ors Tax Act and the Presidential Election Fund Act," November
13, 1966, *Johnson Papers, 1966,* Item 612, pp. 1384–85.

Message (1), *a) "Special Message to the Congress on International
Balance of Payments," February 10, 1965, *Johnson Papers, 1965,*
Item 60, p. 176.

b) "Annual Message to the Congress: The Economic Report of the
President," January 27, 1966, *Johnson Papers, 1966,* Item 34, p.
104.

Legislation (3), Foreign Investors Tax Act of 1966, PL 89-809, 80
Stat. 1539, removes tax deterrents to foreign investment in U.S.

39 President's Commission on the Assassination of President Kennedy
(1963–64)

Statement, *"President's News Conference of November 4, 1966," *Johnson Papers, 1966,* Item 577, p. 1322.

Administrative action (3), The Secret Service was enlarged and its procedures changed to provide for better advance detection of threats to the President, planning and conducting of presidential motorcades, and liaison with other law-enforcement agencies. *Congress and the Nation, 1965–68* (Washington, D.C.: Congressional Quarterly Service, 1969), p. 648.

Legislation (1), PL 89-141, 79 Stat. 580, made it a federal crime to kill, kidnap, or assault the President or other federal officials.

40 Commission on Heart Disease, Cancer and Stroke (1964)

Statement, *"Remarks upon Receiving Report of the President's Commission on Heart Disease, Cancer and Stroke," December 9, 1964, *Johnson Papers, 1963–64,* Item 798, pp. 1650–51.

Message (1), *"Special Message to the Congress: 'Advancing the Nation's Health,' " January 7, 1965, *Johnson Papers, 1965,* Item 5, pp. 16–17.

Legislation (3), Heart Disease, Cancer and Stroke Amendments of 1965, PL 89-239, 79 Stat. 926, program of federal grants to encourage and aid localities in planning and establishing regional medical programs for a specialized attack on heart disease, cancer, stroke, and related diseases. *Congress and the Nation, 1965–68,* pp. 667–69. See, also, "Statement of Dr. Michael De Bakey, chairman of the President's Commission on Heart Disease, Cancer, and Stroke of 1964," in *Hearings* (1971), pp. 298–301, for the details of legislative implementation.

41 National Commission on Technology, Automation and Economic Progress (1964–66)

Message (1), *"Annual Message to the Congress: The Manpower Report of the President," March 8, 1966, *Johnson Papers, 1966,* Item 111, p. 281.

Proposed legislation (3). "For those otherwise unable to find work, the commission recommended that the federal government act as the 'employer of last resort,' by financing a program of jobs to provide needed public services. . . . But an amendment offered in 1967 to the Economic Opportunity Act incorporating the commission's recommendations was defeated in the Senate." *Congressional Quarterly Weekly Report,* June 17, 1972, p. 1479.

42 President's Special Panel on Federal Salaries (1965)

Message (2), *"Special Message to the Congress on Increasing Federal Military and Civilian Pay Rates," May 1, 1965, *Johnson Papers, 1965,* Item 244, pp. 518–21.

Legislation (3), a) Military Pay Act of 1965, PL 89-132, 79 Stat. 545. b) Federal Employees Salary Act of 1965, PL 89-301, 79 Stat. 111. Both of these Acts provided for pay raises greater than the President's request, thereby frustrating one purpose of the panel, which was to pave the way for moderate increases but hold the line against large increases. *Congress and the Nation, 1965–68,* pp. 930–32. c) Postal Revenue and Federal Salary Act of 1967, PL 90-206, 81 Stat. 613, provided for a pay commission and a legislative veto arrangement for pay raises as recommended by the panel.

43 Special Presidential Committee on U.S. Trade Relations with Eastern European Countries and the U.S.S.R. (1965)

Statement, *"Letter in Response to Report on U.S. Trade Relations with East European Countries and the Soviet Union," May 20, 1965, *Johnson Papers, 1965,* Item 266, p. 565.

Proposed legislation (3). Legislation to provide for expanded trade with Eastern Europe and the U.S.S.R. based on the committee's recommendations was introduced as an administration measure in 1965 and followed up on in 1966, 1967, and 1968, but congressional agreement was not forthcoming. *Congress and the Nation, 1965–68,* pp. 64, 76, 96–97, and 110–11.

44 President's Commission on the Patent System (1965–66)

Statement, *"Statement by the President upon Releasing the Report of the President's Commission on the Patent System," December 2, 1966, *Johnson Papers, 1966,* Item 637, pp. 1426–27.

Message (1), "Annual Message to the Congress: The Economic Report of the President," January 26, 1967, *Johnson Papers, 1967,* Item 16, p. 87.

Message (2), *"Letter to the President of the Senate and to the Speaker of the House Transmitting a Proposal to Modernize the Patent System," February 21, 1967, *Johnson Papers, 1967,* Item 65, pp. 214–17.

Proposed legislation (3). The Patent Reform Act of 1967, which embodied many of the recommendations of the commission, was not accepted in the Congress. *Congress and the Nation, 1965–68,* pp. 285–86.

45 President's Commission on Crime in the District of Columbia (1965–66)

Statement, *a) "Statement by the President upon Receiving a Report of the President's Commission on Crime in the District of Columbia," July 23, 1966, *Johnson Papers, 1966,* Item 354, pp. 784–85. *b) "Statement by the President in Response to Report of the President's Commission on Crime in the District of Columbia,"

December 31, 1966, *Johnson Papers, 1966,* Item 656, pp. 1465–66.

Message (1), *a) "Annual Message to the Congress on the District of Columbia Budget," January 25, 1967, *Johnson Papers, 1967,* Item 15, p. 67.

*b) "Special Message to the Congress: 'The Nation's Capital,' " February 27, 1967, *Johnson Papers, 1967,* Item 71, pp. 230–38.

c) "Annual Message to the Congress Transmitting the Budget for the District of Columbia, Fiscal Year, 1969," February 27, 1968, *Johnson Papers, 1968,* Item 95, pp. 282–83.

d) "Special Message to the Congress on the District of Columbia: 'The Nation's First City,' " March 13, 1968, *Johnson Papers, 1968,* Item 133, pp. 384–86.

Administrative action (3), Reorganization of the District of Columbia police department was undertaken. See "Memorandum of Disapproval of the District of Columbia Crime Bill," November 13, 1966, *Johnson Papers, 1966,* Item 611, p. 1383.

Legislation (3), a) An Act Relating to Crime and Criminal Procedure in the District of Columbia, PL 90-226, 81 Stat. 731.

b) District of Columbia Police and Fireman's Salary Amendments of 1968, PL 90-320, 82 Stat. 140, higher police pay, as recommended by the commission.

c) District of Columbia Appropriation Act, 1969, PL 90-473, 82 Stat. 694, authorizes more police for D.C., as recommended by the commission.

d) District of Columbia Court Reform and Criminal Procedure Act of 1970, PL 91-358, 84 Stat. 473, includes court reform and preventive detention, recommended by the commission.

46 President's Commission on Law Enforcement and Administration of Justice (1965–67)

Statement, *a) "Statement by the President Concerning the Report of the President's Commission on Law Enforcement and Administration of Justice," February 18, 1967, *Johnson Papers, 1967,* Item 60, pp. 208–9.

*b) "Remarks to the Delegates to the National Conference on Crime Control," March 28, 1967, *Johnson Papers, 1967,* Item 146, p. 401.

*c) "Remarks to the Lawyers Conference on Crime Control," May 13, 1967, *Johnson Papers, 1967,* Item 221, p. 229.

*d) "Remarks to Members of the National Council on Crime and Delinquency," June 21, 1967, *Johnson Papers, 1967,* Item 276, p. 637.

*e) "Remarks in Kansas City, Missouri, at the Meetings of the

International Association of Chiefs of Police," September 14, 1967, *Johnson Papers, 1967,* Item 382, p. 832.

*f) "Statement by the President Urging Passage of the Safe Streets and Crime Control Act," December 11, 1967, *Johnson Papers, 1967,* Item 530, p. 1116.

*g) "Remarks at the First-Day-of-Issue Ceremony for the Law and Order Postage Stamp," May 17, 1968, *Johnson Papers, 1968,* Item 257, pp. 619–20.

*h) "Statement by the President upon Signing the Omnibus Crime Control and Safe Streets Act of 1968," June 19, 1968, *Johnson Papers, 1968,* Item 320, pp. 725–28.

i) "Remarks upon Signing the Juvenile Delinquency Prevention and Control Act of 1968," July 3, 1968, *Johnson Papers, 1968,* Item 424, p. 855.

j) "Remarks upon Signing the Gun Control Act of 1968," October 22, 1968, *Johnson Papers, 1968,* Item 553, pp. 1059–60.

Message (1), *a) "Annual Budget Message to the Congress, Fiscal Year 1968," January 24, 1967, *Johnson Papers, 1967,* Item 13, p. 56.

*b) "Special Message to the Congress Recommending a 12-Point Program for America's Children and Youth," February 8, 1967, *Johnson Papers, 1967,* Item 39, pp. 157–59.

Message (2), *a) "Special Message to the Congress on Crime in America," February 6, 1967, *Johnson Papers, 1967,* Item 35, pp. 134–45.

*b) "Letter to the President of the Senate and to the Speaker of the House of Representatives Urging Enactment of Gun Control Legislation," September 15, 1967, *Johnson Papers, 1967,* Item 385, pp. 839–41.

c) "Special Message to the Congress on Crime and Law Enforcement: "To Insure the Public Safety,'" February 7, 1968, *Johnson Papers, 1968,* Item 59, pp. 183–96.

d) "Letter to the Majority Leader of the Senate on the Crime Control and Safe Streets Bill," May 9, 1968, *Johnson Papers, 1968,* Item 235, pp. 585–86.

Legislation (3), a) Omnibus Crime Control and Safe Streets Act of 1968, PL 90-351, 82 Stat. 197, grant program to state and local law-enforcement agencies. See, also, Lyndon B. Johnson, *The Vantage Point* (New York: Holt, Rinehart and Winston, 1971), p. 335.

b) Juvenile Delinquency Prevention and Control Act of 1968, PL 90-445, 82 Stat. 462, grants to states for planning and operation of juvenile delinquency programs.

c) Gun Control Act of 1968, PL 90-618, 82 Stat. 1213, bans

interstate shipment of long guns to individuals and prohibits sale to those under twenty-one.

47 National Advisory Commission on Food and Fiber (1965–67)

Statement, *"Remarks Recorded for a Television Program on the Report of the National Advisory Commission on Food and Fiber," December 7, 1967, *Johnson Papers, 1967,* Item 525, pp. 1104–6.

48 National Advisory Commission on Health Manpower (1966–67)

Statement, *a) "Remarks to the Press on Making Public the Report of the National Advisory Commission on Health Manpower," November 20, 1967, *Johnson Papers, 1967,* Item 500, pp. 1062–64.

b) "Statement by the President upon Signing the Health Manpower Act of 1968," August 17, 1968, *Johnson Papers, 1968,* Item 447, pp. 892–93.

Message (2), *"Special Message to the Congress: 'Health in America,' " March 4, 1968, *Johnson Papers, 1968,* Item 111, pp. 328–29.

Legislation (3), Health Manpower Act of 1968, PL 90-490, 82 Stat. 773, provides assistance to schools training health professionals, and scholarships for students in health professions.

49 Presidential Task Force on Career Advancement (1966–67)

Statement, *"Statement by the President upon Signing Order Providing Further Training for Government Employees," April 20, 1967, *Johnson Papers, 1967,* Item 184, pp. 456–57.

Administrative action (3), Executive Order No. 11348, provides for further training for government employees to upgrade their skills.

50 Commission on Marine Science, Engineering and Resources (1966–69)

Message (2), *"Environmental Protection Agency and National Oceanic and Atmospheric Administration," *Weekly Compilation,* 6 (July 13, 1970), pp. 908–16.

Administrative action (3), Executive Order No. 11564, transfers certain programs and activities to the Secretary of Commerce, October 6, 1970, implements Reorganization Plan No. 4 of 1970.

Legislation (3) a) Reorganization Plan No. 4 of 1970, creates National Oceanic and Atmospheric Administration, but not as an independent agency, and not including the Coast Guard as recommended by the commission.

b) Coastal Zone Management Act of 1972, PL 92-583, 86 Stat. 1280.

51 National Advisory Commission on Selective Service (1966–67)

Statement, *"Remarks to the State Directors of the Selective Service System," May 3, 1967, *Johnson Papers, 1967,* Item 205, pp. 503–4.

Message (2), *"Special Message to the Congress on Selective Service," March 6, 1967, *Johnson Papers, 1967,* Item 92, pp. 277–88.

Administrative action (3), a) Executive Order No. 11350, makes changes in representativeness of local draft boards and in appeals procedures, May 3, 1967. See "Remarks to the State Directors of the Selective Service System," May 3, 1967, *Johnson Papers, 1967,* Item 205, pp. 503–4.

b) Proclamation No. 3945, November 26, 1969, and Executive Order No. 11497, November 26, 1969, institute a new order of call, limited draft vulnerability, and a random selection procedure. See the testimony of commission executive director Bradley Patterson and that of Lloyd Cutler, executive director of the National Commission on the Causes and Prevention of Violence (1968–69), in "Presidential Advisory Committees," *Hearings before a Subcommittee of the House Committee on Government Operations,* 91st Cong., 2d Sess. (1970), Part I, p. 94, and Part II, p. 117.

Legislation (3), a) Military Selective Service Act of 1967, PL 90-40, 81 Stat. 100, congressional response to the President's Message and to the commission report, eliminating most of the reforms proposed by the commission and the President and prohibiting the President from implementing some reforms by administrative action.

b) Selective Service Amendment Act of 1969, PL 91-124, 83 Stat. 220, removed the restrictions from the 1967 Act, making it possible for the President to take the administrative actions noted under b) above.

52 National Advisory Commission on Libraries (1966–68)

Legislation (3), National Commission on Libraries and Information Services Act, PL 91-345, 84 Stat. 440. Creation of this permanent commission was one of the principal recommendations of the commission.

53 National Advisory Commission on Rural Poverty (1966–67)

54 National Commission on Urban Problems (1967–68)

Administrative action (3). The Department of Housing and Urban Development began Operation Breakthrough May 8, 1969, to create a mass housing market and to encourage mass production of housing by private industry under the authority of Sec. 108 of the Housing and Urban Development Act of 1968. Jack Rosenthal, "Study Panels Flourish in Capital," *New York Times,* December 14, 1970, p. 60.

Legislation (3), a) Housing and Urban Development Act of 1968, Title I, Sec. 108, "New Technologies in the Development of Housing for Low Income Families," PL 90-448, 82 Stat. 476.

b) Housing and Urban Development Act of 1969, PL 91-152, 83 Stat. 379. According to Howard Shuman, executive director of the commission, the commission had a substantial impact on the content of both of these pieces of legislation. See *Hearings,* Part II (1970), p. 138; and Rosenthal.

55 President's Commission on Budget Concepts (1967)

Message (1) *"Annual Budget Message to the Congress, Fiscal Year 1969," January 29, 1968, *Johnson Papers, 1968,* Item 39, pp. 84, 107–8.

Administrative action (3), Budget format revised in line with the commission's recommendations. See testimony of a commission member, Comptroller General Elmer Staats, *Hearings,* Part I (1970), pp. 57–58; *Congress and the Nation, 1965–68,* pp. 137–38; and Ellsworth H. Morse, Jr., "Report of the President's Commission on Budget Concepts in Retrospect," *Public Administration Review,* 31 (July/August, 1971), pp. 443–50.

56 President's Commission on Postal Organization (1967–68)

Statement, *a) "Statement by the President on the Report of the President's Commission on Postal Organization," July 16, 1968, *Johnson Papers, 1968,* Item 391, pp. 814–15.

b) "Postal Reorganization Act: The President's Remarks at the Signing Ceremony at the Post Office Department," *Weekly Compilation,* 6 (August 12, 1970), pp. 1058–59.

Message (1), *a) "Annual Message to the Congress on the State of the Union," January 14, 1969, *Johnson Papers, 1968,* Item 676, p. 1266.

*b) "Annual Budget Message to the Congress Fiscal Year 1970," January 15, 1969, *Johnson Papers, 1968,* Item 678, p. 1301.

Message (2), *a) "Reform of the Postal Service: The President's Message to the Congress Recommending Legislation to Insure Selection and Promotion of Postal Employees on a Nonpolitical Basis," *Weekly Compilation,* 5 (March 3, 1969), pp. 319–20.

*b) "Reform of the Nation's Postal System: The President's Message to the Congress Transmitting the Proposed Postal Service Act of 1969," *Weekly Compilation,* 5 (May 27, 1969), pp. 752–56.

c) "United States Postal Service: The President's Message to the Congress Recommending Postal Reorganization and Pay Legislation," *Weekly Compilation,* 6 (April 20, 1970), pp. 532–37.

Legislation (3), Postal Reorganization Act of 1970, PL 91-375, 84 Stat. 719, creates an independent U.S. Postal Service and eliminates patronage appointments in the postal service. According to a staff aide of a member of the House Committee on Post Office and Civil Service, "The commission report was used as a model for writing the bill."

57 President's Committee on Urban Housing (1967–69)

Statement, *a) "Memorandum to Secretary Weaver on the Need for a Pilot Program to Stimulate Private Enterprise in Low-Income Housing," August 17, 1967, *Johnson Papers, 1967,* Item 355, pp. 784–85.

*b) "Statement by the President upon Receiving Report of the President's Committee on Urban Housing," January 18, 1969, *Johnson Papers, 1968,* Item 704, p. 1367.

Message (1), *"Special Message to the Congress on Urban Problems: 'The Crisis of the Cities'," February 22, 1968, *Johnson Papers, 1968,* Item 87, pp. 257–58.

Administrative action (2), Pilot program to "stimulate private enterprise to build and manage low-income housing" begun, based on commission recommendations. "Memorandum to Secretary Weaver on the Need for a Pilot Program to Stimulate Private Enterprise in Low-Income Housing," August 17, 1967, *Johnson Papers, 1967,* Item 355, pp. 784–85.

Legislation (3), Housing and Urban Development Act of 1968, Title IX, "National Housing Partnerships," PL 90-448, 82 Stat. 476, program to stimulate investment of private capital in low-income housing. See, also, Johnson, p. 331; and Harold Wolman, *Politics of Federal Housing* (New York: Dodd, Mead & Co., 1971), chapter 4.

58 National Advisory Commission on Civil Disorders (1967–68)

Statement, *a) "Remarks to the Members of the Joint Savings Bank-Savings and Loan Committee on Urban Problems," March 6, 1968, *Johnson Papers, 1968,* Item 114, p. 346.

*b) "President's News Conference of March 22, 1968," *Johnson Papers, 1968,* Item 153, pp. 434–36.

Message (2), *"Special Message to the Congress on Urban Problems: 'The Crisis of the Cities'," February 22, 1968, *Johnson Papers, 1968,* Item 87, pp. 256–57.

Administrative action (2), According to Otto Kerner, the commission chairman, some recommendations to the FBI and the Department of Defense concerning their responses to domestic disorders have been implemented. *Hearings* (1971), pp. 8–9.

Legislation (3), Housing and Urban Development Act of 1968, Title XI, "Urban Property Protection and Reinsurance," PL 90-448, 82 Stat. 476.

59 Commission on Obscenity and Pornography (1967–70)

Statement, *"Statement by the President on the Commission's Report," *Weekly Compilation,* 6 (November 2, 1970), pp. 1454–55.

President Nixon called the conclusions of the report "morally bankrupt" and "totally" rejected them.

Legislation, S. Res. 477, October 13, 1970, Senate rejects the commission report.

60 National Advisory Commission on Health Facilities (1967–68)

Statement, *"Remarks Upon Receiving Report of the National Advisory Commission on Health Facilities," December 12, 1968, *Johnson Papers, 1968,* Item 622, pp. 1183–85.

61 Industry-Government Special Task Force on Travel (1967–68)

Statement, *"Statement by the President upon Designating Robert M. McKinney to Head the President's Foreign Visitor Program," March 6, 1968, *Johnson Papers, 1968,* Item 116, pp. 349–50.

Message (2), *"Letter to the President of the Senate and to the Speaker of the House Proposing a Bill to Simplify the Entry of Foreign Visitors," February 23, 1968, *Johnson Papers, 1968,* Item 88, pp. 263–64.

Proposed legislation (3). Non-Immigrant Visa Act of 1968 was not enacted by the 90th Congress.

Administrative action (1). President designated a coordinator to head the foreign visitors program, and the Civil Aeronautics Board "sanctioned proposals to grant discounts to foreign tourists on domestic airlines." "Statement by the President upon Designating Robert M. McKinney to Head the President's Foreign Visitor Program," March 6, 1968, *Johnson Papers, 1968,* Item 116, pp. 349–50.

62 National Commission on Product Safety (1967–70)

Message (2), *"Consumer Protection: The President's Message to the Congress Outlining His Legislative Program," *Weekly Compilation,* 5 (November 3, 1969), p. 1525.

Administrative action (1). FHA issued regulations requiring safety glass in glass doors. Michael Lemov, "Whatever Happened to Product Safety?" *The New Republic,* 164 (April 3, 1971), pp. 12–13.

Legislation (3), a) Child Protection and Toy Safety Act of 1969, PL 91-113, 83 Stat. 187.

b) Consumer Product Safety Act, PL 92-573, 86 Stat. 1207. "Impetus for creation of the product safety commission [by PL 92-573] stemmed largely from the final report of the National Commission on Product Safety recommending a new agency." *Congress and the Nation,* vol. 3 (Washington, D.C.: Congressional Quarterly, 1973), p. 686. On the Child Protection and Toy Safety Act of 1969, see p. 661.

63 President's Commission on Income Maintenance Programs (1968–69)

64 President's Commission for the Observance of Human Rights Year, 1968 (1968–69)

Statement, *"The President's Letter to Chairman W. Averell Harriman upon Receipt of the Commission's Final Report," *Weekly Compilation,* 5 (May 5, 1969), p. 628.

65 National Commission on the Causes and Prevention of Violence (1968–69)

Proposed legislation (2). Bill to give universities the right to go to federal courts for injunctions to end campus disorders was introduced but not enacted. *Congressional Quarterly Weekly Report,* 27 (June 20, 1969), p. 1066.

66 Committee on Population and Family Planning (1968–69)

Message (2), "Problems of Population Growth: The President's Message to the Congress," *Weekly Compilation,* 5 (July 21, 1969), pp. 1000–1008.

Legislation (2), Commission on Population Growth and the American Future, PL 91-213, 84 Stat. 67.

67 President's Commission on an All-Volunteer Armed Force (1969–70)

Message (2), *"The President's Message to the Congress Outlining Actions and Proposals in a Move Toward Ending the Draft," *Weekly Compilation,* 6 (April 27, 1970), p. 571.

Administrative action (3), "On January 27, 1973, [Secretary of Defense] Laird announced that the administration would not seek renewal of the draft . . . and would henceforth rely on an all-volunteer force." *Congress and the Nation,* vol. 3, p. 252.

Proposed legislation (3). In 1970 an amendment to the annual defense procurement authorization bill (HR 17123) was offered in the Senate. The amendment would have implemented the commission's recommendations, but it was not supported by the administration and it failed.

Legislation (3), Amendments to the Military Selective Service Act of 1967, PL 92-129, 85 Stat. 348, partially implemented the commission's recommendations with the support of the administration.

68 President's Advisory Council on Executive Organization (1969–71)

Statement, *a) "President's Statement on Making Public the Ash Council's Memoranda on the Department of Natural Resources and an Organization for Social and Economic Programs," *Weekly Compilation,* 7 (Feb. 8, 1971), p. 174.

*b) "Statement by the President on Making Public the Ash Council's Study of the Organization and Structure of Seven of the Agencies," *Weekly Compilation,* 7 (Feb. 15, 1971), p. 210.

*c) "Announcement of Resignation of the Council's Members Upon Completion of Its Work," *Weekly Compilation,* 7 (May 10, 1971), pp. 734–35.

Message (1), *a) "Message to Congress: Budget Message," *Weekly Compilation,* 6 (Feb. 2, 1970), p. 116.

b) "Message to Congress: Environmental Quality," *Weekly Compilation,* 6 (Feb. 16, 1970), p. 171.

*c) "President's Message to Congress upon Transmitting Reorganization Plans," *Weekly Compilation,* 6 (July 13, 1970), p. 915.

*d) "Consumer Protection: The President's Message to the Congress Submitting His Legislative Program," *Weekly Compilation,* 7 (March 1, 1971), pp. 288, 290.

*e) "President's Message to Congress: Legal Services Corporation," *Weekly Compilation,* 7 (May 10, 1971), p. 727.

Message (2), *a) "The President's Message to the Congress Transmitting Reorganization Plan 2 of 1970, Implementing Recommendations of the President's Advisory Council on Executive Organization," *Weekly Compilation,* 6 (March 16, 1970), pp. 353–56.

*b) "The President's Message to the Congress Proposing the Establishment of a Department of Natural Resources, Department of Community Development, Department of Human Resources, and Department of Economic Affairs," *Weekly Compilation,* 7 (March 29, 1971), pp. 545–60.

Administrative action (2), *"The President's Memorandum to Heads of Executive Departments and Agencies Calling for Program Evaluation," *Weekly Compilation,* 6 (May 30, 1970), p. 690.

Administrative action (3), *"Statement by the President: Redirecting Executive Branch Management," *Weekly Compilation,* 7 (Jan. 8, 1971), pp. 5–10. Having failed to win congressional approval for the Cabinet reorganization recommended by the commission, the President sought to implement these recommendations by appointing Cabinet members as Special Assistants to the President with broad coordinating responsibility over the areas that would have been consolidated in new departments by the legislation.

Proposed legislation (3). The President proposed legislation for sweeping Cabinet reorganization. See Message (2), b) and Administrative action (3), above.

Legislation (3), a) Reorganization Plan 2 of 1970, creates the Domestic Council and reorganizes the Bureau of the Budget into the Office of Management and Budget.

b) Reorganization Plan 4 of 1970, creates National Oceanic and Atmospheric Administration.

69 Presidential Task Force on International Development (1969–70)

Statement, *"Statement by the President upon Receiving the Task Force's Report on U.S. Foreign Assistance Programs," *Weekly Compilation,* 6 (March 14, 1970), p. 346.

Message (2), *"President's Message to the Congress Proposing Reform of the United States Foreign Assistance Program," *Weekly Compilation,* 6 (Sept. 21, 1970), pp. 1214–25. The Task Force's "report provides the basis for the proposals which I am making today" (p. 1216).

70 President's Task Force on Business Taxation (1969–70)

Administrative action (3), *"Statement by the President upon Announcing Changes in the Depreciation Provisions," *Weekly Compilation,* 7 (Jan. 16, 1971), pp. 58–59.

71 President's Task Force on Improving the Prospects of Small Business (1969–70)

Message (2), *a) "President's Message to the Congress: Small Business," *Weekly Compilation,* 6 (March 23, 1970), pp. 391–94.

b) "President's Message to Congress: Minority Business Enterprise," *Weekly Compilation,* 7 (Oct. 18, 1971), pp. 1400–1404.

Administrative action (2), Executive Order No. 11518, March 20, 1970, "Providing for the Increased Representation of Small Business Concerns before Departments and Agencies of the United States Government." The Message (2) a), above, describes other administrative actions.

Legislation (3), Small Business Act Amendments of 1972, PL 92-595, 86 Stat. 1314.

72 President's Task Force on Model Cities (1969–70)

73 President's Task Force on Rural Development (1969–70)

Legislation (3), Rural Development Act of 1972, PL 92-419, 86 Stat. 657. In his message to Congress on rural development of March 10, 1971, the President recommended a program of special revenue sharing for rural areas. In passing this law reauthorizing and expanding existing programs and creating new categorical programs for rural areas, the Congress acted more in line with the Task Force's recommendations.

74 President's Task Force on Women's Rights and Responsibilities (1969–70)

75 President's Task Force on Higher Education (1969–70)

76 President's Task Force on Science Policy (1969)

77 President's Task Force on Low-Income Housing (1969–70)
78 President's Task Force on the Aging (1969–70)

> Proposed legislation (1). On October 30, 1972, the President pocket-vetoed legislation that would have implemented some of the Task Force's recommendations in the areas of research on the problems of the aging, establishing a federal advisory council on aging, and broadening federal mental health programs to include the aging. *Congress and the Nation*, vol. 3, pp. 572, 621.
>
> Legislation (1), PL 92-258, 86 Stat. 88, amendments to the Older Americans Act of 1965, authorized a program of grants to the states for a nutrition program for the elderly.

79 President's Task Force on Oceanography (1969)

> Message (1), *"President's Message to Congress Upon Transmitting Reorganization Plans," *Weekly Compilation*, 6 (July 13, 1970), p. 915.
>
> Legislation (3), Reorganization Plan 4 of 1970, created National Oceanic and Atmospheric Administration.

80 President's Task Force on the Physically Handicapped (1969–70)
81 President's Task Force on Economic Growth (1969–70)

> Administrative action (1). On June 16, 1970, the President announced the creation of the President's Commission on Financial Structure and Regulation. *Weekly Compilation*, 6 (June 22, 1970), pp. 772–73.
>
> Legislation (2), Reorganization Plan 4 of 1970, created Environmental Protection Agency.

82 President's Task Force on Prisoner Rehabilitation (1969–70)
83 President's Task Force on Urban Renewal (1969–70)
84 President's Task Force on Highway Safety (1969–70)
85 President's Task Force on Air Pollution (1969–70)
86 President's Task Force on the Mentally Handicapped (1969–70)
87 President's Commission on School Finance (1970–72)

> Statement, *"President's Remarks to National Catholic Education Association," *Weekly Compilation*, 8 (April 10, 1972), p. 731.
>
> Message (1), *a) "President's Message to Congress: Educational Opportunity and Busing," *Weekly Compilation*, 8 (March 20, 1972), p. 605.
>
> *b) "President's Message to Congress: Older Americans," *Weekly Compilation*, 8 (March 27, 1972), p. 658.

88 President's Panel on Nonpublic Education (1970–72)

> Proposed legislation (3), A tax credit for the tuition paid for students in non-public non-profit schools was proposed by the President in

1973. *Congressional Quarterly Almanac, 1973* (Washington, D.C.: Congressional Quarterly, 1974) p. 268.

89 Commission on International Trade and Investment Policy (1970–71)

Message (1) *"President's Report to Congress: United States Foreign Policy for the 1970's: The Emerging Structure of Peace," *Weekly Compilation,* 8 (Feb. 14, 1972), pp. 295–96.

Administrative action and legislation (2), PL 92-412, 86 Stat. 644. Export controls are relaxed and statutory authority is given to the Council on International Economic Policy. *Congress and the Nation,* vol. 3, pp. 131–32. The imposition of an import tax and the adoption of more flexible monetary exchange rates were also in line with the commission's recommendations.

90 President's Commission on Campus Unrest (1970)

Statement, *"The President's Letter to Commission Chairman William W. Scranton," *Weekly Compilation,* 6 (Dec. 14, 1970), pp. 1660–63.

Administrative action (1). "The Department of Defense . . . held a series of meetings around the country, between the members of the hierarchy in the Pentagon and the people particularly in the National Guard and the ROTC's, to go over the report thoroughly. . . . [T]hey are now supplying the types of equipment we suggested. And, secondly, they also attempted to do a job on training." Statement of Commission Chairman Scranton in *Hearings* (1971), p. 207.

91 President's Commission on Financial Structure and Regulation (1970–72)

Message (1), *"State of the Union Message," *Weekly Compilation,* (Feb. 4, 1974), pp. 127–28.

Message (2), *"U.S. Financial System: The President's Message to the Congress on Recommendations for Change in the System," *Weekly Compilation,* 9 (Aug. 6, 1973), pp. 953–54.

Proposed legislation (3), Message (2), above, outlines a package of seven legislative proposals which the President subsequently submitted to the Congress as draft legislation.

92 President's Commission for the Observance of the Twenty-fifth Anniversary of the United Nations (1970–71)

Statement, *"United Nations Day, 1971: Proclamation No. 4066," *Weekly Compilation,* 7 (July 12, 1971), p. 1044.

Message (1), *"President's Report to Congress; United States Foreign Policy for the 1970s: The Emerging Structure of Peace," *Weekly Compilation,* 8 (Feb. 14, 1971), pp. 392–93.

Message (2), *a) "United States Participation in the United Nations:
The President's Message to the Congress Transmitting the 25th
Annual Report, Covering Calendar Year 1970," *Weekly Compila-
tion,* 7 (Sept. 25, 1971), pp. 1304–5.

*b) "United States Participation in the United Nations: The Presi-
dent's Message to the Congress Transmitting the 26th Annual
Report, Covering Calendar Year 1971," *Weekly Compilation,* 8
(Sept. 11, 1972), pp. 1351–52.

Administrative action and legislation (3). The administration adopted
a two-China policy as recommended by the commission. With the
support of the Administration, Congress included a provision in the
Departments of State, Justice and Commerce and Related Agencies
Appropriation Act of 1972 (PL 92-544) limiting the U.S. contribution to the U.N. to 25 per cent of the U.N. budget. The administration subsequently negotiated acceptance for this new rate of
contribution with the U.N. *Congress and the Nation,* vol. 3, pp.
890–91.

93 President's Commission on Federal Statistics (1970–71)

94 Commission on American Shipbuilding (1970–73)

95 National Commission on Materials Policy (1970–73)

96 National Commission on State Workmen's Compensation Laws
(1970–72)

Statement, *"Reform of State Workers' Compensation Programs,"
Weekly Compilation, 10 (May 20, 1974), pp. 520–21.

Administrative action (1). In the Statement, noted above, the President announced the creation of a task force to provide technical
assistance to states in their efforts to reform their unemployment
compensation programs and to evaluate these state efforts and
recommend further federal efforts by the end of 1975.

Proposed legislation (3), S. 2008, National Workers' Compensation
Standards Act of 1973, introduced by Senator Williams of New
Jersey and Senator Javits of New York, would impose federal
minimum requirements on state workmen's compensation programs. *Congressional Record* (daily ed., June 18, 1973), pp. S
11286–95.

97 President's Advisory Panel on Timber and the Environment (1971–73)

Statement, *"President's Advisory Panel on Timber and the Environment: Statement by the President upon Receiving the Panel's Final
Report," *Weekly Compilation,* 9 (Sept. 29, 1973), p. 1173.

Administrative action (2). In the Statement, noted above, the President endorses the recommendation of the panel that the national

forests be more extensively harvested to meet national timber supply needs.

98 President's Committee on Health Education (1971–73)

Message (1), *"President's Message to Congress: Health Programs," *Weekly Compilation,* 10 (Feb. 25, 1974), pp. 235–36.

Administrative action (3). According to interviews, both a Bureau for Health Education and an interagency coordinating committee on health education have been established in the Department of Health, Education, and Welfare. In addition, a contract has been let from the Department of Health, Education, and Welfare to the National Health Council to develop a National Center for Health Education. This will presumably lead to HEW funding of a National Center.

99 Presidential Study Commission on International Radio Broadcasting (1972–73)

Statement, *"Statement by the President Upon Transmitting to the Congress the Commission's Report on Radio Free Europe and Radio Liberty," *Weekly Compilation,* 9 (May 14, 1973), p. 655.

Legislation (3), The Board for International Broadcasting Act of 1973, PL 93-129, provides for the continuation of Radio Free Europe and Radio Liberty and for a new International Broadcasting Board to oversee the operations and funds of the stations.

NOTES

CHAPTER ONE

1. These views are expressed in various degrees by Silas Bent, "Mr. Hoover's Sins of Commissions," *Scribner's Magazine,* 90 (July, 1931); Lillian Symes, "The Great Fact-Finding Farce," *Harper's Magazine,* 164 (February, 1932); George B. Galloway, "Presidential Commissions," *Editorial Research Reports,* 1 (May 28, 1931); A. Mervyn Davies, "Brains in Government— Commissions to Find the Facts," *Forum,* 97 (May, 1937); Harvey C. Mansfield, "Commissions, Government," *International Encyclopedia of the Social Sciences,* (New York: Crowell Collier and Macmillan, 1968), vol. 3; Elizabeth Drew, "On Giving Oneself a Hotfoot: Government by Commission," *Atlantic Monthly,* 221 (May, 1968); Jack Rosenthal, "Study Panels Flourish in Capital," *New York Times,* December 14, 1969; Haynes Johnson, "The Study Commission Syndrome," *Washington Post,* June 28, 1970; Frank Popper, *The President's Commissions* (New York: Twentieth Century Fund, 1970), pp. 56–65; Robert Reinhold, "Results Termed Mixed for Study Panels," *New York Times,* May 28, 1971; Art Buchwald, "Costly Reports Viewed Gravely," *The Washington Post,* July 23, 1970, and "Reports of Unrest," *The Washington Post,* October 1, 1970; and William Chapman, "4 Sociologists See Work on President's Study Panels as Futile," *The Washington Post,* August 29, 1973. It is interesting to note that this cynicism and skepticism about commissions has been most frequently expressed in periods of general domestic turmoil: the Depression era, and from the late 1960's into the 1970's when discontent has focused on the Vietnam war and the problems of poverty, urban life, ecological dangers, and the abuse of political power. This suggests that at least some of the criticism of commissions is a function of dissatisfaction with the performance of government as a whole rather than with commissions per se.

2. This poem, "Royal Commissions," *Punch,* August 24, 1955, by Geoffrey Parsons, is a commentary on British Royal Commissions, but it is quoted and applied to American presidential commissions by Harold Seidman, *Politics, Position, and Power: The Dynamics of Federal Organization* (New York: Oxford University Press, 1970), p. 23.

3. *Parade Magazine, The Boston Globe,* July 4, 1971, p. 7.

4. Herbert Hoover, *The Memoirs of Herbert Hoover: 1920–33* (New York: The Macmillan Company, 1952), p. 281.

5. For a brief survey of the elements of the "presidential advisory system," see Thomas Cronin and Sanford Greenberg, eds., *The Presidential Advisory System* (New York: Harper and Row, 1969), pp. xvii–xviii.

6. *Ibid.*, p. 1.

7. On the other hand, there is an immense literature discussing the correctness of the findings of many commissions and the substantive merits of their recommendations.

8. Monographs: Carl M. Marcy, *Presidential Commissions* (New York: King's Crown Press, 1945); and Popper. Essays: Bent; Davies; Drew; Galloway; Johnson; Mansfield; Reinhold; Rosenthal; Symes; Daniel Bell, "Government by Commission," *The Public Interest*, Spring, 1966; Harlan Cleveland, "Inquiry into Presidential Inquirers," *New York Times Magazine*, August 14, 1960; "The Commission: How to Create a Blue Chip Consensus," *Time Magazine*, 95 (January 19, 1970); Alan L. Dean, "Ad Hoc Commissions for Policy Formulation?" in Cronin and Greenberg; Arthur W. Macmahon, "Board, Advisory," *Encyclopedia of the Social Sciences*, (New York: Macmillan Co., 1930), vol. 2; Fritz M. Marx, "Temporary Presidential Advisory Commissions," staff paper, Bureau of the Budget, 1952; Martha Derthick, "Commissionship—Presidential Variety," *Public Policy*, Fall, 1971; and George T. Sulzner, "The Policy Process and the Uses of National Governmental Study Commissions," *Western Political Quarterly*, 24 (September, 1971). Case Studies: Edward Jay Epstein, *Inquest: The Warren Commission and the Establishment of Truth* (New York: The Viking Press, 1966); William R. Hamilton, Jr., "The President's Materials Policy Commission (Paley Commission): A History and Analytical Inquiry into Policy Formation by a Presidential Commission" (Ph.D. diss., University of Maryland, 1962); Donald Herzberg, "Horse and Buggy Election Laws: A Presidential Concern," in *Cases in American National Government and Politics*, ed. Rocco Tressolini and Richard Frost (Englewood Cliffs, N.J.: Prentice-Hall, 1966); Michael Lipsky and David Olson, *Riot Commission Politics* (New York: E. P. Dutton, forthcoming); and Usha Mahajani, "Kennedy and the Strategy of AID: The Clay Report and After," *Western Political Quarterly*, 18 (September, 1965).

9. Dean, pp. 102–3; Thomas E. Cronin, "Political Science and Executive Advisory Systems," in Cronin and Greenberg, pp. 326–28; "The Commission: How to Create a Blue Chip Consensus," p. 22; and Sulzner, p. 438.

10. Drew, p. 45; Popper, p. 7; Marcy, note 4, p. 109; and Cronin and Greenberg, pp. 89–90.

11. Leonard D. White, *The Federalists: A Study in Administrative History, 1789–1801* (New York: The Free Press, 1965), pp. 419–20.

12. Leonard D. White, *The Jacksonians: A Study in Administrative History, 1829–1861* (New York: The Free Press, 1965), p. 428.

13. James MacGregor Burns (*Presidential Government* [Boston: Houghton Mifflin Co., 1965], p. 10) suggests that Alexander Hamilton's studies of manufactures, a national bank, and public credit were the foundation for presidential commissions.

14. Theodore Roosevelt, *An Autobiography* (New York: Charles Scribner's Sons, 1927), pp. 362–65; and Edward Corwin, *The President: Office and Powers*, 4th ed. rev. (New York: New York University Press, 1957), p. 71.

15. See appendix 1 for a description of the number, type, and technique of the interviews. Only since the Federal Register Act of 1935 have presidential executive orders, proclamations, and some directives been promulgated in a single official source. Partial, though extensive, lists of the

executive orders prior to 1935 (by title only) can be found in Works Progress Administration, Historical Records Survey, *Presidential Executive Orders*, 2 vols. (New York: Hastings House, 1944), and in Clifford Lord, ed., *List and Index of Presidential Executive Orders, Unnumbered Series, 1789–1941* (Newark: Works Projects Administration, Historical Records Survey, 1942). Convenient access to executive orders and proclamations (all in one place and in chronological order and not sprinkled among all of the official notices of other executive agencies) is to be found only beginning with *U.S. Code Congressional Service*, 1941–1950; *U.S. Code Congressional and Administrative Service*, 1951; and *U.S. Code Congressional and Administrative News*, 1952 and later (St. Paul: West Publishing Co., 1941–72). A systematic and well-indexed compilation of presidential actions and statements other than executive orders and proclamations begins only with the *Weekly Compilation of Presidential Documents* (Washington, D.C.: Office of the Federal Register, National Archives and Records Service, General Services Administration, August 20, 1965 and after). The official *Public Papers of the President*, which begin with the first year of President Truman's Administration, partially fill the gap in presidential records between 1945 and 1965. They publish only selected documents, but they do contain an appendix listing all White House press releases. These White House press releases, 1945–72, are to be found only in fragmentary library collections or in official government files. Earlier compilations of presidential papers such as Samuel Rosenman, *The Public Papers and Addresses of Franklin D. Roosevelt*, 13 vols. (New York: Random House, 1938–50), and James Richardson, ed., *Messages and Papers of the Presidents, 1789–1897* (Washington, D.C.: Government Printing Office, 1896–99), fill even less adequately the need for comprehensive and systematic publication of the official public acts of Presidents. The situation does not present insuperable research obstacles, and it is noteworthy because this fragmentary and casual publication is of the official public acts of the Presidents and is in marked contrast to the documentation of the official public acts of Congress and most other federal agencies.

16. Marcy, pp. v, 6.

17. Popper, p. 5.

18. For example, "Although every effort has been made to provide a comprehensive list, the paucity or obscurity of records in many instances precludes any claim that this is necessarily complete." Gayle T. Harris, *Advisory Bodies Created by the President and by Congress 1955 through March, 1968* (Washington, D.C.: Library of Congress, Legislative Reference Service, April 17, 1968), p. 2. For an earlier period Carl Marcy notes the "difficulty of rendering a completely accurate statement of the number of commissions, committees, and similar bodies" (Marcy, note 9, pp. 107–8).

19. Macmahon, p. 609.

20. On presidential documents, see note 15 above.

21. The previous efforts in this area are Gayle T. Harris, *Advisory Bodies Created by the President and by Congress 1955 through March, 1968;* Gayle T. Harris, *Committees, Commissions, Boards, Councils and Task Forces Created to Advise the President, the Congress or Executive Agencies Since 1965* (Washington, D.C.: Library of Congress, Legislative Reference Service, August 20, 1968); "Presidential Commissions Appointed Since

1953," *Congressional Quarterly Weekly Report* (February 5, 1960), pp. 206–9; and Popper, pp. 66–67.

22. Macmahon, p. 610.

23. See, for example, Peter Blau, *The Dynamics of Bureaucracy*, 2nd ed. (Chicago: University of Chicago Press, 1963), chapter 7.

24. See chapter 5 on the process of appointment of commission members.

25. The usage of the word "public" is particularly ambiguous and plural. In some contexts it is used as the equivalent of "governmental" as in "public power." In the context of regulatory bodies and labor mediation groups, "public members" are those disinterested persons who approach their task from the point of view of some broader "public" interest. Generally, in the context of advisory bodies, public members are those who are representative of the "public" as opposed to the "government," in terms of their occupations. In this book, the category "public members" refers to all those outside of the sphere of hierarchical control of the President, and it therefore includes many whose occupation is governmental and who are narrowly self-interested rather than public-minded. "Public" in this context means representing any of the President's "publics" or constituencies outside of the Executive Branch.

26. Cronin and Greenberg, pp. xv–xviii.

27. Perhaps most jarring to the reader's image of commissions is the absence of the two Hoover Commissions, created in 1947 and 1953, from the list of presidential advisory commissions in appendix 2. They were formally advisory only to the Congress, and the President appointed only a minority of their members.

CHAPTER TWO

1. See, for example, Elizabeth Drew, "On Giving Oneself a Hotfoot: Government by Commission," *Atlantic Monthly,* 221 (May, 1968); "The Commission: How to Create a Blue Chip Consensus," *Time Magazine,* 95 (January 19, 1970), pp. 22–23; and Frank Popper, *The President's Commissions* (New York: The Twentieth Century Fund, 1970), pp. 9–14.

2. Art Buchwald, "Reports of Unrest," *The Washington Post,* October 1, 1970, p. B1.

3. However, three of them have produced memoirs which were useful: Harry S. Truman, *Memoirs,* 2 vols. (Garden City, N.Y.: Doubleday and Co., 1955–56); Dwight D. Eisenhower, *Mandate for Change* (Garden City, N.Y.: Doubleday and Co., 1963), and *Waging Peace* (Garden City, N.Y.: Doubleday and Co., 1965); and Lyndon B. Johnson, *Vantage Point: Perspectives of the Presidency 1963–1969* (New York: Holt, Rinehart and Winston, 1971).

4. On the collegial nature of the presidency, see James MacGregor Burns, *Presidential Government* (New York: Houghton Mifflin Co., 1965); and Lester Seligman, "Developments in the Presidency and the Conception of Political Leadership," *American Sociological Review,* 20 (December, 1955); and on the institutionalized presidency, see Edward Corwin, *The President: Office and Powers,* 4th ed. rev. (New York: New York University Press, 1957), pp. 299–305; and Lester Seligman, "Presidential Leadership: The Inner Circle and Institutionalization," *Journal of Politics,* 18 (August, 1956).

5. See, for example, Carl M. Marcy, *Presidential Commissions* (New York: King's Crown Press, 1945), chap. 4; Fritz Marx, "Temporary Presidential Advisory Commissions," staff paper, Bureau of the Budget, 1952, pp. 4–8; George B. Galloway, "Presidential Commissions," *Editorial Research Reports,* 1 (May 28, 1931), pp. 359–60; and Harvey C. Mansfield, "Commissions, Government," *International Encyclopedia of the Social Sciences,* vol. 3 (New York: Crowell Collier & Macmillan, 1968), pp. 14–15.

6. See, for example, Popper, pp. 9–14; Drew; and Daniel Bell, "Government by Commission," in Thomas E. Cronin and Sanford D. Greenberg, eds., *The Presidential Advisory System* (New York: Harper & Row, 1969), pp. 120–21.

7. An interesting parallel is the assumption of governmental omnipotence held, according to Epstein, by most commentators on the Warren Commission report. Edward J. Epstein, *Inquest: The Warren Commission and the Establishment of Truth* (New York: The Viking Press, 1966), p. xvii.

8. On revealed goals, see W. Maclean Dickson and Bernard Alpert, "Appointive Committees—A Behavioral Analysis of Committee Effectiveness and Potential for Action," *University of Washington Business Review,* 24 (October, 1964).

9. Executive Order No. 11279, May 12, 1966, 31 F.R. 6947.

10. These quotations are from personal interviews. All of the unattributed quotations in the rest of this work are also from these interviews, which are described in appendix 1.

11. Respectively, Advisory Commission on the Merchant Marine (1947) and Commission on American Shipbuilding (1971–73), President's Commission on a World's Fair (1959), and President's Commission on Registration and Voting Participation (1963).

12. On the window-dressing purpose of commissions, see, also, Avery Leiserson, *Administrative Regulation: A Study in Representation of Interests* (Chicago: University of Chicago Press, 1942), p. 166.

13. The quotation is from Richard Neustadt, *Presidential Power* (New York: New American Library of World Literature, 1964), p. 47.

14. "Address Before a Joint Session of the Congress on Universal Military Training," October 23, 1945, *The Public Papers of the Presidents: Harry S. Truman, 1945* (Washington, D.C.: Government Printing Office, 1961), Item 174, pp. 404–13. All other references to the volumes of presidential papers will be cited by a short form, *Truman Papers, Eisenhower Papers, Kennedy Papers,* and *Johnson Papers,* followed by the year of the volume.

15. President's Advisory Commission on Universal Training, "President's Letter Inviting Members to Serve on Commission," *Program for National Security* (Washington, D.C.: Government Printing Office, 1947), p. 103.

16. Truman, *Memoirs,* vol. 2, p. 55.

17. Letter from Elmer Staats to Don K. Price, December 28, 1961, personal files of Don K. Price. The assistance of Professor Don K. Price, Harvard University, is gratefully acknowledged, for allowing the author access to his personal files dealing with the President's Advisory Panel on Federal Salary Systems (1961–63) and the President's Special Panel on Federal Salaries (1965), on both of which he served as a member.

18. Arthur H. Vandenberg, Jr., ed., *The Private Papers of Senator Vandenberg* (Boston: Houghton Mifflin Company, 1952), p. 375.

19. See, also, Thomas G. Paterson, "The Quest for Peace and Prosperity: International Trade, Communism, and the Marshall Plan," in *Politics and Policies of the Truman Administration*, ed. Barton J. Berstein (Chicago: Quadrangle Books, 1970), p. 97.
20. See, for example, Arthur Maass, *Muddy Waters: The Army Engineers and the Nation's Rivers* (Cambridge, Mass.: Harvard University Press, 1951); and J. Leiper Freeman, *The Political Process: Executive Bureau–Legislative Committee Relations*, rev. ed. (New York: Random House, 1965).
21. President's Citizen Advisers on the Mutual Security Program (Fairless Committee, 1956–57), President's Committee to Study the United States Military Assistance Program (Draper Committee, 1958–59), President's Committee to Strengthen the Security of the Free World (Clay Committee, 1962–63), and Presidential Task Force on International Development (1969–70).
22. See Edward K. Hamilton, "Toward Public Confidence in Foreign Aid," *World Affairs*, 132 (March, 1970), pp. 290–91.
23. This role for the committee is also implied by Sherman Adams, *First-Hand Report* (New York: Harper and Bros., 1961), p. 377.
24. See, also, Gilbert Y. Steiner, *The State of Welfare* (Washington, D.C.: The Brookings Institution, 1971), pp. 249–50.
25. The independence of commissions is discussed in detail in chapter 5.
26. Truman, *Memoirs*, vol. 2, pp. 21–23. A striking example of a presidential window-dressing purpose being foiled is the President's Committee to Strengthen the Security of the Free World (Clay Committee, 1962–63). On the Clay Committee, see Jim F. Heath, *John F. Kennedy and the Business Community* (Chicago: University of Chicago Press, 1969), pp. 109–10; "The Report of the Clay Committee on Foreign Aid: A Symposium," *Political Science Quarterly*, 78 (September, 1963) (particularly the comments of Congressman Otto E. Passman on p. 348); Arthur Schlesinger, Jr., *A Thousand Days* (Boston: Houghton Mifflin Company, 1965), pp. 597–600; and Roger Hilsman, *To Move A Nation: The Politics of Foreign Policy in the Administration of John F. Kennedy* (Garden City, N.Y.: Doubleday, 1967), pp. 394–95.
27. Letter from Eric Goldman to Thomas Wolanin, August 31, 1970.
28. See, also, Donald Herzberg, "Horse and Buggy Election Laws: A Presidential Concern," in *Cases in American National Government and Politics*, ed. Rocco J. Tresolini and Richard T. Frost (Englewood Cliffs, N.J.: Prentice-Hall, 1966), p. 131, concerning the President's Commission on Registration and Voting Participation (1963).
29. See Louis W. Koenig, *The Chief Executive*, rev. ed. (New York: Harcourt, Brace & World, 1968), pp. 3–5; and Fred I. Greenstein, "What the President Means to Americans," in *Choosing the President*, ed. James Barber (Englewood Cliffs, N.J.: Prentice-Hall, 1974).
30. On the background of this commission and its crisis response purpose, see also Paul Tillett and Myron Weiner, *Closing the Newark Airport*, ICP Case Series, no. 27 (University, Ala.: University of Alabama Press, 1955).
31. On the image of presidential power and responsibility, see Thomas E. Cronin, "The Textbook Presidency and Political Science," paper prepared for delivery at the 66th Annual Meeting of the American Political Science Association, 1970; and Grant McConnell, *Steel and the Presidency—1962*

(New York: W. W. Norton & Company, 1963), as well as the works cited in note 29 above. McConnell, particularly in chapters 5 and 6, also provides an excellent case study of the contrast between the image of presidential power and the limits of presidential action.

32. "Presidential Advisory Committees," *Hearings before a Subcommittee of the House Committee on Government Operations,* Part II, 91st Cong., 2d Sess. (1970), p. 137.

33. Howard E. Shuman, "Behind the Scenes and Under the Rug," *The Washington Monthly,* 1 (July, 1969), p. 22. See, also, *Hearings,* Part II (1970), p. 136.

34. See, also, the interchange between Senator Mansfield and former Secretary of Defense Robert A. Lovett, in Senator Henry M. Jackson, ed., *The National Security Council: Jackson Subcommittee Papers on Policy-Making at the Presidential Level* (New York: Praeger, 1965), p. 87.

35. The action response of Presidents to most commission reports is discussed in chapters 7 and 8.

36. President's Committee to Appraise Employment and Unemployment Statistics, *Measuring Employment and Unemployment* (Washington, D.C.: Government Printing Office, 1962), p. 3.

37. "Statement by the President Upon Announcing the Appointment of a Panel to Review Employment Statistics," November 10, 1961, *Kennedy Papers, 1961,* Item 458, p. 711. On the doubt-dispelling purpose of the President's Commission on the Assassination of President Kennedy (Warren Commission, 1963–64), see Epstein, chapters 2 and 10. The commissions to examine the foreign aid program have also had a similar purpose—see notes 21, 22, and 23 above.

38. See chapter 4 on the role of the Congress in creating commissions and prodding the President to create them.

39. See chapter 4 for further discussion of the creation of these two commissions.

40. See, for example, Samuel P. Huntington, "Congressional Responses to the Twentieth Century," *The Congress and America's Future,* ed. David B. Truman (Englewood Cliffs, N.J.: Prentice-Hall, 1965).

41. The role of Congress in stimulating policy initiative by the President is discussed in John R. Johannes, *Policy Innovation in Congress* (Morristown, N.J.: General Learning Press, 1972).

42. These suggestions were raised respectively by Senator William Roth, *Congressional Record* (daily ed., July 24, 1974), pp. S13298-99, and by Paul M. Bator, "A Watergate 'Warren Commission,' " *New York Times,* May 15, 1973, p. 39.

43. On the proposed commission on Vietnam policy, see Hugh Sidey, *A Very Personal Presidency* (New York: Atheneum, 1968), pp. 293–95.

44. On the variety of purposes of the President's Committee on Civil Rights (1946–47), see Truman, *Memoirs,* vol. 2, p. 180; John T. Elliff, "The United States Department of Justice and Individual Rights" (Ph.D. diss., Harvard University, 1967), p. 235; Barton J. Berstein, "The Ambiguous Legacy: The Truman Administration and Civil Rights," in Berstein, ed., pp. 276–81; William C. Berman, *The Politics of Civil Rights in the Truman Administration* (Columbus: Ohio State University Press, 1970), pp. 50–52; and President's Committee on Civil Rights, *To Secure These Rights* (Wash-

ington, D.C.: Government Printing Office, 1947), p. vii. For another example of multiple purposes, see the statement by Eric Goldman, quoted above, concerning the National Advisory Commission on Selective Service (1966–67).
45. Bell, pp. 122–23.

CHAPTER THREE

1. In chapter 8, commissions in the context of competing and supporting initiatives are discussed.

2. These characteristics combine qualitative dimensions and objective features that, to the White House and commission members and staff, are uniquely those of the set of organizations that were isolated by the formal definition. These characteristics are thus the operational definition of presidential advisory commissions held by the political actors as opposed to the researcher's operational definition.

3. The quote is from the White House press release announcing the appointment of the President's Committee to Appraise Employment and Unemployment Statistics (1961–62), November 10, 1961, in President's Committee to Appraise Employment and Unemployment Statistics, *Measuring Employment and Unemployment* (Washington, D.C.: Government Printing Office, 1962), p. 229. Scammon had been director of elections research for the Governmental Affairs Institute and editor of the series *American Votes,* 1 (Washington, D.C.: Governmental Affairs Institute, 1956). Spurr holds a Ph.D. in forest ecology from Yale University and has published extensively in the field of forest ecology and management.

4. For another example from among many, see "Statement by the President Announcing His Appointment of a 15 Member Commission [on Budget Concepts]," *Weekly Compilation of Presidential Documents* (Washington, D.C.: Office of the Federal Register, National Archives and Records Service, General Services Administration, 1967), 3 (March 3, 1967), p. 360. All other references to *Weekly Compilation of Presidential Documents* will be cited as *Weekly Compilation.*

5. For one among many examples, see "Letter Appointing Members of a Special Board of Inquiry on Air Safety," June 15, 1947, *Truman Papers, 1947,* Item 115, p. 278.

6. See, for example, "Letter to the Chairman of the Committee on Equal Opportunity in the Armed Forces," June 24, 1962, *Kennedy Papers, 1962,* Item 257, p. 508. This characteristic of commissions is also noted by George T. Sulzner, "The Policy Process and the Uses of National Governmental Study Commissions," *Western Political Quarterly,* 24 (September, 1971), p. 444.

7. George Meany served as a member of commissions numbered (in appendix 2) 7, 26, 31, 34, 42, 56, 57, and 64.

8. The commentators who talk about proliferating "commissions" are really talking about a more general category of advisory body within the Executive Branch, including permanent staff and planning agencies such as the Council of Economic Advisers, permanent citizen advisory committees reporting either to the President or much more commonly to one of the departments or agencies within the Executive Branch, interagency advisory committees, task forces, and White House conferences, as well as presiden-

tial advisory commissions as defined in this study. See, for example, Elizabeth Drew, "On Giving Oneself a Hotfoot: Government by Commission," *Atlantic Monthly*, 221 (May, 1968); "The Commission: How to Create a Blue Chip Consensus," *Time*, 95 (January 17, 1970), p. 22; and Thomas E. Cronin and Sanford D. Greenberg, eds., *The Presidential Advisory System* (New York: Harper & Row, 1969), pp. xvi–xvii. As of December 31, 1972, there were 1439 "federal advisory committees" in the Executive Branch. *Federal Advisory Committees: First Annual Report of the President* (Washington, D.C.: Government Printing Office, 1973), p. 6.

9. Patrick Anderson's discussion of the work of Eisenhower's press secretary, Jim Hagerty, in *The Presidents' Men* (Garden City, N.Y.: Doubleday & Company, 1968), pp. 180–93, illustrates how a President can be kept prominently in the news even when nothing is happening or when he is not doing anything.

10. For example, see White House press release (Special Presidential Committee on U.S. Trade Relations with Eastern European Countries and the U.S.S.R.), April 5, 1965, p. 2. Although the definition of presidential advisory commissions requires only that one member of a commission be from outside the federal executive branch, in fact only one commissions, the Special Board of Inquiry for Air Safety (1947), had more than 50 per cent of its members from within the Executive Branch, and 95 per cent of all commission members were not employed in the Executive Branch during their commission service.

11. "Letter to Dr. Henry Wriston on His Acceptance of the Chairmanship of the Commission on National Goals," February 7, 1960, *Eisenhower Papers, 1960*, Item 29, p. 158. In discussing his appointment of the President's Commission on the Assassination of President Kennedy, President Johnson remarked, "The commission had to be composed of men who were known to be beyond pressure and above suspicion." Lyndon B. Johnson, *The Vantage Point* (New York: Holt, Rinehart and Winston, 1971), p. 26.

12. This view of commissions is found in the testimony of William Paley, Chairman of the President's Materials Policy Commission (1951–52), "Stockpiling Strategic and Critical Materials," *Hearings Before the Special Subcommittee on Minerals, Materials, and Fuels Economics of The Senate Committee on Interior and Insular Affairs*, 83rd Cong., 1st Sess. (1953), p. 4. Two characteristics of commissions, their limited duration and their non-executive-branch composition, obviously reflect reality as well as image. In chapters 5 and 6 the degree to which the other characteristics ascribed to commissions, particularly their independence and objectivity, are accurate will be examined.

13. Matthew B. Miles, "On Temporary Systems," in *Innovation in Education*, ed. Matthew B. Miles (New York: Bureau of Publications, Teachers College, Columbia University, 1964).

14. The President's Materials Policy Commission (1951–52) was extended by the White House from the original "six to nine months" to the eventual sixteen months that it took to complete the report. William R. Hamilton, "The President's Materials Policy Commission (Paley Commission): A History and Analytical Inquiry Into Policy Formation by a Presidential Commission" (Ph.D. diss., University of Maryland, 1963), pp. 149, 218, 226–27.

15. See, for example, Hamilton, pp. 79–81, 146, 213, and 322.
16. Miles, p. 442.
17. See, for example, Hamilton, p. 109.
18. On the conflicting perceptions of organizational objectives, see Anthony Downs, *Inside Bureaucracy* (Boston: Little, Brown and Company, 1967), pp. 76, 84–87, 134, and 223–38.
19. Miles, p. 453.
20. *Ibid.,* pp. 454–55; and Downs, p. 236.
21. On the greater capacity of small groups to be more effectively goal directed, see Miles, pp. 456–57; Downs, pp. 110–13; and W. Maclean Dickson and Bernard Alpert, "Appointive Committees–A Behavioral Analysis of Committee Effectiveness and Potential for Action," *University of Washington Business Review,* 24 (October, 1964), p. 18. Dickson and Alpert suggest that the optimum committee size is between four and eleven members (p. 18). The mean size of the commissions in this study is thirteen members. The range is from three to fifty members. Forty-seven of the ninety-nine commissions had eleven or fewer members and seventy of them had fourteen or fewer. So a large majority of commissions have been within or near the optimum size range for effective interaction among the members.
22. Miles, pp. 461–63.
23. *Ibid.,* pp. 465–73.
24. *Ibid.,* pp. 473–76. This observation, as well as the above one on the physical and social isolation of commissions, applies most fully to the commission staff and only to a lesser extent to the commission members, who in general devote less than full time to the activities of the commission.
25. The capacity of *ad hoc* committees for problem analysis has been recognized as useful in contexts other than the presidency. See the sources cited by Dickson and Alpert, p. 20; Miles, pp. 486–90; and Arthur W. Macmahon, "Boards, Advisory," *Encyclopedia of the Social Sciences* (New York: The Macmillan Company, 1930), vol. 2, pp. 611–12, as well as David S. Brown, *A Guide to the Use of Advisory Committees* (Washington, D.C.: Department of HEW, Public Health Service, 1959), pp. 1–9; and John D. Lewis, "Some New Forms of Democratic Participation in American Government," in *The Study of Comparative Government,* ed. Jasper Shannon (New York: Appleton-Century-Crofts, 1949).
26. The recruitment of commission members is discussed more fully in chapter 5.
27. The recruitment of commission staff is dicussed more fully in chapter 6.
28. On the quality of the staff of the National Advisory Commission on Selective Service (1966–67), see Harry A. Marmion, *Selective Service: Conflict and Compromise* (New York: John Wiley, 1968), p. 152.
29. See, for example, Commission on International Trade and Investment Policy, "Annex 4," *United States International Economic Policy in an Interdependent World* (Washington, D.C.: Government Printing Office, 1971), pp. 389–94; National Advisory Commission on Civil Disorders, "Appendix E" and "Appendix F," *Report of the National Advisory Commission on Civil Disorders* (Washington, D.C.: Government Printing Office, 1968), pp. 300–304; President's Commission on Law Enforcement and Administration of Justice, "Appendix B," *The Challenge of Crime in a Free*

Society (New York: Avon Books, 1968), pp. 690–710; President's Water Resources Policy Commission, "Appendix 2," *A Water Policy for the American People* (Washington, D.C.: Government Printing Office, 1950), pp. 317–21; and President's Advisory Commission on Universal Training, "Appendix I," *Program for National Security* (Washington, D.C.: Government Printing Office, 1947), pp. 104–10. On the ability of *ad hoc* advisory groups to enlist the advice of the most talented people in their fields, see also the testimony of Robert Cutler in Senator Henry M. Jackson, ed., *The National Security Council: Jackson Subcommittee Papers on Policy-Making at the Presidential Level* (New York: Praeger, 1965), pp. 130–32.

30. Nicholas Katzenbach, "Criminal Justice," *Vital Speeches,* 32 (September 15, 1966), p. 709.

31. Felix Frankfurter, *The Public and Its Government* (New Haven: Yale University Press, 1930), pp. 162–63.

32. See James S. Campbell, "The Usefulness of Commission Studies of Collective Violence," *The Annals,* 391 (September, 1970), p. 171; Sulzner, p. 445; and David B. Truman, *The Governmental Process* (New York: Alfred A. Knopf, 1951), pp. 434–35.

33. "Findings and Recommendations of the President's Commission on Veterans' Pensions (Bradley Commission)," *Hearings before the House Committee on Veterans' Affairs,* 84th Cong., 2d Sess. (1956), p. 3580.

34. Robert E. Lane and David O. Sears, *Public Opinion* (Englewood Cliffs, N.J.: Prentice-Hall, 1964), p. 47.

35. Arthur H. Vandenberg, Jr., ed., *The Private Papers of Senator Vandenberg* (Boston: Houghton Mifflin Company, 1952), p. 375.

36. Lane and Sears, pp. 48–51.

37. Lloyd A. Free and Hadley Cantril, *The Political Beliefs of Americans* (New Brunswick, N.J.: Rutgers University Press, 1967), p. 12.

38. Truman, pp. 159, 512–24. There do not seem to be any empirical studies that explore this question of the standards by which the public evaluates the legitimacy of a decision-making process. The characterization of the normative model offered here is therefore, unfortunately, only a plausible hypothesis.

39. The painstaking seven-month impeachment inquiry undertaken by the House Judiciary Committee before decisions were made on articles of impeachment in July, 1974, is a clear example of a systematic effort to satisfy this public expectation.

40. For a typical example of this elaborate canvassing of opinions, see National Commission on Product Safety, *Final Report of the National Commission on Product Safety* (Washington, D.C.: Government Printing Office, 1970), pp. 131–45. In this respect, the hearings held by commissions serve the same purpose of satisfying "the rules of the game" in making decisions as those held by congressional committees. See Truman, pp. 373–77.

41. Truman, p. 458. The "advisory committees" referred to by Truman are a broader category than presidential advisory commissions as defined in this study. But the point is equally valid solely with respect to the latter.

42. Charles Lindblom, "The Science of 'Muddling Through,' " *Public Administration Review,* 19 (Spring, 1959), pp. 79–81. Other theorists of decision making who suggest the existence of such a normative model are Edward

Banfield, "Ends and Means in Planning," in *Concepts and Issues in Adminis-trative Behavior,* ed. Sidney Mailick and Edward Van Ness (Englewood Cliffs, N.J.: Prentice-Hall, 1962), and Richard Cyert and James March, *A Behavioral Theory of the Firm* (Englewood Cliffs, N.J.: Prentice-Hall, 1963), chapter 2.

43. Marion Greene, "Forum: Should We Oppose the Truman Civil Rights Program?" *Forum,* 109 (June, 1948), p. 352.

44. "The President's News Conference," January 3, 1952, *Truman Papers, 1952,* Item 2, p. 3.

45. *Hearings* (1953), pp. 4–12.

46. *Hearings* (1956), pp. 3601, 3633, 3644, 3756–61, and 3779.

47. *Ibid.,* pp. 3580, 3599–3600.

48. "Regional Medical Complexes for Heart Disease, Cancer, Stroke, and Other Diseases," *Hearings before the House Committee on Interstate and Foreign Commerce,* 89th Cong., 1st Sess. (1965), pp. 120–24, 162–63.

49. See Sulzner, pp. 443–44; Edward Jay Epstein, *Inquest: The Warren Commission and the Establishment of Truth* (New York: The Viking Press, 1966), p. xvii; Gabriel A. Almond and Sidney Verba, *The Civic Culture* (Boston: Little, Brown and Company, 1965), p. 46; and William C. Mitchell, *The American Polity* (New York: The Free Press, 1962), p. 127.

50. Miles, *passim.* The effectiveness of commissions in educating their mem-bers is discussed in chapters 6 and 8.

51. This estimate was arrived at by reading the mandates of commissions and weighing other evidence from interviews and published sources to see whether the problems commissions were called upon to deal with, the manner in which they were directed to handle the problems, and the circumstances of the times indicate that the problems were ones that needed to be basically rethought and that the commissions were intended to do the rethinking. The other estimates in this chapter were arrived at in the same way.

52. "Letter to William S. Paley on the Creation of the President's Materials Policy Commission," January 22, 1951, *Truman Papers, 1951,* Item 19, p. 118.

53. *Ibid.*

54. National Commission on Materials Policy, *Material Needs and the Envir-onment Today and Tomorrow* (Washington, D.C.: Government Printing Office, 1973), pp. 1–4.

55. President's Commission on Veterans' Pensions, "Letter from President Eisenhower to General Bradley," *Findings and Recommendations, Vete-rans' Benefits in the United States* (Washington, D.C.: Government Printing Office, 1956), pp. 413–15.

56. John M. Pfiffner and Robert Presthus, *Public Administration,* 5th ed. (New York: The Ronald Press Company, 1967), p. 306.

57. President's Commission on Income Maintenance Programs, *Poverty Amid Plenty, The American Paradox* (Washington, D.C.: Government Printing Office, 1969), pp. 89–90.

58. "Statement by the President upon Signing the Social Security Amend-ments and upon Appointing a Commission to Study the Nation's Welfare Programs," January 2, 1968, *Johnson Papers, 1968,* Item 3, pp. 14–15.

59. President's Commission on Immigration and Naturalization, *Whom We*

Shall Welcome (Washington, D.C.: Government Printing Office, 1952), p. 263.

60. This idea, for example, was considered by the 1911 Immigration Commission. Roy L. Garis, *Immigration Restriction: A Study of the Opposition to and Regulation of Immigration into the United States* (New York: The Macmillan Company, 1927), p. 122.

61. See, for example, Adam Yarmolinsky, "Ideas into Programs," in Cronin and Greenberg, pp. 91–100; Downs, pp. 195–204; Peter M. Blau, *The Dynamics of Bureaucracy*, rev. ed. (Chicago: University of Chicago Press, 1963), chapter 12; and Victor A. Thompason, "Bureaucracy and Innovation," *Administrative Science Quarterly*, 10 (June, 1965), pp. 1–2. Blau and Downs also argue, quite persuasively, that there are circumstances and forces that are conducive to change and innovation in public bureaucracies. The point here is that while bureaucracies are not totally incapable of some kinds of innovation, they are in general "extraordinarily unfriendly to innovation," particularly if it involves a basic rethinking of organizational goals–that is, "reorienting change." The quote is from Yarmolinsky, p. 91.

62. "Presidential Advisory Committees," *Hearings before a Subcommittee of the House Committee on Government Operations*, 91st Cong., 2d Sess., Part I, p. 92 (1970).

63. For example of relations between agencies and interest groups and their consequences for agency policy, see Arthur Maass, *Muddy Waters: The Army Engineers and the Nation's Rivers* (Cambridge, Mass.: Harvard University Press, 1951); J. Leiper Freeman, *The Political Process: Executive Bureau–Legislative Committee Relations*, rev. ed. (New York: Random House, 1965); Philip Selznick, *TVA and the Grass Roots* (New York: Harper and Row, 1966); and Herbert Kaufman, *The Forest Ranger* (Baltimore: The Johns Hopkins Press, 1960).

64. Howard Shuman, "Behind the Scenes and Under the Rug," *The Washington Monthly*, July, 1969, pp. 18–20.

65. President Johnson hints at this same reason in Johnson, p. 330.

66. Downs, pp. 204–15.

67. *Ibid.*, pp. 211–16.

68. *Ibid.*, pp. 195–97.

69. *Ibid.*, pp. 206–8; and Miles, pp. 443–44.

70. See, for example, Richard Fenno, Jr., *The Power of the Purse* (Boston: Little, Brown and Company, 1966), pp. 315–17.

71. President's Citizen Advisers on the Mutual Security Program (Fairless Committee, 1956–57), President's Committee to Study the United States Military Assistance Program (Draper Committee, 1958–59), President's Committee to Strengthen the Security of the Free World (Clay Committee, 1962–63), Presidential Task Force on International Development (1969–70), and President's Committee to Appraise Employment and Unemployment Statistics (1961–62).

72. The distinction between "old" and "new" post-World War II federal responsibilities is clear in some cases, such as foreign aid. In other cases, a "new" responsibility may be a reassertion of a commitment that was long dormant, such as the protection of the civil rights of individuals, or a major change in the scale, focus, and degree of direct control over an "old" responsibility such as the interstate highway program or the funding of

selected aspects of higher education. In these latter cases, the federal government had been concerned with roads since the legislation in the 1790's dealing with post roads, and involvement with higher education dates from the 1862 Morrill Land Grant Act.

73. President's Committee on Foreign Aid, *European Recovery and American Aid* (Washington, D.C.: Government Printing Office, 1947), pp. 105–14.

74. Harry S. Truman, *Memoirs,* vol. 2 (Garden City, N.Y.: Doubleday & Company, 1956), p. 21.

75. Commission on National Goals, *Goals for Americans* (Englewood Cliffs, N.J.: Prentice-Hall, 1960), pp. 15–20. The President's Committee on Foreign Aid (1947), the President's Committee to Study the United States Military Assistance Program (1958–59), and the President's Commission for the Observance of the Twenty-fifth Anniversary of the United Nations (1970–71) are also possible exceptions to the general absence of commissions concerned with basic foreign policy questions.

76. President's Advisory Commission on Universal Training (1946–47), National Advisory Commission on Selective Service (1966–67), President's Committee on an All-Volunteer Armed Force (1969–70), President's Committee on Integration of the Medical Services of the Government (1945–46), Committee to Review Veterans Hospitals (1950), President's Commission on Veterans' Pensions (1955–56), President's Advisory Panel on Federal Salary Systems (1961–63), President's Special Panel on Federal Salaries (1965), and Committee on Equal Opportunity in the Armed Forces (1962–64).

77. See *The Federalist Papers* (New York: The New American Library, 1961), nos. 69, 70, and 71.

78. William R. Caspary, "The 'Mood Theory': A Study of Public Opinion and Foreign Policy," *American Political Science Review,* 64 (June, 1970), p. 546. Emphasis in original. Even if basic changes in the structure of public attitudes occurred since Caspary wrote, his generalization still applies to most of the period under consideration.

79. Holbert N. Carroll, *The House of Representatives and Foreign Affairs,* rev. ed. (Boston: Little, Brown and Company, 1966), pp. 7–11. See, also, Ernest S. Griffith, *Congress: Its Contemporary Role,* 3rd ed. (New York: New York University Press, 1961), pp. 12, 135–38; and Louis W. Koenig, *The Chief Executive,* rev. ed. (New York: Harcourt, Brace and World, 1968), pp. 125–26.

80. The commissions referred to are, respectively, the President's Commission on Migratory Labor (1950–51), the President's Advisory Commission on Narcotic and Drug Abuse (1963–64), and the Commission on American Shipbuilding (1970–73).

81. A good example of the way in which congressmen can get a grip on military policy through its domestic impact is explained in Lewis A. Dexter, "Congressmen and the Making of Military Policy," in *New Perspectives on the House of Representatives,* ed. Robert L. Peabody and Nelson W. Polsby (Chicago: Rand McNally & Company, 1963). See, also, Robert J. Art, *The TFX Decision: McNamara and the Military* (Boston: Little, Brown and Company, 1968), pp. 2–6. Dexter also describes the perceptions that congressmen have of their lack of competence to make judgments on military policy.

82. See Carroll, p. 8; and Raymond H. Dawson, "Innovation and Intervention in Defense Policy," in Peabody and Polsby, p. 277.
83. President's Committee on Foreign Aid (Harriman Committee, 1947), President's Citizen Advisers on the Mutual Security Program (Fairless Committee, 1956–57), President's Committee to Study the United States Military Assistance Program (Draper Committee, 1958–59), President's Committee to Strengthen the Security of the Free World (Clay Committee, 1962–63), Task Force to Promote Overseas Sale of Securities of U.S. Companies (1963–64), Special Presidential Committee on U.S. Trade Relations with Eastern European Countries and the U.S.S.R. (1965), Industry-Government Special Task Force on Travel (1967–68), Presidential Task Force on International Trade and Investment Policy (1970–71).
84. See, for example, Johnson, p. 472.
85. *Congress and the Nation,* vol. 3 (Washington, D.C.: Congressional Quarterly, 1973), p. 880.
86. Richard Neustadt, "Approaches to Staffing the Presidency: Notes on FDR and JFK," *American Political Science Review,* 57 (December, 1963); and Richard T. Johnson, *Managing the White House* (New York: Harper & Row, 1974).
87. This is remedied only partially by the specially focused staffs in the Executive Office as a whole, such as the Council of Economic Advisers.
88. The Domestic Council was created by Reorganization Plan 2 of 1970 and Executive Order No. 11541 (July 1, 1970).
89. President's Committee on Administrative Management, *Report of the President's Committee on Administrative Management with Special Studies* (Washington, D.C.: Government Printing Office, 1937), p. 5.
90. William D. Carey, "Presidential Staffing in the Sixties and Seventies," in *Hearings,* Part I (1970), p. 165. Emphasis in original.
91. In Cronin and Greenberg, pp. xvii–xviii, some of the major and typical elements of this system are listed.

CHAPTER FOUR

1. Theodore C. Sorensen, *Kennedy* (New York: Bantam Books, 1966), p. 268.
2. See William C. Berman, *The Politics of Civil Rights in the Truman Administration* (Columbus: Ohio State University Press, 1970), p. 51; and Walter White, *A Man Called White* (New York: The Viking Press, 1948), pp. 331–32.
3. See "Presidential Task Forces," Weekly Compilation, 5 (September 27, 1969), p. 1304.
4. Numerous examples can be found in Patrick Anderson, *The President's Men* (Garden City, N.Y.: Doubleday and Company, 1968); and George E. Reedy, *The Twilight of the Presidency* (New York: The World Publishing Company, 1970), especially chapter 7.
5. On the antispending bias of the Bureau of the Budget (since 1970, the Office of Management & Budget), see Arthur Maass, "In Accord with the Program of the President: An Essay on Staffing the Presidency," *Public Policy,* vol. 4 (Cambridge, Mass.: Harvard University Press, 1953).
6. Sec. 103, PL 80–253, 61 Stat. 499.
7. Edward H. Hobbs, *Behind the President: A Study of Executive Office Agencies* (Washington, D.C.: Public Affairs Press, 1954), pp. 156–81.

8. *Ibid.*, pp. 168–69.

9. President's Materials Policy Commission, *Foundations for Growth and Security* (Washington, D.C.: Government Printing Office, 1952), p. 175; and William R. Hamilton, Jr., "The President's Materials Policy Commission (Paley Commission): A History and Analytical Inquiry into Policy Formation by a Presidential Commission" (Ph.D. diss., University of Maryland, 1962), pp. 41–42.

10. The commission, in fact, did recommend that the NSRB oversee an upgraded and expanded federal materials program, and as a necessary corollary that the NSRB and its readiness planning function be upgraded and expanded. However, the NSRB was abolished early in the Eisenhower Administration, and its functions were transferred to the Office of Defense Mobilization by Reorganization Plan 3 of 1953, 67 Stat. 634.

11. Berman, p. 53; and John T. Elliff, "The United States Department of Justice and Individual Rights" (Ph.D. diss., Harvard University, 1967), p. 236.

12. On the circumstances and forces conducive to change in public bureaucracies, see Anthony Downs, *Inside Bureaucracy* (Boston: Little, Brown and Company, 1967), pp. 198–200; and Peter M. Blau, *The Dynamics of Bureaucracy*, rev. ed. (Chicago: University of Chicago Press, 1963), pp. 241–46.

13. See White, pp. 329–32; William C. Berman, "Civil Rights and Civil Liberties," in *The Truman Period as a Research Field*, ed. Richard S. Kirkendall (Columbia: University of Missouri Press, 1967), p. 190; and Barton J. Bernstein, "The Ambiguous Legacy: The Truman Administration and Civil Rights," in *Politics and Policies of the Truman Administration*, ed. Barton J. Bernstein (Chicago: Quadrangle Books, 1970), pp. 276–77.

14. With respect to President Truman and the liberal wing of the Democratic Party, see Bernstein, p. 276; and Berman, *The Politics of Civil Rights*, p. 77. On the conditions for access to government decision makers, see David B. Truman, *The Governmental Process* (New York: Alfred A. Knopf, 1951), pp. 265–70. President Johnson relates that Eugene Rostow of Yale University Law School, columnist Joseph Alsop, and Secretary of State Dean Rusk all suggested the idea of a commission on the assassination of President Kennedy. Lyndon B. Johnson, *Vantage Point* (New York: Holt, Rinehart and Winston, 1971), p. 26.

15. *Congressional Record*, 89th Cong., 1st Sess., p. 19561.

16. *Ibid.*, p. 24377.

17. Other commissions created by statute are a response to initiatives from the President who either wants to have Congress "on board" politically in support of an inquiry into some subject or to have an easier time in funding a commission through the regular appropriation process. The President's Committee on Education Beyond High School (1956–57) is a good example of a commission created by statute at the initiative of the President. In total, nine commissions were created by the Congress: the National Commission on Technology, Automation, and Economic Progress (1964–66), the National Commission on Urban Problems (1967–68), and the National Commission on Product Safety (1967–70), in addition to the President's Committee on Education Beyond High School (1956–57), the Commission on Marine Science, Engineering, and Resources (1966–69), the Commission

on Obscenity and Pornography (1967–70), the Commission on American Shipbuilding (1970–73), the National Commission on Materials Policy (1970–73), and the National Commission on State Workmen's Compensation Laws (1970–72).

18. "Truman Board, Congress Group Will Probe Aviation Industry," *Aviation Week*, 47 (July 28, 1947), p. 11.

19. "Statement by the President upon Signing Executive Order Establishing the Missouri Basin Survey Commission," *Truman Papers, 1952*, January 3, 1952, Item 3, p. 2.

20. Roy F. Nichols, *The Genesis of the Marshall Plan* (The University of Nottingham, England: Montague Burton International Relations Lecture, 1948/49), p. 19.

21. Arthur H. Vandenberg, Jr., ed., *The Private Papers of Senator Vandenberg* (Boston: Houghton Mifflin Company, 1952), pp. 376–77.

22. Richard M. Cyert and James G. March, *A Behavioral Theory of the Firm* (Englewood Cliffs, N.J.: Prentice-Hall, 1963), pp. 120–22.

23. *Ibid.*

24. *Ibid.*, p. 121.

25. *Ibid.*

26. The institutional weakness of the White House as a policy analyst is discussed in chapter 3.

27. For a summary list of the components of the "presidential advisory system," see Thomas E. Cronin and Sanford D. Greenberg, eds., *The Presidential Advisory System* (New York: Harper and Row, 1969), pp. xvii–xviii.

28. See chapter 1 on the historical origins of presidential advisory commissions.

29. The relationship between commissions and types of problems and the circumstances surrounding them was discussed above in chapter 3. The relationship of commissions to presidential style is discussed in chapter 5.

30. Cyert and March, p. 80.

31. For an example of this kind of legal analysis, see James Hart, *The Ordinance Making Power of the President*, (Baltimore: John Hopkins Press, 1925).

32. There are exceptions to this, as to every generalization; for example, Lewis A. Froman, Jr., *The Congressional Process: Strategies, Rules and Procedures* (Boston: Little, Brown and Company, 1967).

33. See *The Federalist Papers* (New York: Mentor Books, 1961), nos. 70, 71, 72, and 73; Theodore Roosevelt, *An Autobiography* (New York: Charles Scribner's Sons, 1927), pp. 362–65; and Edward S. Corwin, *The President: Office and Powers*, 4th ed. rev. (New York: New York University Press, 1957), pp. 10–13.

34. An example of the former is the press release from the White House, April 5, 1965, announcing the creation of the Special Presidential Committee on U.S. Trade Relations with Eastern European Countries and the U.S.S.R. (1965); and an example of the latter is Executive Order No. 10974, November 10, 1961, creating the President's Commission on Campaign Costs.

35. These and other alternative sources of commission funds are discussed in greater detail below.

36. The precise limits of the congressional investigating power have been the subject of extensive debate and commentary, but the existence of the power in general is well established. See *The Constitution of the United States of America: Analysis and Interpretation* (Washington, D.C.: Government Printing Office, 1964), pp. 106–17; Joseph P. Harris, *Congressional Control of Administration* (Garden City, N.Y.: Anchor Books, 1964), chapter 9; and Telford Taylor, *Grand Inquest: The Story of Congressional Investigations* (New York: Ballantine Books, 1955).

37. House Committee on Government Operations, *Executive Orders and Proclamations: A Study of a Use of Presidential Powers*, 85th Cong., 1st Sess. (Committee Print, 1957), p. 1. See, also, Hart, pp. 47–50.

38. Executive Order No. 9808, establishing the President's Committee on Civil Rights (December 5, 1946). This wording was also used in Executive Order No. 10980 establishing the President's Commission on the Status of Women (December 14, 1961). The wording was slightly different in Executive Order No. 10486 creating the Advisory Committee on Government Housing Policies and Programs (September 12, 1953) and Executive Order No. 11513 creating the President's Commission on School Finance (March 3, 1970).

39. The "take care" clause was in fact used in 1842 by President Tyler to justify his creation of a commission to investigate the New York Customs House when his authority to appoint such a commission was questioned in Congress. *Congressional Globe*, 27th Cong., 2d Sess., p. 229. Carl Marcy, *Presidential Commissions* (New York: King's Crown Press, 1945), pp. 7–14, outlines some of the constitutional sources of power by which various kinds of presidential bodies are created.

40. George B. Galloway, "Presidential Commissions," *Editorial Research Reports*, 1 (May 28, 1931), p. 358.

41. *Congressional Globe*, 27th Cong., 2d Sess., p. 481.

42. "Presidential Advisory Committees," *Hearings Before a Subcommittee of the House Committee on Government Operations*, Part I, 91st Cong., 2d. Sess. (1970), p. 78.

43. Roosevelt, p. 417.

44. Act of August 26, 1842, 5 Stat. 533.

45. Act of March 4, 1909, 35 Stat. 1027.

46. Independent Offices Appropriation Act, 1945, 31 U.S.C. 696, 58 Stat. 337.

47. In general, on the obstacles to financing commissions, see Alan L. Dean, "*Ad Hoc* Commissions for Policy Formulation?" in Cronin and Greenberg, pp. 107–9. All of these restrictions clearly apply to a much broader category of Executive Branch bodies than *ad hoc* presidential advisory commissions, but they will be discussed only in terms of their relations to them. What impact, if any, these legislative restrictions had on the use of advisory bodies from President Tyler's time up to the Truman Administration has not been explored in this study. President Theodore Roosevelt flatly states in his *Autobiography* with respect to the Tawney Amendment that "I would not have complied with it" (p. 416). This cavalier attitude, in part perhaps fed on the bravery of no longer being in office, was not emulated by the Presidents in the period 1945–72. They all sought to come

to terms with these provisions in some way other than simply refusing to be bound by them.
48. These are the commissions numbered 19, 21, 45, 46, 47, 53, 55, 56, 57, 63, 65, and 68 in appendix 2. In most of these cases, only appropriations were made, apparently because the commissions were felt to have sufficient authorizations implied under existing legislation.
49. *Hearings,* Part I (1970), p. 38. Staats also noted in the same testimony (pp. 38–39) that this interpretation has been set forth in 11 *Comptroller General* 495 and 27 *Attorney General* 432. The opinion of the Attorney General was rendered in 1909 very shortly after the Tawney Amendment was passed. See, also, Marcy, pp. 17–21, and the testimony of Assistant Attorney General Barnes in "Employment of Experts and Consultants by Federal Agencies," *Hearings Before a Subcommittee of the House Committee on Government Operations,* 84th Cong., 2d Sess. (1956), pp. 137–40.
50. *Hearings,* Part I (1970), p. 39.
51. Second Deficiency Appropriation Act, 1945, PL 79–132, 59 Stat. 414, Emergency Fund for the President.
52. The appropriations for the Emergency Fund for the President are contained in First Supplemental National Defense Appropriation Act, 1943, PL 77–678, 56 Stat. 995, which states: "Emergency fund for the President: To enable the President through appropriate agencies of the Government, to provide for emergencies affecting the national security and defense and for each and every purpose connected therewith, to make all necessary expenditures incident thereto for any purpose for which the Congress has previously made appropriation or authorization and without regard to the provisions of law regulating the expenditure of Government funds or the employment of persons in the Government service. . . ." The Special Projects fund first appears in General Governmental Matters Appropriation Act, 1956, PL 84–110, 69 Stat. 192, which states: "For expenses necessary to provide staff assistance for the President in connection with special projects, to be expended in his discretion and without regard to such provisions of law regarding the expenditure of Government funds or the compensation and employment of persons in Government service as he may specify. . . ."
53. With the obvious exception of those created by statute.
54. The quote is from Executive Order No. 10317, establishing the President's Commission on the Health Needs of the Nation (1951–52). This exemption from the provisions of the Act of 1842 and the Tawney Amendment appears in the executive orders for ten of the fourteen commissions which were created by executive order and which cite funding from one of the two presidential funds. The statement of exemption does not appear in the cases of the four most recent commissions created by executive order and citing funding from one of the two presidential funds, perhaps indicating that these congressional restrictions have atrophied to the point that one need no longer specify that they do not apply. It is also interesting to note that in only one executive order citing funding from one of the two presidential funds is the Russell Amendment specifically waived. This is in Executive Order No. 10095, creating the President's Water Resources Policy Commission (1950). There is no apparent reason for not

continuing to waive it explicitly, as is clearly allowed by the terms of the appropriation for the two funds, unless it has been felt to be wise not to wave a red flag in front of Senator Russell, from whom the amendment takes its name and who was a formidable figure in the Senate until his death in 1971.

55. For example, the President's Advisory Commission on Universal Training (1946–47) was financed from the Emergency Fund for the President. President's Advisory Commission on Universal Training, *Program for National Security* (Washington, D.C.: Government Printing Office, 1947), p. 104.

56. See, for example, "Findings and Recommendations of the President's Commission on Veterans' Pensions (Bradley Commission)," *Hearings Before the House Committee on Veterans' Affairs*, 84th Cong., 2d Sess. (1956), pp. 3622, 3625, and 3640. On the subject of the two unrestricted presidential funds, see, also, the testimony of Comptroller General Staats in *Hearings*, Part I (1970), p. 54.

57. 59 Stat. 134.

58. These are the executive orders creating the commissions numbered 36, 44, 47, 48, 52, 53, and 64 in appendix 2.

59. *Hearings*, Part I (1970), p. 63. Harold Seidman notes that the 1945 act (31 U.S.C. 691) has also been used to get around the provisions of the 1909 Tawney Amendment. *Politics, Position, and Power: The Dynamics of Federal Organization* (New York: Oxford University Press, 1970), p. 174. Mr. Ink also goes on to say, "More recently, however, the Congress enacted a series of restrictive provisions to the 1969 and 1970 appropriation acts which stated 'none of the funds in this act shall be available to finance interdepartmental boards, commissions, councils, committees, or similar groups under section 214 of the Independent Offices Appropriation Act, 1946 (31 U.S.C. 691) which do not have prior and specific congressional approval of such methods of financial support.' The intent of Congress in this instance was to prevent contributory funding of interagency committees, wherein Federal agencies make cash contributions to pay the expenses of certain interagency groups, unless approved by Congress" (p. 63). The impact (if any) of these new restrictions on the funding of commissions was not noticeable in the period under consideration in this study.

60. For example, the President's Commission on Universal Training (1946–47) named nineteen executive agencies which had furnished it with "important materials, studies, or advice." President's Advisory Commission on Universal Training, pp. 101–2. The President's Committee to Appraise Employment and Unemployment Statistics (1961–62) was loaned staff from three federal agencies. President's Committee to Appraise Employment and Unemployment Statistics, *Measuring Employment and Unemployment* (Washington, D.C.: Government Printing Office, 1962), p. 6. Neither of these commissions had members who were officials in the federal Executive Branch.

61. Thus, in this way, a commission indirectly receives a congressional appropriation. See, for example, the testimony of Lloyd Cutler, executive director of the National Commission on the Causes and Prevention of Violence (1968–69) in *Hearings*, Part II (1970), p. 128.

62. For example, nine of the thirteen full-time professional staff members of

the President's Commission on Heart Disease, Cancer, and Stroke (1964) were on loan from the Department of HEW. Commission on Heart Disease, Cancer, and Stroke, *Report to the President: National Program to Conquer Heart Disease, Cancer and Stroke* (Washington, D.C.: Government Printing Office, 1965), pp. 85–86. None of the members of this commission was an HEW official.

63. The quotation is from Executive Order of June 13, 1970, establishing the President's Commission on Campus Unrest (1970).

64. 5 U.S.C. 3109 and 5 U.S.C. 5703. For fourteen of the twenty-nine commissions created by executive order, one or both of these provisions were cited as a source of funds. These two provisions were, respectively, 5 U.S.C. 55a and 5 U.S.C. 73b-2 under an earlier codification. The commissions for which one or both of these provisions is cited are those numbered 35, 36, 45, 46, 47, 48, 51, 52, 53, 56, 58, 64, 87, and 90, in appendix 2.

65. See, for example, National Commission on Higher Education, *Establishing Goals* (Washington, D.C.: Government Printing Office, 1947), p. v; and President's Materials Policy Commission, *The Promise of Technology* (Washington, D.C.: Government Printing Office, 1952), p. xi.

66. See, for example, President's Commission on Migratory Labor, *Migratory Labor in American Agriculture* (Washington, D.C.: Government Printing Office, 1951), p. v; and President's Materials Policy Commission, *Foundations for Growth and Security,* p. 175.

67. See, for example, the testimony by William Paley, Chairman of the President's Materials Policy Commission, in "Stockpiling Strategic and Critical Materials," *Hearings before the Special Subcommittee on Minerals, Materials, and Fuels Economics of the Senate Committee on Interior and Insular Affairs,* 83rd Cong., 1st Sess. (1954), p. 6.

68. See, for example, *Hearings,* Part I (1970), p. 74; and Commission on American Shipbuilding, *Report,* II (Washington, D.C.: Government Printing Office, 1973), p. 11.

69. Commission on National Goals, *Goals for Americans* (Englewood Cliffs, N.J.: Prentice-Hall, 1960), p. iv. The White House had originally hoped to raise $3–5 million for an extensive study patterned on President Hoover's Research Committee on Social Trends. The foundations balked at this idea, and the Commission on National Goals undertook a more limited task with about $400,000 and was delayed for a year in getting organized after it was first announced.

70. For example, the Ford Foundation made grants to both the National Advisory Commission on Civil Disorders (1967–68) (National Advisory Commission on Civil Disorders, *Report of the National Advisory Commission on Civil Disorders* [Washington, D.C.: Government Printing Office, 1968], p. 321) and the National Commission on the Causes and Prevention of Violence (1968–69) (testimony of Robert Cutler, executive director of the Commission, in *Hearings,* Part II [1970], p. 128).

71. These constitutional issues are discussed briefly in Marcy, pp. 17–18, Corwin, pp. 71–72, and *Constitution of the United States: Analysis and Interpretation,* pp. 499–501.

72. Roosevelt, p. 417.

73. PL 89–196, 79 Stat. 827; PL 89–309, 79 Stat. 1151; PL 89–797, 80 Stat. 1502; and Executive Order No. 11236 (July 23, 1965).

74. President's Commission on Law Enforcement and Administration of Justice, *The Challenge of Crime in a Free Society* (New York: Avon Books, 1968), p. 688.
75. PL 92–463, 86 Stat. 770.
76. These topics are discussed in detail in chapters 6, 7, and 8.
77. See Hamilton, p. 225; and Donald Herzberg, "Horse and Buggy Election Laws: A Presidential Concern," in *Cases in American National Government and Politics,* ed. Rocco Tressolini and Richard Frost (Englewood Cliffs, N.J.: Prentice-Hall, 1966), p. 139.
78. Fritz M. Marx, "Temporary Presidential Advisory Commissions," staff paper, Bureau of the Budget, 1952, p. 19.
79. Testimony of Comptroller General Elmer Staats and Assistant Director of the Bureau of the Budget, Dwight Ink, in *Hearings,* Part I (1970), pp. 38–39, 53–54, 62–63, and 73–74.
80. Marx, pp. 16–17; and Hobbs, p. 214.
81. President's Committee on Education Beyond High School, *Second Report to the President* (Washington, D.C.: Government Printing Office, 1957), p. xiii.
82. President's Commission on Postal Organization, *Towards Postal Excellence* (Washington, D.C.: Government Printing Office, 1968), p. 193.
83. Outside the area of purse-string control, the President's Commission on Internal Security and Individual Rights (Executive Order No. 10207, January 23, 1951; abolished by Executive Order No. 10305, November 14, 1951) was killed by the refusal of Senator McCarran's Judiciary Committee to act favorably on a bill granting the commission members an exemption from the stringent conflict of interest laws then in effect. The fullest description of this incident is given by Alan D. Harper, *The Politics of Loyalty: The White House and the Communist Issue, 1946–52* (Westport, Conn.: Greenwood Publishing Corporation, 1969), pp. 179–81. See, also, Marx, pp. 19–21; Berman, in Kirkendall, p. 207; Harry S. Truman, *Memoirs,* II (Garden City, N.Y.: Doubleday & Company, 1956), pp. 285–88; and Cabell Phillips, *The Truman Presidency* (New York: The Macmillan Company, 1966), pp. 392–93.

CHAPTER FIVE

1. For example, the National Security Resources Board played a major role in drafting the mandate of the President's Materials Policy Commission (1951–52). William R. Hamilton, Jr., "The President's Materials Policy Commission (Paley Commission): A History and Analytical Inquiry into Policy Formation by a Presidential Commission" (Ph.D. diss., University of Maryland, 1962).
2. Donald Herzberg, "Horse and Buggy Election Laws: A Presidential Concern," in *Cases in American National Government and Politics,* ed. Rocco Tressolini and Richard Frost (Englewood Cliffs, N.J.: Prentice-Hall, 1966), pp. 135–36, gives an example of such a *pro forma* charge to the President's Commission on Registration and Voting Participation (1963). See, also, "Remarks to the Members of the President's Commission on the Status of Women," February 12, 1962, *Kennedy Papers, 1962,* Item 43, p. 130.
3. For example, John Steelman of the White House staff presented a

message from President Truman at the first meeting of the National Commission on Higher Education (1946–47). George Zook, "President's Commission on Higher Education," *Higher Education*, 3 (September 2, 1946), pp. 1–2. Steelman had helped to formulate the membership of the commission and also served as its White House liaison. Arthur Burns, counsellor to President Nixon, specified the mandate of the President's Task Force on Economic Growth in a letter to its chairman. President's Task Force on Economic Growth, *Politics for American Economic Progress in the Seventies* (Washington, D.C.: Government Printing Office, 1970). The Nixon task forces of 1969 were largely Burns' idea.

4. Executive Order No. 11100 (March 31, 1963) excluded non-voting because of racial discrimination from the mandate of the President's Commission on Registration and Voting Participation (1963). See Herzberg, p. 133.

5. This commission was primarily intended to serve as window dressing for President Truman's national health insurance plan. The A.M.A., the major association of doctors, was the primary opponent of the plan. For the commission to serve the President's purpose effectively, prominent representatives of the A.M.A. had to be included. To assure some chance that they would endorse a national health insurance plan, the criteria of selection described by the White House aide was used.

6. Perhaps the most systematic and vigorous attack on legitimacy and credibility of a commission in terms of the alleged unrepresentativeness of its members and staff occurred in the case of the Commission on Obscenity and Pornography (1967–70). See "Presidential Commissions," *Hearings before the Subcommittee on Administrative Practice and Procedure of the Senate Judiciary Committee*, 92d Cong., 1st Sess. (1971), pp. 24–99.

7. The Occupational Health and Safety Act of 1970 (84 Stat. 1590) specifies in Sec. 27(c)(1) the constituency categories from which the members of the National Commission on State Workmen's Compensation Laws (1970–72) are to be chosen.

8. A similar argument is made in Hamilton, pp. 20, 312.

9. See note 7 in chapter 3 for the commissions on which Meany served. Reuther served on the commissions numbered 14, 41, and 57 in appendix 2.

10. The quotation is from Fritz M. Marx, "Temporary Presidential Advisory Commissions," staff paper, Bureau of the Budget, 1952, p. 13. John McCloy served on the President's Committee to Study the United States Military Assistance Program (1958–59) and the President's Commission on the Assassination of President Kennedy (1963–64); McCone on the Air Policy Commission (1947–48), the National Advisory Commission on Selective Service (1966–67), and the President's Committee on Urban Housing (1967–69); Folsom on the Advisory Committee on the Merchant Marine (1947), the President's Advisory Panel on Federal Salary Systems (1961–63), the Commission on Heart Disease, Cancer and Stroke (1964), and the President's Special Panel on Federal Salaries (1965); Eisenhower on the National Commission on Higher Education (1946–47), the National Commission on the Causes and Prevention of Violence (1968–69), and the Presidential Study Commission on International Radio Broadcasting

(1972–73); and Killian on the President's Communications Policy Board (1950–51), the Commission on National Goals (1960), and the Committee on Public Higher Education in the District of Columbia (1963–64).

11. See, for example, the remarks of White House aide, quoted below, concerning Dr. James Cain, who was a member of the National Advisory Commission on Health Manpower (1966–67).

12. See, for example, the remarks, of a White House aide, quoted below, concerning Thomas Vail, who was a member of the National Advisory Commission on Health Manpower (1966–67).

13. Examples of this type of permanent citizen advisory body are the Citizens Advisory Committee on Recreation and Natural Beauty created in 1966 and the Citizens Advisory Board on Youth Opportunity created in 1967. On the use of appointments to these bodies for patronage, see Rowland Evans and Robert Novak, "Patronage Gap," *Washington Post,* August 1, 1969, p. 10A; and Don Oberdorfer, "Keeping Tab on U.S. Non-Jobs Proves No Mean Job in Itself," Washington Post, *January 15, 1970, p. A17.*

14. See George B. Galloway, "Presidential Commission," *Editorial Research Reports,* 1 (May 28, 1931), pp. 363–64; Avery Leiserson, *Administrative Regulation: A Study in Representation of Interests* (Chicago: University of Chicago Press, 1942), chapter 4; John D. Lewis, "Some New Forms of Democratic Participation in American Government," in *The Study of Comparative Government,* ed. Jasper Shannon (New York: Appleton-Century-Crofts, 1949); and Franklin Smallwood, "Is the Committee in Order?: An Appraisal of the Public Advisory Body in Representative Government" (Ph.D. diss., Harvard University, 1958), pp. 10–13.

15. Hamilton, p. 43.

16. See, for example, Herzberg, p. 131.

17. See, for example, Hamilton, pp. 42–43.

18. See Marx, p. 15; and "Truman Board, Congress Group Will Probe Aviation Industry," *Aviation Week,* 47 (July 28, 1947), p. 12.

19. The naming of one member each was actually delegated to the Republican and Democratic national party chairmen in the case of the President's Commission on Registration and Voting Participation (1963). Herzberg, pp. 131–32.

20. Patrick Anderson, *The Presidents' Men* (Garden City, N.Y.: Doubleday & Company, 1968), gives an example of this kind of political checking, p. 380.

21. Lyndon B. Johnson, *The Vantage Point* (New York: Holt, Rinehart and Winston, 1971), p. 26.

22. Howard E. Shuman, "Behind the Scenes and Under the Rug," *The Washington Monthly,* 1 (July, 1969), p. 16. Richard Scammon participated in the selection of the members of the President's Commission on Registration and Voting Participation (1963) as both an administration official with knowledge of the proposed commission's area of study and then as its prospective chairman. Herzberg, pp. 131–32.

23. The statement by President Truman in his *Memoirs* (Garden City, N.Y.: Doubleday & Company, 1956), vol. 2, p. 21, that "I chose Dr. Paul B. Magnuson . . . to head up the Commission. He selected fourteen representatives from all parts of the country to serve on the Commission," leaves the

impression that Dr. Magnuson did this on his own, without the assistance of the White House. This was not the case; he worked with the White House, but probably exercised more influence over the final choices than most other commission chairmen.

24. The rare exceptions, according to interviews, include several "turn downs" for membership on the President's Committee on Civil Rights (1946–47), including a Southern newspaper editor, and two refusals of the chairmanship of the President's Commission on Law Enforcement and Administration of Justice (1965–67), including a nationally known Republican. In "Ready to Study National Goals," *Business Week* of February 13, 1960, reported that Arthur Burns, the chairman of the Council of Economic Advisers under President Eisenhower, and Chancellor Lawrence Kimpton of the University of Chicago, turned down the chairmanship of the Commission on National Goals (1960) (p. 31). Herbert Hoover turned down the chairmanship of the ill-fated President's Commission on Internal Security and Individual Rights (1951). Alan D. Harper, *The Politics of Loyalty: The White House and the Communist Issue, 1946–52* (Westport, Conn.: Greenwood Publishing Corp., 1969), pp. 174–79.

25. See "Ready to Study National Goals" for a similar statement by the chairman of the Commission on National Goals (1960).

26. Johnson, p. 27.

27. "The Commission: How to Create a Blue Chip Consensus," *Time,* 95 (January 19, 1970): 22. For example, Dr. Howard Rusk served on the President's Committee on Integration of the Medical Services of the Government (1945–46), the Committee to Review Veterans' Hospitals (1950), the President's Committee to Strengthen the Security of the Free World (1962–63), and the Commission on Heart Disease, Cancer and Stroke (1964), under three Democratic Presidents. Anna Rosenberg Hoffman is a fixture on commissions created by Democrats which deal with manpower problems. She served on the President's Advisory Commission on Universal Training (1946–47), the National Commission on Technology, Automation, and Economic Progress (1964–66), the National Advisory Commission on Selective Service (1966–67), and the President's Commission on Income Maintenance Programs (1968–69). Crawford H. Greenwald, President of E. I. du Pont de Nemours, has been chosen as a businessman to serve on the President's Committee on Education Beyond High School (1956–57), the Commission on National Goals (1960), the Special Presidential Committee on U.S. Trade Relations with Eastern European Countries and the U.S.S.R. (1965), and the President's Commission on an All-Volunteer Armed Force (1969–70). J. Irwin Miller, chairman of the board, Cummins Engine Company, is a businessman who was regularly called on by President Johnson. He served as chairman of the Special Presidential Committee on U.S. Trade Relations with Eastern European Countries and the U.S.S.R. (1965) and of the National Advisory Commission on Health Manpower (1966–67), and as a member of the President's Commission on Postal Organization (1967–68) and the President's Committee on Urban Housing (1967–69). Other examples can be found in note 10 above.

28. See, for example, Herzberg, p. 134.

29. *Hearings* (1971), p. 105.

30. See, for example, Hamilton, p. 83, and Herzberg, p. 134.

31. See, for example, *Hearings* (1971), pp. 55–56.

32. The work of the President's Committee on Urban Housing (1967–69) was also used by the White House before the committee issued its final report in formulating the National Housing Partnerships proposal.

33. Shuman, pp. 20–21, describes such a defensive reaction by the White House to the report of the National Commission on Urban Problems (1967–68).

34. The Nixon Administration refused to reconstitute the Commission on Obscenity and Pornography (1967–70) or to attempt to influence its recommendations, although warned long in advance of the nature of its findings and recommendations, which the Administration found distasteful. See Jules Witcover, "Civil War Over Smut," *The Nation,* 210 (May 11, 1970): 550–53. The Administration limited itself to a statement rejecting the report. "Statement on the Commission's Report," *Weekly Compilation,* 6 (November 2, 1970), pp. 1454–55.

35. Elizabeth Drew maintains that commission chairmen and executive directors do receive substantive "suggestions" from presidential assistants. "On Giving Oneself a Hotfoot: Government by Commission," *Atlantic Monthly,* 221 (May, 1968): 49. Another example of testimony to the contrary is given by Robert Cutler, "Presidential Advisory Committees," *Hearings before a Subcommittee of the House Committee on Government Operations,* Part II, 91st Cong., 2d Sess. (1970), p. 115.

36. See chapter 3 and note 6 above for examples of scrutiny of the credibility of commissions in congressional hearings.

37. See testimony of William Carey, *Hearings,* Part I (1970), p. 176.

38. See chapter 4.

39. Drew, p. 47.

40. In chapter 7, the President's Advisory Committee on a National Highway Program (1954–55) and the President's Committee to Strengthen the Security of the Free World (1962–63) are discussed in more detail.

41. See, also, Theodore Sorenson, *Decision-Making in the White House* (New York: Columbia University Press, 1963), pp. 73–74.

42. It was reported that the President's Committee on Foreign Aid (1947), the President's Citizen Advisers on the Mutual Security Program (1956–57), and the National Commission on Technology, Automation, and Economic Progress (1964–65) returned money.

43. Examples are cited in chapter 4.

44. An example is given in chapter 3.

45. *Hearings,* Part II (1970), p. 134.

CHAPTER SIX

1. See Executive Order No. 11513 (March 3, 1970) creating the President's Commission on School Finance, for an example of a very specific mandate, and the President's Advisory Commission on Universal Training, *Program for National Security* (Washington, D.C.: Government Printing Office, 1947), pp. 119–54, for a very detailed list of questions specifying the commission mandate.

2. President's Committee on Civil Rights, *To Secure These Rights* (Washington, D.C.: Government Printing Office, 1947), p. ix.

3. See, also, President's Commission on Financial Structure and Regulation, *Report* (Washington, D.C.: Government Printing Office, 1972), p. 2.

4. See, for example, William R. Hamilton, Jr., "The President's Materials Policy Commission (Paley Commission): A History and Analytical Inquiry into Policy Formation by a Presidential Commission" (Ph.D. diss., University of Maryland, 1962), pp. 66–70; Donald Herzberg, "Horse and Buggy Election Laws: A Presidential Concern," in *Cases in American National Government and Politics,* ed. Rocco Tressolini and Richard Frost (Englewood Cliffs, N.J.: Prentice-Hall, 1966), p. 136; and Air Policy Commission, *Survival in the Air Age* (Washington, D.C.: Government Printing Office, 1948), p. 138.

5. President's Commission on Law Enforcement and Administration of Justice, *The Challenge of Crime in a Free Society* (Washington, D.C.: Government Printing Office, 1967), p. 311.

6. Hamilton, pp. 109–10.

7. Roland Renne, "The President's Water Resources Policy Commission," *Land Economics,* 26 (August, 1950): 296; and President's Water Resources Policy Commission, *A Water Policy for the American People, General Report* (Washington, D.C.: Government Printing Office, 1950), pp. 307–8. For other examples of similar extensive canvassing, see President's Committee on Civil Rights, pp. ix, 178; President's Commission on Veterans' Pensions, *Findings and Recommendations, Veterans' Benefits in the United States* (Washington, D.C.: Government Printing Office, 1956), pp. 26–31; Commission on Marine Science, Engineering and Resources, *Our Nation and the Sea, Plan for National Action* (Washington, D.C.: Government Printing Office, 1969), pp. 280–82; National Advisory Commission on Selective Service, *In Pursuit of Equity: Who Serves When Not All Serve?* (Washington, D.C.: Government Printing Office, 1967), p. 4; and President's Committee on Health Education, *Report* (Washington, D.C.: Department of Health, Education, and Welfare; Health Services and Mental Health Administration; n.d.), p. 14.

8. Books published respectively by the University of Florida Press, Gainesville, 1952, and the Markham Publishing Co., Chicago, 1968.

9. For example, the President's Commission on Immigration and Naturalization (1952) heard 400 witnesses (President's Commission on Immigration and Naturalization, *Whom We Shall Welcome* [Washington, D.C.: Government Printing Office, 1952], pp. xi–xvi); the National Advisory Commission on Libraries (1966–68) heard 404 witnesses (National Advisory Commission on Libraries, *Library Services for the Nation's Needs, Toward Fulfillment of a National Policy* [Bethesda, Md.: Education Resources Information Center, 1968], p. 533; and the President's Commission on Campus Unrest (1970) heard 86 witnesses (President's Commission on Campus Unrest, *Report* [Washington, D.C.: Government Printing Office, 1970], pp. 521–29).

10. President's Commission on Migratory Labor, *Migratory Labor in American Agriculture* (Washington, D.C.: Government Printing Office, 1951), p. vii.

11. President's Advisory Commission on Universal Training, p. 103; Commission on American Shipbuilding, *Report,* vol. I (Washington, D.C.: Gov-

ernment Printing Office, 1973), p. 3; and National Advisory Commission on Civil Disorders, *Report of the National Advisory Commission on Civil Disorders* (Washington, D.C.: Government Printing Office, 1968), p. 319. See, also, Committee to Review Veterans Hospitals, *Report to the President on Veterans' Medical Services* (Washington, D.C.: Government Printing Office, 1950), p. ii; President's Airport Commission, *The Airport and Its Neighbors* (Washington, D.C.: Government Printing Office, 1952), p. 13; Commission on Marine Science, Engineering and Resources, p. 280; and Air Policy Commission, pp. 160–61.

12. Hamilton, pp. 125–27. See, also, President's Committee on Urban Housing, *A Decent Home* (Washington, D.C.: Government Printing Office, 1969), pp. 228–31; and President's Commission on School Finance, *Schools, People, and Money* (Washington, D.C.: Government Printing Office, 1972), pp. 114–19.

13. An explanation of the term "rational-comprehensive" is included in chapter 3.

14. See Michael Lipsky and David Olson, "Riot Commission Politics," *Trans-Action,* July–August, 1969, p. 16, on the concepts of scientific and political legitimacy.

15. See, for example, Lipsky and Olson, p. 14; and the testimony by Howard Shuman, "Presidential Advisory Committees," *Hearings before a Subcommittee of the House Committee on Government Operations,* Part II, 91st Cong., 2d Sess. (1970), p. 139.

16. See, for example, Renne, p. 296.

17. They have not, however, always been successful even in this realm, as witnessed by the extensive and continuing controversy over the facts of the assassination of President Kennedy, the primary focus of the President's Commission on the Assassination of President Kennedy (Warren Commission, 1963–64). See Edward Jay Epstein, *Inquest: The Warren Commission and the Establishment of Truth* (New York: The Viking Press, 1966); and Mark Lane, *Rush to Judgement* (New York: Holt, Rinehart and Winston, 1966).

18. James Q. Wilson argues that the original studies contracted for by the commission do not support the conclusions of the commission which rest on them. "Violence, Pornography, and Social Science," *The Public Interest,* Winter, 1971, pp. 53–57. See, also, Herbert L. Packer, "The Pornography Caper," *Commentary,* 51 (February, 1971), pp. 74–76.

19. Hamilton, p. 294.

20. National Advisory Commission on Selective Service, p. 5.

21. In "On Commissionship–Presidential Variety," *Public Policy,* 19 (Fall, 1971), Martha Derthick provides an insightful analysis of presidential commissions as "instruments of social analysis" (p. 624). Derthick, a political scientist, had the advantage of having served as a member of the President's Commission on Campus Unrest (1970). However, her analysis is limited to "the 'social issue' commissions, those dealing with crime, riots, violence, and campus unrest" (p. 634).

22. Renne, p. 296. The commission lasted for a little more than eleven months.

23. Hamilton, pp. 323–24; Lipsky and Olson, p. 11; Epstein, pp. 100–104; and President's Water Resources Policy Commission, p. 307. Complaints of

inadequate time were particularly frequent from the task forces created by President Nixon in 1969. See, for example, President's Task Force on Economic Growth, *Policies for American Economic Progress in the Seventies* (Washington, D.C.: Government Printing Office, 1970), p. v. In general, on time constraints, see Charles E. Lindblom, *The Policy-Making Process* (Englewood Cliffs, N.J.: Prentice-Hall, 1968), p. 15.

24. See, for example, President's Committee on Education Beyond High School, *Second Report to the President* (Washington, D.C.: Government Printing Office, 1957), p. xi.

25. President's Commission on Law Enforcement and Administration of Justice, p. 311.

26. See, for example, Alice M. Rivlin, *Systematic Thinking for Social Action* (Washington, D.C.: The Brookings Institution, 1971), chapter 5; and the comments of Winifred Bell quoted in Gilbert Y. Steiner, *The State of Welfare* (Washington, D.C.: The Brookings Institution, 1971), p. 40.

27. For example, the President's Commission on Law Enforcement and Administration of Justice (1965–67) made sixteen recommendations for various kinds of research, and also recommended that the pilot use of simulation studies of court systems be expanded (pp. 293–301). The National Commission on the Causes and Prevention of Violence (1968–69) recommended that experimental programs in methadone drug maintenance be conducted and that research into the relation between firearms and violence, as well as into a number of other areas, be conducted (*To Establish Justice, To Insure Domestic Tranquility* [Washington, D.C.: Government Printing Office, 1969], pp. 272–78).

28. See Frank Popper, *The President's Commissions* (New York: Twentieth Century Fund, 1970), pp. 25–26; Lindblom, pp. 12–27; and Charles E. Lindblom, "The Science of 'Muddling Through'," *Public Administration Review,* 19 (Spring, 1959). See the discussion below on the recruitment of staff.

29. On the problems of recruiting academic social scientists, see Raymond W. Mack, "Four for the Seesaw" (paper presented at the Annual Meeting of the American Sociological Association, August 29, 1973), pp. 5–8.

30. Wilson, p. 56. See, also, Rivlin, chapter 5.

31. See, for example, Wilson, p. 58.

32. "Remarks of the President Upon Issuing an Executive Order Establishing a National Advisory Commission on Civil Disorders, July 29, 1967," National Advisory Commission on Civil Disorders, p. 296.

33. National Advisory Commission on Civil Disorders, p. 63.

34. *Ibid.,* pp. 74–77.

35. Lipsky and Olson, p. 20. On complexity as a limit on analysis, see Lindblom, *Policy-Making Process,* pp. 14–15. Commenting on Tolstoy's view of history in his essay on historical causality, *The Hedgehog and the Fox* (New York: Simon and Shuster, 1966), Isaiah Berlin expresses the general problem quite well: "Our ignorance of how things happen is not due to some inherent inaccessibility of the first causes, only to their multiplicity, the smallness of the ultimate units, and our own inability to see and hear and remember and record and co-ordinate enough of the available material. Omniscience is in principle possible even to empirical beings, but, of course, in practice unattainable" (p. 31).

36. Berlin, p. 68. See, also, Thomas S. Kuhn, *The Structure of Scientific Revolutions* (Chicago: University of Chicago Press, 1962), chapter 5.

37. On nonverifiable values, see Lindblom, *The Policy-Making Process,* pp. 16–17; and Herbert A. Simon, *Administrative Behavior,* 2d ed. (New York: The Free Press, 1965), pp. 45–60.

38. Hamilton, pp. 66–68, 182–84, 191–92.

39. On the nature of policy analysis and a contrast between it and more comprehensive analysis, see Yehezkel Dror, "Policy Analysts: A New Professional Role in Government," *Public Administration Review,* 27 (September, 1967).

40. President's Commission on Migratory Labor, pp. 30–31, 35.

41. President's Commission on Law Enforcement and Administration of Justice, pp. 252, 254.

42. National Advisory Commission on Civil Disorders, pp. 81, 157–68, 231–51.

43. The Fort Knox project is specifically mentioned in President's Advisory Commission on Universal Training, pp. 48, 67, 72, 74, and 127.

44. President's Commission on Law Enforcement and Administration of Justice, pp. 131–32.

45. *The Report of the Commission on Obscenity and Pornography* (New York: Bantam Books, 1970), p. 302; and President's Commission on an All-Volunteer Armed Force, *Report* (Washington, D.C.: Government Printing Office, 1970), pp. 165–68.

46. See, for example, the extensive "Review of Existing Programs" in President's Commission on Income Maintenance Programs, *Poverty Amid Plenty: The American Paradox* (Washington, D.C.: Government Printing Office, 1969), pp. 89–141, particularly the rejection of the social services approach to poverty (pp. 139–41).

47. The other decision-making techniques used by commissions and the respective roles of the commission members and staff in making the decisions of commissions are discussed below.

48. Hamilton, p. 292.

49. Wilson, p. 52. Epstein and Lane undertake a detailed and convincing critique of the analysis by the President's Commission on the Assassination of President Kennedy (Warren Commission, 1963–64). See, also, Packer, with respect to the Commission on Obscenity and Pornography (1967–70).

50. On the other hand, in the section of this chapter devoted to the contents of commission reports, and in chapter 5, the biases inherent in the perspectives of commissions are discussed.

51. On the limits of Congress in policy analysis, see Nelson W. Polsby, "Policy Analysis and Congress," *Public Policy,* 18 (Fall, 1969), pp. 68–69.

52. See Lipsky and Olson, p. 12. The commission inquiry, of course, also serves the other functions outlined above.

53. The term is from Epstein, pp. 67–68.

54. Lipsky and Olson, p. 11. See, also, Epstein, p. 67.

55. See, also, Epstein's discussion of the members of the Warren Commission who saw the "dominant purpose" of the commission in terms of dispelling rumors damaging to the national interest, and his analysis of the way in which this attitude led to a failure by the commission to pursue some questions (pp. 31–42 and *passim*).

56. Epstein, pp. 68, 88, and *passim*. Hamilton concludes that despite a major sustained effort, the President's Materials Policy Commission (1951–52) never could establish that shortages existed and that therefore action was necessary to meet them (pp. 293–94).

57. See, for example, Special Board of Inquiry for Air Safety, *Report to the President of the United States* (Washington, D.C.: Government Printing Office, 1947), p. 2; Ernest Lindley, "How Aid to Europe is Being Screened," *Newsweek*, 30 (October 13, 1947), p. 25; Air Policy Commission, p. 161; Renne, p. 297; President's Water Resources Policy Commission, p. 308; "Airport Safety Study Under Way," *Aviation Week*, 56 (March 23, 1952), p. 53; President's Commission on Law Enforcement and Administration of Justice, p. 311; and President's Advisory Panel on Timber and the Environment, *Report* (Washington, D.C.: Government Printing Office, 1973), pp. 123–24.

58. President's Commission on Law Enforcement and Administration of Justice (1965–67), President's Task Force on Prisoner Rehabilitation (1969–70), and President's Commission on Campus Unrest (1970).

59. "Stockpiling Strategic and Critical Materials," *Hearings Before the Special Subcommittee on Minerals, Materials, and Fuels Economics of the Senate Committee on Interior and Insular Affairs*, 83d Cong., 2d Sess. (1954), pp. 8–9.

60. "Findings and Recommendations of the President's Commission on Veterans' Pensions (Bradley Commission)," *Hearings before the House Committee on Veterans' Affairs*, 84th Cong., 2d Sess. (1956), p. 3757.

61. George Zook, "President's Commission on Higher Education," *Higher Education*, 3 (September 2, 1946), p. 3.

62. William C. Berman, *The Politics of Civil Rights in the Truman Administration* (Columbus, Ohio: Ohio State University Press, 1970), p. 56. Carr's Book is *Federal Protection of Civil Rights: Quest for a Sword* (Ithaca, N.Y.: Cornell University Press, 1947).

63. See, for example, Epstein, pp. 11–12.

64. *Ibid.*

65. Hamilton notes that experts were sought for the staff of the President's Materials Policy Commission (1951–52) "chiefly from contacts known to the individuals already involved in the commission effort" (p. 75).

66. Hamilton, pp. 323–34; Fritz M. Marx, "Temporary Presidential Advisory Commissions," Staff Paper, Bureau of the Budget, 1952, pp. 21–22; and *Hearings*, Part II (1970), p. 149.

67. See, for example, Hamilton, pp. 78, 323–24, and Mack.

68. On the quality of commission staffs, see chapter 3. It took the President's Materials Policy Commission (1951–52) about four months to hire its key staff members. Hamilton, pp. 71, 75, 86, 106, 323–24.

69. See, for example, Epstein, pp. 21–22, and Harry A. Marmion, *Selective Service: Conflict and Compromise* (New York: John Wiley & Sons, 1968), p. 75.

70. On goal displacement, see Peter Blau, *The Dynamics of Bureaucracy*, 2d ed. (Chicago: University of Chicago Press, 1963), pp. 231–41, and David L. Sills, "The Succession of Goals," in *Complex Organizations*, ed. Amitai Etzioni (New York: Holt, Rinehart and Winston, 1961), pp. 146–49.

71. See, for example, Hamilton, pp. 149 and 326.

72. In the case of multivolume reports which include staff studies, consultant papers, and technical reports, this generalization and the discussion which follows refer to the volume of general conclusions, analyses, and recommendations. Commission members give much less attention to the supporting volumes. See, for example, President's Materials Policy Commission, p. xiii; and President's Commission on Law Enforcement and Administration of Justice, p. 312.

73. See, for example, President's Advisory Commission on Universal Training, p. 99; President's Materials Policy Commission, p. xii; Commission on Marine Science, Engineering, and Resources, p. 281; "Regional Medical Complexes for Heart Disease, Cancer, Stroke, and Other Diseases," *Hearings before the House Committee on Interstate and Foreign Commerce,* 89th Cong., 1st Sess. (1965), p. 503; *Hearings,* Part II (1970), p. 134; President's Task Force on Rural Development, *A New Life for the Country* (Washington, D.C.: Government Printing Office, 1970), p. 51; and President's Commission on Financial Structure and Regulation, p. 2.

74. *Hearings* (1965), p. 503.

75. Hamilton, pp. 113–15, 154.

76. See, for example, Commission on Marine Science, Engineering, and Resources, p. 281; and *Hearings,* Part II (1970), p. 134.

77. *Hearings* (1965), p. 503.

78. The President's Commission on Heart Disease, Cancer and Stroke (1964) had an average attendance at its subcommittee meetings of over 100 per cent, apparently because commission members who were not part of the basic membership of a subcommittee would frequently attend its meetings. *Hearings* (1965), p. 503.

79. Air Policy Commission, p. 158.

80. Elizabeth Drew, "On Giving Oneself a Hotfoot; Government by Commission," *Atlantic Monthly,* 221 (May, 1968), p. 48.

81. For example, Congresswoman Jessica Weis, member of the President's Commission on the Status of Women (1961–62), *American Women* (Washington, D.C.: Government Printing Office, 1962), p. 85; Jesse Tapp, member of National Advisory Commission on Food and Fiber (1965–67), *Food and Fiber for the Future* (Washington, D.C.: Government Printing Office, 1967), p. x; John Snyder, Jr., member of the National Commission on Technology, Automation and Economic Progress (1964–66), *Technology and the American Economy* (Washington, D.C.: Government Printing Office, 1969), p. iii; and W. Braddock Hickman, member of President's Commission on Federal Statistic (1970–71), *Federal Statistics* (Washington, D.C.: Government Printing Office, 1970).

82. See, for example, Commission on Marine Science, Engineering and Resources, p. 281; and the testimony of Howard Shuman, executive director of the National Commission on Urban Problems (1967–68), Lloyd Cutler, executive director of the National Commission on the Causes and Prevention of Violence (1968–69), and Col. William G. McDonald, administrative officer of the National Commission on the Causes and Prevention of Violence, in *Hearings,* Part II (1970), pp. 137, 121, and 134.

83. See, for example, Hamilton, pp. 180–81 and 218–19, and Herzberg, pp. 137–39. Epstein reports that "some chapters [of the Warren Commission Report] were rewritten as many as twenty times. . . ." (p. 26).

84. Hamilton, pp. 284–87, and Marmion, pp. 90–91. See, also, Herzberg, pp. 137–39.

85. Hamilton, pp. 77, 131, 175.

86. *Ibid.,* p. 156.

87. See, for example, with respect to the National Commission on Urban Problems (1967–68) and the National Commission on the Causes and Prevention of Violence (1968–69), *Hearings,* Part II (1970), pp. 150, 118.

88. Lipsky and Olson, p. 13.

89. See, for example, Drew, p. 48; Lipsky and Olson, pp. 14–16; and Hamilton, pp. 284–87.

90. On the liberalizing effect of the commission experience on the members, see chapter 7.

91. See, for example, Lipsky and Olson, pp. 15–16.

92. See, also, the comments of General Bradley, chairman of the President's Commission on Veterans' Pensions (1955–56), and Michael March, a member of the commission staff, in *Hearings* (1956), pp. 3580, 3599, and 3701; and the statement in the *Report* of the Commission on American Shipbuilding, Vol. II, "This Report is a direct product of the Commission's deliberations" (p. 11).

93. See, for example, *Hearings,* Part II (1970), p. 115.

94. On the "unfreezing" of role definitions, see Matthew B. Miles, "On Temporary Systems," in *Innovation in Education,* ed. Matthew B. Miles (New York: Bureau of Publications, Teachers College, Columbia University, 1964), pp. 465–67.

95. "Presidential Commissions," *Hearings before the Subcommittee on Administrative Practice and Procedure of the Senate Judiciary Committee,* 92d Cong., 1st Sess. (1971), p. 224.

96. On "policy side payments," see Richard Cyert and James March, *A Behavioral Theory of the Firm* (Englewood Cliffs, N.J.: Prentice-Hall, 1963), pp. 30–31.

97. See, for example, Herzberg, pp. 137–39; Epstein on "the battle of the adjectives," pp. 150–51; and Derthick, p. 625.

98. See above for examples of "hobby horse" recommendations reflecting the interests of commission members.

99. In "The Quaker Way Wins Adherents," *New York Times Magazine,* June 17, 1951, Morris L. Cooke, chairman of the President's Water Resources Policy Commission (1950), discusses the sense-of-the-meeting technique for reaching decisions and its successful use in achieving a unanimous report by the commission.

100. See, for example, Lipsky and Olson, p. 14; Hamilton, p. 283; and Derthick, p. 624. The lack of success of divided reports is discussed in chapter 8.

101. On this general phenomenon, see Miles, pp. 167–73.

102. See, for example, Herzberg, p. 136.

103. See, for example, Lipsky and Olson, pp. 17, 21.

104. See, for example, Hamilton' p. 237.

105. See chapter 5 on the types of members chosen for commissions.

106. On social and task leaders, see Sidney Verba, *Small Groups and Political Behavior* (Princeton, N.J.: Princeton University Press, 1961), chapters 6 and 7. Verba describes them as "affective" and "instrumental" leaders.

107. See, for example, Herzberg's description of the "Scammon compromise," p. 137.

108. See, for example, on the role of Milton Eisenhower, chairman of the National Commission on the Causes and Prevention of Violence (1968–69), *Hearings,* Part II (1970), p. 118.

109. See chapter 2 on the availability of commissions as a White House option.

110. The Federal Advisory Committee Act (PL92-463, 1972) attempts to impose some structural and procedural uniformity on advisory commissions. Its impact in this area remains to be seen.

111. The President's Committee on Civil Rights (1946–47), for example, was modeled after the National Commission on Law Observance and Enforcement (Wickersham Commission, 1929–31), the Commission on National Goals (1960) after the Research Committee on Social Trends (1929–33), and the President's Commission on Income Maintenance Programs (1968–69) after the Committee on Economic Security (1934–35). On the President's Committee on Civil Rights and the National Commission on Law Observance and Enforcement, see Berman, p. 55. On the Commission on National Goals and the Research Committee on Social Trends, see "Annual Message to Congress on the State of the Union," January 9, 1959, *Eisenhower Papers, 1959,* Item 6, pp. 10–11.

112. The large jump in the number of commissions per year in Nixon's first term is largely a function of the seventeen task forces created under the auspices of Arthur Burns, counsellor to the President, in 1969 (numbered 70–86 in appendix II).

113. The decrease in the average duration of commissions in Nixon's first term again reflects the seventeen task forces created in 1969, most of which were two to four months long.

114. See chapter 8 on the Executive Branch process of review of commission reports and chapter 4 on the methods of financing commissions.

115. The exceptions to this generalization are, first, the few crisis-response commissions which found that the fears and suspicions of the public were excessive. The President's Airport Commission (1952) and the President's Commission on the Assassination of President Kennedy (1963–64) fall in this category. The other exceptions are the commissions which reviewed foreign aid and also the President's Committee to Appraise Employment and Unemployment Statistics (1961–62), which found that the government programs under attack were not ineffective, mismanaged, or biased, as critics had charged.

116. Even though commissions as temporary systems are not preoccupied with institutional maintenance, they are not immune to the desire to perpetuate themselves as permanent advisory bodies.

CHAPTER SEVEN

1. Art Buchwald, "Costly Reports Viewed Gravely," *Washington Post,* July 23, 1970, p. A19.

2. Elizabeth Drew, "On Giving Oneself a Hotfoot: Government by Commission," *Atlantic Monthly,* 221 (May, 1968), p. 49.

3. "Presidential Commissions," *Hearings before the Subcommittee on Ad-*

ministrative Practice and Procedure of the Senate Committee on the Judiciary, 92d Cong., 1st Sess. (1971), p. 3.

4. The commissions are identified by a short title. Their corresponding full title can be found following the same capital numeral in appendix 2 or appendix 3.

5. These were: "Letter to the Director, Bureau of the Budget," White House press release, June 18, 1946, in which President Truman rejected one of the major recommendations of the President's Committee on Integration of the Medical Services of the Government (1945–46) and "Statement on the Commission's Report," *Weekly Compilation,* 6 (November 2, 1970), pp. 1454–55, in which President Nixon "totally" rejected the report of the Commission on Obscenity and Pornography (1967–70) and characterized it as "morally bankrupt." The Senate also passed a resolution (S. Res. 477, Oct. 13, 1970) rejecting the pornography report. In "The President's Letter to Commission Chairman William W. Scranton," *Weekly Compilation,* 6 (December 14, 1970), pp. 1660–63, President Nixon responded to the call from the President's Committee on Campus Unrest for greater presidential "leadership" by noting that "Moral authority in a great and diverse nation such as ours does not reside in the Presidency alone" (p. 1663). Thus Art Buchwald and Elizabeth Drew are correct about *when* Presidents do not adopt commission recommendations: they usually "ignore" or "bury" them rather than explicitly rejecting them.

6. In appendix 3, a piece of legislation that was passed does not appear twice, as proposed legislation and as legislation. Only those pieces of legislation which were not passed are listed as "proposed." For the purposes of this list and table 5, reorganization plans have been classified as legislation, although they are hybrids of legislation and administrative action. In one case, the authoritative action was legislation in line with the recommendations of a commission but clearly contrary to the policies of the President. The case was that in which the Air Policy Commission (1947–48) recommended a seventy-group Air Force for which money was appropriated over the opposition of President Truman.

7. These figures are again probably low, because of the limited data from which they are drawn. In particular, many other statements were probably made public as press releases but not included in the *Public Papers of the Presidents* or the *Weekly Compilation.*

8. The cases where legislation was introduced over presidential opposition or at the initiative of Congress are excluded in evaluating the level of *presidential* support. These cases are noted by (C) in table 5.

9. The average score of level of public presidential support is 1.99.

10. To be included, the government action must have occurred within about four years of the commission's final reporting. Looked at over a longer perspective, other commissions have had many of their recommendations implemented; for example, the President's Committee on Civil Rights (1946–47) by the civil rights Acts of the 1960's and the President's Commission on Immigration and Naturalization (1952) by the Immigration and Nationality Act Amendments of 1965, PL 89-236, 79 Stat. 911.

11. The average score of level of authoritative government action is 1.74.

12. The importance of presidential support as well as other factors, in

determining the degree of success enjoyed by a commission is described in detail in the following chapter.

13. The impact of changes in legislation that appear insignificant in the broad terms of public debate but that are of major importance in their effect is lucidly demonstrated in the case studies in James L. Sundquist, *Politics and Policy: The Eisenhower, Kennedy, and Johnson Years* (Washington, D.C.: The Brookings Institution, 1968).

14. Numerous examples of the use of commission reports in the testimony of administration witnesses and examples of the testimony of commission members and staff in congressional hearings can be found in the hearings that are part of the legislative history of the laws cited in appendix 3.

15. See, for examples of criticism of the two crisis commissions, Michael Lipsky and David Olson, "Riot Commission Politics," *Trans-Action,* July/August, 1969; and *One Year Later: An Assessment of the Nation's Response to the Crisis Described by the National Advisory Commission on Civil Disorders* (Washington, D.C.: Urban Coalition, 1969).

16. Lipsky and Olson, p. 21; and *One Year Later,* pp. 114–18.

17. "Statement by the President Concerning the Report on the Relationship Between the CIA and Private Voluntary Organizations," March 29, 1967, *Johnson Papers, 1967,* Item 147, pp. 403–4. The report referred to is that of a high-level government review committee. This statement announced that the commission composed of private citizens would also study the problem and follow up on the intragovernment study.

18. See *Congress and the Nation, 1965–68* (Washington, D.C.: Congressional Quarterly Service, 1969), p. 852.

19. On the President's Budget and State of the Union messages and the Congress, see Richard Neustadt, "Presidency and Legislation: Planning the President's Program," *American Political Science Review,* 49 (December, 1955).

20. Coretta Scott King, *My Life With Martin Luther King, Jr.* (New York: Holt, Rinehart, and Winston, 1969), p. 109.

21. James A. and Nancy F. Wechsler, "The Road Ahead for Civil Rights: The President's Report; One Year Later," *Commentary,* 6 (October, 1948), pp. 303–4. Nancy Wechsler was counsel to the committee. For other comments in the same vein, see Charles W. Shull review of the President's Committee on Civil Rights, *To Secure These Rights,* in *The Annals,* 256 (March, 1948), p. 186; Robert S. Allen and William V. Shanley, *The Truman Merry-Go-Round* (New York: the Vanguard Press, 1950), p. 31; and Walter White, *A Man Called White* (New York: The Viking Press, 1948), p. 333.

22. Various positions in this debate are expressed in "Federal Aid Without Controls," *Commonweal,* 47 (February 13, 1948); "Tides of Mediocrity," *Time,* 51 (February 23, 1948); Robert Hutchins, "Double Trouble," *Saturday Review of Literature,* 31 (July 17, 1948); and William Tolley, "Some Observations on the Report of the President's Commission on Higher Education," *Educational Record,* 29 (October, 1948).

23. Gail Kennedy, ed. (Boston: D. C. Heath and Company, 1952).

24. What these responses were and the process by which they were worked out is described in Sundquist, chapters 5 and 6.

25. See, for example, Burton Levy, "Effects of 'Racism' on the Racial

Bureaucracy," *Public Administration Review,* 32 (September/October, 1972), p. 480.

26. President's Commission on Veterans' Pensions, *Veterans' Benefits in the United States* (Washington, D.C.: Government Printing Office, 1956), p. 10.

27. See Gilbert Y. Steiner, *The State of Welfare* (Washington, D.C.: The

28. United Automobile, Aerospace, and Agricultural Implement Workers of America, *Songs for a Better Tomorrow* 1963 (recording). Quoted by permission of The Labor Education Division, Roosevelt University.

29. National Commission on Technology, Automation and Economic Progress, *Technology and the American Economy* (Washington, D.C.: Government Printing Office, 1966), chapter 2.

30. *The AFL-CIO Platform Proposals: Presented to the Republican and Democratic Conventions* 1968 (n.d.), p. 11.

31. The Paley approach was the application of economic analysis to resource problems. It is succinctly described by Arthur Maass in "Review: *Resources For Freedom,*" *American Political Science Review,* 47 (March, 1953), p. 206, and "Conservation: Political and Social Aspects," *International Encyclopedia of the Social Sciences,* vol. 3 (New York: The Macmillan Company and the Free Press, 1968), p. 273. It should really be called the "Mason approach" after Edward Mason, the commission member who was its primary architect.

32. William Paley, the commission chairman, was one of the original directors of Resources for the Future. Several members of the commission staff also joined the new organization. *New York Times,* November 17, 1952, p. 26.

33. *Congress and the Nation, 1945–64* (Washington, D.C.: Congressional Quarterly Service, 1965), p. 175.

34. See, also, Jack Rosenthal, "Study Panels Flourish in Capital," *New York Times,* December 14, 1969, p. 60.

35. President's Commission on Veterans' Pensions, chapter 3.

36. "Presidential Advisory Committees," *Hearings before a Subcommittee of the House Committee on Government Operations,* Part II, 91st Cong., 2d Sess. (1970), p. 127. See, also, Rosenthal; and James S. Campbell, "The Usefulness of Commission Studies of Collective Violence," *The Annals,* 391 (September, 1970).

37. Advisory Committee on Government Housing Policies and Programs, *Recommendations on Government Housing Policies and Programs* (Washington, D.C.: Government Printing Office, 1954).

38. Quoted in Rosenthal. See also the comments of commission chairman Katzenbach in *Hearings* (1971), p. 165.

39. "Presidential Commissions and Social Change: A Brown University Symposium," March 11, 1971 (transcript mimeographed), p. 6. See also the comments of David Ginsburg, Judge Otto Kerner, and Dr. Milton Eisenhower in *Hearings* (1971), pp. 16, 23, 147–48, and 155.

40. Brown Symposium, p. 30.

41. The reports of the Commission on National Goals (1960), the President's Commission on the Assassination of President Kennedy (1963–64), the President's Commission on Law Enforcement and Administration of Justice (1965–67), the National Advisory Commission on Civil Disorders (1967–

68), the Commission on Obscenity and Pornography (1967–70), and the National Commission on the Causes and Prevention of Violence (1968–69) have appeared in commercial paperback editions. Staff reports of the Violence Commission also were published in this form. See the testimony of Lloyd Cutler, executive director of the National Commission on the Causes and Prevention of Violence, and Howard Shuman, executive director of the National Commission on Urban Problems (1967–68), *Hearings,* Part II (1970), pp. 116, 149.

42. *Hearings* (1971), p. 145.
43. Sundquist, p. 195.
44. The quotation is from Lillian Symes, "The Great Fact-Finding Farce," *Harper's Magazine,* 164 (February, 1932), p. 360.
45. See National Commission on Urban Problems, *Building the American City* (Washington, D.C.: Government Printing Office, 1968), p. 1; and *Hearings,* Part II (1970), pp. 137–38.
46. See, also, *Hearings,* Part II (1970), p. 139, in which Howard Shuman accounts for the unanimity of the National Commission on Urban Problems (1967–68) in the same way.
47. The importance of a unanimous report is discussed in chapter 8.
48. Kenneth Trombley, *The Life and Times of a Happy Liberal: A Biography of Morris Llewellyn Cooke* (New York: Harper and Brothers, 1954), p. 243.
49. Nicholas Katzenbach, "Criminal Justice," p. 711; Richard Stolley, "Crisis Worse Than Anyone Imagined: Report," *Life,* 62 (February 24, 1967), p. 25; and Robert Reinhold, "Results Terms Mixed for Study Panels," *New York Times,* March 28, 1971, p. 48. See also, with respect to the President's Commission on Registration and Voting Participation (1963), Donald Herzberg, "Horse and Buggy Election Laws: A Presidential Concern," in *Cases in American National Government and Politics,* ed. Rocco Tressolini and Richard Frost (Englewood Cliffs, N.J.: Prentice-Hall, 1966), p. 141.
50. Rosenthal.
51. Brown Symposium, p. 26.
52. *One Year Later,* p. 62.
53. Ronald Kahn, "The Politics of Roads: National Highway Legislation in 1955–56" (Master's thesis, University of Chicago, 1967), pp. 88–90.
54. Otto E. Passman in "The Clay Committee: A Symposium," *Political Science Quarterly,* 78 (September, 1963), p. 350.
55. Arthur Schlesinger, Jr., *A Thousand Days* (Boston: Houghton Mifflin Company, 1965), p. 599.
56. *Ibid.;* Theodore Sorenson, *Kennedy* (New York: Harper & Row, 1965), p. 393; Jim F. Heath, *John F. Kennedy and the Business Community* (Chicago: University of Chicago Press, 1969), pp. 109–10; Usha Mahajani, "Kennedy and the Strategy of AID: The Clay Report and After," *Western Political Quarterly,* 18 (September, 1965); and Roger Hilsman, *To Move A Nation* (Garden City, N.Y.: Doubleday & Company, 1967), pp. 394–95.
57. Quoted in Rosenthal.
58. *Hearings* (1971), p. 215.
59. This view is expressed in "The Commission: How to Create a Blue Chip Consensus," *Time,* 95 (January 17, 1970), p. 23.
60. *Hearings* (1971), p. 161.

CHAPTER EIGHT

1. The exceptions are the commissions instituted by legislation and those which got some or all of their resources from specially designated appropriations or from private sources. See chapter 4.

2. Again, with the exception of those commissions created by statute, which are in most cases technically advisory to both the President and the Congress.

3. As measured and defined in chapter 7.

4. See appendix 3.

5. Howard R. Bowen, "Technology and Employment: Address," *Vital Speeches,* 32 (May 1, 1966), p. 439.

6. "Address Before a Joint Session of the Congress," November 27, 1963, *Johnson Papers, 1963–64,* Item 11, p. 9.

7. These were the President's Council on Pennsylvania Avenue (1962–64), the Committee on Equal Opportunity in the Armed Forces (1962–64), the President's Advisory Commission on Narcotic and Drug Abuse (1963–64), the President's Commission on Registration and Voting Participation (1963), the Committee on Public Higher Education in the District of Columbia (1963–64), and the Task Force to Promote Overseas Sale of Securities of U.S. Companies (1963–64). See appendix 3 for the responses they received.

8. "Statement by the President on the Report of the President's Materials Policy Commission," July 1, 1952, *Truman Papers, 1952–53,* Item 191, pp. 454–55; and "Letter to the President of the Senate and to the Speaker of the House Transmitting Report of the President's Materials Policy Commission," July 1, 1952, *Truman Papers, 1952–53,* Item 192, pp. 455–56.

9. "Annual Budget Message to the Congress: Fiscal Year 1952," January 5, 1951, *Truman Papers, 1951,* Item 13, p. 85.

10. "Annual Budget Message to the Congress: Fiscal Year 1953," January 21, 1952, *Truman Papers, 1952–53,* Item 18, p. 87.

11. See table 5 in chapter 7.

12. See chapter 7.

13. "Statement on the Commission's Report," *Weekly Compilation,* 6 (November 2, 1970), pp. 1454–55.

14. See below for another reason why the commission's report was not acted upon.

15. Howard E. Shuman, "Behind the Scenes and Under the Rug," *The Washington Monthly,* 1 (July, 1969), pp. 21–22.

16. See Avery Leiserson, *Administration Regulation: A Study in Representation of Interests* (Chicago: University of Chicago Press, 1942), p. 167.

17. Ruth P. Morgan, *The President and Civil Rights: Policy Making by Executive Order* (New York: St. Martin's Press, 1970), p. 63.

18. *Congress and the Nation, 1965–68* (Washington, D.C.: Congressional Quarterly Service, 1969), pp. 574–75. See, also, Harry A. Marmion, *Selective Service: Conflict and Compromise* (New York: John Wiley & Sons, 1968) on the weakening of the National Advisory Commission on Selective Service's recommendation on student deferments because the commission was divided.

19. Garth Mangum and Frazier Kellogg had worked for the committee.

20. The Missouri Basin Survey Commission (1952–53), the President's Commission on the Status of Women (1961–62), the Commission on the Assassination of President Kennedy (1963–64), the President's Commission on Budget Concepts (1967), the National Advisory Commission on Civil Disorders (1967–68), and the National Commission on the Causes and Prevention of Violence (1968–69) had congressmen among their members. The Commission on Marine Science, Engineering, and Resources (1966–69) had a group of "congressional advisers." Several other commissions have had former congressmen as members, for example, the President's Commission on Campaign Costs (1961–62), the President's Advisory Panel on Federal Salary Systems (1961–63), and the National Commission on Urban Problems (1967–68).

21. See "Special Message to Congress on Urban Problems: 'The Crisis of the Cities,' " February 22, 1968, *Johnson Papers, 1968,* Item 87, pp. 257–58.

22. Alfred Steinberg, *The Man From Missouri: The Life and Times of Harry S. Truman* (New York: Putnam, 1962), p. 303; Robert S. Allen and William V. Shanley, *The Truman Merry-Go-Round* (New York: The Vanguard Press, 1950), pp. 58–64; and William C. Berman, *The Politics of Civil Rights in the Truman Administration* (Columbus, Ohio: Ohio State University Press, 1970), pp. 72–73.

23. "Statement by the President on the Report of the President's Materials Policy Commission," July 1, 1952, *Truman Papers, 1952–53,* Item 191, pp. 454–55.

24. See Arthur Maass, *Muddy Waters: The Army Engineers and the Nation's Rivers* (Cambridge, Mass.: Harvard University Press, 1951). The assistance of Professor Arthur Maass, Harvard University, is gratefully acknowledged, in allowing me access to his personal files and providing stimulating and perceptive comment and discussion of the events discussed in this case study. The responsibility for the analysis and conclusions is, of course, mine alone.

25. "Letter to Department and Agency Heads on the Report of the Water Resources Policy Commission," March 14, 1951, *Truman Papers, 1951,* Item 55, p. 185.

26. Arthur Maass, Draft, Water Policy Paper, January 2, 1953 (Maass files).

27. See Arthur Maass, "In Accord with the Program of the President?: An Essay on Staffing the Presidency," *Public Policy* (Cambridge, Mass.: Graduate School of Public Administration, 1953), pp. 82–83; and Arthur Maass, "Public Investment Planning in the United States: Analysis and Critique," *Public Policy,* 18 (Winter, 1970), pp. 221–23.

28. Letter from Secretary of Interior Oscar Chapman to Frederick Lawton, Director of the Bureau of Budget, April 17, 1952 (Maass files).

29. Letter from Elmer B. Staats, Assistant Director of the Bureau of the Budget, to the Secretary of the Interior, May 29, 1952 (Maass files).

30. *Ibid.*

31. *Ibid.*

32. For example, letter from Vernon D. Northrop, Acting Secretary of the Interior, to Frederick J. Lawton, Director of the Bureau of the Budget, September 3, 1952 (Maass files).

33. For example, letter and "Memorandum of Comment" from Vernon D.

Northrop, Acting Secretary of the Interior, to Frederick J. Lawton, Director of the Bureau of the Budget, November 20, 1952 (Maass files).

34. Memorandum from Assistant Secretary Warne to Secretary Chapman, December 29, 1950 (Maass files).

35. Minutes, second meeting of the Departmental Task Force to Consider the Report of the President's Water Resources Policy Commission, January 8, 1951 (Maass files).

36. Memorandum from Assistant Secretary Warne to Secretary Chapman, December 29, 1950 (Maass files).

37. January 19, 1953, *Truman Papers, 1952–53,* Item 388, pp. 1208–15.

38. See "Annual Budget Message to the Congress: Fiscal Year 1952," January 5, 1951, *Truman Papers, 1951,* Item 13, p. 85; "Annual Budget Message to the Congress: Fiscal Year 1953," January 21, 1952, *Truman Papers, 1952–53,* Item 18, p. 89; and "Address in Arkansas at the Dedication of the Norfolk and Bull Shoals Dams," July 2, 1952, *Truman Papers, 1952–53,* Item 194, pp. 459–60.

39. Before its termination the commission prepared its own draft Water Resources Act of 1951, which was one of the documents used by the Budget Bureau's Interagency Water Policy Review Committee. The commission's draft Act was made public on February 18, 1952, probably as a means to bring pressure on the Budget Bureau to complete the drafting of its Water Resources Policy Act of 1952. "Water Resources Policy Commission Recommendations for Legislation," February 11, 1952, includes a letter from Morris L. Cooke, Chairman, President's Water Resources Policy Commission, to President Truman, February 12, 1951, and the draft Water Resources Act of 1951 (Maass files).

40. See Arthur Maass, *Muddy Waters;* and *Congress and the Nation, 1945–64* (Washington, D.C.: Congressional Quarterly Service, 1965), pp. 771–931.

41. See Raymond Bauer, Ithiel de Sola Pool, and Lewis Dexter, *American Business and Public Policy* (New York: Atherton Press, 1967), chapters 11, 12, 25, and 26; David Truman, *The Governmental Process* (New York: Alfred A. Knopf, 1951), chap. 4 and p. 511; and James Q. Wilson, "Innovation in Organizations: Notes Toward a Theory," quoted in Anthony Downs, *Inside Bureaucracy* (Boston: Little, Brown and Company, 1967), p. 201.

42. Truman, pp. 268–70.

43. Another example of bureaucratic bias contrary to the recommendations of a commission, and its consequences for the implementation of those recommendations, is the fate of the top priority recommendation of the Commission on Marine Science, Engineering and Resources (1966–69). The commission proposed that a new agency, the National Oceanic and Atmospheric Agency (NOAA), be created to administer civil marine and atmospheric programs. NOAA would be independent and report directly to the President. It would contain the Coast Guard from the Department of Transportation, the Environmental Science Services Administration from the Commerce Department, the Bureau of Commercial Fisheries and some functions of the Bureau of Sport Fisheries and Wildlife from the Interior Department, several programs from the National Science Foundation, and the U.S. Lake Survey from the Army Corps of Engineers. As recommended

by the President and accepted by the Congress, NOAA was not independent
and was placed in the Department of Commerce, and it did not contain the
Coast Guard, which would have constituted 75 per cent of its manpower as
proposed. The most important reasons for this severe cutback and altera-
tion of the NOAA proposal were the desire of the Executive Branch
agencies to protect their empires, to prevent erosion of their jurisdictions
and hence their political power, their desire to, if possible, build their
power by capturing the new agency, and the inability or unwillingness of
the President to overcome these strong agency positions. This interpretation
is persuasively argued and documented by Marc Tipermas, "Bureaucratic
Imperialism in the NOAA Controversy" (paper, prepared for Prof. Harvey
Sapolsky's course, Public Management of Science, Massachusetts Institute
of Technology, 1971).

44. "Presidential Commissions," *Hearings before the Subcommittee on Administrative Practice and Procedure of the Senate Committee on the Judiciary,* 92d. Cong., 1st Sess. (1971), p. 311.
45. See testimony of William D. Carey, "Presidential Advisory Committees,"
*Hearings Before a Subcommittee of the House Committee on Government
Operations,* Part I, 91st Cong., 2d Sess. (1970), pp. 167–69.
46. See, also, Marmion, pp. 98, 126, 156, and 167.
47. "Task Forces of the Johnson Administration," mimeographed (n.d.), lists
111 task forces when each of five groups is excluded as either a cabinet
committee, an interagency committee, or a presidential advisory commission.
48. On the general increase of central clearance through the White House
rather than the Budget Bureau, see Robert S. Gilmour, "Central Legislative
Clearance: A Revised Perspective," *Public Administration Review,* 31
(March/April, 1971).
49. *Congress and the Nation, 1965–68,* pp. 64, 76, 96–97, and 110–11.
50. Another example is the initiatives in support of the President's Commission on Law Enforcement and Administration of Justice (1965–67). See
James Vorenberg, "Presidential Crime Commission," *Federal Rules Decisions,* 44 (May, 1968), pp. 76–77.
51. *Congress and the Nation, 1965–68,* pp. 881–90; and Marmion, pp. 87,
139, 141, 149, and 155.
52. Another example is the advisory group set up by the Department of
Housing and Urban Development, to compete with the National Commission on Urban Problems (1967–68), according to its executive director,
Howard Shuman. *Hearings,* Part II (1970), pp. 141–42.
53. Niccolo Machiavelli, *The Prince* (New York: New American Library,
1952), p. 50.
54. See chapters 3 and 6.
55. "On Commissionship—Presidential Variety," *Public Policy,* Fall, 1971, p.
624.
56. Another example with respect to the President's Commission on Registration and Voting Participation (1963) is provided by Donald Herzberg,
"Horse and Buggy Election Laws: A Presidential Concern," in *Cases in
American National Government and Politics,* ed. Rocco Tressolini and
Richard Frost (Englewood Cliffs, N.J.: Prentice-Hall, 1966), p. 137.
57. This generalization does not contradict the previous observation that the

recommendations of commissions are consistent with the existing dominant values and institutions. There is ample room in this paradigm for new, unorthodox, innovative and, by some definitions, radical proposals to be adopted without fundamentally altering these values and institutions.

58. Dwight D. Eisenhower, *Waging Peace* (Garden City, N.Y.: Doubleday & Company, 1965), p. 221. The Gaither Committee was a secret citizen task force created by President Eisenhower to make a general study of the nation's defense effort. The major findings and conclusions of the report became known, and the President was forced to respond. See Morton H. Halperin, "The Gaither Committee and the Policy Process," *World Politics*, 13 (April, 1961).

59. In "On Temporary Systems," Matthew Miles identifies "linkage failure" between "temporary systems" and their permanent parent system as a "crucial problem" in the successful use of this type of institution. He explains that "the very detachment and euphoria which make time-limited systems so fascinating and productive help to blind the participants to what they will be up against when they return to 'ordinary' life with its role conflicts, work pressures, and vested interests." In *Innovation in Education*, ed. Matthew B. Miles (New York: Bureau of Publications, Teachers College, Columbia University, 1964), p. 483.

60. See, for example, Herzberg, p. 141.

61. *Hearings*, Part II (1970), p. 116. See, also, the statement by commission chairman Milton Eisenhower, in "Presidential Commissions and Social Change: A Brown University Symposium," March 11, 1971 (mimeographed transcript), pp. 33–34; and *Hearings* (1971), pp. 104, 145, 147–48.

62. See, also, *Hearings*, Part II (1970), p. 150.

63. See, for example, Michael Lipsky and David Olson, "Riot Commission Politics," *Trans-Action*, July–August, 1969; and *One Year Later: An Assessment of the Nation's Response to the Crisis Described by the National Advisory Commission on Civil Disorders* (Washington, D.C.: Urban Coalition, 1969).

64. See Jack Rosenthal, "Study Panels Flourish in Capital," *New York Times*, December 14, 1969, p. 60.

65. See, for example, Lloyd Cutler's testimony, *Hearings*, Part II (1970), p. 117.

66. See, for example, the statements by Otto Kerner, chairman of the commission, and Milton Eisenhower, chairman of the National Commission on the Causes and Prevention of Violence (1968–69), in Brown Symposium, pp. 6, 30, and 33.

67. The Brown Symposium and the hearings on presidential commissions held by Senator Edward Kennedy's Subcommittee on Administrative Practice and Procedure of the Senate Judiciary Committee in 1971, at both of which Chairman Kerner was a prominent participant, are evidence of the continuing impact of the commission more than three years after its report was issued.

68. See appendix 3.

69. *Hearings* (1971), p. 18.

70. Lyndon B. Johnson, *The Vantage Point* (New York: Holt, Rinehart and Winston, 1971), pp. 172–73, 451.

71. National Advisory Commission on Civil Disorders, *Report of the Na-*

tional Advisory Commission on Civil Disorders (Washington, D.C.: Government Printing Office, 1968), p. 1.

CHAPTER NINE

1. "Presidential Commissions," *Hearings Before the Subcommittee on Administrative Practice and Procedure of the Senate Committee on the Judiciary,* 92d Cong., 1st Sess. (1971), p. 5.
2. PL 92-463, 86 Stat. 770.
3. See testimony of David S. Brown and Howard Shuman, "Presidential Advisory Committees," *Hearings before a Subcommittee of the House Committee on Government Operations,* Part II, 91st Cong., 2d Sess. (1970), pp. 47, 50, and 153.
4. See Chapter 5.
5. Clinton Rossiter, "The Constitutional Significance of the Executive Office of the President," *American Political Science Review,* Vol. 43 (December, 1969), pp. 1215–16.

INDEX

Abel, I. W., 76
Adams, Sherman, 87
Advisory Commissions. *See* Commissions, Presidential Advisory Aging, President's Task Force on the: impact, 137, 242; data on, 213
Agriculture, Department of, 172
Air Policy Commission: purpose of, 24; recommendations, 50; initiative from Congress, 58; task of, defined, 97; inquiry by, 105; membership, 112; impact, 134, 218; data on, 206
Air Pollution, President's Task Force on: impact, 137, 242; data on, 214
Airport Commission, President's: impact, 134, 162, 195, 220–21; data on, 206
Air Safety, Special Board of Inquiry for: membership, 78; impact, 134, 218; data on, 205
All-Volunteer Armed Force, President's Commission on an: membership, 78, 113; inquiry by, 105; recommendations, 133; impact, 136, 239; data on, 212
American Council on Education, 83, 109
American Jewish Committee, 150
American Medical Association, 75, 80
Army Corps of Engineers, 172
Arthur D. Little, Inc., 98
Assassination of President Kennedy, President's Commission on the: purpose of, 22; membership, 79, 84, 85, 123; inquiry by, 107; impact, 135, 195, 229–30; data on, 209

Ball, George, 85
Battelle Institute, 98
Beirne, Joseph, 81
Bissell, Richard, 167

Bradley, Omar, 36, 79, 82
Brewster, Kingman, 30, 115
British Royal Commissions, 5, 197–98
Brooke, Edward, 76
Brown, Francis, 109
Budget Concepts, President's Commission on: proposed, 55; impact, 136, 236; recommendations, 141, 142; data on, 211
Bunting, Mary, 81
Bureau of the Budget (also Office of Management and Budget), 17, 55, 82, 107, 161, 171–76, 181, 199
Burns, Arthur, 55, 164
Business Taxation, President's Task Force on: impact, 136, 241; data on, 212
Byrne, William, 118

Cahill, Thomas, 30
Cain, James, 80–81
Califano, Joseph, 74, 180
Campaign Costs, President's Commission on: proposed, 54–55; membership, 77, 79, 82–83, 113, 122; report, writing of, 114; impact, 135, 165, 182, 185, 225; data on, 208
Campus Unrest, President's Commission on: purpose of, 22; "runaway," 94; decision making by, 118; membership, 123; impact, 131, 137, 144, 145, 155, 185, 193, 243; data on, 214–15
Career Advancement, Presidential Task Force on: impact, 135, 234; data on, 210
Carr, Robert, 109
Census Bureau, 34
Central Intelligence Agency, 144
Civil Disorders, National Advisory Com-

291

DESIGNED BY EDGAR J. FRANK
COMPOSED BY THE COMPOSING ROOM, GRAND RAPIDS, MICHIGAN
MANUFACTURED BY THOMSON-SHORE, INC., DEXTER, MICHIGAN
TEXT IS SET IN PRESS ROMAN, DISPLAY LINES IN CASLON

Library of Congress Cataloging in Publication Data
Wolanin, Thomas R   1942–
Presidential advisory commissions.
Includes bibliographical references and index.
1. Executive advisory bodies—United States.
2. United States—Politics and government—1945-
I. Title.
JK468.C7W64   353.09'3   74-27317
ISBN 0-299-06860-9